U

GRID COMPUTING FOR BIOINFORMATICS AND COMPUTATIONAL BIOLOGY

BICENTENNIAL
1807
⊕WILEY
2007
BICENTENNIAL

THE WILEY BICENTENNIAL—KNOWLEDGE FOR GENERATIONS

*E*ach generation has its unique needs and aspirations. When Charles Wiley first opened his small printing shop in lower Manhattan in 1807, it was a generation of boundless potential searching for an identity. And we were there, helping to define a new American literary tradition. Over half a century later, in the midst of the Second Industrial Revolution, it was a generation focused on building the future. Once again, we were there, supplying the critical scientific, technical, and engineering knowledge that helped frame the world. Throughout the 20th Century, and into the new millennium, nations began to reach out beyond their own borders and a new international community was born. Wiley was there, expanding its operations around the world to enable a global exchange of ideas, opinions, and know-how.

For 200 years, Wiley has been an integral part of each generation's journey, enabling the flow of information and understanding necessary to meet their needs and fulfill their aspirations. Today, bold new technologies are changing the way we live and learn. Wiley will be there, providing you the must-have knowledge you need to imagine new worlds, new possibilities, and new opportunities.

Generations come and go, but you can always count on Wiley to provide you the knowledge you need, when and where you need it!

WILLIAM J. PESCE
PRESIDENT AND CHIEF EXECUTIVE OFFICER

PETER BOOTH WILEY
CHAIRMAN OF THE BOARD

GRID COMPUTING FOR BIOINFORMATICS AND COMPUTATIONAL BIOLOGY

Edited by

El-Ghazali Talbi
University of Lille, Lille, France

Albert Y. Zomaya
University of Sydney, Sydney, Australia

WILEY-INTERSCIENCE

A JOHN WILEY & SONS, INC., PUBLICATION

Library of Congress Cataloging-in-Publication Data:
Grid computing for bioinformatics and computational biology / edited by
El-Ghazali Talbi, Albert Y. Zomaya.
   p. cm.
   Includes index.
   ISBN 978-0-471-78409-8 (alk. paper)
   1. Bioinformatics. 2. Computational biology. 3. Computational grids (Computer systems)
I. Talbi, El-Ghazali, 1965 - II. Zomaya, Albert Y.
   QH324.2.G75 2007
   570.285–dc22

                                                               2007019075

Printed in the United States of America
10 9 8 7 6 5 4 3 2 1

To my daughter Besma, you are my sweet little girl with an impressive intelligence.
To my mother Zehour for her infinite sacrifice.
To my father Ammar who continues to support me in my academic research.
In memory of my uncle Djerabi Hocine. He was like a Big Brother to me.

Prof. E-G. Talbi

To my students for teaching me so many things.

Prof. A.Y. Zomaya

CONTENTS

PREFACE

Bioinformatics is fast emerging as an important discipline for academic research and industrial applications. Research and development in bioinformatics and computational biology create and develop advanced information and computational techniques to manage and extract useful information from the DNA/RNA/protein sequence being generated by high-throughput technologies (e.g., DNA microarrays, DNA sequencers). It is the comprehensive application of mathematics (e.g., probability and graph theory), statistics, science (e.g., biochemistry), and computer science (e.g., computer algorithms and machine learning) to the understanding of living systems. These techniques are extremely computationally or data intensive, providing motivation for using grids.

Grids are an enabling technology that permits the transparent coupling of geographically dispersed resources (machines, networks, data storage, visualization devices, and scientific instruments) for large-scale distributed applications. Grids provide several important benefits for users and applications to share: computing and data storage, knowledge, instruments, and so on.

This book not only presents grid algorithms and applications, but also presents software frameworks and libraries that integrate bioinformatics and computational biology applications. Many researchers in this field are not aware of the existence of these frameworks which encourages the reusing of existing code with a high level of transparency in the target grid platform.

The intended audience is mainly in research, development, and some industrial fields (pharmaceutical, biotechnology, etc.). Research and development concerns many domains: bioinformatics, computational biology, grid computing, data mining, and so on. Many biological researchers are also using grids in problem solving.

Many undergraduate courses worldwide on bioinformatics and grid computing would be interested in the contents because of the introductory part of each chapter and the additional information on Internet topical resources. In addition, Ph.D. courses related to grid for bioinformatics are a direct target for this book.

This book's purpose is to serve as a single up-to-date source for grid issues to the bioinformatics and computational biology communities. Its text provides details on modern and ongoing research on grid applications for bioinformatics and computational biology and is organized following two different categories grid platforms and grid algorithms.

Some beginning chapters present a state-of-the-art on data and computational grid platforms devoted to some challenging problems in bioinformatics and computational biology: docking and conformational analysis (Chapter 8), sequence analysis and phylogenetics (Chapter 4), pairwise sequence alignment (Chapter 5), heterogeneous biomedical data grids (Chapter 7), RNA folding (Chapter 11), and biological sequence comparison (Chapter 13).

Other chapters illustrate grid services such as OpenMolGRID (open computing grid for molecular sciences and engineering, Chapter 1), WISDOM (molecular docking, Chapter 9), interactive visualization and analysis of biomedical data (Chapter 10), and semantic mediation architecture for a clinical data grid (Chapter 12), and biomedical network modeling (Chapter 16).

Grid algorithms for well-known problems in bioinformatics and computational biology are presented: sequence alignment (Chapter 2), multiple sequence alignment for protein sequences (Chapter 3), phylogenetics (Chapter 6), protein threading (Chapter 14), and DNA fragment assembly (Chapter 15).

EL-GHAZALI TALBI
ALBERT Y. ZOMAYA

Lille, France
Sydney, Australia
September 2007

ACKNOWLEDGMENTS

Thanks to all the contributors for their cooperation in bringing this book to completion.

Professor Talbi would like to thank all the members of his research team DOLPHIN: J-C. Boisson, M. Basseur, C. Boutroue, J. Brongniart, F. Clautiaux, C. Dhaenens, G. Even, L. Jourdan, N. Jozefowiez, M. Khabzaoui, J. Lemesre, A. Liefooghe, C. Luit, N. Melab, N. Mezmaz, A. Tantar, and E. Tantar. Also, he would like to dedicate this book to the memory of his Ph.D. student, S. Cahon.

Professor Zomaya would like to acknowledge the support of his research team at the Advanced Networks Research Lab at Sydney University.

Finally, we are grateful to the support and patience of the team from John Wiley & Sons, without their help this book would not have been possible.

CONTRIBUTORS

ENRIQUE ALBA, Department of Computer Language and Science, ETSI Informatica, Campus Teatinos, Malaga, Spain.

RUMEN ANDONOV, IRISA, Campus de Beaulieu, Rennes, France.

RYUZO AZUMA, RIKEN Genomic Sciences Center, Tsurumi, Yokohama, Kanagawa, Japan.

ADAM L. BAZINET, Center for Bioinformatics and Computational Biology, University of Maryland, College Park, Maryland.

EMILIO BENFENATI, Mario Negri Institute of Pharmaceutical Research, Milano, Italy.

SIEGFRIED BENKNER, Institute of Scientific Computing, University of Vienna, Wien, Austria.

AZZEDINE BOUKERCHE, University of Ottawa, Ontario, Canada.

VINCENT BRETON, IN2P3 CNRS, LPC Clermont-Ferrand, Aubière, France.

MARIAN BUBAK, Institute of Computer Science, AGH, Krakow, Poland.

GUILLAUME COLLET, IRISA, Campus de Beaulieu, Rennes, France.

MICHAEL P. CUMMINGS, Center for Bioinformatics and Computational Biology, University of Maryland, College Park, Maryland.

VIPIN CHAUDHARY, Department of Computer Science and Engineering, The State University of New York, Buffalo, New York.

CHUNXI CHEN, School of Computer Engineering, Nanyang Technology University, Singapore.

HANS DE STERCK, Department of Applied Mathematics, University of Waterloo, Waterloo, Ontario, Canada.

W. DUBITZKY, School of Biomedical Sciences, University of Ulster, Coleraine, United Kingdom.

G. ENGELBRECHT, Institute of Scientific Computing, University of Vienna, Wien, Austria.

JOCHEN FINGBERG, C&C Research Laboratories, NEC Europe, Ltd., St. Augustin, Germany.

J-F. GIBRAT, Mathematics Information and Genome Unit, INRA, Joue-en-Josas, France.

MICAH HAMADY, Department of Computer Science, University of Colorado, Boulder, Colorado.

NICOLAS JACQ, IN2P3 CNRS, LPC Clermont-Ferrand, Aubière, France.

VINOD KASAM, IN2P3 CNRS, LPC Clermont-Ferrand, Aubière, France.

ROB KNIGHT, Department of Chemistry and Biochemistry, University of Colorado, Boulder, Colorado.

AKIHIKI KONAGAYA, RIKEN Genomic Sciences Center, Tsurumi, Yokohama, Kanagawa, Japan.

FUMIKAZU KONISHI, RIKEN Genomic Sciences Center, Tsurumi, Yokohama, Kanagawa, Japan.

KAI KUMPF, Department of Bioinformatics, Fraunhofer-Institute for Algorithms and Scientific Computing (SCAI), Schloss Birlinghoven, St. Augustin, Germany.

JOSEPH LANDMAN, Scalable Informatics LLC, Canton, Michigan.

WEIGUO LIU, School of Computer Engineering, Nanyang Technology University, Singapore.

GABRIAL LUQUE, Department of Computer Language and Science, ETSI Informatica, Campus Teatinos, Malaga, Spain.

ALBA CRISTINA MAGALHAES ALVES DE MELO, University of Brazil, Rio de Janeiro, Brazil.

A. MARIN, IRISA, Campus de Beaulieu, Rennes, France.

KAZUMI MATSUMURA, RIKEN Genomic Sciences Center, Tsurumi, Yokohama, Kanagawa, Japan.

NOUREDINE MELAB, LIFL, University of Lille, INRIA, CNRS, Lille, France.

DANIEL S. MYERS, Center for Bioinformatics and Computational Biology, University of Maryland, College Park, Maryland.

ANTONIO J. NEBRO, Department of Computer Language and Science, ETSI Informatica, Campus Teatinos, Malaga, Spain.

SHINGO OHKI, RIKEN Genomic Sciences Center, Tsurumi, Yokohama, Kanagawa, Japan.

ALEKS PAPO, Department of Applied Mathematics, University of Waterloo, Waterloo, Ontario, Canada.

VINCENT POIRRIEZ, LAMIH, University of Valenciennes, Valenciennes, France.

MATHILDE ROMBERG, School of Biomedical Sciences, University of Ulster, Coleraine, United Kingdom.

JEAN SALZEMANN, IN2P3 CNRS, LPC Clermont-Ferrand, Aubière, France.

BERTIL SCHMIDT, School of Computer Engineering, Nanyang Technology University, Singapore.

PETER M. A. SLOOT, Informatics Institute, University of Amsterdam, Amsterdam, The Netherlands.

EL-GHAZALI TALBI, LIFL, University of Lille, INRIA, CNRS, Lille, France.

ALEXANDRU-ADRIAN TANTAR, LIFL, University of Lille, INRIA, CNRS, Lille, France.

ALFREDO TIRADO-RAMOS, Informatics Institute, University of Amsterdam, Amsterdam, The Netherlands.

Denis Trystram, ID-IMAG, Grenoble, France.

Ryo Umetsu, RIKEN Genomic Sciences Center, Tsurumi, Yokohama, Kanagawa, Japan.

Bharadwaj Veeravalli, Department of Electrical & Computer Engineering, The National University of Singapore, Singapore.

John Paul Walters, Institute for Scientific Computing, Wayne State University, Detroit, Michigan.

Chen Wang, School of Information Technology, University of Sydney, Sydney, Australia.

Alexander Wöhrer, Institute for Scientific Computing, University of Vienna, Wien, Austria.

N. Yanev, University of Sofia, Sofia, Bulgaria.

Sumi Yoshikawa, RIKEN Genomic Sciences Center, Suehiro, Tsurumi Yokohama, Kanagawa, Japan.

Chen Zhang, Department of Computer Science, University of Waterloo, Waterloo, Ontario, Canada.

Jaroslaw Zola, Institute of Computer & Information Sciences, Czestochowa University of Technology, Poland.

Albert Y. Zomaya, School of Information Technology, University of Sydney, Sydney, Australia.

Bing Bing Zhou, School of Information Technology, University of Sydney, Sydney, Australia.

1

OPEN COMPUTING GRID
FOR MOLECULAR SCIENCES

Mathilde Romberg, Emilio Benfenati, and Werner Dubitzky

All substances are poisons; there is none that is not a poison. The right dose differentiates a poison from a remedy.

Paracelsus (1493–1541)

1.1 INTRODUCTION

The number of chemicals in society is largely increasing, and therewith the risk of being exposed to chemicals increases. Knowledge of possible toxic effects of these chemicals is vital, as are the measurement and assessment of the effects and related risks. Within the European Union, the Registration, Evaluation, and Authorisation of Chemicals (REACH) legislation [1] places responsibility on the chemical industries to properly assess the risks associated with their products. It has been estimated that about 30,000 new chemicals will be put on the European market in the coming years. The assessment of these chemicals would cost billions of euros and involve the use of millions of animals. REACH also aims to ensure that risks from substances of very high concern (SVHC) are properly controlled or that the substances are substituted. To match REACH requirements, fast and reliable methods with reproducible results are crucial, and regulatory bodies would be able to approve results. Property prediction and modeling will play an important role in this case [2].

Toxicology, the study of harmful interactions between chemicals and biological systems [3], uses more and more computer models. These models are based on already available data and help to reduce *in vivo* testing. Toxicity modeling and its data have many applications such as characterizing hazards, assessing environmental risks, and identifying potential lead components in drug discovery. A well-established method for toxicity modeling is quantitative structure–activity relationship (QSAR) or quantitative structure–property relationship (QSPR) [4,5]. On the basis of the available measured and calculated properties or activities and descriptors of compounds, predictive models for a certain property are built, which are then used to predict that

Grid Computing for Bioinformatics and Computational Biology. Edited by E.-G. Talbi and A.Y. Zomaya.
Copyright © 2008 John Wiley & Sons, Inc.

property for new compounds. An example for a property is the lethal dose (LD50), which is the amount of a substance that kills 50% of the population exposed to it. This property is mainly used to compare the toxicity of different compounds and to classify them, for example, for hazard warnings.

Classical QSAR models have been based on a very limited number of parameters, which have been measured (such as simple physicochemical properties) or calculated. The model target has been to find a relationship between these parameters and the property within a very limited congeneric series of chemicals. These chemicals share a common skeleton, and a few fragments are linked to it. In more recent years, there has been a significant change in the QSAR scenario: The interest has shifted from the identification of the relationship between the parameters and the property to a more practical use, the prediction of the properties of new chemicals. This calls attention to the predictive power of the model, since previously a model was not verified but was simply assessed with statistical measurements evaluating the fitting of the calculated values. Meanwhile, the challenge has become to model larger sets of compounds, and in addition the number of calculated chemical descriptors or fragments has drastically increased to several thousands. Finally, new more powerful algorithms are used, and these tools also introduce the possibility to extract new knowledge from the data instead of simply leading the algorithms toward well-known parameters based on *a priori* knowledge or hypotheses.

Classical bioinformatics applications such as data warehousing and data mining are a major part of the model development as a result of the following:

(a) The available data are stored in very different sources such as published journal papers, spreadsheets, and relational databases in different formats and notations with different nomenclature and

(b) Relations between the data are mined and used for building predictive models of various kinds such as multilinear regression (MLR), partial least squares (PLS), or artificial neural networks (ANNs).

Other applications applied within the process of prediction model development belong to the field of molecular modeling. Calculating certain properties of a molecule on the basis of its two- and three-dimensional structures provides the basis for the prediction of an endpoint such as LD50. Currently, the model-building and prediction process includes a variety of steps that a toxicologist or a pharmacologist would perform manually step by step by taking care of data selection, parameter setting, data format conversions and data transfer between each pair of subsequent steps, and so on.

Pharmaceutical industry and regulatory bodies together with environmental agencies are very interested in finding fast, cost-effective, easy, and reliable ways to identify compounds with respect to their toxicity. The process of determining lead compounds for a new drug takes years [6,7] in the laboratory, and in addition about 90% of the potential drugs entering the preclinical phase fail in further process due to their toxicity [8,9]. In recent years, pharmaceutical companies along with research initiatives have investigated modeling and prediction methods together with grid computing to streamline and speed up processes. The prominent interest of industries lies in cost reduction, for example, reducing failure rate and using in-house PCs' idle time to run modeling tasks [10,11]. Software providers offer matching grid solutions [12,13] for the latter. These approaches exploit the embarrassingly parallel[1] nature of the applications and offer sophisticated scheduling mechanisms. They are deployed as in-house systems, that is, they do not span multiple organizations, mainly for security reasons. Companies do not risk their data and methods being exposed to outsiders.

Publicly funded research projects in bioinformatics investigate data and computational grid methods to integrate huge amounts of data, develop ontologies, model workflows, efficiently integrate application software including legacy codes, define standards, and offer easy-to-use and efficient tools [14–21].

Section 1.2 of this chapter will highlight grid systems in toxicology and drug discovery and their main characteristics. Section 1.3 will give an in-depth overview of the European OpenMolGRID approach, while Section 1.4 will conclude with an outlook for future developments.

1.2   GRIDS FOR TOXICOLOGY AND DRUG DISCOVERY

Toxicology covers important issues in life and environmental sciences. It is essential that the characteristics of a chemical be identified before producing and releasing it into the environment. In drug discovery, one aim is to exclude toxic, chemically unstable and biologically inactive compounds from the drug discovery [22,23] early on in the process. Therefore, models are being developed for predicting which compounds are liable to fail at a later stage of the process. In this context, QSAR models are one of the most popular methods. Another goal is to identify compounds that would bind to a given biological receptor. The area of docking is important to understand biological processes and find cures that succeed by activating or by inhibiting protein actions [24]. The docking studies require the modeling of the enzyme (which has to be known) in addition to the modeling of the small chemical compounds to be studied (ligand). However, these docking studies are more complex and do require a careful tridimensional description of the ligand. This is not always necessary in the case of QSAR models. For this reason, faster and simpler screening based on easier methods is often performed by drug companies, and the detailed docking studies are performed only for a limited number of chemicals. However, grid technologies introduce new possibilities.

The major objectives for using grid technology [25,26] to support biomathematics and bioinformatics approaches in drug discovery and related fields are to shorten the time to solution and reduce its costs. Users of such technology are (computational) biologists, pharmacologists, and chemists, who are usually not computer system experts. To bridge this gap, providing a user-friendly system is crucial. It allows

---

[1]An application is called embarrassingly parallel if no particular effort is needed to split it into a large number of independent problems that can be executed in parallel, and these processes do not need to communicate with each other.

the user to solve the biochemical problem without the knowledge about the details of the underlying system. Users require access to their private and publicly available data, execution of legacy software, and visualization of results. In cases where users develop their own application software, it should also be easily integratable.

There exist quite a few initiatives, projects, and systems that exploit grid methods for chemoinformatics, bioinformatics, and computational biology, and some of which focus on applications relevant to this chapter. One of the early grid projects in drug discovery is the Virtual Laboratory [27]. In the beginning of this century, the Virtual Laboratory project set up an infrastructure based on the Globus Toolkit 2.4 [28] and the Nimrod-G resource broker [29], specifically designed for parametric studies. The Virtual Laboratory environment provides software tools and resource brokers that facilitate large-scale molecular studies on geographically distributed computational and data grid resources. This is used for examining or screening millions of chemical compounds (molecules) in the Chemical Data Bank (CDB) to identify those having potential use in drug design. The DOCK software package [30] is integrated for molecular docking calculations and for access to the CDB, and the data replica catalogs are provided. The user interface allows us to specify input and output data sets and locations, set parameters for the DOCK software, submit jobs, and retrieve output. This command-line interface has recently been replaced by a Web portal within the Australian BioGrid initiative [31].

DDGrid [32] is a subproject of the China grid initiative that also focuses on docking. Its goal is to analyze chemical databases and identify compounds appropriate for a given biological receptor. It offers access to a variety of databases such as Specs (chemically available compounds' structure database), MDL Comprehensive Medicinal Chemistry 3D (pharmaceutical compounds), National Cancer Institute Database (NCI)-3D (structures with corresponding 3D models), China Natural Products Database, Traditional Chinese Medicinal Database (TCMD), and ZINC-ChemBridge (chemical structures). The user is provided with tools for preprocessing of data (Combimark), for visualization, for structure search, and for encrypting and decrypting of data. The core middleware layer is based on the Berkeley Open Infrastructure for Network Computing (BOINC, [33]), which is a well-established base for the group of "at home" systems. For example, Rosetta@home [34] uses PCs all over the world to model protein structures and interactions to understand diseases and find cures. Rosetta@home distinguishes itself from other grid initiatives in drug discovery by using voluntarily donated free CPU cycles to execute the Rosetta program. The "users" of these systems have no influence on the application. They download the software that uses the free CPU cycles to run the application set up by a research group, which in this case was David Baker's group at the University of Washington in Seattle [35].

Within the UK e-Science program, the e-Science Solutions for the Analysis of Complex Systems (eXSys) project [36] studies drug discovery from the angle of interaction networks. It analyzes protein interaction networks to identify sets of proteins in a bacterium that, if they were inhibited, would destroy the bacterium but not affect its host organism. These proteins qualify as potential drug targets. eXSys tackles data access and integration issues by building local data sets for intracellular metabolic or protein interaction networks from heterogeneous resources such as the Database of Interacting Proteins (DIP, [37]), the Kyoto Encyclopedia of Genes and Genomes (KEGG, [38]), the Swissprot protein databank [39], and publications. A project internal common data format is established in which all data are integrated. The necessary network analysis programs plus their integration as grid services are developed. A graphical user interface allows users to select interaction networks from a local database, analyze them, and visualize the results. myGrid [40] and OGSA-DAI/OGSA-DQP [41] are used for data access and analysis of various data sources. The myGrid infrastructure offers a workbench well suited for bioinformaticians. It includes workflow generation and enactment, as well as a variety of services for data integration such as knowledge annotation and verification of experiments (KAVE), semantic discovery (Feta), and life science identifier (LSID) services for data handling.

The aspects of workflows for the drug design pipeline are also dealt with in the Wide *In Silico* Docking On Malaria (WISDOM) data challenge [42], a project to challenge the infrastructure built by the Enabling grids for e-Science (EGEE) project [43]. WISDOM seeks to find new inhibitors for a family of proteins by using *in silico* docking on the grid. During the 6-week data challenge in mid-2005, a terabyte of data was produced using 80 CPU years. These data from over 40 million docked ligands are now being further analyzed.

While most of the drug-discovery-related grid projects and systems deal with simulations and modeling of docking ligands to proteins and the identification of protein functions, it is also important to identify and optimize lead molecules with the targeted therapeutic potential. Pharmaceutical companies set up in-house grid systems to also cover this aspect. Little is published about these grid systems, but information can be found in case studies of software vendors [10] and press releases [44–46]. Key to this approach is workflow modeling, semantic Web technologies, and data management.

The approaches described use a variety of grid middleware or infrastructure systems, including grid service and pregrid-service versions of the Globus Toolkit, gLite (basis of the EGEE test bed), Web services, network computing (desktop grid), myGrid, and the pregrid-service version of UNICORE. With respect to middleware, all further developments aim at a service-oriented architecture (SOA), whatever type of resource is being used. The Open grid Services Architecture (OGSA [47]) has been defined by the Open grid Forum [48] to achieve a standardized grid framework. For drug discovery, the topics workflow modeling, application integration, standards for data structures, metadata and ontologies, and data integration are equally important.

Recently, a series of activities has addressed both the issues of databases of chemical compounds used in the world and how to predict their environmental and toxic properties. The European Commission's Joint Research Centre is considering the strategic development of a general system to predict properties of industrial chemicals. The U.S. Environmental Protection Agency (EPA), which adopts predictive tools for the property predictions of chemicals for decades, is also enlarging its set of tools. The Danish EPA predicted properties of tens of thousands of chemicals using a set of software. All these initiatives show the deep interest in a more powerful approach capable to cope with a problem that involves many programs, databases, and resources, which would surely benefit from an integrated strategy supported by grid.

The following section will detail these characteristics taking the OpenMolGRID system as an example.

1.3 EXAMPLE OpenMolGRID

The Open Computing grid for Molecular Sciences and Engineering (OpenMolGRID, [49]) system has been developed to support the lead component identification in drug discovery and designed in an open manner to be of immediate use for other applications in biochemistry and pharmacology. The objectives of this project are to

- Develop tools that permit end users to securely and seamlessly access, integrate, and use relevant globally distributed data resources;
- Develop tools that permit end users to securely and seamlessly access, use, and schedule globally distributed computational methods and tools; and
- Provide foundations and design principles for developing and constructing next-generation molecular engineering systems.

The selected underlying grid middleware UNICORE [50] offers well-designed interfaces for application software integration both on the user client side and on the execution server side. It provides data access and data transfer together with workflow modeling, execution, and monitoring. To facilitate the development of prediction model and prediction workflows, the OpenMolGRID project developed abstraction layers to easily integrate application software and to access different publicly available relevant databases (e.g., ECOTOX [51], NTP [52]), and built a data warehouse from that data [53]. It includes automated workflow support that simplifies the task of the user by including support steps such as data conversion and data transfer into the workflow, by automatically assigning appropriate execution servers, and by exploiting parallelism [54,55].

The general architecture underlying the OpenMolGRID system is depicted in Fig. 1.1. The abstract resource interfaces are the key to flexibility providing a common interface accessible by the UNICORE server and a resource-specific interface on the resource side. Each resource has an XML resource description attached to inform the server and the client about input and output characteristics and behavior. The challenges addressed in the OpenMolGRID project are as follows:

- Molecular design and engineering are computationally very demanding, and they generates huge amounts of data.
- Data from a variety of different sources need to be integrated using data warehousing techniques, and the data need to be accessible seamlessly.
- The scientific workflows involve heterogeneous data, compute, and application resources.

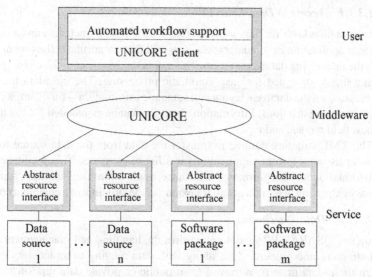

Figure 1.1. OpenMolGRID high-level architecture.

- The scientific workflows are fairly complex and involve multiple dependent steps.

These challenges become obvious when analyzing, for example, the QSAR model-building process: First, relevant experimental (toxicity) data are searched from one or multiple sources, which requires that all sources be accessible through the system and that the relevant data can be extracted. The structural information is then extracted and a 3D structure is generated for each molecule. Application software such as MOL-GEO [56] is used to accomplish this task. In the next step, the generated molecular geometry is optimized using the molecular modeling software for example, MOPAC [57]. These applications process a single structure at a time so that the tasks can easily be distributed. This is also true for the next step in the workflow, the calculation of descriptors, for example, using the molecular descriptor analyzer (MDA) module from the Codessa [58] software package. The results from all structures serve as input to model development software—for example, the best multilinear regression (BMLR) analysis module of Codessa. The following sections will describe the OpenMolGRID solutions in detail.

1.3.1 Data Management

Besides storage of data, the major challenge in data management is the access to every kind of data source containing data relevant to drug discovery, toxicology, pharmacology, and, of course, the interpretation and integration of these data.

1.3.1.1   Access to Data Sources

The abstraction layer for data sources is realized as a set of metadata and a server-side wrapper application called database access tool that encapsulates the communication with the underlying database system. The output data are sent to the client in an XML format that is designed for easy automatic processing. The metadata file contains information on the database layout and semantic information—for example, database name, access restrictions, information about the database intended for the user, table names, field names, and types.

The XML structure defined to transfer the data from the data source to the user client or as input to other applications is a list of elements. This facilitates an easy transformation to other formats, for instance, application software input formats, and for easy extraction of certain fields, for example, the structure of a chemical compound.

1.3.1.2   Data Warehouse

Predictive QSAR/QSPR modeling requires the handling and management of chemical structure and property data, along with data relating to molecular descriptors. Often these data must be retrieved from public or private data repositories as well as integrated and formatted so that it is amenable to data mining methods such as linear regression methods, artificial neural networks, and decision tree algorithms. Data warehousing [59] provides the data integration and formatting functionality required by data mining applications. It is employed to integrate, cleanse, normalize, and consolidate data from different sources and to map them onto "ready-to-use" data structures (e.g., by denormalizing relational database tables). Within the OpenMol-GRID system, a grid-enabled data warehouse for molecular engineering environments has been developed [53]. Its main purpose is to provide integrated and consolidated data originating from selected data resources relevant to molecular engineering. The following data resources have been integrated:

- National Toxicology Program database, which provides information regarding potentially toxic chemicals to health regulatory and research agencies, the scientific and medical communities, and the public NTP [52]
- ECOTOX (ecotoxicology) databases Aquire and Terretox, which provide chemical toxicity information for aquatic and terrestrial life, respectively [51]
- Multidrug resistance (MDR) data set, proprietary
- G-protein-coupled receptor (GPCR) data set, proprietary

The databases integrated in the data warehouse are harvested from the sources mentioned above and are mapped into the warehouse and its physical repository. A detailed view of the OpenMolGRID data warehouse and its relation to the Web and other OpenMolGRID components is depicted in Fig. 1.2. The warehouse processes follow the typical extract, transform, and load scheme (also known as ETL). According to reflect updates in the underlying databases, the warehousing process is performed periodically. The extract component transfers the database from its public Web site as single or multiple files (depending on the database) to the data warehouse. Each

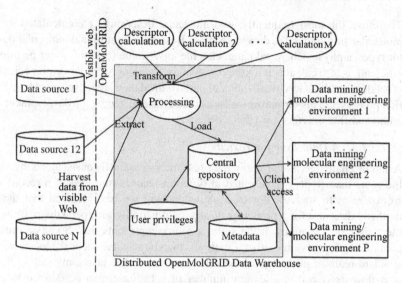

Figure 1.2. OpenMolGRID data warehouse and related components.

database has its own implementation-specific format from which the data are extracted and mapped into the data transformation environment. Within this environment, the data are denormalized from relational databases, cleansed (inconsistent entries are removed), enriched, and standardized based on the requirements of the molecular engineering environments. New fields are computed to facilitate different types of analyses. For example, the log inverse of the measured dosage of a chemical's toxicity is often more useful for some calculations and models than that of the toxicity value itself. By providing this value within the warehouse's data structures, the user does not have to perform this calculation and can focus on the more intricate aspects of the modeling task at hand. Data normalization may involve, for example, missing value imputation, mean centering, or alignment to canonical units. In addition, complex data transformations (descriptor calculations) are integrated into the warehouse again to offer values the users would have to calculate otherwise.

The transformed data are then loaded into the data warehouse's physical data storage, a PostgreSQL relational database. Client access to data in the OpenMolGRID data warehouse is enabled via the generic database access tool mentioned above. Inputs and outputs are encapsulated in an OpenMolGRID-specific XML syntax and data are easily identifiable due to being associated with generic data types defined especially for OpenMolGRID's data needs. These data types are used throughout all applications in the OpenMolGRID system.

The data warehouse's transformation environment includes the calculation of certain descriptor values as mentioned. Specialized software is required to perform these calculations and they are expensive to compute, especially if there are a large number of chemicals and several representations of the same chemical. From a data warehouse perspective, these descriptor calculations are complex data transformations.

Therefore, the most frequently used molecular descriptors are calculated for each molecular structure in the data warehouse. Besides the traditional molecular descriptor types, a physicochemical parameter, the log P value (octanol–water partition coefficient), is also calculated for the compounds. Essentially, the descriptor calculation procedure amounts to virtualization of parts of the data warehouse's data transformation processes. This virtualization functionality is realized by the development of the command-line interface for UNICORE.

1.3.1.3   A Data Type for Toxicity

A major challenge is that many data resources contain inconsistencies by way of the same data (types) represented in different records (the idea of a record varies from source to source). For example, supposing we have decided that the standardized data unit for a particular dosage field is milligrams per kilogram (mg/kg), there may be variations in the style, a source represents this. Some records may contain Mg/kg (or some other variation), thereby causing inconsistencies with the standard realized in the OpenMolGRID warehouse. The taxonomy step in the process flow described enables any number of substitutions to be defined to ensure that consistency is maintained within, and between, data resources entering the warehouse. Characteristic of many data sources is the idea that each data field contains a value from a set of allowable values. This can be problematic when a number of resources are being integrated into a data warehouse. For example, a dosage field can have several measurement units associated with it—for example, g/kg, mg/kg, or µg/kg—which have to be aligned to be usable for data mining. In the absence of a data warehouse, this must be performed manually, but in the OpenMolGRID data warehouse, anautomated mechanism is required. The mechanism was developed based on canonical units or primitives. Measurement units can be broken down into several categories—for example, length, weight, and time. Each of these categories has an associated base unit, the unit primitive—for example, kilograms for weight. For the conversion between various forms of the same measurement category, scaling factors (which can be more complex mathematical formulations) are defined, in both directions, to enable dynamic conversion from one unit to another.

1.3.1.4   Data Storage

Besides the data warehouse that contains the cleaned and transformed data from available data sources, space to store (intermediate) results is required. A relational database has been set up to support the complete molecular engineering process. It is capable of handling all data generated in the OpenMolGRID system (molecules, descriptors, models, experimental property values, predicted property values, etc.). It is set up as a read/write store, while the data warehouse is read-only from the end users' perspective.

Very important for a data store for molecular sciences is a structure and substructure search capability that has been developed. This function is necessary for identifying the best subset of data (chemical compounds) to be used for further analysis and is fundamental in chemical and related communities. The substructure search is realized

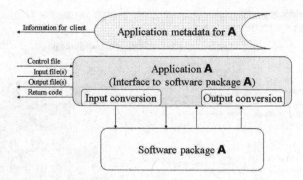

Figure 1.3. Application interface.

as a two-part process with two different queries. The first query aims to select a subset of structures that may contain the substructure. This is performed using a fingerprinting approach, which significantly accelerates the search. Fingerprints of the structures are matched against the fingerprint of the substructure, and those structures that cannot possibly match are removed from the set. The second query is performed within the matching subset to select structures that actually contain the full chemical substructure. The comparison is computationally expensive, which makes it important to use the first step to reduce the input set for the second query and thereby make the overall process more efficient.

1.3.2   Application Integration

Similar to the integration of data sources through metadata and access software (database access tool), all kinds of applications can be integrated into the system as shown in Fig. 1.3. The abstract interface is realized as a wrapper to existing software modules. It provides the description of the application (its metadata) and the input/output (I/O) data format conversion routines from the standard data format to the proprietary and vice versa. The metadata also define the interface and I/O format information used by clients. As a result, a well-defined application on the server side can be addressed on the user client side by an application-specific interface as shown in the following section.

1.3.3   User Interface

OpenMolGRID, being based on the UNICORE grid middleware [60], includes the UNICORE graphical client (see Fig. 1.4), which is shown here with the detailed workflow for model building (for the description of the coarse-grained workflow, see introduction to Section 1.3). It is a Java application offering job creation and monitoring for complex multistep and multisite jobs. Jobs are composed of subjobs, tasks, and dependencies reflecting temporal and data dependencies. Jobs are represented by acyclic directed graphs with tasks and subjobs as vertices and dependencies

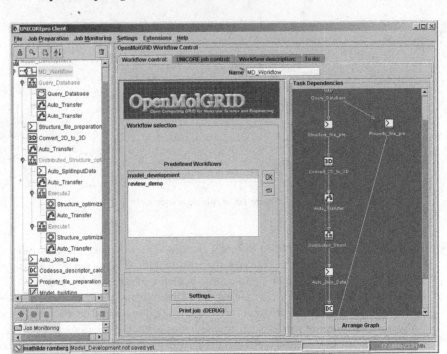

Figure 1.4. User client.

as edges. UNICORE jobs representing subjobs are associated with a target system (vsite), where the (part of the) job should be executed. The basic tasks the client provides are *import* of input data files, *export* of output data files, *transfer* of data between subjobs, *execute* of a program, and dependencies for simple sequential dependency, *if-then-else*, *while*, *repeat*, and *hold*. The most important feature in the OpenMol-GRID context is the client's plugin interface to integrate application-specific plugins that represent new flavors of the execute task. The application-specific plugins correspond to defined application resources on the server side as described in Section 1.3.2.

1.3.4 Workflow Modeling

The specification and execution of complex workflows such as those in molecular design and engineering using grid resources is still under research [61]. Workflow solutions exist mostly for business processes. Languages to describe business processes are, for example, BPEL4WS (Business Process Execution Language for Web Services, see Reference 62) and WPDL (Workflow Process Definition Language; see Reference 63). The modeling of complex workflows in the scientific arena is mostly performed manually using the tools the existing grid middleware offers [64,65]. The key to automated generation of workflows is the description of software resources available on grid computing resources. In the OpenMolGRID system, this is provided by the application's abstraction layer. These descriptions can be used for automated application identification and inclusion in multistep workflows. The following paragraphs will describe the solution for automated workflow specification and processing developed within the OpenMolGRID project.

Workflow Specification. Workflows consist of task or process elements with logical, temporal, and data dependencies. Tasks may also be independent of other tasks in a workflow. As described in Section 1.3.3, OpenMolGRID uses the UNICORE client that offers graphical workflow specification to build up complex jobs. Existing workflow description languages do not match the UNICORE model with respect to application software resources. As these play the most important role within the automatic job generation, a workflow specification language has been developed that enables a high-level definition of various scientific processes containing sufficient information for the automatic generation of complete UNICORE jobs. This includes the tasks and their dependencies, as well as the necessary resources. XML has been selected as a specification language for the workflow. A core element in a workflow is the task, which is described by

- A string, the task's function to be fulfilled by an application resource and supported by a client plugin
- A string, the UNICORE task identifier in the job tree
- An integer, the unique numerical task identification within the workflow
- A boolean, the export flag specifying whether result files are to be exported to the user's workstation
- A boolean, the split flag specifying whether the task is data parallel and can be distributed onto several execution systems
- A string, the identifier of an application that is capable of splitting the input data for this task into *n* chunks (splittertask)
- A string, the identifier of an application that is capable of joining the *n* result files into one file (joinerTask)
- A set of options to feed the application with parameter settings

A set of resources is specified for a task requesting runtime, number of nodes, number of processors, and memory. The target system for the execution of all tasks within a UNICORE (sub)job can be specified by usite and vsite.

The following shows the XML workflow specification for the model development process:

```
<?xml version="1.0" ?>
<!- *** Model Multi-Drug resistance on OpenMolGRID data warehouse data ***
-- >
<workflow xmlns="http://www.openmolgrid.org/namespaces/2004/Workflow
  Description" xmlns:rd="http://www.openmolgrid.org/namespaces/2004/
  SimpleResources" >
  <group type="subjob" identifier="Query Database" id="1" >
```

```
<!-- wrapper group to allow easy datasource selection -->
  <task name="DataBaseRequest" identifier="Query Database" id="11"
  export="false" split="false" >
  <option name="query" value="SELECT chemical.moldw_id,
  chemical.structuretype, chemical.fileformat,chemical.
  molecularstructure,property.propertyid,property.propertyname,
  property.loginverse FROM (chemical LEFT JOIN property ON
  chemical.moldw_id=property.moldw_id) WHERE chemical.
  molecularstructure!=" and property.propertyname like 'Multi-Drug%'" />
  </task>
  <task name="DataBaseRequestToPLF" identifier="Property file
  preparation" id="3" export="false" split="false" />
  <task name="DataBaseRequestToSLF" identifier="Structure file
  preparation" id="2" export="false" split="false" />
  <resourceRequest>
    <rd:node usite="Ulster OMG" vsite="MOLDW" />
  </resourceRequest>
</group>
<task name="2Dto3Dconversion" identifier="Convert 2D to 3D" id="21"
export="false" split="false" />
<task name="SemiempiricalCalculation" identifier="Structure optimization"
id="25" export="false" split="true" splitterTask="SplitStructureList"
joinerTask="JoinStructureLists" >
  <option name="keywords" value="AM1 PRECISE 1SCF NOINTER" />
</task>
<task name="DescriptorCalculation" identifier="Codessa descriptor
calculation" id="29" export="false" split="false" />
<task name="ModelBuilding" identifier="Model building" id="40"
export="false" split="false">
  <resourceRequest>
    <rd:resources runTime="3600" />
  </resourceRequest>
</task>
<dependency pred="11" succ="2" />
  <!-- db request to structure extract -->
<dependency pred="11" succ="3" />
  <!-- db request to property extract -->
<dependency pred="3" succ="40" />
  <!-- property extract to model building -->
<dependency pred="2" succ="21" />
  <!-- struct extract to 2d to 3d -->
<dependency pred="21" succ="25" />
  <!-- 2d to 3d to semiempirical -->
<dependency pred="25" succ="29" />
  <!-- semiempirical to descriptor calc -->
<dependency pred="3" succ="40" />
  <!-- property extract to model building -->
<dependency pred="29" succ="40" />
  <!-- descriptor calc to Modelbuilding -->
<resourceRequest>
  <rd:node usite = "Tartu OMG" vsite = "VSite1"/ >
</resourceRequest>
</workflow>
```

Workflow Processing. A workflow specified as described serves as input to the MetaPlugin, a special plugin to the UNICORE client. The MetaPlugin parses the XML workflow, creates the corresponding UNICORE job, and assigns target systems and resources to it. These tasks include a number of sophisticated actions:

- Subjobs are introduced into the job wherever necessary, for example, when requested applications are not available on the same target system.
- Transfer tasks are introduced into the job to transmit data from one target system to another, which is the execution system of a subjob.
- Data conversion tasks are added between two tasks where the output format (specified in XML according to the application metadata) of one task does not match the input format of the successor task.
- Splitter and transfer tasks are added to the workflow as predecessor tasks of a splitable task for input data preparation.
- Subjobs are created around split tasks for each selected target system and a transfer task to transfer the output data back to the superordinate subjob.
- Joiner tasks are added to join the output data of split tasks.
- The directed acyclic graph of dependencies between all tasks (the Explicit ones from the workflow specification and the automatically generated ones) is set up.

The MetaPlugin uses the resource information provided by the target system (vsite), the metadata of the applications, and information about the plugins available to the client. A resource information provider component has been developed to support the MetaPlugin in resource selection. It returns the client plugin handling the function, the target systems offering the corresponding application, and the I/O formats. Currently, the MetaPlugin does resource selection at a basic level, but a more sophisticated resource broker component can easily be added. The main advantage of this mechanism is that a user who wants to do model building can name the coarse-grained tasks and their dependencies in an XML workflow, thereby avoiding the tedious job of the step-by-step preparation of the complex workflow of the corresponding UNICORE job. The latter would demand detailed knowledge about, for example, I/O formats for the inclusion of data conversion tasks and the manual splitting and distribution of tasks onto appropriate target systems. The automatic UNICORE job creating gives the flexibility to the system to adapt to the actual grid layout and resource availability and helps to avoid human errors.

Figure 1.4 shows on the left-hand side the UNICORE job the MetaPlugin generated from the workflow detailed. All tasks starting with "Auto_" have been added as are the groups "Execute1" and "Execute2," where the semiempirical calculation is distributed among systems offering the necessary application software. "Auto_Transfers" are used, for example, to transfer data from the database to the systems where the structure conversion and the model development are to be executed. The "Auto_SplitInputData" and "Auto_Join_Data" tasks have been included to partition the input data for the semiempirical calculation to allow for its distributed execution and to join the result files after the execution is completed.

1.3.5   Experience

One of the most noteworthy outcomes of the OpenMolGRID project is that it paves the way for standardization of model-building and prediction processes. Within Open-MolGRID, we checked that results obtained with the automatic process are equivalent to those obtained by manual modeling, both for the chemical descriptor calculation and for the QSAR results. This shows that OpenMolGRID has practical potential as a regular tool for QSAR modeling. It is important to note the advantages in this direction offered by the OpenMolGRID approach for models for regulatory purposes. Indeed, in the case of scientific applications the automatic simplified process is surely convenient and appealing, and it speeds up the application. But for regulatory purposes, it becomes necessary to get the same result independently of the user. So far in most of the cases QSAR models, except those within the classical approach with a few simple parameters, require manual steps that produce variable results due to optimization differences and the lack of sufficient details. The availability of automatic QSAR modeling tools would surely cover the need for more reproducible results, which is a requirement for results to be used within a regulatory context: The implementation of a candidate protocol for QSAR modeling as a workflow would achieve reproducibility, easy models, and suitability for regulatory purposes [66].

Mazzatorta et al. [67] obtained stable and thoroughly validated QSARs using the OpenMolGRID system, and Maran et al. [68] detailed the use of OpenMolGRID for the development of QSAR models for the prediction of HIV-1 protease inhibition ability of potential inhibitors. They pointed out that building the model is accomplishable within 1 h using the system instead of 1 day because of automation of the workflow and parallel execution of tasks. This shows that the objective to shorten the time to solution has been achieved. Especially the automatic distribution of a task onto the available systems and the automated output/input format conversion account for this.

During the development of the system, application integration has proved to be easy because the application software itself does not need to be adapted, only a wrapper implementing the abstract interface has to be developed. The data warehouse's transformation process has been significantly improved by the provision of a command-line interface and a queuing component to the UNICORE system. The data warehouse uses these components to submit descriptor calculation to grid resources and retrieve the output. Indirectly, this also speeds up the user's workflows because values that every user requires are already calculated up-front and provided in the data warehouse.

The current lack of an XML editor to generate the workflows makes it difficult for the toxicologists to prepare their own workflows. These have to be prepared by someone familiar with XML and the workflow schema which can easily be covered for standard workflows that are prepared initially and made available to everyone—for example, the model development process, but not for, for example, experimental workflows.

A set of open issues has arisen from data handling. Standard formats should be used wherever possible, but, for example, there is not yet an established standard for globally unique identifiers for molecular descriptors. How to store the predictive models has not yet been resolved because PMML (predictive model markup language, [69]) is not sufficient, and it cannot be used to describe PLS (partial least square) or PCR (principal components regression) models. An extension to PMML could be a solution. For a molecular structure, multiple conformations can exist, and the handling of these multiple data including their storage, selection, and processing has not yet been resolved in chemoinformatics. These topics will, among others, be dealt with in the EC-funded project Chemomentum [70].

1.4 SUMMARY AND OUTLOOK

QSAR modeling, *in silico* modeling, is a prominent method in toxicology and pharmacology. Important is the quality of the models; for example, the REACH legislation requires a clear estimation of the quality of a model, its accuracy, before it can be used for REACH purposes. The European Chemical Bureau is coordinating an action on QSAR [71] in support of prediction modeling for regulatory purposes. Within drug discovery, it is vital to have significant models for the prediction of ADMET (absorption, distribution, metabolism, excretion, and toxicity) properties [72]. The mathematical modeling is supported by grid computing because it helps speed up the process of model building through parallelization and user-friendliness. Pharmaceutical companies save further costs with in-house grids using their idle desktop PC cycles instead of investing in additional compute power. The emerging service-oriented architectured grid systems allow interoperability and thereby support for true global sharing of all kinds of resources (CPU cycles, data, knowledge, applications, etc.). This enables collaboration and may lead to synergy in achieving better and quicker results. Data and knowledge management are key to interoperability. The data from different sources need to be interpretable, requiring ontologies to be further developed to enable "understanding." The Semantic grid [73] offers the necessary framework. It can be used to automate the integration of data from different sources and their transformation into knowledge. The CombeChem UK e-Science project [74] demonstrates the advantages of Semantic grid for data from chemistry. On the basis of a chemistry ontology and RDF (Resource Description Framework) graphs using XML data descriptions, it provides a flexible data structure for data integration and knowledge management. Drug development and toxicology are going to gain from the smart laboratory that has developed. An aspect to be covered is data privacy and security, especially for company-owned data or medical records. These data would not be allowed to leave the source, but it may be allowed to mine the data locally and transfer only the results. Therefore, distributed data mining is another topic needing further research [75]. In addition to security issues, it may not be feasible to transfer data to an execution server because of their sheer volume.

In the future, grid computing will further impact procedures in toxicology and pharmacology. Having standard procedures will help regulatory bodies in their decisions. High-quality prediction models will reduce the amount of *in vitro* and *in vivo* testings. Nanotoxicology [76], the research on toxic effects of nanoparticles (particles of nanometer size), will need computational and prediction models and procedures for determining physicochemical parameters and effects and for risk assessment. Drug development will extend its use of computational methods and knowledge exploitation to find cures. The systems, biology approach to simulate all processes in a biological system—for example, a cell—is used to further understand the way the system works and can be influenced, which may improve drug discovery [77].

ACKNOWLEDGMENTS

This work has partially been funded by the European Commission under Grants IST-2001-37238 and FP6-2005-IST-5-033437.

REFERENCES

1. EU Chemicals Legislation—REACH (Registration, Evaluation and Authorisation of Chemicals). http://ec.europa.eu/enterprise/reach/index_en.htm.

2. M.T.D. Cronin, J.S. Jaworska, J.D. Walker, M.H.I. Comber, C.D. Watts, A.P. Worth, Use of QSARs in international decision-making frameworks to predict health effects of chemical substances, *Environmental Health Perspectives* **111**(10), 1391–1401, 2003.

3. J. Timbrell, *Introduction to Toxicology*, third edition, Taylor & Francis, Boca Raton, FL, 2002.

4. C. Hansch, A. Leo, Exploring QSAR: *Fundamentals and Applications in Chemistry and Biology*, Vol. 1, American Chemical Society, Washington, DC, Chapters 6 and 11, 1995.

5. J.D. McKinney, A. Richard, C. Waller, M.C. Newman, F. Gerberick, The practice of structure activity relationships (SAR) in toxicology, *Toxicological Sciences* **56**(1), 8–17, 2000.

6. American Association for the Advancement of Science. http://www.aaas.org/international/africa/gbdi/mod1c.html.

7. PPD Corporate Information. http://www.ppdi.com/corporate/faq/about_drug_development/home.htm.

8. UK Department of Trade and Industry (DTI), call for research proposals. http://www.technology programme.org.uk/site/DTISpring06/Spring06Docs/BioscienceHealthcare06.pdf.

9. J.A. DiMasi, Risks in new drug development: Approval success rates for investigational drugs, *Clinical Pharmacology & Therapeutics* **69**(5), 297–307, 2001.

10. Novartis Grid MP case study. http://www.ud.com/resources/files/cs_novartis.pdf.

11. ADMEToxGrid project. http://www.lpds.sztaki.hu/index.php?loadproject s/current/comgenex.php.

12. United Devices Grid MP on Intel Architecture. http://www.ud.com/resources/files/wp_intel_ud.pdf.

13. Platform Computing products for life sciences. http://www.platform.com/Life.Sciences/CustomersCaseStudies.htm.

14. North Carolina bioportal. http://www.ncbiogrid.org.

15. Workflow management for bioinformatics (pegasys). http://bioinformatics.ucb.ca/pegasys.

16. Cancer biomedical informatics grid (cagrid). https://cabig.nci.nih.gov/workspaces/Architecture/caGrid.

17. BioPAUÁ. http://www.biopaua.lncc.br/ENGL/index.php.

18. Open bioinformatics grid. http://www.obigrid.org.

19. Asia Pacific biogrid initiative. http://www.apbionet.org/apbiogrid.

20. Genegrid—virtual bioinformatics laboratory. http://www.qub.ac.uk/escience/dev/article.php, section projects.

21. OpenMolGrid project. http://www.openmolgrid.org/.

22. Drug Discovery Process, graphics by Novartis.
    http://www.nibr.novartis.com/images/OurScience/drug.discovery_graph.jpg.

23. Genelabs' Drug Discovery Process. http://www.genelabs.com/research/discoveryProcess.html.

24. E.A. Lunney, Computing in drug discovery: The design phase, *IEEE Computing in Science and Engineering* **3**(5), 105–108, 2001.

25. I. Foster, C. Kesselman (Eds.), *The Grid: Blueprint for a New Computing Infrastructure*, Morgan Kaufmann Publishers, San Francisco, CA, 1998.

26. I. Foster, C. Kesselman (Eds.), *The Grid 2: Blueprint for a New Computing Infrastructure*, second edition, Morgan Kaufmann Publishers, San Francisco, CA, 2004.

27. R. Buyya, K. Branson, J. Giddy, D. Abramson, The virtual laboratory: enabling molecular modelling for drug design on the World Wide Grid, *Concurrency and Computation: Practice and Experience* **15**(1), 1–25, 2003.

28. Globus Toolkit 2.4 Overview. http://www.globus.org/toolkit/docs/2.4/overview.html.

29. R. Buyya, D. Abramson, J. Giddy, Nimrod/G: An architecture for a resource management and scheduling system in a global computational grid, in: *Proceedings of the HPC ASIA 2000, Beijing, China*, IEEE Computer Society Press, Los Alamitos, CA, 2000.

30. B. Shoichet, D. Bodian, I. Kuntz, Molecular docking using shape descriptors, *Journal of Computational Chemistry* **13**(3), 380–397, 1992.

31. H. Gibbins, K. Nadiminti, B. Beeson, R. Chhabra, B. Smith, R. Buyya, The Australian BioGrid Portal: Empowering the Molecular Docking Research Community. Technical Report, GRIDS-TR-2005-9, Grid Computing and Distributed Systems Laboratory, University of Melbourne, Australia, June 13, 2005.

32. W. Zhang, J. Shen, Drug Discovery Grid (DDGrid), Second Grid@Asia Workshop, Shanghai, China, February 20–22, 2006.

33. Berkeley Open Infrastructure for Network Computing (BOINC). http://boinc.berkeley.edu/.

34. O. Schueler-Furman, C. Wang, P. Bradley, K. Misura, D. Baker, Progress in modeling of protein structures and interactions, *Science* **310**, 638–642, 2005.

35. The Baker Laboratory. http://depts.washington.edu/bakerpg/.

36. e-Science Solutions for the Analysis of Complex Systems (eXSys).
    http://www.neresc.ac.uk/projects/eXSys.

37. Database of Interacting Proteins (DIP). http://dip.doe-mbi.ucla.edu/.

38. KEGG: Kyoto Encyclopedia of Genes and Genomes. http://www.genome.ad.jp/kegg/.

39. UniProtKB/Swiss-Prot Protein Knowledgebase. http://www.ebi.ac.uk/swissprot/.

40. R. Stevens, A. Robinson, C.A. Goble, my Grid: personalised bioinformatics on the information grid, *Bioinformatics* **19**(Suppl. 1), i302–i304, 2003.

41. Open Grid Services Architecture—Data Access and Integration. http://www.ogsadai.org.uk/.

42. Initiative for grid-enabled drug discovery against neglected and emergent diseases.
    http://wisdom.eu-egee.fr/.

43. Enabling Grids for e-Science. http://www.eu-egee.org/.

44. Will LION and IBM succeed with the drug research Grid solution?
    http://www.gridtoday.com/02/1111/100708.html.

45. Platform partners with Matrix Science to accelerate drug discovery for pharmaceutical companies.
    http://www.hoise.com/primeur/02/articles/weekly/AE-PR-12-02-38.html.

46. Output of e-Science project helps GSK speed up drug discovery.
    http://www.rcuk.ac.uk/escience/news/ahm9.asp.

47. The Open Grid Services Architecture, Version 1.0. 2005. Global Grid Forum, http://www.gridforum.org/documents/GFD.30.pdf.

48. The Open Grid Forum (former Global Grid Forum and Enterprise Grid Alliance). http://www.ogf.org.

49. M. Romberg (Ed.), *OpenMolGRID—Open Computing Grid for Molecular Science and Engineering*, NIC series No. 29, Forschungszentrum Julich, ISBN 3-00-016007-8, July 2005.

50. UNICORE—Uniform Interface to Computing Resources. http://unicore.sourceforge.net.

51. ECOTOXicology Database. http://www.epa.gov/ecotox.

52. National Toxicology Program. http://ntp-server.niehs.nih.gov.

53. W. Dubitzky, D. McCourt, M. Galushka, M. Romberg, B. Schuller, Grid-enabled data warehousing for molecular engineering, *Parallel Computing* **30**(9–10), 1019–1035, 2004.

54. B. Schuller, M. Romberg, L. Kirtchakova, Application Driven Grid Developments in the Open-MolGRID Project, in: P.M.A. Sloot, A.G. Hoekstra, T. Priol, A. Reinefeld, and M. Bubak (Eds.), *Advances in Grid Computing—EGC 2005*, LNCS 3470: February 23–29, 2005.

55. S. Sild, U. Maran, M. Romberg, B. Schuller, E. Benfenati, OpenMolGRID: Using automated workflows in GRID computing environment. in: P.M.A. Sloot, A.G. Hoekstra, T. Priol, A. Reinefeld, and M. Bubak (Eds.), *Advances in Grid Computing—EGC 2005*, LNCS 3470, pp. 464–473, February 2005.

56. E.V. Gordeeva, A.R. Katritzky, Rapid conversion of molecular graphs to three-dimensional representation using the MOLGEO program, *Journal of Chemical Information and Computer Sciences* **33**, 102–111, 1993.

57. J.J. Stewart, MOPAC: A semiempirical molecular orbital program, *Journal of Computer-Aided Molecular Design* **4**, 1–45, 1990.

58. COmprehensive DEscriptors for Structural and Statistical Analysis (Codessa) QSPR/QSAR Software, http://www.codessa-pro.com/index.htm.

59. L. Moss, A. Adelman, Data warehousing methodology, *Journal of Data Warehousing* **5**, 23–31, 2000.

60. D. Erwin (Ed.), UNICORE Plus Final Report—Uniform Interface to Computing Recources, Joint Project Report for the BMBF Project UNICORE Plus Grant Number: 01 IR 001 A-D, ISBN 3-00-011592-7. Available at http://www.unicore.org/documents/UNICOREPlus-Final-Report.pdf.

61. Open Grid Forum (OGF) Research Group on Workflow Management (WFM-RG). https://forge.gridforum.org/projects/wfm-rg/.

62. Business Process Execution Language for Web Services. Version 1.0. July 31, 2002. http://www-106.ibm.com/developerworks/library/ws-bpel1/.

63. M. zur Muehlen, J. Becker, WPDL: State-of-the-art and directions of a meta-language for workflow processes, in: Lothar Bading, Boris Pettkoff, August-Wilhelm Scheer, Siegfried Wendt (Eds.), *Proceedings of the 1st Know-Tech Forum*, Potsdam, 1999.

64. D. Hull, K. Wolstencroft, R. Stevens, C. Goble, M.R. Pocock, P. Li, T. Oinn, Taverna: A tool for building and running workflows of services, *Nucleic Acids Research* **34**(Web Server issue):W729–W732, doi:10.1093/nar/gkl320, 2006.

65. S. Majithia, M.S. Shields, I.J. Taylor, I. Wang, Triana: A graphical web service composition and execution toolkit, *In Proceedings of the IEEE International Conference on Web Services* (ICWS '04), IEEE Computer Society, Los Alamitos, CA, pp. 514–524, 2004.

66. E. Benfenati, Modelling Aquatic Toxicity with Advanced Computational Techniques: Procedures to Standardize Data and Compare Models, in: J.A. López, E. Benfenati, and W. Dubitzky (Eds.), *Proceedings of International Symposium Knowledge Exploration in Life Science Informatics 2004* (KELSI 2004), Lecture Notes in Computer Science, LNCS 3303, Springer, New York, pp. 235–248, 2004.

67. P. Mazzatorta, M. Smiesko, E. Lo Piparo, E. Benfenati, QSAR model for predicting pesticide aquatic toxicity, *Journal of Chemical Information Model*, **45**, 1767–774, 2005.

68. U. Maran, S. Sild, I. Kahn, K. Takkis, Mining of the chemical information in GRID environment, Future Generation Computer Systems, in press, Corrected Proof, Available online 5 July 2006.

69. Predictive Model Markup Language. http://www.dmg.org/pmml-v3-1.html.

70. Chemomentum (Grid Services based Environment to enable Innovative Research). http://www.chemomentum.org.

71. Computational Toxicology (including QSARs) Joint Research Centre (JRC) Action no1321 of the European Chemicals Bureau (ECB). http://ecb.jrc.it/QSAR/.

72. I.V. Tetko, P. Bruneau, H.-W. Mewes, D.C. Rohrer, G.I. Poda, Can we estimate the accuracy of ADME-Tox predictions? *Drug Discovery Today*, **11**(15–16), 700–707, 2006.

73. D. De Roure, N.R. Jennings, N.R. Shadbolt, The Semantic Grid: A Future e-Science Infrastructure, in: F. Berman, A.J.G. Hey, and G. Fox (Eds.), *Grid Computing: Making the Global Infrastructure a Reality,* John Wiley & Sons, Hoboken, NJ, 2003, pp. 437–470.

74. K.R. Taylor, J.W. Essex, J.G. Frey, H.R. Mills, G. Hughes, E.J. Zaluska, The semantic grid and chemistry: experiences with combechem, *Journal of Web Semantics* **4**(2), 84–101, 2006.

75. D.B. Skillicorn, Distributed Data-Intensive Computation and the Datacentric Grid, White Paper, School of Computing, Queen's University, Kingston, Canada, 2003.

76. A. Bassan, S. Eisenreich, B. Sokull-Kluettgen, A. Worth, The role of ECB in the risk assessment of nanomaterials. Is there a future for "computational nanotoxicology"? Poster, The 12th International Workshop on QSAR in Environmental Toxicology.
http://ecb.jrc.it/DOCUMENTS/QSAR/INFORMATION_SOURCES/
PRESENTATIONS/Bassan_Lyon_0605_poster.pdf.

77. E.C. Butcher, Can cell systems biology rescue drug discovery? *Nature Reviews Drug Discovery* **4**(6), 461–467, 2005.

2

DESIGNING HIGH-PERFORMANCE CONCURRENT STRATEGIES FOR BIOLOGICAL SEQUENCE ALIGNMENT PROBLEMS ON NETWORKED COMPUTING PLATFORMS

Bharadwaj Veeravalli

> *Realizing the power of the Supreme is via pondering over our built-in life-code—the simple, yet magnificent DNA!*
>
> Bharadwaj Veeravalli

2.1 INTRODUCTION

Designing high-performance algorithms for aligning biological sequences is always a challenging problem. Biological sequences are made up of residues. In DNA (deoxyribonucleic acid) sequences, these residues are nucleic acids, while in protein sequences, these residues are amino acids. Aligning or comparing biological sequences is a computationally intensive operation because we need to take into consideration that biological sequences may mutate or evolve over time. The process of aligning two or more sequences is often an imperative step to quantify the quality of the samples under consideration. For instance, in the case of protein structure predictive methods and structure comparison methods, sequence alignment for maximum similarity score is often one of the crucial steps. As such, in aligning biological sequences, residues can be inserted, deleted, or substituted from either of the two sequences to

Grid Computing for Bioinformatics and Computational Biology. Edited by E.-G. Talbi and A.Y. Zomaya.
Copyright © 2008 John Wiley & Sons, Inc.

obtain the optimum alignment. For two sequences with k number of residues each, it was shown in the literature that there are as much as $(1 + \sqrt{2})^{2k+1}\sqrt{k}$ possible alignment combinations. Hence, over the years, various algorithms have been proposed in order to speed up the alignment process. The outcome of the alignment can be correlated to derive conclusions on aspects that are common to the two species (or families of the species from where they come from), common functionalities (in the case of proteins), ancestral relationships (in the case of DNA), and other wealth of information pertaining to the two chosen sequences. In fact, for protein sequences, a class of algorithms that are designed to determine their structures primarily use sequence comparison methods. The amount of DNA/protein sequence data accrued every year seem to be overwhelming on public databases like GenBank, PDB, and so on. Not only animate species are concerned, but gene data about inanimate species also seem to be of immense use to drug industries. These are primarily used by researchers, bioinformaticians, and medical researchers, among others, to understand the functional behavior, how proteins interact, location of genes in a particular sequence, origin of protein coming from the genes, and so on. Drug industries as of today use more than 8 TB of sequence data, and large pharmaceutical industries use data close to 30 TB for their research and drug manufacturing purposes.

High-performance algorithms tend to promise a significant speedup and cater to the needs of the application in a highly customized way. While there are studies concerning parallelization of sequencing algorithms and hardware and/or software realizations, opening up such methodologies on public portals or on Internet-like networks seem to be missing; if not, only a few exist. Most of the methods use conventional algorithms and fine-tuned versions of standard well-known algorithms (BLAST, FASTA, Clustal W, etc.) to prescribe a matching that maximizes the alignment score. In this chapter, we shall employ a very generic version of sequence-matching algorithm, referred to as Smith–Waterman algorithm in all our analysis and implementations.

In this chapter, we are concerned with realizing efficient distributed strategies when sequence alignment problems are to be handled on networked computing systems. Thus, we more or less envisage computations that carry over delay-sensitive networks and can be designed for public use via Internet- and Intranet-like networks. Although sequence search process can be carried out comfortably on loosely coupled systems using general-purpose computers,[1] for a collaborative computing requirement, explicit sophisticated algorithms to handle (dependent) computations and communications must be in place. Another factor that influences the performance of such realizations is the level of *granularity* that one considers. Interestingly, there are hardware realizations using FPGA and also via VLSI technology on special-purpose architectures that are solely used for sequence-matching problems. It may be finally noted that there are several variants that exist in carrying out the sequence-matching process, either for local alignment problems or for global alignment problems. These include FASTA, BLAST, MEGABLAST (uses a special XDrop alignment algorithm specifically for DNA sequences), PSI-BLAST (gives special considerations and

---

[1]This is owing to independent search process.

alters the scoring matrices), ClustalW (multiple sequence alignment process), ClustalW with MPI, Silicon Graphics version HT ClustalW, and Multiclustal, among other processes. We will present the required mathematical background and the reader is referred to several textbooks and Web simulations to understand the basic mechanics of sequence matching/alignment problems. Although several textbooks start with Needleman–Wunsch algorithm, a dynamic programming recursion, we use Smith–Waterman algorithm because it is generic and easy for implementation.

2.1.1 Mathematical Underpinnings and Smith–Waterman Algorithm

We first briefly introduce an improved version, a very generic version, of Smith–Waterman algorithm proposed by Gotoh as well as some characteristics of the matrix generated by the algorithm. In the process of aligning two sequences, denoted by *SqA* and *SqB* of length α and β, respectively, the algorithm generates three separate matrices, denoted by **S**, **h**, and **f**. Each row and column of these matrices represents a residue of *SqA* and *SqB*, respectively. Given $s(a_x, b_y)$, a substitution score[2] for replacing the *x*th residue from *SqA* with the *y*th residue from *SqB*, z as the penalty for introducing a gap, and v as the penalty for extending a gap, the **S**, **h**, and **f** matrices are related by the following recursive equations:

$$S_{0,y} = S_{x,0} = h_{0,y} = f_{x,0} = 0 \tag{2.1}$$

$$S_{x,y} = \max \left\{ h_{x,y}, \quad S_{x-1,y-1} + s(a_x, b_y), \quad f_{x,y} \right\} \tag{2.2}$$

$$h_{x,y} = \max \left\{ S_{x-1,y} + z, \quad h_{x-1,y} + v \right\} \tag{2.3}$$

$$f_{x,y} = \max \left\{ S_{x,y-1} + z, \quad f_{x,y-1} + v \right\} \tag{2.4}$$

for the range $1 \leq x \leq \alpha$, $1 \leq y \leq \beta$, where $S_{x,y}$, $h_{x,y}$, and $f_{x,y}$ represent the matrix elements in the *x*th row and *y*th column of the matrices **S**, **h**, and **f**, respectively. In this computation process, residues in *SqA* and *SqB* are tested for a best possible alignment in a recursive fashion. The computation of the above-mentioned matrices leads to possible alignment of the respective sequences. The score of the matrix element $S_{x,y}$ quantifies the quality of alignment (from the first residue of *SqA* and *SqB*, respectively) up to the *x*th residue of *SqA* and the *y*th residue of *SqB*. Thus, the higher the score at $S_{x,y}$, the better the alignment between the sequences up to those residues. The details of this algorithm can be found in Reference 1. The **S** matrix contains all the alignment scores of *SqA* and *SqB*, and it is used to determine the optimal alignment. As we can see from the equations above, the matrix element $S_{x,y}$ is dependent on the $(x - 1, y - 1)$, $(x - 1, y)$, and $(x, y - 1)$ elements from the **S**, **h**, and **f** matrices, respectively. This is illustrated in Fig. 2.1. Due to this dependency, the **S** matrix

---

[2]The score defines the similarities between two residues. The scores can be found in substitution score matrices such as the identity score matrix for DNA or the PAM250 matrix for protein. These substitution score matrices are predefined based on biological factors.

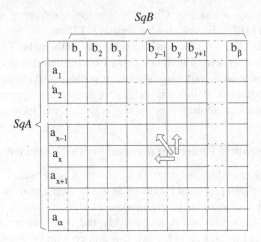

Figure 2.1. Illustration of the computational dependency of the element (x, y) in the **S** matrix.

elements cannot be computed independently, either columnwise or rowwise. Nevertheless, the elements along the diagonal line given by $S_{x+1,y-1}$, $S_{x,y}$, and $S_{x-1,y+1}$ are independent of each other and, hence, they can be calculated independently. In our strategy we exploit this property and attempt to distribute the computations of the matrix elements across several processors in our cluster/high-performance system. After the **S** matrix has been generated, it is necessary to interpret the results to generate the aligned sequences. Thus, one has to run a "traceback process" on the **S** matrix to obtain an optimal alignment. We shall give a brief introduction on this traceback process now.

2.1.1.1 Traceback Process

The traceback process[3] is used to determine an optimal alignment between two sequences. The process utilizes the fact that every matrix element in the **S** matrix represents the maximum alignment score of the sequences until the respective residues. For example, when aligning *SqA* and *SqB*, the $S_{x,y}$ in the **S** matrix represent the maximum score of aligning $a_1, \ldots, a_x$ and $b_1, \ldots, b_y$, where a_x and b_y are the xth and yth residues of *SqA* and *SqB*, respectively. Hence, to obtain an optimum alignment, we start from the bottom right of the **S** matrix and move toward the upper left of the matrix. At each matrix element, we are only allowed to move to the adjacent element in three different directions: They are, up, left, or diagonal (upper left). The choices are determined by the largest values among them. Moving up and left represents the introduction of a "gap" in *SqA* and *SqB*, respectively, while moving diagonally represents a "substitution" where no gap is added. Hence, moving diagonally is preferred if there is a tie between the score for the up/left and diagonal directions.

---

[3]Refer to Reference 1.

It may be noted that the above explained process is for aligning two sequences. However, very often need arises to align multiple sequences. Several implementations are now in place on Web servers such as ClustalW(http:/mason.csse.uwa.edu.au), ClustalW-MPI, BLAST and BLAST ++, FASTA and its parallel version, MPI implementations of FASTA, and systolic array implementations. The algorithms and the methodologies to be presented in this chapter can easily adopt these versions.

2.1.2 Divisible Load-Scheduling Paradigm and Network Topologies

There have been several implementations of the above SW algorithm and its versions on networked systems. However, these are predominantly on systems that are dedicated and/or tightly coupled systems with almost no external network data traffic interference. A direct implication of this is that communication delays are often negligible, if not completely absent. In such systems, when one attempts to run multiple sequence alignment (MSA) algorithms, division of labor (number of sequences) among the processing nodes is more or less balanced and identical. It may be noted that in running MSA algorithms, by simply concatenating a set of aligned sequences from processors does not warrant a global alignment. Most of the available Web servers that undertake this task do not accommodate more than few tens of sequences at a time, as of now. Thus, running a MSA algorithm instance will seldom be more than 30–40 sequences. The methodologies proposed in this chapter consider both problems—aligning two sequences (on bus/Ethernet networks) and MSA (on mesh networks). The implementations attempted in the literature so far employ strategies that are more suited for dedicated multiprocessor systems or workstations. We attempt to develop high-performance algorithms using divisible load paradigm,[4] a model that is shown to be robust, particularly suitable for handling large-size loads on a networked computing system.[5] In this model, a large-size load is assumed to be arbitrarily divisible and partitioned into several smaller chunks. Also, we assume that each chunk can be executed on any computing node, and it bears no dependence on any other chunk. The communication and computation delays by the links and computing nodes/processors in the system are assumed to vary in a linear fashion with respect to the size of the load. Thus, the load distribution takes into account the proportion of the load to be assigned to each computing node toward the goal of minimizing the overall processing time of the load. A monograph by Bharadwaj et al. [3] serves as a basic reference, and recent survey articles[6] detail the model and the usefulness and applicability of DLT paradigm to such large scale problems.

In the subsequent sections, we present our experiences with modeling, analysis, and implementation of DLT-based algorithms for such biological sequencing problems on two different widely used network topologies—bus (Ethernet) network and a mesh network. Although the methodologies developed for the former topology is primarily

---

[4]Divisible load theory (DLT), also referred to as divisible load scheduling.
[5]Specifically, DLT modeling becomes an advantage when communication delays are nonzero and are very large in systems.
[6]See References 2 and 3.

meant for two-sequence alignment problem, we describe a procedure to realize a full-fledged multiple sequence alignment engine to virtually handle any number of sequences using mesh topology.

2.2   SEQUENCE MATCHING ON BUS NETWORKS

We consider a loosely coupled bus-based multiprocessor system, interconnected by a bus communication link, as shown in Fig. 2.2, with m processors denoted by $P_1, P_2, P_3, \ldots, P_m$. It may be noted that in such a bus network, at any time instant, only one communication process is possible, as the link will be fully utilized by any two communicating processors. Further, we assume that the processors have front ends. A front end is a coprocessor that off-loads its communication task so that a processor can communicate and process at the same time instant.

Our objective is to design a strategy such that the *processing time*, defined as the time from when the computation starts until it ends, is a minimum. The processing time involves generating the **S**, **h**, and **f** matrices, as presented in Section 2.1.1 and distributing the intermediate results among the respective processors. Finally, when the **S** matrix is generated, an optimum alignment can be determined by postprocessing by a traceback process. In our strategy, the complete **S** matrix will be finally in processor P_m, and hence the constant time taken for traceback process will not be a part of our processing time.

We denote the two sequences to be aligned as *SqA* and *SqB* with lengths α and β, respectively. We assume that all processors, $P_1, \ldots, P_m$, already have *SqA* and *SqB* in their local memories, or can be initialized in this way. Note that this communication time is again not a part of the processing time, as per our definition above. Further, in the case of the clustering strategy for multisequence alignment, the Berger–Munson algorithm, where multiple pairwise alignments are to be performed, sequences are often compared with each other more than once. On the basis of this comparison, the sequences are realigned with minor differences. One of the research attempts by Trelles et al. [5] (1998) identifies only special sequences among several sequences, referred to as the "special interest group" (SIG), by randomly choosing a sequence and comparing it with all other sequences, in a pairwise manner. According to these sequence similarities, sequences are either dropped or grouped into two different groups. Sequences within these two groups are then compared against each other.

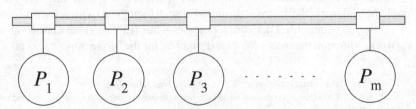

Figure 2.2. Bus network/cluster architecture with m processors.

This procedure is repeated until one of the groups becomes empty. To carry out such a procedure in a multiprocessor environment, it would only be cost-effective when all the processors keep a copy of all sequences in their local memories and only small modifications on the sequences need to be broadcast. Thus, with this notion, it should be clear at this stage that we are concerned with the design of the strategy to minimize the processing time for aligning two sequences and do not consider the problem of initially broadcasting the sequences to the respective processors.

We shall now introduce an index of definitions and notations that are used throughout for analysis on bus and mesh networks.

Notations and Definitions

m:	The total number of processors in the system.
P_i:	The ith processor, where $i = 1, \ldots, m$.
E_i:	The total time taken for P_i to compute a matrix element (x, y) of each of the matrices $\mathbf{S}, \mathbf{h}$, and $\mathbf{f}$, respectively, that is, the time taken to compute $S_{x,y}, h_{x,y}$, and $f_{x,y}$ values.
C:	Time taken for the link(bus) to communicate one matrix element (x, y).
α:	Length of SqA or the number of residues in SqA.
β:	Length of SqB or the number of residues in SqB.
Q:	Total number of iterations used to compute the $\mathbf{S}, \mathbf{h}$, and $\mathbf{f}$ matrices.
α_j:	Total number of residues of SqA assigned to P_j, where $\sum_{j=1}^{m} \alpha_j = \alpha$.
$\beta^{(k)}$:	Total number of residues of SqB considered for alignment with α_j by each processor $j = 1, \ldots, m$ in the k th iteration, where $\sum_{k=1}^{Q} \beta^{(k)} = \beta$.
$L_{i,k}$:	Submatrix of $\mathbf{S}, \mathbf{h}$, and $\mathbf{f}$ that is assigned to P_i for computation in the kth iteration. Note that each submatrix of $\mathbf{S}, \mathbf{h}$, and $\mathbf{f}$ is of same dimension $\alpha_i \times \beta^{(k)}$.
$T(m)$:	The *processing time*, defined as the time from when the process of generating the $\mathbf{S}$ matrix starts until the end, with m processors.

2.2.1 Design and Analysis of Distributed Processing Strategy

First, let us consider the distribution of the task of generating the $\mathbf{S}$ matrix. It may be noted that when we mention generating the $\mathbf{S}$ matrix, we also take into account the generation of other two required matrices $\mathbf{h}$ and $\mathbf{f}$, as generating $S_{x,y}$ demands computing the elements of $h_{x,y}$ and $f_{x,y}$ as well. The $\mathbf{S}$ matrix is partitioned into submatrices $L_{i,k}, i = 1, \ldots, m, \ k = 1, \ldots, Q$, where each submatrix consists of a portion of SqA and SqB. We assign the computation of the submatrices $L_{i,k}, i = 1, \ldots, m$, and $k = 1, \ldots, Q$, respectively, in Q iterations to processor P_i. The distribution pattern is as illustrated in Fig. 2.3. During to the characteristics of the $\mathbf{S}$ matrix (as discussed in Section 2.1.1), submatrices $L_{i,k}$ with the same value of $(i + k)$ can be calculated concurrently. Thus, for instance, submatrices $L_{1,3}, L_{2,2}$, and $L_{3,1}$ can be calculated in parallel as all three $L_{i,k}$ have the same value $(i + k) = 4$.

Note that computing the values of a submatrix $L_{i,k}$ means we compute the values of the submatrices of the matrices $\mathbf{S}, \mathbf{h}$, and $\mathbf{f}$, respectively. At this stage, it may be noted that, due to data dependency, P_i needs the values of submatrix $L_{i-1,k}$ from P_{i-1} in order to start computing $L_{i,k}$. To be more precise, P_i requires only the data from the last row of $L_{i-1,k}$ (of the $\mathbf{S}$ and $\mathbf{h}$ matrices) to start computing $L_{i,k}$. Note that the size of the last row (number of columns) of each of the submatrices of $\mathbf{S}$ and

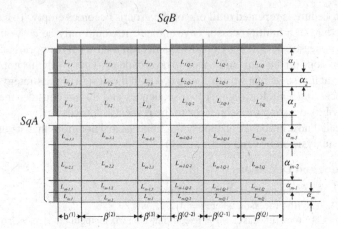

Figure 2.3. Distribution pattern for matrices **S**, **h**, and **f**.

h, with processor P_{i-1}, is $\beta^{(k)}$. Hence, on the whole, we need to transmit $2\beta^{(k)}$ values (last rows of **S** and **h** matrices from $L_{i-1,k}$) to P_i before initiating the computation of $L_{i,k}$. Lastly, it may be noted that P_i does not require the values of **f** from P_{i-1}, since the computation $L_{i,k}$ in every iteration uses values of **f** generated within the same processor.

Now, the question that remains unanswered is the number of residues from SqA, that is, the value of α_i, $i = 1, \ldots, m$, that should be assigned for each processor P_i such that a high degree of parallelism can be achieved. Further, we need to determine the amount of residues of SqB, the value at $\beta^{(k)}$, $k = 1, \ldots, Q$, that should be considered in each iteration for matching with each of the assigned residues of SqA. We shall discuss these issues in the following section.

2.2.1.1 Actual Load Distribution Process

DLT paradigm can be beneficial in deciding the quantum of load, in this case, the number of residues of SqA that should be given to each processor, as well as the number of residues that should be considered from SqB in each iteration. The distribution strategy is shown in the timing diagram in Fig. 2.4. In the timing diagram, the x-axis represents the time and the y-axis represents the processors. We represent the communication by the striped blocks and computation by the shaded box. The block $L_{i,k}$ represents the computation of $L_{i,k}$, that is, the submatrix to be computed by P_i at the kth iteration. The distribution strategy is as follows. First, P_1 will compute $L_{1,1}$. After it has finished computing $L_{1,1}$, it will continue processing $L_{1,2}$, since it only requires the results from $L_{1,1}$. At the same time, it will send the last row of $L_{1,1}$ to P_2 so that P_2 may start processing $L_{2,1}$ from time $\alpha_1\beta^{(1)}E_1 + 2\beta^{(1)}C$. Note that by the time P_2 finishes computing $L_{2,1}$, it would have received the last row of $L_{1,2}$ (from P_1); hence, it can start computing $L_{2,2}$ continuously right after completing the computation of $L_{2,1}$. At the same time instant, it will send the last row of $L_{2,1}$ to P_3. This process continues until P_m.

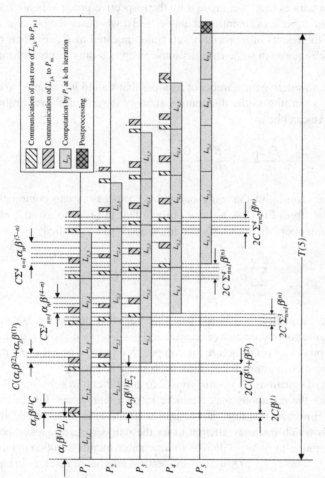

Figure 2.4. Timing diagram of the distribution strategy when $m = 5$ and $Q = 5$.

The legend in the figure reads:

- Communication of last row of $L_{j,k}$ to P_{j+1}
- Communication of $L_{j,k}$ to P_m
- $L_{j,k}$ Computation by P_j at k-th iteration
- Postprocessing

From the timing diagram, we note that there are two phases of communication processes involved for P_i, $i = 1, \ldots, m - 1$: (a) sending the last row of $L_{i,k}$ (**S** and **h** matrices), of total size $2\beta^{(k)}$, to P_{i+1}, and (b) sending $L_{i,k}$ (**S** matrix only), of size $\alpha_i \beta^{(k)}$, to P_m. As stated in the previous section, phase (a) is required for $P_{i+1}, i = 1, \ldots, m - 1$, to start its computation. On the contrary, phase (b) is required so that P_m can have the complete **S** matrix to perform any necessary postprocessing such as the traceback process to determine an optimal alignment. In our strategy, each of the submatrices that is computed by the respective processors are transmitted to P_m right after phase (a) mentioned above. Thus, whenever the bus is available after phase (a), the results of a processor are communicated to P_m. Further, note that (b) may not be required in some cases as some postprocessing can be done at individual processors.

We can now derive the number of residues that should be assigned to each P_i, $i = 1, \ldots, m$, according to the distribution strategy described above. From the timing diagram, we can obtain

$$\alpha_i = \alpha_{i-1} \frac{\beta^{(k)}}{\beta^{(k-1)}} \frac{E_{i-1}}{E_i} + 2 \frac{\beta^{(k)}}{\beta^{(k-1)}} \frac{C}{E_i} - 2 \frac{C}{E_i} , \ i = 2, \ldots, m , \ k = 2, \ldots, Q \quad (2.5)$$

With our constraint that only one pair of processors can communicate at any time instant, from Fig. 2.4, we can observe that in order to avoid communication overlap/contention, the following condition needs to be satisfied:

$$\sum_{i=1}^{m-1} \alpha_i \beta^{(k-i)} C + 2 \sum_{i=1}^{m-1} \beta^{(k-i)} C \leq \alpha_1 \beta^{(k)} E_1 \quad (2.6)$$

The above inequality is captured using the fact that during the kth iteration, $k = 1, \ldots, Q$, the communication phases (a) and (b) described above must be completed by all the processors at or before the computation process of P_1, as P_1 needs to send the last row of $L_{1,k}$ immediately after processing $L_{1,k}$ to P_2.

The set of equations (2.5) satisfying (2.6) are difficult to solve to yield an optimal solution, as the equations may generate inconsistent values for the unknowns α_i and $\beta^{(k)}$. However, this does not restrict us from deriving a practically realizable solution in which one may attempt to fix the number of residues to be considered in each iteration in order to deliver an acceptable quality solution. Thus, by setting $\beta^{(k)} = \beta / Q, k = 1, \ldots, Q$, we use an identical number of residues in each iteration. With this modification, we will be able to solve (2.5) together with the fact that $\sum_{i=1}^{m} \alpha_i = \alpha$, to determine the value of $\alpha_i, i = 1, \ldots, m$, as

$$\alpha_i = \frac{1}{E_i} \frac{\alpha}{\sum_{j=1}^{m} \frac{1}{E_j}}, \ i = 1, \ldots, m \quad (2.7)$$

However, to solve (2.5), we assume that Q is a fixed or a known parameter. As far as the choice of the value of Q is concerned, we set it to the largest possible value, that is, $Q = \beta$ (implying that $\beta^{(k)} = 1$), to maximize the degree of parallelism that can be achieved. Note that one may have $Q < \beta$, which will degrade the quality of the solution (speedup) as shown in Theorem 1.

Theorem 1.[7] *The processing time for a m-processor system to complete q iterations is strictly greater than the processing time for the system completing $q + 1$ iterations.*

As for condition (2.6) mentioned above, since we consider $\beta^{(k)} = 1, k = 1, \ldots, Q$ (as we have set $Q = \beta$), alternatively, we have

$$C \leq \frac{\alpha}{\sum\limits_{i=1}^{m} \dfrac{1}{E_i} \left(\sum\limits_{j=1}^{m-1} \alpha_j + 2(m-1) \right)} \tag{2.8}$$

Hence, before we begin aligning *SqA* and *SqB*, we first check if (2.8) can be satisfied. If (2.8) holds, then we will distribute and compute the **S** matrix as proposed above. The processing time is

$$T(m) = \alpha_1 \beta E_1 + 2C(m-1) + \sum_{i=2}^{m} \alpha_i E_i \tag{2.9}$$

with α_i derived from (2.7). However, it may happen that (2.8) may not be satisfied, that is, typically when communication link is too slow. This is also equivalent to a situation where processor speeds are much faster than the link speeds. In such cases, we will need to resolve using alternate (heuristic) strategies. We shall propose two heuristic strategies and an illustrative example in the following section to demonstrate their workings.

2.2.2   Discussion on Some Heuristic Strategies for Bus Networks

In the literature, few heuristic strategies are proposed. We shall briefly describe them here. These will be used when (2.8) cannot be satisfied. The key idea in these strategies is that both of them attempt to provide more communication bandwidth/time for each P_i by introducing sufficient time gaps in between, which will sustain the computation process without large processor idle times. The key difference between the strategies is that the first one attempts to retain all the available processors in the hope of achieving maximum possible speedup, whereas the second strategy attempts to judiciously consider the number of processors that can be used at every step whenever necessary. In the first strategy, a critical condition similar to (2.8) is derived, which is simple to satisfy. However, even when this condition cannot be met, we switch to use the second strategy for processing that guarantees that processing will be completed. In

---

[7]Interested readers can refer to a formal proof from Wong and Bharadwaj [6].

the latter strategy, it is guaranteed that there will be at least one processor to complete the processing in the worst case scenario.

2.2.2.1 Idle-Time Insertion Strategy

As mentioned above, we attempt to "insert" an optimal (minimum time gap required) redundant idle time into the computation process to compensate for the slow communication link. One can follow similar treatment in constructing a timing diagram and it has been shown that, in this case, following condition needs to be satisfied:

$$C \leq \frac{\alpha}{\sum\limits_{i=1}^{m} \frac{1}{E_i} \left(\sum\limits_{j=1}^{m-1} \alpha_j + 2(m-1) \right) - \sum\limits_{k=2}^{m-1} \frac{4}{E_k}} \tag{2.10}$$

As we can see, the condition (2.10) is easier to satisfy than (2.8); hence, this heuristic strategy can work even if (2.8) is not satisfied. When (2.10) is satisfied, the processing time is given by

$$T(m) = \frac{\alpha(\beta + m - 1)}{\sum\limits_{i=1}^{m} \frac{1}{E_i}} + 2C(m-1) + \frac{(\beta + m - 1)}{\sum\limits_{j=1}^{m} \frac{1}{E_j}} \left(4C \sum\limits_{k=2}^{m-1} \frac{1}{E_k} \right) - 4C(m-2)$$

$$\tag{2.11}$$

Thus, in a way, this strategy is conservative in its working style by attempting to use all the processors and by calculating the required idle times to insert during the computation process.

2.2.2.2 Reduced Set-Processing Strategy

In this heuristic strategy, we attempt to use maximal number of processors such that (2.8) is satisfied. Since large communication time consumption is what is responsible for violation of (2.8), using fewer available processors for processing is expected to solve the problem with an increase in the computation time of each processor.

The reduced set processing heuristic strategy is an iterative process and simple to implement, but it is shown that it may leave a large number of processors unutilized. In order to utilize more processors, it is possible to sort the processors as per their speeds and use them, from fastest to the slowest. This may improve the overall performance of the heuristic strategy as the slower processors will be eliminated before the faster ones.

2.2.2.3 Hybrid Strategy

As each of the above methods have advantages and disadvantages, we attempt to utilize both the strategies in an alternating fashion. The procedure is repeated until either (2.8) or (2.10) is satisfied, and it is guaranteed to work with a maximal set of fast processors. This method is particulary recommended when the system can afford to spend additional computational time, especially while handling non-time-critical jobs.

2.2.3   Performance Evaluation of the Strategies for Bus Networks and Discussions

To quantify and understand the performance of the strategies, rigorous simulation experiments were performed to compare the processing time of our strategy with the direct implementation of Smith–Waterman algorithm using a single machine (nonparallel version). It may be noted that the resources we have used, the network and nodes, are dedicated in our experiments. Thus, it is expected that the speedup, defined below and measured in our experiments, serves as an upper bound. We define speedup by

$$\text{Speedup} = \frac{T(1)}{T(m)} \qquad (2.12)$$

where $T(m)$ is the processing time of our strategy on a system using m processors. $T(1)$ is the processing time using a single processor and is given by

$$T(1) = \alpha\beta E_1 \qquad (2.13)$$

In our experiments, we consider several influencing parameters such as length of the sequences, communication link speeds, computation speeds, and the number of processors in the system. We categorize the experiments in a systematic fashion and describe them as follows.

2.2.3.1   Effect of Available Communication Bandwidth and Speedup

As stated in Section 2.2, we consider a loosely coupled multiprocessor system where communication delays or equivalently the bandwidth is taken into account. From (2.8), we can sense that large delays owing to the presence of slow communication links is one of the major factors that limits the use of processors, that is, when the "reduced set processing" strategy is used. We performed some experiments to observe the effect of the communication link speed on the performance of our strategy.

In this simulation, we considered a homogeneous system with the number of processors varying from $m = 3$ to 25 with $E_x = E_y = E$ chosen in the range (15, 45) time units/element, $\forall x \neq y$ following a uniform probability distribution. We varied the link speed parameter in the range (1, 10) time units/element. We considered two real-life DNA samples in our experiments. The first sample is the DNA of house mouse mitochondrion (*Mus musculus* mitochondrion, NC_001569, denoted as *SqA*) consisting of 16,295 residues. The DNA of human mitochondrion (*Homo sapiens* mitochondrion, NC_001807, denoted as *SqB*), consisting of 16,571 residues (both samples are obtainable from the GenBank), was the second sample. The choice of these DNA samples is very typical of sequence alignment studies reported elsewhere as drug manufacturers often use a mouse model to test their products and understanding the differences and similarities between the two species is of the utmost important. The results are as shown in Fig. 2.5.

Thus, when link delays dominate, heuristic strategies may be in place for processing, as (2.8) may not hold. This fact can be captured from our experiments when $C \approx 5$ time units/element, since the speedup increases linearly with respect to m until

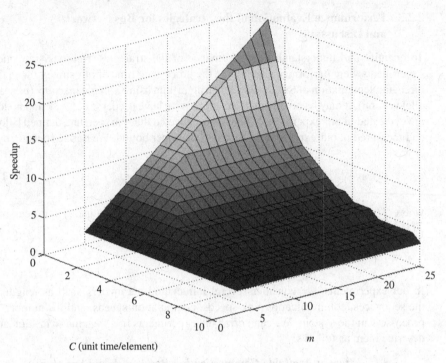

Figure 2.5. Effect of communication link speed and number of processors on the speedup.

the point where $m > 7$, and then it starts to saturate. This clearly shows that beyond $m = 7$, the use of additional processors to share the processing load becomes pointless. From a theoretical standpoint, this is due to the fact that (2.8) and (2.10) are both violated in this case when $m > 7$ and hence redundant processors are not being utilized. Nevertheless, as we can see, when the communication link speed increases, the speedup increases exponentially. In other words, when the communication link is very fast, the speedup will increase linearly with the number of processors used. This can be seen by substituting (2.13) and (2.9) into (2.12), and using (2.7) we obtain

$$\text{Speedup} = \frac{\alpha\beta E_1 \sum_{i=1}^{m} \frac{1}{E_i}}{\alpha\beta + \alpha(m-1) + 2C(m-1)\sum_{i=1}^{m} \frac{1}{E_i}} \tag{2.14}$$

Finally, if we consider a homogeneous system, $E_1 = E_2 = \cdots = E$, with very fast communication links, where $C \to 0$, we can then simplify the above equation to

$$\text{Speedup} = \frac{\beta m}{(\beta + m - 1)} \tag{2.15}$$

Since $\beta \gg m$, we then have speedup $\approx m$. As a result, when the communication link is very fast, that is, $C \to 0$, the speedup will be able to increase linearly with the number of processors.

It may be noted that even if one uses a heterogeneous platform comprising machines of different speeds, it should not be surprising that DLT outperforms ELP approach. This is due to the fact that when ELP is used, faster processors will be forced to wait for slower processors due to the data dependency operations discussed earlier. On the contrary, when DLT is used, the numbers of residues (from SqA) assigned to the processors are inherently adjusted so that each processor's idle time is kept to a minimum. Thus, for all values of C and m, the speedup performance (and hence the processing time) delivered by DLT is expected to be better than that of the ELP strategy. Finally, by varying the length of the sequences from $\alpha = \beta = 100$ to 15,000 in steps of 100 residual units, it was shown that the unutilized processing time of the processors remained less than 16% even while processing shorter sequences of length 100. In real-life situations, it may be noted that sequences of length 100 residues may be unlikely to exist; however, the results demonstrate the efficiency of the strategies even in handling short sequences. When sequence lengths are more than 100,000, it was shown that the unutilized processing time drops to less than 0.4%.

2.2.4   Shared-Memory MIMD Versus DLT Approach

As our system is basically a loosely coupled multiprocessor system, it would be of direct interest to compare the performance of our strategy on this bus network system with that of a shared-memory MIMD system. Thus, when we consider the case where the submatrices generated are not required to be sent to the last processor, the processing time of such implementation in an MIMD system, $T_{MIMD}(m)$, with m process elements (PE) is as follows:

$$T_{MIMD}(m) = \left(\alpha + \frac{\alpha(\beta - 1)}{m} \right) E_1 + 2C(m + \beta - 1) \qquad (2.16)$$

where $E_1 = E_2 = \cdots = E_m$. The PEs in the MIMD system are such that they (a) are not able to execute both computation or communication at the same time instant, (b) are able to send and receive data simultaneously, and (c) can have multiple communication in parallel.

These assumptions are slightly different from what we have considered in this chapter (Section 2.2). Although the assumptions (b) and (c) give the MIMD system a significant advantage, it was shown that the strategy described in this chapter is still able to yield a better processing time (less that an amount equal to $2C/\beta$ when compared to $T_{MIMD}(m)$). Although only two processors are allowed to communicate at any time instant in our strategy, the performance seems to be comparatively good against an MIMD system.

2.3 MULTIPLE SEQUENCE MATCHING ON MESH TOPOLOGY

The previous section had conclusively demonstrated the usefulness and applicability of DLT paradigm to handle such computationally intensive sequence-matching problems. We now extend this idea to address the problem of aligning multiple (protein) sequences. As aligning multiple protein sequences is a study that is a part of drug targeting applications and is also used to understand certain functions that are common to structures, protein sequences are usually considered in the MSA problems. In this case, a natural choice of topology would be a mesh architecture.

For mesh topology, we shall now present some of the required technical background material first before we present our approach. We know that the element $S_{x,y}$ is dependent on the $(x - 1, y - 1)$, $(x - 1, y)$, and $(x, y - 1)$ elements from the **S**, **P**, and **Q** matrices, respectively, as shown in Fig. 2.1. Due to this dependency, the **S** matrix elements cannot be computed independently (either columnwise or rowwise), but the elements along the diagonal line with the same $(x + y)$ values can be computed independently. This property will be exploited in our strategy in the attempt to distribute computations among several processors in the mesh. Second, the mesh network, by virtue of its physical topological arrangement of processors, offers natural advantage to handle multiple sequences in a concurrent fashion. In our scheme, every row of processors is allowed to handle a set of sequences. We use [1] clustering strategy for multiple protein sequence alignment. It must be stressed that the choice of this strategy is due to its simplicity in implementation; and in our strategy, any clustering strategy could be used in the place of Taylor's method. Basically, Taylor's strategy makes use of the similarity scores obtained via SW and orders the sequences into a cluster by decreasing similarity scores. Third, divisible load paradigm is employed to partition the computational space among the processors in the mesh to enable simultaneous processing in order to achieve higher speedup.

We now describe the underlying mesh architecture, as in Fig. 2.6. We envisage our mesh architecture as a tightly coupled (no communication delays) structure comprising $N \times M$ processing nodes (or processors/CPUs) as shown in the figure. We designate each row as $R_i, i = 1, 2, \ldots, N$, and the processors on each row as $P_k, \quad k = 1, \ldots, M$. Each row has a master node that coordinates the activities of the processors in that row. We assume that a process that starts an instance of MSA retrieves a set of sequences to be aligned from a database and injects to the mesh following the distribution strategy to be described in the following sections. The main sequence pool **O** (see Fig. 2.7) is divided equally among all the rows so that each row handles the same number of sequences, say, Q. Thus, each row of the mesh will be processing a subset of sequences and arrive at an alignment that is best for that subset. All master nodes of a each row will collate the results to recommend an ultimate aligned sequence set.

As mentioned above, the process of consolidating all the locally aligned subset of sequences can be via a certain heuristic approach (one of the methods by Taylor, Martinez, Barton, and Sternberg can be used). We consider the heuristic approach by Taylor to align the sequences. Then, the output of the Taylor's method, a set of locally aligned sequences, is passed to another module, referred to as an *Improved Taylor's*

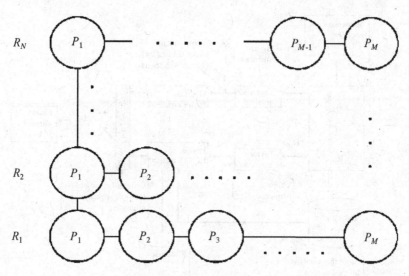

Figure 2.6. $N \times M$ mesh structure.

Method (ITM), to align all the locally aligned sequences from each row to improve the overall score. This overall aligned set (only the indices or name tags [8]) is temporarily stored for comparing the quality of the output from the next iteration. We redesignate the sequences following this aligned order and randomly form a set of sequences Q for each row of the mesh for the next iteration for obtaining a refined score. The process is repeated until a satisfactory score and performance gain is achieved. Figure 2.7 shows this entire process. It is assumed that all the processors that are involved in the computation of the Smith–Waterman matrices will be furnished with an information on the respective subset of sequences involved, in their local memories. Below, we list some additional index of notations and terminology that are used (apart from the notation introduced earlier in Section 1.2) throughout for our analysis.

R_i: Row number, $i = 1, \ldots, N$.

P_k: kth processor on a row, $k = 1, \ldots, M$.

α_k: Length/computation space of $Seq1$ processed by P_k, where $\sum_{k=1}^{M} \alpha_k = \alpha$.

β_k: Length/computation space of $Seq2$ processed by P_k, where $\sum_{k=1}^{M} \beta_k = \beta$.

ω_k: Inverse of speed of processor P_k (in seconds/load).

2.3.1   Design and Analysis of MSA Strategies for Mesh Networks

2.3.1.1   *Load Distribution Strategy*

Actual processing-time computation involves capturing the time taken to generate the **S, P,** and **Q** matrices. All M processors in a row will be involved in the alignment of any one pair of sequences at any particular time. Thus, the matrices will be partitioned

---

[8]We can store the FASTA name tags associated with each sequence in the order.

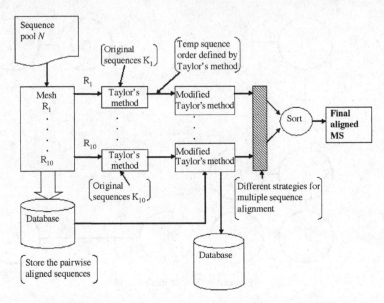

Figure 2.7. Design and implementation of our mesh-based MSA engine.

into M sections, both in row- and columnwise directions. All three matrices are partitioned into submatrices $L_{k,l}$, $k = 1, \ldots, M; l = 1, \ldots, M$(as shown in the previous section), with each submatrix containing a portion of $Seq1$ and $Seq2$.

Computation starts at L_{11}. Since L_{12} and L_{21} has dependency on L_{11} as described in previous sections (see Fig. 2.3), they cannot begin computation until L_{11} is completed. This applies to the rest of the matrix entries as well. The effect of this dependency will be seen in the processing time calculation procedure later in this section.

Following the DLT paradigm, the amount of computational load allocated to each processor will be proportional to its speed, so that all the processes will complete its computation at the same instant.

The computation space is partitioned as follows. All processors are assigned an identical amount of computational space along $Seq2$ (β/M) following an equal load partitioning (ELP) strategy, whereas the number of rows is derived using DLT paradigm, along $Seq1$ direction. Thus, our aim is to have on each row R_i,

$$\alpha_k \omega_k = \alpha_{k+1} \omega_{k+1}, \quad k = 1, \ldots, M-1 \qquad (2.17)$$

with $\sum_{k=1}^{M} \alpha_k = \alpha$. Solving these equations, the net computation space assigned to processor k is

$$\alpha_k = \frac{\alpha}{1 + \sum_{j=1}^{M-1} \left(\frac{\omega_M}{\omega_j} \right)} \left(\frac{\omega_M}{\omega_k} \right) \qquad (2.18)$$

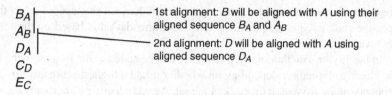

Figure 2.8. Improved Taylor's method illustration 1.

Thus, this effectively completes the task of load distribution to the various processors. ELP is a subset of the DLT problem, in which all the loads are partitioned equally. This applies to the division of computation space of $Seq2$, where $\beta_k = \beta_{k+1}$. This means only α_k values will differ while β_k values are constant (for a particular $N \times M$ mesh).

2.3.2 Fine-tuning the Taylor's Method for MSA

In the original Taylor's MSA method, the alignment of multiple sequences is done on the basis of the next highest score available in the local database. However, it is easy to realize that this alignment might not be an optimal alignment.

Therefore, an *improved Taylor's method* (ITM) that is proposed aims to align every sequence to the previously aligned set. A sequence is realigned with its highest similarity score partner (whose alignment has already been done in the initial all-pairs sequence pairing step) to produce better results. Thus, instead of placing an aligned sequence, say D, with a sequence, say A, denoted as (D_A) below A_B(assuming A and B are already aligned initially), the original sequence D is now realigned with A_B, producing (D_{A_B}). This is shown (Fig. 2.8) to produce a more accurate MSA, as an altered alignment of sequences is considered rather than original sequences. We use this modified alignment process in our strategy.

2.3.3 Heuristic Approach to Align Subsets of Sequences

While individual rows align a subset of sequences, we need to align all these subsets to generate a fully aligned set of sequences. One can follow a simple concatenation of sequences; however, in this case there is no influence or exchange of knowledge of sequences between rows of mesh so as to generate a final alignment that has a better score. In other words, if final alignment involves a comparison among the scores secured by each row, then the quality of the solution can be improved. Our method, referred to as "center-to-center" heuristic strategy (CCS) is proposed to carry out this ordering. In this strategy, the center sequence[9] in all the clusters is extracted into a set and are aligned against each other, similar to a single cluster alignment process. An ITM is then used to decide the positioning of these sequences, that is, ordering is carried out. Once individual positions of these (center) sequences

---

[9] Assume that we have odd number of sequences for the ease of understanding.

are determined, we consider ordering the individual subsets according to their respective center sequence positions. Our recommendation is based on the following observation.

In the Taylor's methodology, a sequence can be added to the front or to the back of the already aligned set depending on whether it had a highest score affinity with the sequence at the front or at the back of the set. As such, there is no certainty on whether the sequence with the highest similarity score (i.e., the one that is aligned at the very beginning) would end up at the front, back, or center. However, the probability of it being in the center of the cluster is higher than being either at the beginning or the end of the cluster. Thus, this approach is prescribed.

2.3.4 Overall Processing Time Calculations and Speedup

We will describe the methods we have used to compute the serial and parallel processing times. As in the parallel processing literature, there exist several flavors of speedup defined in the literature, and we define our metrics below.

2.3.4.1 Serial Processing Time

The serial time $T(s)$ is defined as the time taken by the fastest processor available on the entire mesh to process all the sequences. This is done to evaluate whether the parallel times are always better compared to serial times, especially when the architecture has fastest serial processors in place for such large scale problems.

2.3.4.2 Parallel Processing Time

There are two approaches in deriving this parallel processing time.

(1) *DLT approach.* As described in the above sections, the multiprocessor strategy essentially parallelizes the computation. However, even with DLT paradigm in place, all the computations cannot proceed simultaneously, due to the dependency in matrix information, as described in Section 2.1. Only submatrices with the same diagonal values of $(k + l)$ can be computed concurrently. Therefore, the total processing time, referring to Fig. 2.9 is $T(p) = t_1 + t_2 + t_3 + t_4 + t_5$.

(2) *ELP approach.* Here the ELP approach will be used as a benchmark against the DLT approach, to observe any advantage gained in using DLT. In ELP, the computation space of a sequence will be divided equally among all processors, and thus, time taken for each processor to complete their load will vary. Hence, all processes will be limited by the speed of the slowest processor involved. Only when the slowest processor completes its load may the processing in the next computation segment begin. Therefore, the total processing time, referring to Fig. 2.10, is $T(p) = t_1 + t_2 + t_2' + t_3 + t_3' + t_4 + t_4' + t_5$.

The overall parallel time, taking into consideration N rows, is defined to be

$$\text{Overall parallel time, } T'(p) = \max\{T_i(p)\}, \quad i = 1, \ldots, N \qquad (2.19)$$

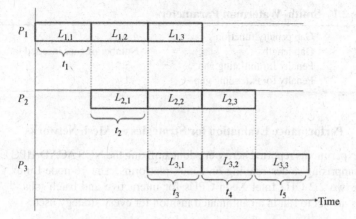

Figure 2.9. Parallel time by DLT for a three-processor problem.

where $T_i(p)$ is parallel time obtained from row i. Thus, speedup can now be defined as

$$\text{Speedup} = \frac{T(s)}{T'(p)} \qquad (2.20)$$

where $T(s)$ and $T'(p)$ are as defined above. We will use this metric to quantify the performance of the strategies.

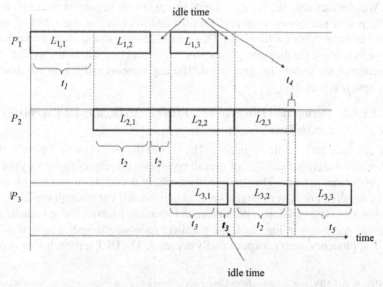

Figure 2.10. Parallel time by ELP for a three-processor problem.

Table 2.1   Smith–Waterman Parameters

w_k	Gap penalty function	$u + vk$
k	Gap length	Number of gaps inserted into sequence
u	Penalty for initiating gap	-5
v	Penalty for extending gap	-1

2.3.5   Performance Evaluation for Strategies on Mesh Networks

The experiments reported here were done utilizing the NUS ACAD-HPC Linux Cluster comprising nodes running on Linux platforms. The 16-node Linux Cluster has thirty-two 2.2-GHz Intel Xeon CPUs for interactive and batch jobs.[10] All experiments are set to run in an automated fashion for every strategy used.

2.3.5.1   Simulation Settings

In our experiments, the $N \times M$ mesh size was fixed, with N, the number of rows in the mesh, set to be 10 and M, the number of processors in a row, set to vary from 2 to 10. The cluster nodes comprises heterogeneous processors, whose speeds are set with one of the values 2, 4, 6, 8, and 10. The sequences used for this simulation are homologous protein sequences derived from the *Rattus norvegicus* and *Mus musculus* databases of olfactory receptors and have an average length of approximately 300 amino acid residues each. A total of 200 sequences is used in the serial time, parallel time, and speedup computations. Sequences used for this simulation have been collected from GenBank. Each simulation run is carried out for 100 times and average results are reported. The Smith–Waterman constants (described in Section 2.1.1) used are as in Table 2.1.

We conduct simulation experiments to study two important issues—one on the influence of number of sequences on time and the other on the effect of mesh size (network scalability), while using DLT and ELP techniques. These two experiments serve to analyze the different parameters and factors that affects the parallel time and speedup of the system in our context. The experiments and results are described in the next two sections.

2.3.5.2   Results and Discussions—Effect of Mesh Size, DLT versus ELP on Finish Time

We consider 200 protein sequences. The size of the mesh is varied from a 10×2 to 10×10 to analyze the effect of overall speedup with respect to the varying number of processors per row. This study is particularly useful when number of sequences to be handled grows very large. Simulation is carried out for both the ELP and DLT techniques. The serial, parallel times, and speedup for both the approaches are observed. As shown in Fig. 2.11, the parallel processing times for both the DLT and ELP approaches seem to exponentially decrease. The DLT approach always produces

---

[10]NUS ACAD-HPC stands for National University of Singapore academic and high-performance computing provided by the Supercomputing & Visualisation Unit of the Computer Centre.

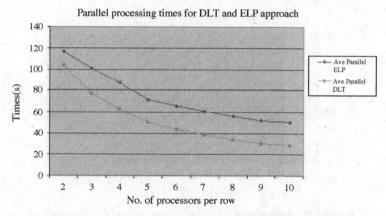

Figure 2.11. Parallel processing times of DLT and ELP approach.

a lower finish time than the ELP approach. This is due to the fact that when ELP is used, the faster processors always have to wait for the slowest processor to complete the task in a row (generating longer idle times) due to the computational dependency operations. On the contrary, DLT approach gains an advantage of partitioning the computation space according to a processor's speed to minimize the delay experienced, if at all any exist. Figure 2.12 illustrates speedup performance for both DLT and ELP methods. The speedup exhibited seems approximately linear in both the cases. The DLT approach, however, delivers a higher speedup—almost as a function of number of processors per row—compared to the ELP approach, again due to the data dependency as described before. Figure 2.13 essentially compares the serial and parallel processing times in a row because each row processes a total of 20 protein sequences, with a total of 200 sequences in the 10 rows of the mesh.

In Fig. 2.13, it may be observed that the serial time is found to be faster than both parallel approaches at first; however, the DLT approach eventually guarantees better finish times than the serial and parallel ELP strategies. The reason for this

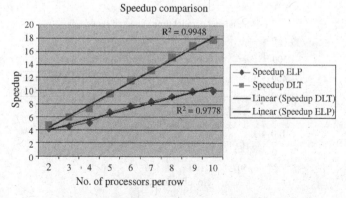

Figure 2.12. Speedup through DLT and ELP approach.

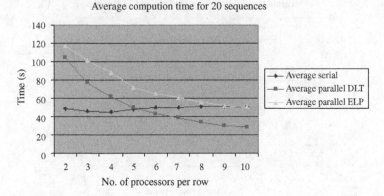

Figure 2.13. Average serial and parallel processing times for 20 sequences per row.

behavior initially is due to the heterogeneity (random spread of heterogenous processors) throughout the mesh cluster. For example, with two processors per row, there is no guarantee that their speeds match the fastest processor in the mesh. However, the chances are that they may be slower. Thus, the processing time, although running in parallel, could be higher than the serial time. However, increasing the number of processors actually increases the chances of higher and faster computing power, resulting in minimum processing time.

As observed for bus networks, here too, for ELP approach, the processing time always depends on the slowest processor involved. Further, due to network heterogeneity, it is very unlikely that the ELP approach will surpass even the serial time. In this set of results (averaged), the ELP reaches the serial approach when 10 processors per row is used.

2.3.5.3   Effect of Number of Sequences on Finish Time

In this study, we vary the number of sequences to be processed, while the mesh size is kept constant at 10×10 (100 nodes). The number of sequences ranges from 50 to

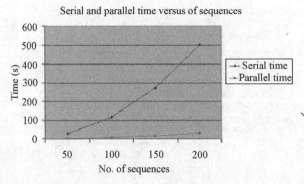

Figure 2.14. Serial and parallel time with respect to varying number of sequences.

Table 2.2   Number of Sequence Comparisons

Number of Sequences	Number of Comparisons
50 (5 per row/cluster)	$^{5}C_2 \times 10 \, \text{rows} = 100$
100 (10 per row/cluster)	$^{10}C_2 \times 10 \, \text{rows} = 450$
150 (15 per row/cluster)	$^{15}C_2 \times 10 \, \text{rows} = 1050$
200 (20 per row/cluster)	$^{20}C_2 \times 10 \, \text{rows} = 1900$

200. This is done to analyze the effects on serial and parallel times with respect to the number of sequences.

As shown in Fig. 2.14, both serial and parallel times increase when the number of sequences becomes large. It may be noted that the tendency is not strictly linear. This is essentially due to the fact that the amount of computation (i.e., in this case the number of comparisons and score generation) involved in processing a larger set of sequences does not scale up in a linear fashion with the increasing number of sequences, as shown in Table 2.2. Therefore, as the number of comparisons needed increases exponentially, the finish time (both serial and parallel) is also found to be increasing exponentially.

2.4   CONCLUDING REMARKS

We considered the problem of aligning large biological sequences, which is an important study in several bioinformatics applications. We proposed an efficient multiprocessor solution on loosely coupled bus and mesh topologies. Although there have been studies proposing high-performance methodologies, this is the first time that divisible load paradigm is attempted on such biological sequence related problems. The performance of our findings were testified by means of rigorous simulations on real-life DNA and protein samples. The modeling and results have conclusively demonstrated the applicability and usefulness of the DLT paradigm in terms of achieving a significant speedup and utilization of resources. Our study also highlighted the effect of several influencing parameters such as communication bandwidth (slow and fast links) and processing delays on the speedup performance. Modeling and capturing the delay components being crucial for carrying out intensive computations on networked systems, the performance using DLT paradigm has been shown to be convincing. Immediate extensions to this work can be in an attempt to practically implement these strategies and to open up a portal for public use. This venture is currently underway. Further, more accurate and comprehensive work can be done on how the processing time is calculated including all overheads and also the distribution of load to processors in the real-life implementation on a network. First, the communication delay time between processors can be factored out to give a more realistic representation of the processing time involved. Second, the computational space (load) can be made to be distributed on a wider scale, which means that one can attempt distributing at a much finer level of computation involving both the rows and the columns, in the case of mesh networks. Following this, sophisticated heuristic methods can be designed to improve the overall alignment of sequences. Finally, a portal for public use to submit a batch of requests, each demanding a batch of MSA, can also be designed.

ACKNOWLEDGMENTS

The author likes to thank Professor David Bader, College of Computing, Georgia Institute of Technology Atlanta, USA, for reading and commenting on the contributions on mesh topology. Also, the author wishes to thank the editing support rendered by Mr. Jingxi Jia of the Department of ECE, NUS, Singapore.

BIBLIOGRAPHIC NOTES

Genomic and protein data can be found in several public databases: GenBank— http://www.ncbi.nlm.nih.gov; EMBL (European Molecular Biology Laboratory) Nucleotide Sequence Database—http://www.ebi.ac.uk/embl; DNA Data Bank of Japan—http://www.ddbj.nig.ac.jp; to quote a few. Fundamental Needleman–Wunsch Algorithm description and analysis can be found in Reference 7. Dynamic programming recursion and analysis of Smith–Waterman algorithm and its variant used in this chapter can be read in Reference 1. While variants of the basic dynamic programming recursion for implementation, such as FASTA, BLAST, MEGABLAST, PSI-BLAST, ClustalW, ClustalW with MPI and Silicon Graphics version HT ClustalW, MULTI-CLUSTAL, can be found in recent bioinformatics books and on the Web; parallel implementations for deriving high throughput and speedups can be found in References 8 and 9. There have been studies that attempt to parallelize such variants. For example, the study in Reference 10 attempts to port BLAST on shared and distributed memory architectures. Similarly, FASTA's performance was studied on clusters— PARAM 10000 in Reference 11. Parallel FASTA is particularly useful when long genome sequences are to be searched in large volume bio databases. Studies that focus on building specific architectures also play a key role in improving the overall performance. FPGA implementations are becoming popular owing to their flexibility in supporting reconfigurable computations. One of the recent attempts is reported in Reference 12 using FPGAs with more than 125 processing elements for homology detection application. Their implementation demonstrates that the solution seek time is 300 times faster than that obtained from computing on a PC with Pentium III (1 GHz). A sixfold speedup is also reported in Reference 9 for SW algorithm implementation. State-of-the-art parallel computing for bioinformatics can be found in Chapter 21 of a recent compilation by Zomaya [13]. Distributed implementations using network infrastructure seem to be very few in the literature. There are very few engines on the Web that could encourage submitting tens of sequences but not on a massive scale. The divisible load paradigm that is used in this chapter is shown to be simple yet robust and applicable to handling large volume data processing on networked environments [3,14]. The paradigm models computation and communication components explicitly and allows a node to decide on the amount of computation it needs to perform without sacrificing the solution time. With no delays scenario, the partitioning of load could be trivial if there are no dependent computations. However, with different topologies, amidst nonzero network delays, scheduling computations on compute nodes is seldom trivial. The study in Reference 6 provides a detailed version of the performance on bus architecture presented in this chapter. Reference 15 and a technical report available with the author presents details on MSA alignment using mesh.

REFERENCES

1. T.K. Yap, O. Frieder, R.L. Martino, *High Performance Computational Methods for Biological Sequence Analysis*, Kluwer Academic Publishers, Dordrecht, 1996.

2. T.G. Robertazzi, Ten reasons to use divisible load theory, *Computer* **36**(5), 63–68, 2003.

3. V. Bharadwaj, D. Ghose, V. Mani, T.G. Robertazzi, *Scheduling Divisible Loads in Parallel and Distributed Systems*, IEEE Computer Society Press, Los Alamitos, CA, 1996.

4. M.P. Berger, P.J. Munson, A novel randomized iteration strategy for aligning multiple protein sequences, *Computer Applications in the Bioscience* **7**, 479–484, 1991.

5. O. Trelles, M.A. Andrade, A. Valencia, E.L. Zapata, J.M. Carazo, Computational space reduction and parallelization of a new clustering approach for large groups of sequences, *Bioinformatics* **14**(5), 439–451, 1998.

6. H.M. Wong, V. Bharadwaj, Aligning biological sequences on distributed bus networks: A divisible load scheduling approach, *IEEE Transactions on Information Technology in BioMedicine* **9**(4), 1910–1924, 2005.

7. I. Eidhammer, I. Jonassen, W.R. Taylor, *Protein Bioinformatics: An Algorithmic Approach to Sequence and Structure Analysis*, John Wiley & Sons, Hoboken, NJ, 2004.

8. D. Pekurovsky, I.N. Shindyalov, P.E. Bourne, A case study of high-throughput biological data processing on parallel platforms, *Bioinformatics* **20**, 1940–1947, 2004.

9. T. Rognes, S. Erling, Six-fold speed-up of Smith–Waterman sequence database searches using parallel processing on common microprocessors, *Bioinformatics* **16**, 699–706, 2001.

10. A. Julich, Implementations of BLAST for parallel computers, *Computer Applications in the Biosciences* **11**(1), 3–6, 1995.

11. C. Janaki, R.R. Joshi, Accelerating comparative genomics using parallel computing, *Silico Biology* **3**(4), 429–440, 2003.

12. Y. Yamaguchi, T. Maruyama, A. Konagaya, High speed homology search with FPGAs, *Pacific Symposium on Biocomputing* **7**, 271–282, 2002.

13. A.Y. Zomaya, *Parallel Computing for Bioinformatics and Computational Biology*, John Wiley & Sons, Hoboken, NJ, 2006.

14. V. Bharadwaj, D. Ghose, T.G. Robertazzi, Divisible load theory: A new paradigm for load scheduling in distributed systems, special issue on Divisible Load Scheduling in Cluster Computing **6**(1), 2003.

15. D.H.P. Low, B. Veeravalli, D. Bader, On the design of high-performance algorithms for aligning multiple protein sequences on mesh-based multiprocessor architectures, *Journal of Parallel Distrib. Computing* **67**, 1007–1017, 2007.

3

OPTIMIZED CLUSTER-ENABLED HMMER SEARCHES

John Paul Walters, Joseph Landman, and Vipin Chaudhary

3.1 INTRODUCTION

Protein sequence analysis tools to predict homology, structure, and function of particular peptide sequences exist in abundance. One of the most commonly used tools is the profile hidden Markov model algorithm developed by Eddy and co-workers [1,2]. These tools allow scientists to construct mathematical models (hidden Markov models or HMM) of a set of aligned protein sequences with known similar function and homology, which is then applicable to a large database of proteins. The tools provide the ability to generate a log-odds score as to whether or not the protein belongs to the same family as the proteins that generated the HMM or to a set of random unrelated sequences.

Due to the complexity of the calculation and the possibility to apply many HMMs to a single sequence (Pfam search), these calculations require significant numbers of processing cycles. Efforts to accelerate these searches have resulted in several platform and hardware specific variants including an Altivec port by Lindahl [3], a GPU port of *hmmsearch* by Horn et al. of Stanford [4], and several optimizations performed by the authors of this chapter. These optimizations span a range between minimal source code changes with some impact upon performance to recast the core algorithms in terms of a different computing technology, thus fundamentally altering the calculation. Each approach has specific benefits and costs. Detailed descriptions of the author's modifications can also be found in References 5 and 6.

The remainder of this chapter is organized as follows: In Section 3.2, we give a brief overview of HMMER and the underlying plan-7 architecture. In Section 3.3, we discuss several different strategies that have been used to implement and accelerate HMMER on a variety of platforms. In Section 3.4, we detail our optimizations and provide performance details. We conclude this chapter in Section 3.5.

Grid Computing for Bioinformatics and Computational Biology. Edited by E.-G. Talbi and A.Y. Zomaya.
Copyright © 2008 John Wiley & Sons, Inc.

3.2 BACKGROUND

HMMER operations rely upon accurate construction of an HMM representation of a multiple sequence alignment (MSA) of homologous protein sequences. This HMM may then be applied to a database of other protein sequences for homology deter- mination or grouped together to form part of a protein family set of HMMs that are used to test whether a particular protein sequence is related to the consensus model, and annotate potential functions within the query protein from what is known about the function of the aligned sequence from the HMM (homology transfer and func- tional inference). These functions in HMMER are based upon the profile HMM [1] architecture. The profile HMM architecture is constructed using the plan-7 model as depicted in Fig. 3.1.

This architecture encodes insertion, deletion, and match states, all relative to a consensus sequence model. The plan-7 architecture is a Viterbi algorithm [7] and the code implementing the plan-7 architecture is constructed as such. Viterbi algo- rithms involve state vector initialization, comparison operations to compute the most probable path to the subsequent state, and thus at the end of the algorithm the most probable/maximum likelihood (Viterbi) path through the state model. The application of the previously constructed HMM to the protein sequence data will generate the aforementioned log-odds score and an optimal alignment represented by the Viterbi path.

Most homology searches perform alignments in either a local or global fashion. The Smith–Waterman algorithm [8], for instance, is intended for local alignments while the Needleman–Wunsch algorithm [9] performs global alignments. The purpose of a global alignment is to find the similarities between two entire strings without regard to the specific similarities between substrings. A local alignment search, however, as- sumes that the similarities between two substrings may be greater than the similarities between the entire strings. In practice, local alignments are typically preferred.

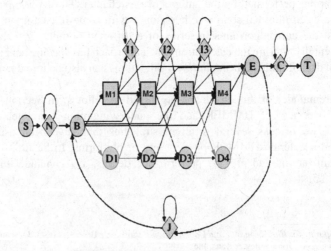

Figure 3.1. Plan 7 HMM model architecture.

Unlike typical homology searches, HMMER does not perform local or global alignments. Instead, the HMM model itself defines whether local or global alignment searches are performed. Typically, alignments are performed globally with respect to an HMM and locally with respect to a sequence [10].

HMMER actually is not a single program, but rather a collection of several programs that perform different tasks to facilitate protein sequence analysis. Among the functionalities they provide are aligning sequences to an existing model, building a model from multiple sequence alignments, indexing an HMM database, searching an HMM database for matches to a query sequence, or searching a sequence database for matches to an HMM. The last two functionalities (i.e., the searches) are among the most frequently used and often require long execution times, depending on the input sequence or HMM and the size of database being searched against. These functionalities are provided by *hmmpfam* and *hmmsearch*, respectively.

3.3 TECHNIQUES FOR ACCELERATING HMMER

As we mentioned in Section 3.1, there have been a variety of techniques used to both implement and accelerate HMMER searches. They range from typical high-performance computing (HPC) strategies such as clustering to Web services and even extending the core HMMER algorithm to novel processing architectures. In this section, we discuss in greater depth the various strategies used in both implementing and accelerating HMMER.

3.3.1 Network and Graphics Processors

3.3.1.1 JackHMMer

We begin with a discussion of *JackHMMer* [11], where network processors are used in place of a general-purpose processor in order to accelerate the core Viterbi algorithm. Specifically, *JackHMMer* uses the Intel IXP 2850 network processor. Like many network processors, the Intel IXP 2850 is a heterogeneous multicore chip; that is, several different processing elements are integrated into a single chip. In this case, sixteen 32-bit microengines (MEs) are paired with a single XScale ARM-compatible processor. Each microengine runs at 1.4 GHz while the XScale CPU runs at a peak rate of 700 MHz. Other processing elements such as memory controllers and interconnect also run at 700 MHz.

JackHMMer essentially uses the IXP 2850 as a single-chip cluster with the XScale CPU functioning as the head node. Like a typical cluster, the XScale CPU is responsible for distributing jobs to the individual microengines. In *JackHMMer*, each job takes the form of a *Viterbi packet*. A database of HMMs is divided into a series of *Viterbi packets* with each packet corresponding to an individual database model [11]. The XScale processor distributes the *Viterbi packets* to the microengines where each microengine then independently performs the Viterbi algorithm on the packet. In the standard HMMER implementation, this computation is performed by hmmpfam.

Despite the IXP's apparently slow clock speed, the authors of Reference 11 claim a speedup of 1.82× compared to a P4 running at 2.6 GHz. However, it is important to note that the algorithm implemented in *JackHMMer* is not the full Viterbi algorithm as implemented in HMMER. A small amount of processing time is saved by not computing the postprocessing portion of the HMMER reference implementation. In addition, Wun et al. note that up to 25% of the initial time was spent in a preprocessing stage in which HMM models are converted into log-odds form as required by the Viterbi algorithm. Instead, they precompute the log-odds data ahead of time and store it on disk for future use. This technique could also be used in a standard HMMER implementation.

3.3.1.2   ClawHMMER

A second technique that has gained prominence in sequence analysis is the use of streaming/graphics processors. While actual streaming processors are not yet widely available, graphics processors bear a close resemblance with regard to functionality. Unlike traditional general-purpose processors, graphics hardware has been optimized to perform the same operation over large streams of input data. This is similar to the SIMD operations of general-purpose CPUs, but with greater width and speed.

Unlike the SIMD approach to optimizing HMMER, *ClawHMMER* [4] operates over multiple sequences rather than vectorizing the computation of individual sequences. The key to *ClawHMMER*'s speed is that sequences many sequences are computed simultaneously. The time to process a group of sequences is essentially the time to process the longest sequence in the batch. Therefore, is it advantageous to group sequences into similar-sized chunks (on the basis of sequence length). Unlike *JackHMMer*, *ClawHMMER* implements the *hmmsearch* function of the standard HMMER implementation.

In Reference 4, Horn et al. demonstrate the speed of *ClawHMMER* with an implementation of their streaming Viterbi algorithm on a 16-node rendering cluster. The cluster consisted of 16 nodes with a Radeon 9800 Pro GPU in each node. Since each sequence is independent of the others, the Viterbi algorithm is highly parallel. Thus, Horn et al. are able to demonstrate nearly linear speedup with their streaming Viterbi algorithm.

3.3.2   DeCypherHMM

For the fastest possible sequence analysis, a custom processor is a necessity. Typically, such customized hardware comes in the form of an FPGA (field programmable gate array). Historically, FPGAs have been difficult and time consuming to program. They require expertise in hardware/CPU design and are quite costly. However, they are often able to achieve 10–100× the speed of a general purpose CPU or cluster.

Timelogic provides an FPGA HMM protein characterization solution named *DeCypherHMM* [12]. The DeCypher engine is deployed as a standard PCI card into an existing machine. Multiple DeCypher engines can be installed in a single machine, which according to TimeLogic results in near-linear speedup.

3.3.3   Web Services

Web-based sequence analysis tools are becoming popular for all areas of bioinformatics research. In this section, we detail two of the most popular Web-based toolkits for facilitating HMMER searches, *SledgeHMMER* and the *MPI Bioinformatics Toolkit*.

3.3.3.1   SledgeHMMER

SledgeHMMER [13] is a Web service designed to allow researchers to perform Pfam database searches without having to install HMMER locally. To use the service, a user submits a batch job to the *SledgeHMMER* Web site. Upon completion of the job, the results are simply emailed back to the user.

In addition to being available via the Web, *SledgeHMMER* also includes three optimizations to expedite Pfam searches. The first optimization is their use of pre-calculated search results. Those queries that match entries held within the *SledgeHMMER* database can be quickly returned. Matching entries are found using an MD5 hashing strategy.

For those results that are not already contained within the *SledgeHMMER* database, *SledgeHMMER* uses a parallelized *hmmpfam* algorithm. Rather than using MPI or PVM to perform the distributed search, *SledgeHMMER* relies on a Unix-based file-locking strategy. This not only allows nodes to leave/join as they become available but also requires a shared file system from which all nodes access a lock file. This lock file acts as an iterator and returns indexes that correspond to query sequences. By using a lock file, *SledgeHMMER* ensures that all sequences are distributed exactly once.

The final optimization employed by *SledgeHMMER* is to read the entire Pfam database stored into memory before performing the batch search. In a typical scenario the entire Pfam database will be read for each query sequence in the batch search. This can be extremely time-consuming. To alleviate this problem, the Pfam database is read and stored into memory upon startup and can be referenced throughout the computation without accessing the disk.

3.3.3.2   The MPI Bioinformatics Toolkit

The *MPI* (Max Planck Institute) *Bioinformatics Toolkit* [14] is a Web-based collection of bioinformatics tools that is freely accessible to researchers. The toolkit makes two major contributions to Web-based bioinformatics services.

The first contribution is the toolkit's vast collection of tools, all of which are available on a single Web site. These tools not only include HMMER searches, but BLAST [15,16] ClustalW [17], and MUSCLE [18] searches also (among others) in addition to many tools developed in-house. Some of these tools, specifically HMMER, include optimizations to accelerate the searching of sequences. In the case of HMMER, the *MPI Bioinformatics Toolkit* reduces HMMER searches to ~10% of their original. This is done by reducing the database with a single iteration of PSI-BLAST.

The second major contribution made by the *MPI Bioinformatics Toolkit* is to allow the user to pipeline searches from one tool to another automatically. This allows the results of an initial search to be fed into a secondary search (e.g., from a sequence analysis tool to a formatting tool or classification tool). Furthermore, a user can store customized databases on the *MPI Bioinformatics Toolkit* server for future use.

3.4   CONVENTIONAL CPU OPTIMIZATIONS

In this section we detail three optimizations made by the authors of this chapter. In the first case, we evaluate changes made through absolute minimal changes in source code. In this case, the changes were designed to allow the compiler to perform its optimizations in a more efficient manner. Such changes also benefit from portability as well. Our second strategy was to manually add SSE2 code to the P7Viterbi function. This required the addition of in-line assembly code resulting in nonportable, but accelerated code. Our final strategy was to recast the computation in terms of MPI such that multiple nodes could be used simultaneously. The MPI implementation is portable across standard-compliant MPI implementations.

3.4.1   Hardware/Software Configuration

The experiments in this chapter were performed on a university cluster. Each node is an SMP configuration consisting of two 2.66-GHz Pentium 4 Xeon processors with 2.5 GB of total system memory per node. 100-Mbit ethernet facilitates communication between each node.

Each node runs the Rocks v3.3.0 Linux cluster distribution. In addition, each node is loaded with both MPICH version 1.2.6 [19,20] and PVM version 3.4.3 [21]. All nodes are identical in every respect.

For testing purposes, most experiments were performed using the *nr* sequence database compared against *rrm.hmm* (*rrm.hmm* is included in the HMMER distribution). The *nr* database is 900 MB in size. A smaller version of the *nr* database was used to verify our results against smaller databases. To demonstrate the applicability of our *SSE2* optimizations in *hmmpfam*, we also ran tests using the *Pfam* database.

In Section 3.4.2, tests were performed using BBSv3 [22] tests on a 64-bit AMD Opteron. The binaries were compiled with threading disabled.

3.4.2   Minimal Source Changes

Profiling of the code down to the line level with long test cases indicated that the conditionals and the loop in the P7Viterbi routine were consuming approximately 30% and 60%, respectively, of the execution time of this routine. Carefully examining the loop, several issues were immediately obvious. First, the variable *sc* was superfluous and forced a memorization of the value of an intermediate calculation. Without a complete aliasing analysis on the part of the compiler, there would be little opportunity for the optimizer to remove the variable and leave the intermediate results in a register.

Second, the use of variable *sc* resulted in creating artificial dependencies between different sections of the loop and between iterations of the loop. The former would prevent the optimizer from moving statements around to reduce resources. The latter would impede automatic unrolling.

Finally, the conditional within the loop is always executed except for the last iteration. This implies that this loop can be refactored into two loops, one with k incrementing from 1 to $M - 1$ over the main loop block (MLB) with no conditional needed to execute the conditional block (CB), and one main loop block with $k = M$ without the conditional block; that is, we alter the structure of the loop from Listing 3.1 to that of Listing 3.2.

Listing 3.1. The most time-consuming portion of the P7Viterbi algorithm.

```
for (k = 1; k <= M; k++) {
  mc[k] = mpp[k-1]   + tpmm[k-1];
  if ((sc = ip[k-1]   + tpim[k-1]) > mc[k])
    mc[k] = sc;
  if ((sc = dpp[k-1] + tpdm[k-1]) > mc[k])
    mc[k] = sc;
  if ((sc = xmb   + bp[k])          > mc[k])
    mc[k] = sc;
  mc[k] += ms[k];
  if (mc[k] < -INFTY) mc[k] = -INFTY;

  dc[k] = dc[k-1] + tpdd[k-1];
  if ((sc = mc[k-1] + tpmd[k-1]) > dc[k])
    dc[k] = sc;
  if (dc[k] < -INFTY)
    dc[k] = -INFTY;

  if (k < M) {
    ic[k] = mpp[k] + tpmi[k];
    if ((sc = ip[k] + tpii[k]) > ic[k])
      ic[k] = sc;
    ic[k] += is[k];
    if (ic[k] < -INFTY)
      ic[k] = -INFTY;
  }
}
```

Listing 3.2. Removing the conditional from the innermost loop.

```
for (k = 1; k < M; k++) {
  ...

  ...

  ...

    ic[k] = mpp[k] + tpmi[k];
    if (( ip[k] + tpii[k]) > ic[k])
      ic[k] = ip[k] + tpii[k];
    ic[k] += is[k];
    if (ic[k] < -INFTY)
      ic[k] = -INFTY;

}

    k = M;
    sc1 = mpp[k-1]   + tpmm[k-1];
    if (( ip[k-1]   + tpim[k-1]) > sc1)
        sc1 = ip[k-1]   + tpim[k-1] ;
    if (( dpp[k-1] + tpdm[k-1]) > sc1)
        sc1 = dpp[k-1] + tpdm[k-1] ;
    if (( xmb   + bp[k])           > sc1)
        sc1 = xmb   + bp[k] ;
    sc1 += ms[k];
    if (sc1 < -INFTY) sc1 = -INFTY;
    mc[k] = sc1;

    dc[k] = dc[k-1] + tpdd[k-1];
    if (( mc[k-1] + tpmd[k-1]) > dc[k])
        dc[k] = mc[k-1] + tpmd[k-1] ;
    if (dc[k] < -INFTY) dc[k] = -INFTY;
```

Removing the conditional from the loop lets the compiler generate better code for the loop as long as the artificial loop iteration dependency was broken by removing the memorization of *sc* and using a register temporary. After making these changes, the HMMER regression tests included with the code distribution were rerun, and the benchmark output was inspected to ensure correctness of the calculations.

This set of changes resulted in a binary approximately $1.8\times$ faster than the binary built from the original source tree. An interloop dependency still exists with the use of the *sc*1 variable. However, the only time memory traffic that will be observed will be when the assignment conditional is true, which should allow the cached value of *sc*1 to be used without requiring repeated memoization where it is not required. Additional work was performed on the function to remove the *sc* variable from other conditionals so as to avoid the artificial dependencies.

Combining these changes with the preceding changes yielded a binary approximately $1.96\times$ faster than the Opteron baseline binary provided by the HMMER download site. Subsequent tests on end-user cases have yielded a range from $1.6\times$ to $2.5\times$ baseline performance, depending in part upon which database and how the HMM was constructed for the tests.

3.4.2.1   Performance Results of the Minimal Changes

The binary generated by the changes was compared to the standard downloadable Opteron binary, running the BBSv3 tests. No special efforts were undertaken to make the machine quiescent prior to the run, other than to ascertain whether or not another user was running jobs. The test binary used *hmmcalibrate* to test the efficacy of the Viterbi improvements.

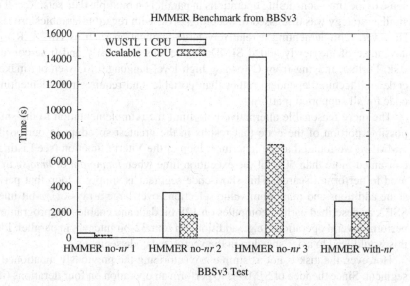

Figure 3.2. BBSv3 results.

From Fig. 3.2, we can see that modest improvements can be gained from seemingly minor source code changes. Such changes, while small, can have a dramatic effect on the compiler's ability to optimize the source code. In cases where most of the compute time is spent in a single function, such compiler optimizations can be particularly useful.

3.4.3   Inline Assembly/SSE2

The *SSE2* [23] instructions are among a series of Intel *Single Instruction Multiple Data (SIMD)* extensions to the x86 Instruction Set Architecture (ISA). The first was the *MultiMedia eXtension (MMX)* that appeared in the Pentium MMX in 1997 [24]. MMX provides a series of packed integer instructions that work on 64-bit data using eight MMX 64-bit registers. MMX was followed by the *Streaming SIMD Extensions (SSE)* that appeared with Pentium III. SSE adds a series of packed and scalar single-precision floating-point operations, and some conversions between single-precision floating point and integers. SSE uses 128-bit registers in a new XMM register file, which is distinct from the MMX register file. The *Second Streaming SIMD Extensions (SSE2)* appeared with the Pentium IV. SSE2 adds a series of packed and scalar double-precision floating-point operations. In addition, SSE2 provides integer operations similar to those available with MMX except that they work on 128-bit data and use the XMM register file. SSE2 also adds a large number of data type conversion instructions. More recently, a third set of extensions, *SSE3* [25], was added to enable complex floating-point arithmetic in several data layouts. *SSE3* also adds a small set of additional permutes, and some horizontal floating point adds and subtracts.

Like other applications dealing with processing large arrays of data, HMMER seemingly has a strong potential to benefit from SIMD instructions by performing some of the time-consuming operations in parallel on multiple data sets. Recall that a similar strategy was discussed in Section 3.3.1.2 with regard to graphics processors. However, reimplementing a relatively large application such as HMMER to take advantage of the newly added SIMD instructions is a costly and time-consuming task. Further, moving from C (or any high level language) to assembly makes the code architecture dependent rather than portable, and requires reimplementing the code for all supported platforms.

The more reasonable alternative is to limit the reimplementation to the smallest possible portion of the code that results in the greatest speedup. In our profile of HMMER, we found that the innermost loop of the Viterbi function (see Listing 3.1) consumed more than 50% of the execution time when *hmmpfam* or *hmmsearch* are used to perform a search. This short-code segment is simply a loop that performs some additions and maximum value selections over large arrays of 32-bit integers. SSE2, as described earlier, computes on 128-bit data and enables the programmer to perform several operations (e.g., addition) on four 32-bit integers in parallel. Ideally, this would lead to a 4× speedup in the vectorized code segment.

However, the task is not as simple as vectorizing the previously mentioned code segment. Since the idea of SIMD is to perform an operation on four iterations (items) in parallel at the same time, the first problem is *interiteration dependencies*, that is, an operation in iteration i requires a result from iteration $i - 1$ (or earlier iterations) to be performed. To resolve interiteration dependencies in our loop, we had to split the loop into three loops. This may appear to add additional overhead, but each loop now iterates only 25% of the number of iterations in the original loop. We still achieve reasonable speedup, but not quite the ideal case as described above.

Splitting the loop is not the only overhead that can affect the overall reduction in execution time. We also encountered another problem: the lack of packed max/min instructions that works on 32-bit integers, similar to PMAXUB/PMINUB and PMAXSW/PMINSW that work on 8-bit and 16-bit data, respectively. Implementing a replacement for that missing instruction costs five SSE2 instructions for each occurrence. Assume that the data to be compared are initially in registers XMM3 and XMM4, where each register contains four integer items, and the maximum item of each pair is required to be in register XMM3 by the end of the task. If we have that "desired instruction" (let us call it PMAXD), the task can be performed simply by one instruction "PMAXD XMM4, XMM3." The replacement code is simply

- MOVDQA XMM3, XMM5
  copying the content of XMM3 into XMM5;
- PCMPGTD XMM4, XMM5
  comparing contents of XMM4 and XMM5 and for each pair, if the item in XMM4 is greater than that in XMM5, the item in XMM5 is replaced with 0s, otherwise it is replaced by all 1s. By the end of this step, each of the four items in XMM5 will be either 0x00000000 or 0xFFFFFFFF. The original data in XMM5 are lost, and that is why we copied them in the previous step;
- PAND XMM5, XMM3
  bitwise AND the content of the two registers and put the results in XMM3. Since XMM3 has the same contents as those of XMM5 before the previous step, this step will keep only the maximum values in XMM3 and replace those which are not the maximum in their pairs by 0s;
- PANDN XMM4, XMM5
  invert XMM5 (1's complement) and AND it with XMM4. That will have a similar result as in the previous step, but the maximum numbers in XMM4 will be stored in XMM5 this time;
- POR XMM5, XMM3
  this will gather all the maximums in XMM5 and XMM3 and store them in XMM3. The task is done.

Fortunately, even with these five instructions replacing the desired instruction, we can still achieve reasonable speedup over the non-SSE2 case. With no SIMD the maximum selection consists of three instructions: Compare, Jump on a condition, and then a move instruction that will be executed only if the condition fails. Assuming equal probabilities for the fail and the success of the condition, that means an average of 2.5 instructions for each pair of items, that is, 10 instructions for four pairs compared to the five when the SSE2 instructions are used.

We should note that the Altivec architecture provides the needed instruction in the form of VMAXSW and VMAXUW (vector max signed/unsigned max). This is used in the Erik Lindahl [3] port to achieve excellent speedup on the PowerPC architecture.

Finally, an additional overhead is shared, typically by several SSE2 instructions: that is, data alignment and the moving of data into the 128-bit XMM registers. However, once the data are in these registers, many SSE2 operations can be performed on them, assuming an efficiently written code and that the entire alignment and loading cost can be shared. Even if this is not the case some speedup can still be observed over the non-SIMD case.

3.4.3.1   SSE2 Evaluation and Performance Results

We begin our evaluation by noting that approximately 50% of the runtime of our code can be vectorized using the *SSE2* instructions. We can therefore use Amdahl's law to compute the theoretical maximum speedup possible, given 50% parallelizable code. We start from Amdahl's law:

$$\text{Speedup} = \frac{1}{(1 - P) + \frac{P}{N}} \tag{3.1}$$

From Equation (3.1), we have P is the percentage of the code that can be parallelized. $1 - P$ is therefore the percentage of code that must be executed serially. Finally, from Equation (3.1), N represents the number of processors. In this case, N actually represents the number of elements that can be executed within a single SSE2 instruction, 4.

Theoretically, the expected speedup of the loop is 4, This should therefore result in an expected speedup of

$$\text{Speedup} = \frac{1.0}{50\% + \frac{50\%}{4}} = 1.6 \tag{3.2}$$

In other words, the overall reduction in execution time is expected to be

$$1 - \frac{1}{1.6} = 37.5\% \tag{3.3}$$

Our analysis shows a reduction in the execution time even considering the overhead described in Section 3.4.3. The loop was then reimplemented using the SSE2

Table 3.1   Effect of SSE2 on HMMER Execution Time

	Average Execution Time, s		Reduction in Execution Time
	Original Code	with SSE2	
Sample 1	1183	909	23.2%
Sample 2	272	221	18.8%
Sample 3	1919	1562	18.6%

instructions, and *hmmpfam* and *hmmsearch* were used to compare the results. Many samples were used in searches against the *Pfam* and *nr* databases [26,27]. The Pfam database is a large collection of multiple sequence alignments and hidden Markov models covering many common protein families. The *nr* database is a nonredundant database available from Reference 27. Each search was repeated several times and the average was found for each search both when the original code and the modified code using SSE2 are used. The reduction in execution time varies from around 18% up to 24% depending on the sample and the percentage of time spent in the reimplemented code. Table 3.1 shows the results of three Samples. Samples 1 and 2 were taken from *hmmpfam* searches while sample 3 was taken from *hmmsearch* searches. The corresponding speedups are from around 1.2 up to 1.3.

Implementing more code using the SSE2 may have resulted in more speedup, but would have been a much more costly task. The advantage of this speedup is that it is cost-free, no new hardware is required, and no real development time is needed; just a small portion of the code needs to be reimplemented and maintained over the original implementation. This disadvantage is the lack of portability.

3.4.4   Cluster/MPI Parallelism

In this section, we describe our HMMER MPI implementation. Unlike the SIMD/SSE2 and minimal source-change implementations, the MPI implementation takes advantage of the parallelism between multiple sequences rather than the instruction level parallelism used by the SSE2 technique. The advantage in this case is that greater parallelism can be achieved by offloading the entire *P7Viterbi()* function to compute nodes, rather than simply vectorizing the most time-consuming loop.

3.4.4.1   Parallelizing the Database

Rather than the instruction-level parallelism described in Section 3.4.3, we now distribute individual sequences to cluster nodes. Each cluster node then performs the majority of the computation associated with its own sequence and returns the results to the master node. This is the method by which the original PVM implementation of HMMER performs the distribution. It is also the basis from which we began our MPI implementation. To understand the distribution of computation between the master node and the worker nodes, we provide pseudocode in Listings 3.3, 3.4, and 3.5. The important point to note is that the *P7Viterbi()* function accounts for greater than 90% (see Table 3.2) of the runtime, thus it is imperative that it be executed on the worker nodes if any effective parallelism is to be achieved.

3.4.4.2   Enhancing the Cluster Distribution

While the strategy demonstrated above does indeed yield reasonable speedup, we found that the workers were spending too much time blocking for additional work. The solution to this problem is twofold. First, the workers should be using a nonblocking, double buffering strategy rather than their simple blocking techniques. Second, the

Listing 3.3. Pseudocode of each sequence iteration.

```
while (ReadSeq(...)){
  dsq = DigitizeSequence(...);
  if (do_xnu && Alphabet_type
        == hmmAMINO)
    XNU(...);
  sc = P7Viterbi(...);
  if (do_forward) {
    sc  = P7Forward(...);
    if (do_null2)
      sc -= TraceScoreCorrection(...);
  }
  pvalue = PValue(hmm, sc);
  evalue = thresh->Z ?
      (double) thresh->Z * pvalue :
      (double) nseq * pvalue;
  if (sc >= thresh->globT &&
        evalue <= thresh->globE){
    sc = PostprocessSignificantHit(...);
  }
  AddToHistogram(histogram, sc);
}
```

workers can reduce the communication time by processing database chunks rather than individual sequences.

Our double buffering strategy is to receive the next sequence from the master node while the current sequence is being processed. The idea behind double buffering is to overlap as much of the communication as possible with the computation, hopefully hiding the communication altogether.

In keeping with the strategy used in the PVM implementation, the master does not also act as a client itself. Instead, its job is to supply sequences as quickly as possible to the workers as newly processed sequences arrive. Therefore, a cluster of N nodes will actually have only $N - 1$ worker nodes available with one node reserved as the master.

While double buffering alone improved the speedup immensely, we also sought to reduce the communication time in addition to masking it through double buffering. To

Listing 3.4. Pseudocode of the master node.

```
while (ReadSeq(...)){
     /* receive output */
   pvm_recv(slave_tid, HMMPVM_RESULTS);
     /* send new work */
   dsq = DigitizeSequence(...);
   if (do_xnu) XNU(...);
   pvm_send(slave_tid, HMMPVM_WORK);


     /*process output */
   if (sent_trace){
     sc = PostprocessSignificantHit(...);
   }
   AddToHistogram(...);
}
```

this end, we simply bundled several sequences (12, in our experiments) to each worker in each message. We settled on 12 sequences by simply observing the performance of *hmmsearch* for various chunk sizes. Sending 12 sequences in each message maintained a reasonable message size and also provided enough work to keep the workers busy while the next batch of sequences was in transit.

3.4.4.3 MPI Performance Results

Beginning from Equation (3.1), we can derive a formula for the expected speedup of *hmmsearch* for a given number of CPUs. For example, let us assume that the number of CPUs is 2. From Equation (3.1), we can express the potential speedup as

$$\frac{1}{(1-P) + \frac{P}{2}} \tag{3.4}$$

Again, P is the percentage of code executed in parallel and $(1 - P)$ is the serial code. In order to find the fraction of code capable of being parallelized, we profiled *hmmsearch* using the *nr* database. Table 3.2 lists our results of the profile.

We notice that the *P7Viterbi* function accounts for nearly all of the runtime of *hmm-search*. Furthermore, of the functions listed in Table 3.2, the first 3 are all run on the worker node. Therefore, our P from Equation (3.4) can be reasonably approximated

Listing 3.5. Pseudocode of the worker node.

```
for (;;){
/*receive work*/
  pvm_recv(master_tid, HMMPVM_WORK);


/*compute alignment*/
  sc = P7Viterbi(...);
  if (do_forward) {
    sc  = P7Forward(...);
    if (do_null2)
      sc -= TraceScoreCorrection(...);
  }


  pvalue = PValue(...);
  evalue = Z ? (double) Z * pvalue :
               (double) nseq * pvalue;
  send_trace = (tr != NULL &&
               sc >= globT
               && evalue <= globE)
               ? 1 : 0;


     /* return output
      */


  if (send_trace) PVMPackTrace(...);
  pvm_send(master_tid, HMMPVM_RESULTS);
}
```

Table 3.2   Profile Results of *hmmsearch*

Function	Percentage of Total Execution
P7Viterbi	97.72
P7ViterbiTrace	0.95
P7ReverseTrace8	0.25
addseq	0.23
other	0.85

Table 3.3 Actual Speedup Compared to Optimal Speedup (non-*SSE2*)

N CPU	Actual Speedup	Optimal Speedup
1	1	1
2	1.62	1.98
4	3.09	3.87
8	6.44	7.44
16	11.10	13.77

as 98.92%. For two worker processors, this leaves us with an expected speedup of

$$\frac{1}{(1 - 0.9892) + \frac{0.9892}{2}} = 1.98 \tag{3.5}$$

with an expected increase in execution time of 49%.

From Table 3.3, we can see that the actual speedup of two CPUs is 1.62 or approximately a 38% decrease in runtime. Considering that the implementation requires message passing over a network and that the messages and computation cannot necessarily be overlapped entirely, we feel that the actual speedup is rather respectable.

In Fig. 3.3, we provide our raw timings for *hmmsearch*, comparing our *MPI* and *MPI+SSE2* code against the *PVM* code provided by the HMMER source distribution. In Table 3.4 we translate the numbers from Fig. 3.3 into their corresponding speedups and compare them against one another.

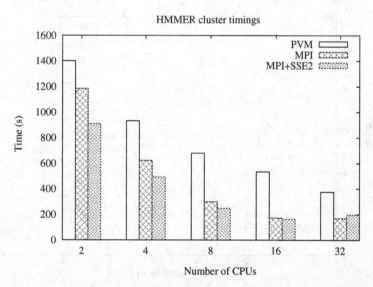

Figure 3.3. Comparative timings of *PVM*, *MPI*, and *MPI* + *SSE2* implementations.

Table 3.4 Speedups of *hmmsearch* for 100-MB Database

# CPU	PVM	MPI	MPI+SSE2
2	1.39	1.69	2.21
4	2.28	3.38	3.84
8	4.05	5.81	6.65
16	4.56	5.90	7.71

To verify that our techniques work in the case of smaller databases, we also tested *hmmsearch* with a smaller (100 MB) version of the *nr* database. The smaller database was created by simply taking the first 100 MB of *nr*. Our results are summarized in Table 3.4. From Table 3.4 we can see that both the *MPI* and the *SSE2* techniques yield reasonable speedup from even fairly small databases. By examining Fig. 3.4 and Table 3.4, we can also see that our speedup increases with larger databases.

As can be seen in Fig. 3.3, our MPI implementation clearly outperforms the PVM implementation by a fairly wide margin. As the number of nodes increases, the MPI implementation improves the runtime by nearly a factor of 2. And adding SSE2 improves upon the MPI implementation. Figure 3.4 clearly shows that our MPI implementation scales much better than the current PVM implementation. In addition, some of the speedup may be, at least in part, due to the underlying differences between PVM and MPI.

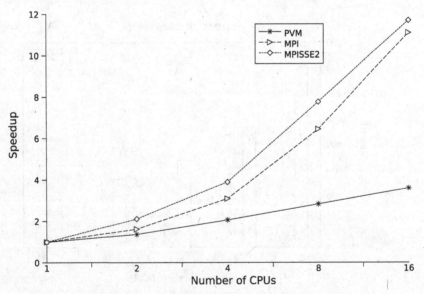

Figure 3.4. Figure 3.3 translated into the corresponding speedups.

3.5 CONCLUSIONS

We have discussed the many ways in which HMMER has been accelerated and improved through a variety of mechanisms. These include novel hardware solutions, Web services, and conventional CPU acceleration techniques. Owing to its popularity, HMMER has inspired a wealth of freely available Web services that enable the linking of multiple sequence analysis tools into a single service. We have also shown how HMMER can be effectively accelerated on typical hardware in order to more effectively utilize the resources that are already available. Our acceleration strategies ranged from minimal source code changes to inline assembly and MPI. We have further demonstrated large improvements in the clustered implementation of HMMER by porting the client and server to use MPI rather than PVM. Furthermore, our MPI implementation utilized an effective double buffering and database chunking strategy to provide performance increases beyond that which would be achieved by directly porting the PVM code to MPI code. Our results show excellent speedup over and above that of the PVM implementation and beyond that of any conventional hardware. The techniques that we have implemented could prove useful beyond the cluster implementation. Indeed, even the Web services will soon find the need to cluster-enable their computational back ends. Our accelerations could therefore easily be used within a Web-based sequencing package for high scalability.

REFERENCES

1. S. Eddy, Profile hidden Markov models, *Bioinformatics* **14**(9), 755–763, 1998.
2. R. Durbin, S. Eddy, A. Krogh, A. Mitchison, *Biological Sequence Analysis: Probabilistic Models of Proteins and Nucleic Acids*, Cambridge University Press, New York, 1998.
3. E. Lindahl, Altivec-accelerated HMM algorithms, 2005. http://lindahl.sbc.su.se/.
4. D.R. Horn, M. Houston, P. Hanarahan, ClawHmmer: A streaming HMMer-search implementation. in: *IEEE International Conference on High Performance, Computing, Networking Storage, and Analysis*, Seattle, 2005.
5. J. Landman, J. Ray, J.P. Walters. Accelerating Hmmer searches on Opteron processors with minimally invasive recoding, AINA '06, in: *Proceedings of the 20th International Conference on Advanced Information Networking and Applications*, Vol. 2 (AINA '06), IEEE Computer Society, Washington, DC, pp. 628–636, 2006.
6. J.P. Walters, B. Qudah, V. Chaudhary, Accelerating the Hmmer sequence analysis suite using conventional processors, AINA '06, in: *Proceedings of the 20th International Conference on Advanced Information Networking and Applications*, Vol. 1 (AINA '06), IEEE Computer Society, Washington, DC, pp. 289–294, 2006.
7. A.J. Viterbi, Error bounds for convolutional codes and an asymptotically optimum decoding algorithm, *IEEE Transactions on Information Theory* **IT-13**, 260–269, 1967.
8. T.F. Smith, M.S. Waterman, Identification of common molecular subsequences, *Journal of Molecular Biology* **147**, 1981.
9. S. Needleman, C. Wunsch, A general method applicable to the search for similarities in the amino acid sequence of two sequences, *Journal of Molecular Biology* **48**(3), 443–453, 1970.
10. S. Eddy, HMMER: Profile HMMs for Protein Sequence Analysis, 2006. http://hmmer.wustl.edu.

11. B. Wun, J. Buhler, P. Crowley. Exploiting coarse-grained parallelism to accelerate protein motif finding with a network processor, PACT '05, in: *Proceedings of the 2005 International Conference on Parallel Architectures and Compilation Techniques*, 2005.

12. TimeLogic BioComputing Solutions, DecypherHMM, 2006. http://www.timelogic.com/.

13. G. Chukkapalli, C. Guda, S. Subramaniam. SledgeHMMER: A web server for batch searching the Pfam database, *Nucleic Acids Research*, **32**, W542–544, 2004 (Web server issue).

14. A. Biegert, C. Mayer, M. Remmert, J. Soding, A. Lupas, The MPI bioinformatics toolkit for protein sequence analysis, *Nucleic Acids Research* **34**, W335–339, 2006 (Web server issue).

15. S.F. Altschul, W. Gish, W. Miller, E.W. Myers, D.J. Lipman, Basic local alignment search tool, *Journal of Molecular Biology* **215**(3), 403–410, 1990.

16. S.F. Altschul, T.L. Madden, A.A. SchÃ/ffer, J. Zhang, Z. Zhang, W. Miller, D.J. Lipman, Gapped blast and psi-blast: A new generation of protein database search programs, *Nucleic Acids Research* **25**(17), 3389–3402, 1997.

17. J.D. Thompson, D.G. Higgins, T.J. Gibson, Clustal w: Improving the sensitivity of progressive multiple sequence alignment through sequence weighting, position-specific gap penalties and weight matrix choice, *Nucleic Acids Research* **22**(22), 4673–4680, 1994.

18. R.C. Edgar, Muscle: Multiple sequence alignment with high accuracy and high throughput, *Nucleic Acids Research* **32**(5), 1792–1797, 2004.

19. Argonne National Lab MPICH-A Portable Implementation of MPI, 2006. http://www-unix.mcs.anl.gov/mpi/mpich/.

20. W. Gropp, E. Lusk, N. Doss, A. Skjellum. A high-performance, portable implementation of the MPI message passing interface standard, *Parallel Computing* **22**(6), 789–828, 1996.

21. V.S. Sunderam, PVM: a framework for parallel distributed computing, *Concurrency: Practice and Experience* **2**(4), 315–339, 1990.

22. J. Landman, 2006. Bbsv3. //www.scalableinformatics.com/bbs.

23. Intel Corporation, SSE2: Streaming SIMD (Single Instruction Multiple Data) Second Extensions, 2006a. http://www.intel.com.

24. Intel Corporation, MMX: MultiMedia eXtensions, 2006b, http://www.intel.com.

25. Intel Corporation, SSE3: Streaming SIMD (Single Instruction Multiple Data) Third Extensions, 2003. www.intel.com.

26. Pfam, The PFAM HMM library: A large collection of multiple sequence alignments and hidden Markov models covering many common protein families, 2006. http://pfam.wustl.edu.

27. NCBI, The NR (non-redundant) database, 2006. ftp://ftp.ncbi.nih.gov/blast/db/FASTA/nr.gz.

4

EXPANDING THE REACH OF GRID COMPUTING: COMBINING GLOBUS- AND BOINC-BASED SYSTEMS

Daniel S. Myers, Adam L. Bazinet, and Michael P. Cummings

4.1 INTRODUCTION

Grid computing is a relatively recent formulation of distributed computing, and although there are more formal definitions [1], we use the following description [2]: Grid computing is a model of distributed computing that uses geographically and administratively disparate resources. In Grid computing, individual users can access computers and data transparently without having to consider location, operating system, account administration, and other details. In Grid computing, the details are abstracted and the resources are virtualized.

At present, Grid computing systems can be broadly classified into two types. The first type might be considered the "classical" computational Grid system used by the computer science research community. Such heavyweight systems provide rich feature sets (e.g., resource discovery services and multiuser authentication) and tend to concern themselves primarily with providing access to large-scale, intra- and interinstitutional-level resources such as clusters or multiprocessors.

The second general class of Grid computing systems is the desktop Grid, in which cycles are scavenged from idle desktop computers. The power of desktop systems has increased dramatically in recent years, and there has been a concomitant shift away from centralized client/server computing to a decentralized model. Although individual desktops remain inferior to "big iron" machines in many ways, the combined power of hundreds to many thousands of desktop systems united in a desktop Grid represents a substantial computing resource. Desktop Grids excel at embarrassingly parallel problems, and they have become particularly popular in the natural sciences, where they have been used in research areas as diverse as radio

Grid Computing for Bioinformatics and Computational Biology. Edited by E.-G. Talbi and A.Y. Zomaya.
Copyright © 2008 John Wiley & Sons, Inc.

astronomy [3], phylogenetics [4,5], structural biochemistry [6], and anti-HIV drug discovery [7].

In contrast to classical computer science research Grid systems, lightweight desktop Grids provide only a thin layer of abstraction over the resources they manage. This is largely a function of their origins: systems such as SETI@home [3] (and its relatives and descendants) were initially conceived to solve immediate research problems, not as objects of study themselves. Note that we specifically exclude Condor [8] and similar systems from our definition of desktop Grids. Although Condor is a distributed computing system that uses cycles from idle computers, the individual computers typically reside wholly within a single institution and administrative domain.

Many computational biology problems are well-suited to processing by desktop Grids for two main reasons. First, many computational biology problems require considerable CPU time to solve, and provisioning a cluster or a symmetric multiprocessor to provide reasonable response times for a large number of such jobs can be prohibitively expensive and lead to massive overprovisioning during periods of low load. Second, many computational biology algorithms exhibit extremely coarse-grained parallelism, and many existing applications do not take advantage of parallel hardware. In these cases, the fast interconnect of a cluster or a symmetric multiprocessor is simply wasted. Hence, many computational biology problems would be well-served by desktop Grid systems if such systems could be made available and easy to use.

Thus, we have two largely separate models of Grid computing. One provides a rich feature set for accessing large-scale resources; the other provides a minimal feature set but can utilize resources as informal as personal computers in suburban homes. Ideally, We would like the best of both worlds: We would want to apply the features of the first model over the scope of the latter. Here, we describe middleware that allows us to realize this goal. We present an interface between the Globus Toolkit [9] and the Berkeley Open Infrastructure for Network Computing (BOINC) [10]. First, however, we provide an overview of the two software toolkits.

4.1.1 Globus

The Globus Toolkit [9] is the paradigmatic example of a heavyweight Grid system. Its Grid Security Infrastructure (GSI) provides for strong distributed authentication of mutually distrustful parties, and its Community Authorization Service (CAS) provides robust authorization capabilities. The Monitoring and Discovery System (MDS) allows for on-the-fly resource discovery. Additionally, the Grid Resource Allocation and Management (GRAM) service provides an abstraction layer that allows jobs to be submitted to computational resources without prior knowledge of the underlying job submission and queuing systems used by those resources.

Globus operates on a push model: Work is sent from some submitting node to some computational resource, which then accepts and processes the job, returning the results to the submitter. Moreover, these jobs can be arbitrary: Globus resources are able (although perhaps not always willing) to execute user-supplied code. Input and result files may be automatically transferred between the submitting node and the computing resources.

Finally, newer versions of Globus (version 3 and onward) support the concept of Grid services, which are closely related to standard Web services in both design and implementation. Globus Toolkit 4 is completely compliant with the Web Services Resource Framework (WSRF), so its Grid services are, in fact, sanctioned Web services. Grid services provide a clean way of representing operations that the Grid can perform on behalf of its users; they represent a higher level of abstraction than that of individual computational jobs, and they allow Globus-based Grids to serve as more than large queuing systems.

4.1.2 BOINC

The Berkeley Open Infrastructure for Network Computing [10] is the direct descendant of the SETI@home project. Developed by the same group at the University of California, Berkeley that developed SETI@home, BOINC is a generalized implementation of the master/worker Internet-scale model that SETI@home made famous. BOINC implements a public-computing desktop Grid: It harnesses resources outside the bounds of direct institutional control.

As in SETI@home, BOINC clients (i.e., desktop personal computers) contact a server that acts as a central repository of work to retrieve jobs to execute: In contrast to Globus, which uses a push model, here clients pull work from a server. Moreover, although BOINC is generalized in the sense that it can manage any arbitrary project, it is limited in that it expects to manage a small number of very large, well-defined projects: Its aim is to allow individual research groups to manage SETI@home-style projects without developing their own software [11]. As such, BOINC does not provide mechanisms for executing arbitrary jobs on the fly, for determining which users may modify which jobs, or for any of the other functions which one would expect a normal queuing system to provide.

Although BOINC does not support many of the features that Globus does, it does provide the more limited functionality required by its model. For example, BOINC can automatically match work to be processed with hosts suitable to execute it, taking into account estimated memory and disk requirements as well as architecture and operating system constraints. Moreover, given that BOINC compute clients are expected to be unreliable, BOINC includes support for redundant computing, in which multiple copies of the same computation are performed by different clients, and then cross-checked for agreement.

Finally, it is useful to define some BOINC-related terms that we use throughout this chapter. In BOINC, a work unit defines a unit of computation to be executed. A result unit is an instance of a work unit; that is, due to redundant computing, a BOINC server might create five result units for a given work unit. These five (not yet processed) result units are sent to clients, which process and return them. Once a quorum is reached (e.g., three matching result units have been received from clients), one result unit becomes the canonical result for the work unit. For simplicity, we may sometimes refer to "the result" of a work unit in which the quorum/canonical designation process is subsumed.

4.2   CHALLENGES IN COMBINING GLOBUS AND BOINC

As previously described, Globus and BOINC differ significantly in their assumptions regarding the need they seek to fill and in the features that they provide. Any attempt to join these two systems must thus reconcile these differences. Here, we discuss some of the concrete challenges that must be overcome.

4.2.1   Job Submission

BOINC was designed to allow a single coordinated group to manage large-scale distributed computing projects. As such, BOINC has a number of assumptions about the way in which it will be used. In particular, BOINC has no concept of users and thus no concept of remote users, there is simply a single local entity that provides work for the system. Globus, on the contrary, expressly allows multiple distributed users to submit jobs. Thus, BOINC must somehow gain multiuser functionality.

4.2.2   Job Specification

GRAM, the protocol Globus uses to manage jobs, was designed assuming that jobs would execute on conventional UNIX systems (i.e., systems with UNIX-like file systems where programs are executed by specifying a path, a command, and some arguments). BOINC, on the contrary, has no concept of paths but only a loose conception of a file system. Thus, a Globus job description document (JDD) will specify something like "<executable>/usr/bin/foo</executable>." In a Grid system where this request could be tasked to a desktop computer using the Windows operating system without foo installed, what is the meaning of "/usr/bin/foo?" This request needs to be mapped into the file-system-less universe of BOINC.

4.2.3   Data and Executable Staging

Globus is able to stage both data and executable files from submitting systems to the host on which the job executes. In particular, this means that Globus compute resources are able to execute arbitrary user-supplied codes. Thus, there needs to be a mechanism to handle the staging of data all the way down to the BOINC clients, and the issue of arbitrary code execution on a desktop Grid needs to be addressed.

4.2.4   Reporting of Results

Globus can also stage result data and program output back to the submitting node from the compute node(s). Therefore, there needs to be some way to take files generated by BOINC clients and return them to the Globus submitting node.

   In the next section, we provide a general overview of our approach to integrating BOINC and Globus.

4.3 MEETING THE CHALLENGES — GENERAL IMPLEMENTATION

4.3.1 Job Submission

By design, Globus provides mechanisms and procedures for integrating new types of resources: By placing an abstraction layer (GRAM) over its resources, it reduces the task of integrating a new resource type to that of writing a GRAM-compliant interface for that resource. Therefore, we have written a GRAM scheduler interface (commonly known as a job manager) for BOINC. The job manager in this case is more complicated than in others, however, because the BOINC model is significantly different from other more traditional queuing systems.

Globus provides a Perl base class from which job managers may derive, and by extending this base class, BOINC gains the ability to accept jobs from the outside world, thus acquiring multiuser functionality. Although this achieves many of the capabilities of a true multiuser system, it does not provide robust production-grade authentication and authorization capabilities. Rather than grafting authentication and authorization onto BOINC, we choose to leave these tasks to a Grid meta-scheduler such as Condor-G [12] or, in the case of our current system [13], to a meta-scheduler of our own design. In either case, the component is tightly integrated with the Globus security infrastructure. It is our belief that this represents a much preferred solution than forcing the concept of "BOINC local users" onto BOINC or making BOINC aware of Grid credentials. Note, however, that our design does provide, through Globus, multiuser authentication and authorization not heretofore available to BOINC.

The other three challenges require somewhat more complicated solutions, and we discuss them below.

4.3.2 Job Specification

One of the primary tasks of a Globus job manager is to translate the job description documents used by GRAM into a native format that the managed resource can understand. In many cases, this can be a straightforward mapping between corresponding fields. In our case, however, more work is required to generate a BOINC work unit from a job description document.

Globus job description documents contain a few fields of particular interest in this context. First, we have the executable field that specifies the program to execute. This could be either a fully qualified pathname or a simple executable name. As discussed earlier, however, BOINC does not have a UNIX-like execution environment, and it certainly does not have a shell capable of resolving a non-path-qualified name to a specific executable. Thus, we need to map the executable field manually.

The closest BOINC concept to an executable file is an application. Essentially, each BOINC project is composed of one or more applications, which represent computations that clients may perform. Each application in turn is composed of one or more application versions, which are executables implementing the computation for specific client architectures. Thus, we establish a mapping between the JDD *executable* field and the BOINC *application_name* field. To do so, we remove any path information from the *executable* field and look for a BOINC application matching the remainder.

If we find a match, we designate it as the application to use. If a matching application cannot be found, we reject the job submission and return an error to Globus. Note that this requires applications to be preregistered with the BOINC server; we do not allow user-supplied code. Although user-supplied code could be supported, our design specifically excludes this capability because of security concerns, as BOINC lacks mechanisms to protect clients from malicious programs.

Resource limits constitute another set of difficult mappings from Globus to BOINC. There are trivial mappings between certain resource limits, such as maximum memory required. However, BOINC and Globus measure computing requirements in fundamentally different ways. Globus measures them in the minutes of CPU time, whereas BOINC measures them in the number of floating-point operations required. Moreover, for Globus, CPU time limits are entirely optional, whereas in BOINC, operation counts rest at the core of the scheduling process. BOINC work units have an "estimated number of floating-point operations" field that is used to estimate how long the job will take to run on any given BOINC client. This allows BOINC to send work only to those clients who are able to complete it before the *delay_bound*, or maximum permissible elapsed wall clock time, expires. So, if estimated CPU time is not correctly set, BOINC scheduling will work suboptimally. Further complicating the matter, the WS-GRAM job description schema has a field to set maximum permissible CPU time, but it does not have one for expected CPU time.

Our solution is twofold. First, using standard Globus extension mechanisms, we introduce a new JDD parameter, estCpuTime, which is defined to be the estimated CPU time (in minutes) required by the job on a computer capable of one gigaflop. (Such a computer is identical to the reference computer used by BOINC when calculating expected real execution times from the estimated number of required floating-point operations.) If this parameter is supplied, it is used to compute the number of floating-point operations required by multiplying it by 60×10^9. (We choose to express estCpuTime in minutes instead of in operations so as to maintain consistency with the other Globus CPU time parameters.) If a value for estCpuTime is not given, it defaults to one-half the maximum permissible CPU time.

The other JDD fields of particular interest are those relating to file staging or the copying of files to and from the submitting node. These fields need to be added as <file_info> and <file_ref> sections to BOINC work units so that file staging can be extended all the way through to the BOINC clients. We discuss file staging in more detail in Section 4.3.3.

Once the various required parameters have been determined, a BOINC work unit based on those data may be written and submitted to the BOINC work database using the BOINC create_work command, which completes the translation from a generic Globus job description to a resource native format.

4.3.3 Data and Executable Staging

File staging between the BOINC server and the submitting node is handled by standard Globus file transfer components. However, there is a need to extend file staging all the way down to the BOINC clients that actually execute the computations.

As expected, BOINC provides support for clients to exchange files with the server, so we simply need to ensure that the right files are sent to the right places at the right times. This is a two-part problem: files need to be copied to the correct locations on the BOINC server, and BOINC clients need to be instructed to conduct the correct sequence of uploads and downloads.

Globus jobs have a private working directory into which files are staged in from remote systems and out of which files are staged to remote systems. When a Globus job is sent to the BOINC server, files specified in the JDD as to-be-staged-in are automatically downloaded using Globus file transfer mechanisms. BOINC, on the contrary, has two file staging directories shared by all jobs and by all clients (one for staging files to clients—referred to as the "download" directory—and the other for staging files from clients—referred to as the "upload" directory). Files staged to the BOINC server by Globus thus need to be copied from the Globus staging directory to the BOINC download directory, and they need to be renamed so as to ensure uniqueness, as BOINC requires all files to have unique names. Similarly, when BOINC clients upload their results to the upload directory on the BOINC server, files need to be uniquely named, and they need to be copied back to the Globus staging directory with the filenames that Globus expects them to have.

Our job description documents include a unique ID field that may be trivially used to generate unique filenames for job files. This is sufficient to handle the original name to unique name mapping required at job submit time. The reverse mapping, required at job completion time is somewhat more difficult to handle, however; it requires additional techniques discussed more fully in Section 4.3.4.

Once BOINC has been provided the job files, clients are instructed to transfer them by <file_info> and <file_ref> blocks in the work unit created for the job. Assigning the client an executable appropriate for its architecture is also handled by BOINC.

4.3.4   Reporting of Results

Without the ability to return results from the BOINC server to the Globus submitting node, our combined-model Grid system would be of little use. Returning results comprise two distinct tasks: returning any required output files to the submitting Globus node and returning any standard output and standard error associated with the job to the submitting node. First, note that by default BOINC does not trap the standard output of the processes it executes. Thus, applications executing under BOINC need to send their standard output to the file *boinc_stdout*, which we arrange to have copied back to the BOINC server (our application compatibility library, discussed in Section 4.5, automatically redirects standard output). The task then becomes one of copying these files to the correct locations.

First, Globus looks for the standard output of a job in a specific file, so by simply copying the standard output file returned from the BOINC client to that location, we can utilize the normal mechanisms provided by Globus to return standard output to the submitting node. Note that this design does not support the real-time streaming of standard output to the submitting node: standard output is buffered until the job terminates. Similarly, by copying output files from the BOINC upload directory to the Globus file staging directories, we can utilize the default Globus file staging mechanism. However, a problem now occurs: How do we know the location to which we need to copy our files? The file copying must be implemented by BOINC, not by the Globus job manager, because the Globus job manager should not (as a design decision) have to access BOINC internal data structures to locate these files. Moreover, BOINC will delete the work unit output files after it detects that the work unit has finished and that the associated cleanup code is executed. BOINC has no knowledge of Globus, and thus no way of knowing where to copy the data.

Our solution is as follows. When a job is first submitted, the BOINC job manager writes out a Perl script containing the correct commands to copy files from the BOINC upload directory to the Globus locations (even though these files do not yet exist); as part of Globus, the job manager has access to these locations. We provide cleanup code for the BOINC server that calls this Perl script when a work unit completes. Files are thus placed in the correct locations at the correct times.

4.4   EXAMPLES

Here, we present the flow of control for a job dispatched to a more typical Globus resource, such as a cluster managed by the portable batch system (PBS) [14] and for a job dispatched to a BOINC server as a Globus resource. As an example application, we use SSEARCH from William Pearson's FASTA [15] suite of DNA and protein sequence analysis programs, which are important bioinformatics applications. SSEARCH uses the Smith–Waterman algorithm [16] to search a library of DNA or amino acid sequences (lib.fa in our examples) for sequences similar to a query sequence (seq.fa in our examples).

4.4.1   Portable Batch System

1. Globus user executes globusrun-ws -submit -Ft PBS -c /usr/bin/ssearch -O results.txt seq.fa lib.fa.
2. A Globus job description file is generated and passed to the Globus installation running on a PBS cluster node.
3. Globus copies seq.fa and lib.fa from the submitting host to a job-specific staging directory on the PBS cluster.
4. Submit method of the job manager executes that it writes a PBS job description file from the supplied JDD and submits it using qsub.
5. PBS eventually executes the job, and the job completes.
6. The PBS job manager recognizes that the job has completed and returns results.txt and any associated standard output to the submitting node. The job scratch directory is removed from the PBS cluster.

4.4.2   BOINC-Based Desktop Grid

1. Globus user executes globusrun-ws -submit -Ft BOINC -c /usr/bin/ssearch -O results.txt seq.fa lib.fa.

2. A Globus job description file is generated and passed to the Globus installation running on the BOINC server.

3. Globus copies seq.fa and lib.fa from the submitting host to a job-specific staging directory on the BOINC server.

4. The submit method of the job manager executes the following:

   (a) It strips "/usr/bin/" from "/usr/bin/ssearch" and checks to see if an "ssearch" application exists. It exits with an error condition if not.

   (b) It determines that lib.fa and seq.fa need to be staged to the BOINC client.

   (c) It determines that results.txt needs to be staged back from the BOINC client.

   (d) It copies lib.fa and seq.fa to the BOINC download directory, giving them new names on the basis of the unique ID present in the job description.

   (e) It writes a work unit containing the arguments to ssearch and the file handling blocks for lib.fa, seq.fa and results.txt; it submits the work unit to BOINC. BOINC produces multiple result units for redundant computation.

   (f) It writes a Perl script to be called on work unit completion that will copy the BOINC files corresponding to results.txt and boinc_stdout back to Globus-accessible directories.

5. Once per result unit, a BOINC client downloads the unit, lib.fa, seq.fa, and an ssearch binary caching the executable for future use.

6. Once per result unit, the BOINC client executes ssearch and returns results.txt to the server.

7. BOINC detects enough result units that are returned and designates one as canonical. It locates the callback script written by the job manager and executes it.

8. Files corresponding to results.txt and boinc_stdout in the BOINC server upload directory are copied back to the locations and names expected by Globus.

9. BOINC deletes its copies of the result files associated with the work unit.

10. The BOINC job manager recognizes that the job has completed and returns results.txt and any associated standard output to the submitting node. The job scratch directory is removed from the BOINC server.

4.5 ADAPTING APPLICATIONS FOR USE WITH BOINC

Although we do not allow arbitrary code from Globus to run on the BOINC-managed desktop Grid, it is desirable to minimize the effort required to port an application to BOINC in order to make BOINC a somewhat more general-purpose resource. BOINC has an application programming interface (API) that it expects applications to call; this API handles tasks such as mapping between application-expected filenames and BOINC required unique filenames. Thus, porting an application to BOINC could require making extensive changes to its source code, which can present a significant hindrance to deploying applications on the BOINC-based desktop Grid.

In order to ease the task of porting a large number of existing bioinformatics applications, we have written compatibility libraries that allow programs written in C or C++ to run under BOINC; these libraries wrap C library functions so that the requisite calls to the BOINC API are made automatically. Under Windows, we use the Microsoft Detours package [17], and existing binaries may be used unmodified. Under UNIX-like systems (such as Linux and Macintosh OS X), only relinking is required. For more information on these procedures, please see our technical report [18].

4.6 GRID-ENABLED APPLICATIONS RUNNING ON BOINC

We have built more than 20 grid services implementing bioinformatics and computational applications using the Grid Services Base Library (GSBL) [19] as part of The Lattice Project Grid system [13], and of these grid services, 15 can run on BOINC. Each of these programs is available to be run on our Grid system, which provides researchers access to more resources than they would otherwise have. Thus, large amounts of work can be done in a relatively short time. The following is a list of applications that runs on BOINC and some information about each one.

ClustalW: A program for multiple DNA or protein sequence alignment based on a progressive alignment strategy where more similar sequences are aligned first to produce groups of aligned sequences and then these groups are aligned together [20].

CNS: Crystallography and NMR system (CNS) is a program that has been designed to provide a flexible multilevel hierarchical approach for the most commonly used algorithms in macromolecular structure determination [21].

IM: Isolation with migration (IM) is a program for the fitting of an isolation model with migration to haplotype data drawn from two closely related species or populations [22].

LAMARC: Likelihood analysis with Metropolis algorithm using random coalescence (LAMARC) is a package of programs for computing population parameters, such as population size, population growth rate, and migration rates by using likelihoods for samples of data (sequences, microsatellites, and electrophoretic polymorphisms) from populations [23–25]. LAMARC provides both maximum likelihood and Bayesian estimates, and it uses a coalescent theory approach taking into account the history of mutations and the uncertainty of the genealogy.

MDIV: A program that simultaneously estimates divergence times and migration rates between two populations under a infinite-site model or under a finite-site model [26].

MIGRATE-N: MIGRATE estimates population parameters, effective population sizes, and migration rates of n populations using genetic data [27,28].

MIGRATE provides both maximum likelihood and Bayesian estimates, and it uses a coalescent theory approach taking into account the history of mutations and the uncertainty of the genealogy.

Modeltest: A program that assists in evaluating the fit of a range of nucleotide substitution models to DNA sequence data through a hierarchical series of hypothesis tests [29]. Two test statistics, likelihood ratio and Akaike information criterion (AIC), are provided to compare model pairs that differ in complexity. The program is used together with PAUP* [30], typically as part of data exploration prior to a more extensive phylogenetic analysis.

MrBayes: A program for phylogenetic analysis of nucleotide or amino acid sequence data using a Bayesian approach [31]. A Metropolis-coupled Markov Chain Monte Carlo (MCMCMC) algorithm is used with multiple chains, all but one of which is heated. The chains are used to sample model space through a process of parameter modification proposal and acceptance/rejection steps (also called cycles or generations). A choice of several commonly used likelihood models is available as are the choices for starting tree (user defined and random), data partitions (e.g., by codon position), and Markov Chain Monte Carlo parameters.

ms: A program that generates random independent sequence samples according to a simple Wright–Fisher neutral model [32]. If invoked with a minimum of options, it produces samples under a panmictic equilibrium model without recombination. By specifying various options on the command line, the model can include recombination, island-model-type structure, gene conversion, and simple population size changes in the past.

Muscle: A program for multiple DNA or protein sequence alignment [33].

PHYML: A program for phylogenetic analysis of sequence data using maximum likelihood methods [34].

Pknots: PKNOTS implements a dynamic programming algorithm for predicting optimal RNA secondary structure, including pseudoknots [35]. The implementation generates the optimal minimum energy structure for a single RNA sequence, using standard RNA folding thermodynamic parameters augmented by a few parameters describing the thermodynamic stability of pseudoknots.

Seq-Gen: Seq-Gen is a program that will simulate the evolution of nucleotide or amino acid sequences along a phylogeny using common models of the substitution process [36].

Snn: A program that performs the "nearest neighbor test" to detect genetic differentiation [37]. Given a matrix of pairwise differences between sampled sequences, Snn can determine genetic differentiation among local sample groups.

SSEARCH: A program for doing Smith–Waterman search for similarity between a query sequence and a group of sequences of the same type (nucleic acid or protein) [16]. This may be the most sensitive method available for similarity searches. It is the part of the FASTA package [15].

4.7 PERFORMANCE

Given that the middleware provided here is quite thin, it is unsurprising that it has negligible impact on performance. The elapsed time between using globusrun-ws to submit a job to the BOINC server and seeing the work unit corresponding to that job appear in the queue on the sever is minimal, on the order of 1 or 2 s, and timing runs have shown this delay to be attributable to overhead associated with Globus.

Depending on the number of jobs and on their data requirements, it is conceivable that the BOINC server could find itself required to store and forward large amounts of data. BOINC is able to support multiple data servers, so perhaps default GRAM behavior could be changed such that files are transferred from the submitting node to a cluster of such data servers from which BOINC clients would then download.

4.8 PRODUCTION USE—EXAMPLES

This middleware has been tested and used extensively in our Globus Toolkit-based development and production Grid system, the Lattice Project [13]. We have scaled up to thousands of jobs running concurrently under this framework as described. BOINC was designed to accommodate this type of load, readily scaling up to millions of work units. The limiting variable for this system thus becomes the number of concurrent GRAM jobs that can be effectively managed, and this is something the Globus team continues to improve. To help in this regard, we are currently working to add support for managing batches of similar work units in a single GRAM job instance.

The Lattice Project Grid system has been used to complete several research projects in computational biology using BOINC as the primary computing resource. Our Globus–BOINC-based Grid system performed approximately 17.5 CPU years of computation over several months, during which users submitted jobs intermittently.

Ranjani Varadan in the laboratory of David Fushman ran thousands of protein–protein docking simulations using the CNS Grid service. When driven by experimentally derived constraints, these simulations help in modeling the structures of large multisubunit proteins and the interactions of such proteins with various ligands. An example is the analysis of the structural determinants for recognition of a polyubiquitin chain [38]. The computations consumed approximately 12.4 CPU years.

Holly Mortensen and Floyd Reed in the laboratory of Sarah Tishkoff have run many analyses using the MDIV and IM Grid services. These analyses are for studies of human population genetics that use DNA sequence polymorphism to estimate the times of divergence and migration rates among ethnically diverse populations in Africa [39]. The computations consumed approximately 5.1 CPU years.

4.9 SOFTWARE AVAILABILITY

The current version of our middleware is available for download from our Grid research Web site, http://lattice.umiacs.umd.edu/. This software is free; you can redistribute it and/or modify it under the terms of the GNU General Public License as published by the Free Software Foundation; use either version 2 of the License or (at your option) any later version. Please credit the original authors and cite relevant publications where appropriate.

4.10   SUMMARY

We have developed middleware allowing the Globus Toolkit to dispatch work to a desktop Grid managed by BOINC, tested it using real-world applications used extensively in bioinformatics, and used it in a production Grid system for a variety of computational biology problems. This middleware, though conceptually simple, serves as a bridge between two very different models of Grid computing.

By joining these two models, we deliver substantial advantages to users of both. On the Globus side, Grid users may gain access to a much wider pool of potential resources than was previously possible. On the BOINC side, Grid users may gain a more full-featured system; indeed, one could imagine using Globus outside of a full-scale Grid system simply to provide a convenient interface to a stand-alone BOINC-based desktop Grid.

Finally, we believe that the integration of the BOINC and the Globus Toolkit will foster a transformation in public computing. Previously, public computing infrastructures were exclusively domain-specific pieces of software and establishing a public computing project required significant time and experience. Even using BOINC, one still has to develop custom scripts and interfaces so as to be able to manage the flow of work into and out of the BOINC server, which takes significant effort. Our middleware provides a tremendous enhancement to public computing: it allows public computing resources to be accessed using feature rich and widely used standard protocols. It thus dramatically decreases the overhead associated with starting subsequent public computing projects once the initial infrastructure is established. It is our hope that this will allow public computing to be a viable option for a much wider range of research projects than it is currently.

ACKNOWLEDGMENTS

We thank Andrew Younge for his assistance in recently upgrading this software; Deji Akinyemi, John Fuetsch, Jonathan Howard, Stephen McLellan, and Christopher Milliron for developing some of the grid services; Karl Chen (University of California, Berkeley) for his help in installing BOINC; the members of the Globus developer-discuss mailing list for their help with Globus; the members of the Condor group at the University of Wisconsin, Madison for the help with Condor-G; and the UMIACS systems staff, who were of great help in setting up the software and the hardware used in this project.

References

1. Z. Németh, V. Sunderam, Characterizing grids: Attributes, definitions, and formalisms, *Journal of Grid Computing* 1, 9–25, 2003.

2. M.P. Cummings, J.C. Huskamp, Grid computing, *EDUCAUSE Review* **40**, 116–117, 2005.

3. D.P. Anderson, J. Cobb, E. Korpela, M. Lebofsky, D. Werthimer, SETI@home: An experiment in public-resource computing, *Communications of the ACM* **45**, 56–61, 2002.

4. M.P. Cummings, S.A. Handley, D.S. Myers, D.L. Reed, A. Rokas, K. Winka, Comparing bootstrap and posterior probability values in the four taxon case, *Systematic Biology* **52**, 477–487, 2003.

5. D.S. Myers, M.P. Cummings, Necessity is the mother of invention: A simple Grid computing system using commodity tools, *Journal of Parallel Distributed Computing* **63**, 578–589, 2003.

6. S.M. Larson, C.D. Snow, M. Shirts, V.S. Pande, Folding@Home and Genome@Home: using distributed computing to tackle previously intractable problems in computational biology, in: R. Grant (Ed.), *Computational Genomics: Theory and Applications*, Horizon Scientific Press, Norfolk, VA, 2004.

7. http://fightaidsathome.scripps.edu/.

8. M. Litzkow, M. Livny, M. Mutka, Condor—a hunter of idle workstations, in *Proceedings 8th International Conference of Distributed Computing Systems*, San Jose, 1988.

9. I. Foster, C. Kesselman, Globus: A toolkit-based Grid architecture, in I. Foster, C. Kesselman (Eds.), *The Grid: Blueprint for a New Computing Infrastructure*, Morgan Kaufmann, Los Altos, CA, 1999.

10. http://boinc.berkeley.edu/.

11. D.P. Anderson, Public computing: Reconnecting people to science, Conference on Shared Knowledge and the Web, Residencia de Estudiantes, Madrid, Spain, November 17–19, 2003.

12. J. Frey, T. Tannenbaum, I. Foster, M. Livny, S. Tuecke, Condor-G: A computation management agent for multiinstitutional Grids, *Journal of Cluster Computing* **5**, 237–246, 2002.

13. A.L. Bazinet, M.P. Cummings, The Lattice Project: A grid research and production environment combining multiple grid computing models, in M.H.W. Weber (Ed.), *Distributed & Grid Computing— Science Made Transparent for Everyone, Principles, Applications and Supporting Communities*, Tectum (to appear).

14. Altair Engineering, Portable Batch Systems, http://www.openpbs.org/

15. W.R. Pearson, Flexible sequence similarity searching with the FASTA3 program package, *Methods of Molecular Biology* **132**, 185–219, 2000.

16. T.F. Smith, M.S. Waterman, Identification of common molecular subsequences, *Journal of Molecular Biology* **147**, 195–197, 1981.

17. G. Hunt, D. Brubacher, Detours: Binary interception of Win32 functions, *Proceedings of 3rd USENIX Windows NT Symposium*, Seattle, WA, July 1999. USENIX.

18. D.S. Myers, A.L. Bazinet, Intercepting arbitrary functions on Windows, UNIX, and Macintosh OS X platforms, Center for Bioinformatics and Computational Biology, Institute for Advanced Computer Studies, University of Maryland, CS-TR-4585, UMIACS-TR-2004-28, 2004.

19. A.L. Bazinet, D.S. Myers, J. Fuetsch, M.P. Cummings, Grid services base library: A high-level, procedural application programing interface for writing Globus-based grid services, *Future Generation Computer Systems* **23**, 517–522, 2007.

20. J.D. Thompson, D.G. Higgins, T.J. Gibson, Clustal W: Improving the sensitivity of progressive multiple sequence alignment through sequence weighting, position-specific gap penalties and weight matrix choice, *Nucleic Acids Research* **22**, 4673–4680, 1994.

21. A.T. Brünger, P.D. Adams, G.M. Clore, W.L. DeLano, P. Gros, R.W. Grosse-Kunstleve, J.-S. Jiang, J. Kuszewski, M. Nilges, N.S. Pannu, R.J. Read, L.M. Rice, T. Simonson, G.L. Warren, Crystallography & NMR system: A new software suite for macromolecular structure determination, *Acta Crystallographica* **D54**, 905–921, 1998.

22. J. Hey, R. Nielsen, Multilocus methods for estimating population sizes, migration rates and divergence time, with applications to the divergence of *Drosophila pseudoobscura* and *D. persimilis*, *Genetics* **167**, 747–760, 2004.

23. M.K. Kuhner, J. Yamato, J. Felsenstein, Estimating effective population size and mutation rate from sequence data using Metropolis-Hastings sampling, *Genetics* **140**, 1421–1430, 1995.

24. M.K. Kuhner, J. Yamato, J. Felsenstein, Maximum likelihood estimates of population growth rates based on the coalescent, *Genetics* **149**, 429–434, 1998.

25. M.K. Kuhner, J. Yamato, J. Felsenstein, Maximum likelihood estimation of recombination rates from population data, *Genetics* **156**, 1393–1401, 2000.

26. R. Nielsen, J. Wakeley, Distinguishing migration from isolation. A Markov chain Monte Carlo approach, *Genetics* **158**, 885–896, 2001.

27. P. Beerli, J. Felsenstein, Maximum likelihood estimation of migration rates and effective population numbers in two populations using a coalescent approach, *Genetics* **152**, 763–773, 1999.

28. P. Beerli, J. Felsenstein, Maximum likelihood estimation of a migration matrix and effective populations sizes in *n* subpopulations by using a coalescent approach, *Proceedings of the National Academy of Science of the United States of America* **98**, 4563–4568, 2001.

29. D. Posada, K.A. Crandall, Modeltest: Testing the model of DNA substitution, *Bioinformatics* **14**, 817–818, 1998.

30. D.L. Swofford, PAUP*: Phylogenetic analysis using parsimony (*and other methods), version 4, Sinauer Associates, Sunderland, MA, 2003.

31. F. Ronquist, J.P. Huelsenbeck, MrBayes 3: Bayesian phylogenetic inference under mixed models, *Bioinformatics* **19**, 1572–1574, 2003.

32. R.R. Hudson, Generating samples under a Wright–Fisher neutral model of genetic variation, *Bioinformatics* **18**, 337–338, 2002.

33. R.C. Edgar, MUSCLE: multiple sequence alignment with high accuracy and high throughput, *Nucleic Acids Research* **32**, 1792–1797, 2004.

34. S. Guindon, O. Gascuel, A simple, fast, and accurate algorithm to estimate large phylogenies by maximum likelihood, *Systematic Biology* **52**, 696–704, 2003.

35. E. Rivas, S.R. Eddy, A dynamic programming algorithm for RNA structure prediction including pseudoknots, Journal of Molecular Biology **285**, 2053–2068, 1999.

36. A. Rambaut, N.C. Grassly, Seq-Gen: An application for the Monte Carlo simulation of DNA sequence evolution along phylogenetic trees, *Computer Applications in the Biosciences*, **13**, 235–238, 1997.

37. R.R. Hudson, A new statistic for detecting genetic differentiation, *Genetics* **155**, 2011–2014, 2000.

38. R. Varadan, M. Assfalg, S. Raasi, C. Pickart, D. Fushman, Structural determinants for selective recognition of a Lys48-linked polyubiquitin chain by a UBA domain, *Molecules and Cells* **18**, 687–698, 2005.

39. S.A. Tishkoff, M.K. Gonder, B.M. Henn, H. Mortensen, N. Fernandopulle, C. Gignoux, G. Lema, T.B. Nyambo, P.A. Underhill, U. Ramakrishnan, F.A. Reed, J.L. Mountain, History of click-speaking populations of Africa inferred from mtDNA and Y chromosome genetic variation, *Molecular Biology and Evolution* in press.

5

HIERARCHICAL GRID COMPUTING FOR HIGH-PERFORMANCE BIOINFORMATICS

Bertil Schmidt, Chunxi Chen, and Weiguo Liu

5.1 INTRODUCTION

Hierarchical grid computing describes the combination of several geographically distributed compute clusters within one architecture using grid infrastructure. The driving force and motivation behind hierarchical grid computing is the price/performance ratio. Using PC clusters as in the Beowulf approach is currently one of the most efficient and simple ways to gain computing power at a reasonable price. Combining several existing PC clusters can further increase the price/performance ratio significantly. The development or adaptation of parallel applications for the hierarchical grid architecture is made challenging by the often heterogeneous nature of the resources involved. In this chapter, we present how three popular bioinformatics algorithms can be mapped efficiently onto a hierarchical grid system. These three algorithms are as follows:

(1) *Pairwise alignment of long DNA sequences:* We present an efficient parallel implementation of the linear space Smith–Waterman algorithm for optimal pairwise sequence alignment. In addition, our solution can compute near-optimal nonintersecting alignments, since not only the optimal alignment but also suboptimal alignments are biologically significant. We show that this approach generates high quality alignments and leads to significant run-time savings on a hierarchical grid system. In order to achieve a high efficiency on this type of architecture, we investigate static and dynamic load-balancing approaches. On the basis of this analysis, we propose a new dynamic load-balancing approach named scheduler–worker technique, which can achieve better performance under disturbance and for low intercluster bandwidth.

Grid Computing for Bioinformatics and Computational Biology. Edited by E.-G. Talbi and A.Y. Zomaya.
Copyright © 2008 John Wiley & Sons, Inc.

(2) *Construction of large suffix trees:* The suffix tree is a key data structure for biological sequence analysis, since it permits efficient solutions to many string-based problems. Constructing large suffix trees is challenging because of high memory overheads and poor memory locality. Even though efficient suffix tree construction algorithms exist, their runtime is still very high for long DNA sequences such as whole human chromosomes. In this chapter, we are using a hierarchical grid system as a computational platform in order to reduce this runtime significantly. To achieve an efficient mapping onto this type of architecture, we introduce a parallel suffix tree construction algorithm that makes use of a new data structure called the common prefix–suffix tree. Using this algorithm together with a dynamic load balancing strategy, we show that our distributed grid implementation leads to significant runtime savings.

(3) *Protein folding with the HP lattice model:* Genetic algorithms are a general problem-solving technique that has been widely used in computational biology. We present a framework to map hierarchical parallel genetic algorithms for protein-folding problems onto hierarchical grids. By using this framework, the two level communication parts of hierarchical parallel genetic algorithms are separated. Thus, both parts of the algorithm can evolve independently. This permits users to experiment with alternative communication models on different levels conveniently. The underlying programming technique is based on generic programming, a programming technique suited for the generic representation of abstract concepts. This allows the framework to be built in a generic way at the application level and thus provides good extensibility and flexibility.

The rest of this chapter is organized as follows. We discuss the hierarchical grid computing concept and the hierarchical grid system used in our research in Section 5.2. In Section 5.3, we present an adaptive hierarchical grid implementation of long DNA sequence alignment. Section 5.4 shows how human chromosome size suffix trees can be efficiently constructed on a grid. The efficient mapping of hierarchical parallel genetic algorithms for protein folding onto a hierarchical grid is presented in Section 5.5. Finally, Section 5.6 concludes our chapter.

5.2 HIERARCHICAL GRID COMPUTING

The computational grid enables resource sharing among geographically distributed sites all over the world. These sharing resources may reside in different administrative domains, run different software, be subjected to different access control policies, and be connected by networks with widely varying performance characteristics. Therefore, computational grids are a hierarchical and heterogeneous environment [1].

The grid system used in our research consists of three Linux PC clusters. The three clusters are located at two different research centers (PDCC, parallel and distributed computing center; and BIRC, bioinformatics research center) at Nanyang Technological University. Two clusters are in PDCC (8 nodes for one cluster: Intel PIII 733-MHz processor with 750 MB memory; and 8 nodes for the other cluster: Intel Xeon 2.6-GHz processor with 1-GB memory) and one cluster is in BIRC (8 nodes: Intel Itanium-1 processor 733 MHz). Each cluster is internally connected by a Myrinet (the intracluster connection), and an Ethernet switch is used as an intercluster connection. The normal application-level bandwidth inside each cluster is about 190 MB/s. The normal application-level intercluster bandwidth is about 8 MB/s. In order to evaluate different intercluster bandwidths, we run an application that only sends or receives data packages between the clusters. We can control the sizes and frequencies of the data packages to get different levels of intracluster bandwidth. The experimental test bed is similar to a real wide-area grid system.

The software architecture is shown in Fig. 5.1. It can be divided into two layers. The upper layer is the MPICH-G2 [2,3] layer that runs on the control node of each cluster. This allows (slow) intercluster communication. The lower one is the MPICH [4] layer that runs on all nodes within a cluster. This allows (fast) intracluster communication. Each cluster has an Sun Grid Engine (SGE) [5] installed. The SGE is a Distributed Resource Management (DRM) software. It can allocate parallel tasks from the control node to execution nodes inside a cluster. Each parallel task is first distributed to the control nodes of each cluster. Then, Sun Grid Engine allocates the task from the control node to another execution node within the cluster, complying with its scheduling strategy. Parallel processes can communicate via MPICH-G2 (between clusters) or with MPICH (within the same cluster). Applications based on MPI run in the grid systems just like inside a cluster from the view of a programmer.

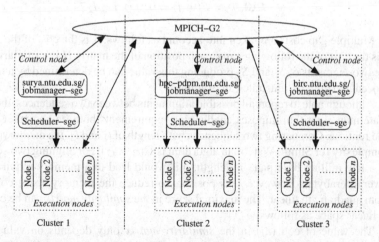

Figure 5.1. The hierarchical parallel-programming environment consisting of MPICH-G2, MPICH, and Sun Grid Engine.

5.3   ADAPTIVE GRID IMPLEMENTATION OF DNA SEQUENCE ALIGNMENT

5.3.1   Smith–Waterman Algorithm

The Smith–Waterman algorithm [6] finds the most similar subsequences of two sequences (the local alignment) by dynamic programming. Consider two strings S_1 and S_2 of length l_1 and l_2. To identify common subsequences, the Smith–Waterman algorithm computes the similarity $H(i,j)$ of two sequences ending at position i and j of the two sequences S_1 and S_2. The computation of $H(i,j)$ is given by the following recurrences:

$$H(i, j) = \max \begin{cases} 0 \\ E(i, j) \\ F(i, j) \\ H(i - 1, j - 1) + sbt(S_1[i], S_1[i]) \end{cases}$$

$$E(i, j) = \max \begin{cases} H(i, j - 1) - \alpha \\ E(i, j - 1) - \beta \end{cases}$$

$$F(i, j) = \max \begin{cases} H(i - 1, j) - \alpha \\ F(i - 1, j) - \beta \end{cases}$$

where $1 \leq i \leq l_1, 1 \leq j \leq l_2$, and Sbt is a character substitution cost table. Initialization of these values is given by

$$H(i, 0) = E(i, 0) = 0, 0 \leq i \leq l_1$$

$$H(0, j) = F(0, j) = 0, 0 \leq j \leq l_2$$

Multiple gap costs are taken into account as follows: α is the cost of the first gap; β is the cost of the following gaps; each position of the matrix H is a similarity value; the two segments of S_1 and S_2 producing this value can be determined by a traceback procedure (Fig. 5.2 illustrates an example).

Although able to report all possible alignments between two sequences, the Smith–Waterman algorithm imposes challenging requirements both on computer memory and runtime. Comparing two sequences with length of l_1 and l_2, the memory and time complexity for Smith–Waterman algorithm is $O(l_1 \times l_2)$. For aligning two sequences of a few million base pairs in length, this would lead to a memory requirement of several terabytes. However, it is possible to reduce the memory space complexity from quadratic to linear. The maximal score in the *similarity matrix* can be computed in linear space as follows.

The value of cell (i,j) in the *similarity matrix* only depends on values of the cells $(i - 1, j - 1)$, $(i - 1, j)$, and $(i, j - 1)$. Thus, the ith row can be computed by overwriting values for the $(i - 1)$th row in a left-to-right sweep. As the matrix is being

		A	T	C	T	C	G	T	A	T	G	A	T	G
	0	0	0	0	0	0	0	0	0	0	0	0	0	0
G	0	0	0	0	0	0	2	1	0	0	2	1	0	2
T	0	0	2	1	2	1	1	4	3	2	1	1	3	2
C	0	0	1	4	3	4	3	3	3	2	1	0	2	2
T	0	0	2	3	6	5	4	5	4	5	4	3	2	1
A	0	2	2	2	5	5	4	4	7	6	5	6	5	4
T	0	1	4	3	4	4	4	6	5	9	8	7	8	7
C	0	0	3	6	5	6	5	5	5	8	8	7	7	7
A	0	2	2	5	5	5	5	4	7	7	7	10	9	8
C	0	1	1	4	4	7	6	5	6	6	6	9	9	8

Figure 5.2. Example of the Smith–Waterman algorithm to compute the local alignment between two DNA sequences ATCTCGTATGATG and GTCTATCAC. The matrix $H(i, j)$ is shown for the computation with gap costs $\alpha = 1$ and $\beta = 1$, and a substitution cost of $+2$ if the characters are identical and -1 otherwise. From the highest score ($+10$ in the example), a traceback procedure delivers the corresponding alignment (shaded cells), the two subsequences being TCGTATGA and TCTATCA.

built, we keep track of the maximum score as well as the index of the corresponding cell (i_{max}, j_{max}). The indices i_{max} and j_{max} specify the end positions of the optimal local alignment of the sequences S_1 and S_2. To find the starting positions i_{start} and j_{start}, the algorithm can be executed with the sequences in reversed order.

However, this approach will only find the maximal score and start and end points; it will not find the actual alignment. Hirschberg [7] and Myers and Miller [8] presented a recursive divide-and-conquer algorithm for computing this alignment in linear space. The central idea is to find the "midpoint" of an optimal conversion using a "forward" and a "reverse" application of the linear space cost-only variation. Then, an optimal conversion can be delivered by recursively determining optimal conversions on both sides of this midpoint.

5.3.2 Finding Near-Optimal Alignments in Linear Space

The Smith–Waterman algorithm computes the highest-scoring or optimal local sequence alignment. However, there may be other biological important alignments with scores close to the optimal one. These near-optimal alignments may be alternate paths back through the dynamic programming matrix starting at the same high-scoring position. These alignments will use some of the same aligned base pairs (or amino acids for protein sequences) that were also used in the optimal alignment. Other alignments may use the same base pairs but have them aligned differently. Yet a third kind of alternative alignment may use entirely different base pairs to achieve a range of possible alignments. For the comparison of long DNA sequences, the detection of near-optimal (or high-scoring) nonintersecting local alignments is particularly useful [9,10]. Definition 1 gives the concept of nonintersecting.

Definition 1. *Two local alignment paths in the similarity matrix are said to be nonintersecting if they do not share any cell in matrix H.*

Definition 2. *For each cell (i,j) in the similarity matrix H, define st(i,j) to be the cell index of the starting position of the local alignment ending at (i,j) that has the score H(i,j).*

The values $st(i,j)$ are calculated by the following recurrences:

$$st(i, j) = \begin{cases} (i, j), & \text{if } H(i, j) = 0 \text{ or } i = 0 \text{ or } j = 0 \\ st(i - 1, j - 1), & \text{if } H(i, j) = H(i - 1, j - 1) + sbt(S_1[i], S_2[j]) \\ st(i, j - Eg(i, j)), & \text{if } H(i, j) = E(i, j) \\ st(i - Fg(i, j), j), & \text{if } H(i, j) = F(i, j) \end{cases}$$

where

$$Eg(i, j) = \begin{cases} 1, & \text{if } E(i, j) = H(i, j - 1) - \alpha \text{ or } j = 1 \\ Eg(i, j - 1) + 1, & \text{if } E(i, j) = E(i, j - 1) - \beta \end{cases}$$

$$Fg(i, j) = \begin{cases} 1, & \text{if } F(i, j) = H(i - 1, j) - \alpha \text{ or } j = 1 \\ Fg(i - 1, j) + 1, & \text{if } F(i, j) = F(i - 1, j) - \beta \end{cases}$$

The start point $st(i_{max}, j_{max})$ of the maximal score at end point (i_{max}, j_{max}) can be easily computed in linear space. In order to determine k near-optimal nonintersecting alignments, the k highest similarity scores (together with the corresponding start/end points) that have different start points are stored during the linear-space computation of the *similarity matrix*. Thus, for the calculated k highest scores, $H(i_1, j_1), \ldots, H(i_k, j_k)$ holds $st(i_m, j_m) \neq st(i_n, j_n)$ for all $1 \leq m, n \leq k$. Theorem 3 shows that these alignments do not intersect for each $m \neq n$. Subsequently, the divide-and-conquer algorithm is applied k times to compute the actual alignments from the lower-right neighbor of $st(i_n, j_n)$ to (i_n, j_n) for $m = 1, \ldots, k$. The detected alignments of this algorithm using $k = 4$ and the sequences and parameters of Fig. 5.2 is displayed in Fig. 5.3.

5.3.3 Mapping onto the Hierarchical Grid Architecture

Grid systems typically have a heterogeneous nature. Therefore, the following three aspects have to be taken into account when running a parallel application in a multi-clustered grid environment [11–13].

(1) Resources have different computational power.
(2) Resources are shared, that is, there are several users' tasks running at the same time; therefore, the effective CPU time of an application depends on the number of jobs running on the node at that time.
(3) Resources in a grid system are usually connected by networks with widely varying performance characteristics. Furthermore, the intercluster connection is by one or two orders of magnitude slower than the intracluster connection.

		C=0	C=1	C=2	C=3	C=4	C=5	C=6	C=7	C=8	C=9	C=10	C=11	C=12
		A	T	C	T	C	G	T	A	T	G	A	T	G
R=0		0	0	0	0	0	0	0	0	0	0	0	0	0	0
R=1 G	0	0	0	0	0	0	2	1	0	0	2	1	0	2
R=2 T	0	0	2	1	2	1	1	4	3	2	1	1	3	2
R=3 C	0	0	1	4	3	4	3	3	3	2	1	0	2	2
R=4 T	0	0	2	3	6	5	4	5	4	5	4	3	2	1
R=5 A	0	2	2	2	5	5	4	4	7	6	5	6	5	4
R=6 T	0	1	4	3	4	4	4	6	5	9	8	7	8	7
R=7 C	0	0	3	6	5	6	5	5	5	8	8	7	7	7
R=8 A	0	2	2	5	5	5	5	4	7	7	7	10	9	8
R=9 C	0	1	1	4	4	7	6	5	6	6	6	9	9	8

Figure 5.3. Example of the computation of highest-scoring nonintersecting local alignments using $k = 4$ and DNA sequences, substitution cost, and gap penalties as in Fig. 5.2. The four calculated start/end points are (1,3)/(8,11), (0,5)/(6,12), (4,0)/(9,5), and (1,1)/(8,8). The corresponding alignments computed by the divide-and-conquer methods are displayed as shaded cells. Note that the algorithm only requires linear space, that is, the complete matrix H does not need to be stored.

In order to parallelize an application efficiently on a hierarchical grid architecture, the program should comply with the following rules:

(1) Reduction of intercluster data transfer, since the intercluster link is usually very slow.
(2) Amount of work allocated to a processor should depend on the computational power that the processor allocates to the application at that time. This assures that no processor becomes the bottleneck.

5.3.3.1 Parallelization of Sequence Alignment

Parallelization of long DNA sequence alignment consists of two parts:

(1) parallelization of the *similarity matrix* computation in order to calculate the k best start/end points;
(2) parallelization of the divide-and-conquer algorithm to calculate the actual alignments.

The parallelization of the *similarity matrix* calculation is based on the wavefront communication pattern. Figure 5.4 displays the dependency relationship: Each cell (i, j) of the *similarity matrix* is computed from the cells $(i - 1, j)$, $(i, j - 1)$, and $(i - 1, j - 1)$. The wavefront moves in antidiagonals as depicted in Fig. 5.4a; that is, the shift direction is from northwest to southeast.

On coarse-grained architectures like grids, it is efficient to assign an equal number of adjacent columns to each processor as shown in Fig. 5.5a. In order to reduce communication time further, matrix cells can be grouped into blocks. Processor i then computes all the cells within a block after receiving the required data from

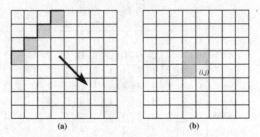

Figure 5.4. Wavefront computation of the *similarity matrix*: (**a**) shift direction, (**b**) dependency relationship.

processor $i - 1$. Figure 5.5 shows an example of the computation for four processors, eight columns, and a block size of 2×2.

Calculation of the actual alignment between a start/end point pair is parallelized as follows: Let us define special columns as the last columns of the parts of the *similarity matrix* allocated to each processor, except the last processor. If we can identify the intersection of an optimal path with the special columns, we can split the problem into subproblems and solve them sequentially on each processor using linear space algorithm. The solutions of the subproblems are then concatenated to get the optimal alignment.

5.3.3.2 Mapping onto the Hierarchical Grid Using Static Load Balancing

In this approach, the mapping has two levels of partitioning. First, the matrix is divided into parts of adjacent columns equal to the numbers of clusters. Second, the part within each cluster is further partitioned. The computation is then performed in the same way as shown in Fig. 5.5b. This reduces the intercluster data transfer to a single column per iteration step. In order to avoid bottlenecks on the heterogeneous hierarchical grid architecture, the number of columns assigned to each cluster depends on its computational capabilities. The order of the partitioning depends on the intercluster bandwidths. Figure 5.6 displays the partitioning on our architecture.

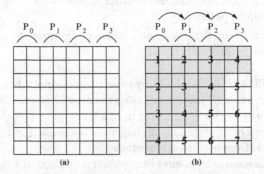

Figure 5.5. (**a**) Column-based division of an 8×8 matrix using four processors; (**b**) wavefront computation for four processors, eight columns, and a 2×2 block size. The complete 8×8 matrix can then be computed in seven iteration steps.

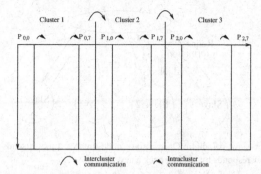

Figure 5.6. Partitioning of the wavefront computation on the hierarchical grid architecture. The number of columns assigned to each cluster is determined by its performance to execute the Smith–Waterman algorithm using MPI.

The static load-balancing approach can achieve good performance under the condition that there is no disturbance from other applications. Figure 5.11 (left) shows the speedups of different number of processors and different intercluster bandwidths. If the execution of a job is disturbed by another application in a node, it might become the bottleneck for the whole system. An experiment is therefore designed to measure the performance degradation.

In order to scale the extent to which a disturbance affects the application performance, we define PDRD (performance degradation ratio under disturbance) as [14]:

$$\text{PDRD} = \left(\frac{T' - T}{T} \right) \times 100\%$$

where T' denotes the execution time under disturbance and T denotes the execution time without any disturbance. Smaller PDRD values indicate a better robustness of the application to disturbance.

Figure 5.11 (right) shows the effect of disturbance by an application running on the CPU that uses around 50% CPU time.

5.3.3.3 Mapping onto the Hierarchical Grid Using Dynamic Load Balancing

(1) Traditional Master–Slave Paradigm. The master–slave paradigm is a widely used technique to implement dynamic load balancing. It works like a server–client model as illustrated in Fig. 5.7.

The implementation of long DNA sequence alignment on the hierarchical grid using this approach works as follows: The *similarity matrix* is divided into rectangular blocks as shown in Fig. 5.8. The computation of a rectangular block is assigned by the *master* to an available *slave*. This requires the sending of the left column and upper row of the block to be computed to the *slave*. The *slave* then returns the right column and bottom row of the computed block to the *master*. Compared to static load-balancing

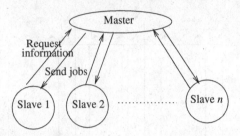

Figure 5.7. Master–slave paradigm. Once a slave node finishes a job, it sends a request to the *master* process. The *master* responds by sending back a new job.

implementation, the advantage of this approach is its robustness under disturbance (see the right part of Fig. 5.12). Unfortunately, it requires much more communication. For example, for a *similarity matrix* size of $100k \times 100k$ and a block size of 1250×1250, the overall data to be transferred sequentially through intercluster link are around 240 MB. This makes the approach very sensitive to the intercluster bandwidth (see the left part of Fig. 5.12).

(2) New Scheduler–Worker Technique. We present a new technique named scheduler–worker in order to achieve good robustness under disturbance as well as high performance for low intercluster bandwidth. The *worker*s report their computing performances to the *scheduler* every time they finish a piece of work. The *scheduler* then produces a new job allocation form depending on every node's performance and broadcasts it to each *worker*. The new job allocations are implemented by exchanging data among *worker*s. In the case of DNA sequence alignment, the data transfer for rearranging jobs only happens between two neighboring processes (see Fig. 5.9).

An example of this technique is shown in Fig. 5.10. Initially, the *similarity matrix* is partitioned in the same way as in the static load-balancing approach. During the

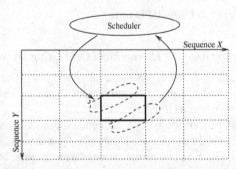

Figure 5.8. Data transfer between *master* and *slave* for finishing a subjob. The *slave* has to receive the upper row and left column from the *master* in order to start computing a new block. Afterward, the *slave* returns the right column and bottom row of this block to the *master*.

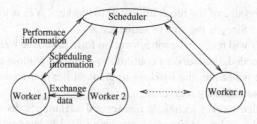

Figure 5.9. Scheduler–worker technique.

computation each *worker* reports it performance to the *scheduler*. We define *NP* (*node performance*) as

$$NP_i = \frac{SB_i}{T}$$

where SB_i denotes the size of the block assigned to worker$_i$ and T denotes the time for finishing the computation of this block. NP values describe the currently available computing power in a node.

The *scheduler* judges whether a new job allocation is needed depending on all the *NP*s. If there exits a disturbance in one node, the sizes of blocks will be rearranged. The equation is as follows:

$$SB_i = \frac{Size_x}{\sum\limits_{j=0}^{N} \frac{NP_i}{NP_j}}$$

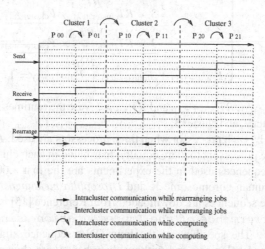

Figure 5.10. Example of the scheduler–worker technique. After each *worker* reports its computing performance to the *scheduler* every time it finishes a piece of work (such as at *send*), the *master* then produces a new job allocation form depending on all these performance and sends it to each *worker* (such as at *receive*). The *worker*s implement the job rearrangement by exchanging data between neighboring *worker*s.

where SB_i is the size of the block allocated to worker$_i$, NP_i is the node performance of worker$_i$, and Size$_x$ is the size of sequence X.

The *worker*s will receive the job allocation form produced by the *master*. If no new allocation is needed, the *worker*s continue to compute without any interruption. If a new allocation is needed, the *worker*s implement the rearrangement by exchanging data between neighboring *worker*s.

The scheduler–worker technique has several advantages. Its speedup without disturbance is only slightly slower than the static load-balancing implementation (see the left part of Fig. 5.13). However, it achieves much better PDRD values (see the right part of Fig. 5.13). It has only slightly worse PDRD values compared to the implementation using the master–slave approach. However, because of the significantly reduced data transfer, it achieves much higher speedups for low intercluster bandwidths.

5.3.4   Performance Evaluation

5.3.4.1   Speedup and PDRD

One of the goals of the paper is to investigate the performance of applications on grid systems with different intercluster connection bandwidth. In our experiments, intracluster application-level bandwidth is almost 190 MB/s. We investigate the speedups of each implementation on the grid system with four different application-level intercluster bandwidths: 8, 1, 0.5, and 0.3 MB/s. How to construct this kind of test environment is described in Section 5.2. The method used for computing speedup is

$$
\begin{cases}
\text{speedup} = \dfrac{3 \times RT_{\text{cluster } 1(1)} \times F_{\text{cluster } 1(1)}}{RT_{\text{real}}} \\[2mm]
\quad = \dfrac{3 \times RT_{\text{cluster } 1(2)} \times F_{\text{cluster } 2(1)}}{RT_{\text{real}}} \\[2mm]
\quad = \dfrac{3 \times RT_{\text{cluster } 3(1)} \times F_{\text{cluster } 3(1)}}{RT_{\text{real}}} \\[2mm]
F_{\text{cluster } 1(1)} + F_{\text{cluster } 2(1)} + F_{\text{cluster } 3(1)} = 1
\end{cases}
$$

where $RT_{\text{cluster } 1(1)}$, $RT_{\text{cluster } 2(1)}$, and $RT_{\text{cluster } 3(1)}$ are the runtimes for one processor in cluster 1, cluster 2, and cluster 3; $F_{\text{cluster } 1(1)}$, $F_{\text{cluster } 2(1)}$, $F_{\text{cluster } 3(1)}$ are the fractions of tasks finished by each processor when three processors are used; RT_{real} is the runtime when multiple processors that are equally distributed in each cluster are used.

The two sequences used in the experiments are the first 3,000,000 Mbp subsequences on human chromosome X and *Drosophila melanogaster* chromosome X. These genome sequences are downloaded from Reference [15].

(1) Performance of the Implementation using Static Load Balancing. The speedups of the long DNA sequence alignment application, using static load balancing and without disturbance, are shown in the left part of Fig. 5.11. The right part of Fig. 5.11 shows the PDRDs when one application is running in one CPU and uses around 50% CPU time to disturb the execution of our application.

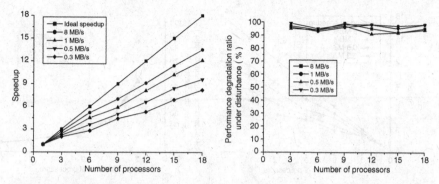

Figure 5.11. Speedups and PDRDs of the implementation, using static load balancing and without disturbance, on the grid system with different application-level intercluster bandwidths (8, 1, 0.5, and 0.3 MB/s).

(2) Performance of the Implementation Using Master-Slave. The execution times and speedups of the long DNA sequence alignment application, using master–slave load balancing and without disturbance, are shown in left part of Fig. 5.12. The right part of Fig. 5.12 shows the PDRDs when one application is running in one CPU and uses around 50% CPU time to disturb the execution of our application.

(3) Performance of the Implementation using Scheduler-Worker. The execution times and speedups of the long DNA sequence alignment application, using scheduler–worker load balancing and without disturbance, are shown in the left part of Fig. 5.13. The right part of Fig. 5.13 shows the PDRDs when one application is running in one CPU to disturb the execution of our application. The disturbance frequency is once every 3 min.

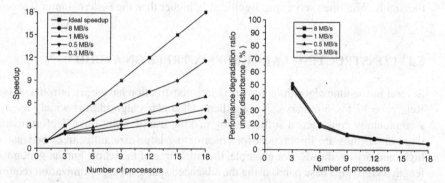

Figure 5.12. Speedups and PDRDs of the implementation, using master–slave dynamic load balancing and without disturbance, on the grid system with different application-level intercluster bandwidths (8, 1, 0.5, and 0.3 MB/s). The *similarity matrix* is divided into blocks of size 30,000 × 30,000 cells.

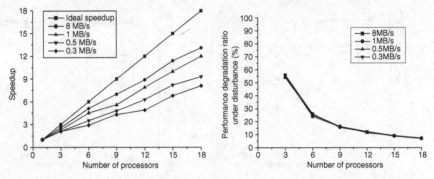

Figure 5.13. Speedups and PDRDs of the implementation, using scheduler–worker load balancing and without disturbance, on the grid system with different application-level intercluster bandwidths (8, 1, 0.5, and 0.3 MB/s).

5.3.4.2   Quality of Produced Alignments

We have compared the outputs of our system to the alignments produced by Pattern-Hunter II. PatternHunter is a new generation of spaced seed-based method for general-purpose homology search. PatternHunter II claims to approach Smith–Waterman sensitivity at a speed 3000 times faster than Smith–Waterman [16]. However the comparison between PatternHunter II and Smith–Waterman performed in Reference 16 is based on relatively short EST sequences. We have performed experiments comparing these two approaches using much larger sequences. The sequences used are the first 3 Mbp DNA sequence of human chromosome X and the *drosophila_melanogaster* genome. Each of the 3 Mbp DNA sequences is divided equally into three segments of length 1 Mbp each. Since the genomes are relatively unrelated, we are using the following scoring scheme: match = 2, mismatch = −1, gapopen = −10, gapextension = −1. Table 5.1 shows the top scores of the alignments found by our Smith–Waterman grid implementation and by PatternHunter II. It can be seen that the Smith–Waterman scores are significantly higher than the PatternHunter II scores.

5.4   CONSTRUCTING LARGE SUFFIX TREES ON A GRID

Several linear-time algorithms for suffix tree construction have been introduced (see Reference 17 for summary). Among them, Ukkonen's algorithm is widely used. It incrementally constructs a suffix tree by making use of suffix links. Unfortunately, these algorithms are impractical for constructing large-size suffix trees because of high memory overheads. For example, the suffix tree of the whole human genome of length 3 Gbp (giga base pairs) using the advanced space-saving optimization requires 30 to 50 GB of memory [18]. Therefore, new suffix tree construction approaches are required because genomic sequences typically have very large-size and sequence datasets are growing at a rapid rate [19].

TABLE 5.1   The Top Scores of Alignments for Aligning Segments of Length 1 Mbp of the Human Chromosome X and the *Drosophila_Melanogaster* Genome by our Grid System and by PatternHunter II using the Score Scheme: Match = 2, Mismatch = −1, Gapopen = −10, Gapextension = −1. The Parameter "−o 64" is used in Running PatternHunter II to Optimize its Alignments

Sequence₁	Sequence₂	Top Score by Our System	Top Score by PatternHunter II
human_chro_x_segment_1	drosophila_chro_x_segment_1	9,336	323
human_chro_x_segment_1	drosophila_chro_x_segment_2	6,046	408
human_chro_x_segment_1	drosophila_chro_x_segment_3	1,016,789	285
human_chro_x_segment_2	drosophila_chro_x_segment_1	6,536	277
human_chro_x_segment_2	drosophila_chro_x_segment_2	6,123	377
human_chro_x_segment_2	drosophila_chro_x_segment_3	1,009,670	a
human_chro_x_segment_3	drosophila_chro_x_segment_1	9,331	a
human_chro_x_segment_3	drosophila_chro_x_segment_2	6,640	299
human_chro_x_segment_3	drosophila_chro_x_segment_3	1,016,338	a

[a] After using about 500 MB memory, PatternHunter II exits with the information "PatternHunter has exceeded its memory limits."

We are introducing a new data structure with a corresponding linear-time algorithm for constructing large suffix trees. The data structure is called the *common prefix–suffix tree* (CPST). All suffixes in a CPST share a common prefix. A standard suffix tree can be divided into a number of CPSTs. Each CPST can be tackled independently by one node in a parallel environment. In order to map these independent tasks efficiently onto a heterogeneous hierarchical grid system, we use a dynamic load-balancing strategy based on the master–slave paradigm.

5.4.1   Suffix Trees and Suffix Links

Let S be a nonempty string over a finite alphabet Σ, that is, $S \in \Sigma^+$. $S[i \cdots j]$ denotes the substring of S that starts at position i and ends at position j. In particular, $S[i \cdots n]$ is the suffix of S that begins at position i and $S[1 \cdots i]$ is the prefix of S that ends at position i, where n is the length of S. Furthermore, $S[i]$ denotes the ith character of S. A suffix tree Υ for an n-character string S is defined as follows:

- Υ is a rooted directed tree with exactly n leaves numbered 1 to n.
- Each internal node, other than the root, has at least two children and each edge is labeled with a nonempty substring of S.
- No two edges out of a node can have edge labels beginning with the same character.
- For any leaf i, the concatenation of the edge labels on the path from the root to leaf i exactly spells out the suffix of S that starts at position i, that is, it spells out $S[i \cdots n]$.

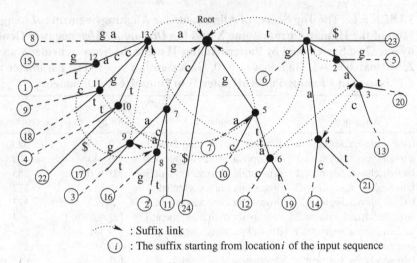

: Suffix link

(i) : The suffix starting from location i of the input sequence

Figure 5.14. The suffix tree with corresponding suffix links for $S = accattgaagcgttaccagttat\$$.

The *label of a path* from the root that ends at a node is the concatenation, in order, of the substrings labeling the edges of that path. The *path label of a node* is the label of the path from the root of Υ to that node. For an internal node υ with path-label $x\alpha$, where $x \in \Sigma$ and $\alpha \in \Sigma^*$, if there is another node $s(\upsilon)$ with path-label α, then a pointer from υ to $s(\upsilon)$ is called a *suffix link*. On the basis of the properties of a suffix tree, it can be shown (see, e.g., Reference 17) that every internal node of a suffix tree in fact has a suffix link from it (if α is empty, then the suffix link goes to the root node). Figure 5.14 shows the suffix tree with corresponding suffix links for $S = accattgaagcgttaccagttat\$$.

5.4.2 CPST: Common Prefix Suffix Tree

In order to map the suffix tree construction problem efficiently onto a computational grid architecture, we partition the suffixes into groups according to their prefixes.

Definition 3. Common prefix-suffix tree (CPST): *Let Υ be the suffix tree for S and compre be a substring of S. The common prefix suffix tree for S and compre, denoted as $CPST(S, compre)$, is the subtree of Υ representing all suffixes of S starting with prefix compre, and its root is the internal node of Υ with path-label compre (if it exists, otherwise it is the original root).*

For $|\Sigma| = k$, the number of CPSTs for common prefixes of length l is k^l. In particular, for the DNA alphabet $\Sigma = \{a, c, g, t\}$, the number of CPSTs with common prefixes length of l is 4^l.

Once all the CPSTs have been constructed, the standard suffix tree for S can be easily derived by concatenating the roots of every CPST with the virtual root of the standard suffix tree. In Section 5.4.3, we will show that most operations on standard suffix trees can be efficiently adapted to a collection of distributed CPSTs. Hence, it is not necessary to gather all CPSTs in one processor.

Ukkonen's algorithm makes use of suffix links to efficiently construct a suffix tree. Unfortunately, suffix links can be connected to nodes that are in general located within different CPSTs. Assuming that we want to use individual processors to construct each CPST in parallel, the use of suffix links would introduce communication and synchronization between them. This, in turn, would lead to inefficiencies in heterogeneous and loosely coupled architectures such as grid systems. Therefore, we will take advantage of another type of link called the *compre suffix link* in the CPST construction process. The compre suffix link has the property that it is always connected to nodes within the same CPST. The corresponding definitions and construction algorithm is explained in the following.

Definition 4. `Suffix chain`: *For each internal node of a suffix tree, there exists a directed chain of suffix links starting from this node and ending at the root node. This directed chain is called suffix chain.*

For example in Fig. 5.14, the *suffix chain* for internal node 3 is $3\rightarrow4\rightarrow13\rightarrow root$.

Definition 5. `Compre suffix link`: *Given are two internal nodes A and B inside the same CPST. We define a compre suffix link from A to B, if A and B are part of the same suffix chain in the standard suffix tree, where A is before B and no other internal node of the CPST lies between A and B on this suffix chain. We also define a compre suffix link from B to the root of the CPST, if no other node inside the CPST is part of the suffix chain between B and the root of the standard suffix tree.*

Figure 5.15 shows all compre suffix links for $CPST(S, a)$, $CPST(S, c)$, $CPST(S, g)$, and $CPST(S, t)$ for the string $S = accattgaagcgttaccagttat\$$.

In order to simplify the description, let $len(compre)$ denote the length of the substring *compre* and $CPST\_pathlabel(N)$ denote the path label from the CPST root to the internal node N. Furthermore, if the ith suffix of S starts with the prefix *compre*, we say that suffix i is *valid* for $CPST(S, compre)$. The edge characters on a directed path from node A to node B are denoted as $e(A, B)$.

Our algorithm constructs a CPST through orderly inserting *valid* suffixes for the CPST. In Reference 17, the introduction of suffix links permits the usage of the skip/count trick. On the basis of this trick, Ukkonen's algorithm can achieve linear time complexity. The compre suffix link in CPSTs is the counterpart of the suffix link in standard suffix trees. Using them, we can locate the next node in the CPST by using the skip/count trick instead of traversing the CPST from its root. The algorithm of constructing $CPST(S, compre)$ can be described as follows:

CPST construction algorithm.
```
Input:    String S = α$, where α ∈ Σ*, $ ∉ Σ, and Σ is a finite alphabet.
          Common prefix compre ∈ Σ* with |compre| < |α|
Output:   CPST(S, compre)

N = number_of_valid_suffixes(S, compre);
IF (N == 0) RETURN (nil);
FOR i = 1 TO N BEGIN
      v(i) = starting position of the ith valid suffix in S;
END
```

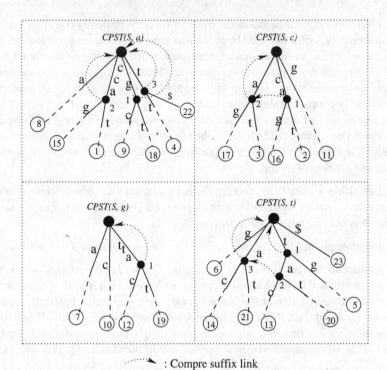

..............➤ : Compre suffix link

(i) : The suffix starting from location i of the input sequence

Figure 5.15. *CPST(S, a)*, *CPST(S, c)*, *CPST(S, g)*, and *CPST(S, t)* for the string *S = accattgaagcgtt-accagttat*$ with corresponding compre suffix links.

```
current_node = CPST_root;
lemma2_flag_node = CPST_root;
FOR i = 1 TO N BEGIN
    IF((current_node == CPST_root)||(lemma2_flag_node == CPST_root))
        new_node_info = traversal(current_node, v(i), S);
    ELSE
        new_node_info = skip_count(lemma2_flag_node, current_node.edge_labels);
        IF (new_node already exists)
            /* v(j) is a new location in S */
            new_node_info = traversal(new_node, v(j), S);
    create_new_node(new_node_info)
    create_new_CompreSuffixLink(new_internal_node, old_internal_node)
    current_node = new_internal_node;
    lemma2_flag_node = current_node.father.compre_suffix_link;
END
RETURN (CPST_root);
```

We are giving an example to show how algorithm 1 works. In order to simplify the description, we consider the two-symbol alphabet $\Sigma = \{a, c\}$ and the input string $S = aaccaacaacac$\$. Figure 5.16 shows the process of constructing *CPST(S, a)*. For the *valid* suffix 1, 2, 5, 6, and 8, we need to traverse the CPST from its root in order

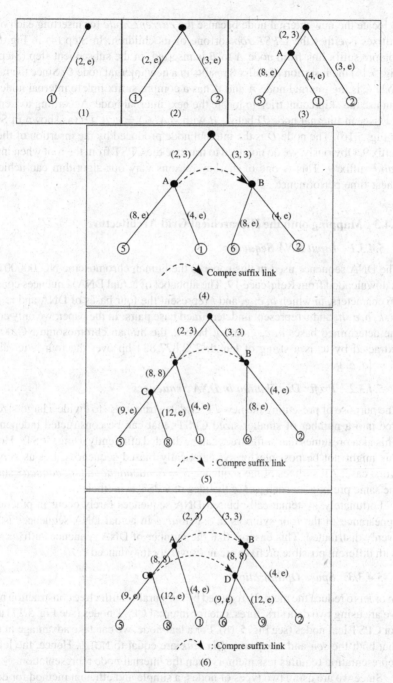

Figure 5.16. Example for constructing *CPST(S, a)*, where *S = aaccaacaacac*$. Every step shows the state of inserting a *valid* suffix: Step (1) shows inserting suffix 1; Step (2) shows inserting suffix 2; Step (3) shows inserting suffix 5; Step (4) shows inserting suffix 6; Step (5) shows inserting suffix 8; and Step (6) shows inserting suffix 9.

to locate the new internal node because the *current_node* for inserting each of these suffixes is either the *CPST_root* or one of its children. In Step (4) in Fig. 5.16, a compre suffix link from node *A* to *B* is inserted. In the subsequent step (Step (5) in Fig. 5.16) the insertion of suffix 8 results in a new internal node *C*. Since the father of node *C* is the internal node *A* and *A* has a compre suffix link to internal node *B*, we can use the skip/count trick to locate the next internal node. According to Lemma 2, it exists an internal node *D* below *B* with $e(A, C) = e(B, D)$ (as shown in Step (6) in Fig. 5.16). The node *D* is the internal node produced by the insertion of the *valid* suffix 9. Obviously, we do not need to traverse the CPST from the root when inserting *valid* suffix 9. This is one of the key reasons why our algorithm can achieve the linear-time performance.

5.4.3   Mapping onto the Hierarchical Grid Architecture

5.4.3.1   Input DNA Sequence

The DNA sequence used in this paper is the human chromosome NC_000001.4 that is downloaded from Reference 19. The alphabet of actual DNA sequences consists of 16 characters, in which *a*, *c*, *g*, and *t* represent the four bases of DNA and *r*, *y*, *w*, *s*, *m*, *k*, *b*, *d*, *h*, and *v* represent undetermined base pairs. In the paper, we only consider the determined bases *a*, *c*, *g*, and *t*. Hence, the human chromosome NC_000001.4 extracted by us is a string of length 222,827,884 bp over the four-letter alphabet $\Sigma = \{a, c, g, t\}$.

5.4.3.2   Prefix Distribution in DNA Sequences

The purpose of presenting the new CPST data structure is to divide a large-size suffix tree into a number of smaller-sized CPSTs that can be constructed independently. This idea presumes that suffix trees can be divided efficiently using CPSTs. However, this might not be possible for systematically biased sequences. Let us consider a worst case: All suffixes of the sequence $S = aaaaaaaaaaaaaaaaaaaaaaaa\$$ start with the same prefix *a*. In such a case the idea of CPST is inefficient.

Fortunately, systematically biased DNA sequences rarely occur in practice. The appearance of the four symbols *a*, *c*, *g*, *and g* in actual DNA sequences is almost evenly distributed. This ensures that the number of DNA sequence suffixes starting with different possible prefixes are not severely imbalanced.

5.4.3.3   Space Optimization

In order to reduce the memory required by our parallel suffix tree construction method, we are using two data structures, one for internal CPST nodes (see Fig. 5.17) and one for CPST leaf nodes (see Fig. 5.18). For a leaf node, we can take advantage of the fact that both the *son* and *compre_suffix_link* are equal to NULL. Hence, the leaf node representation requires less memory than the internal node representation.

Since we are using two types of nodes, a simple and efficient method for deciding whether a node pointer points to an internal node or a leaf node would be useful. Given a string *S* and a prefix *compre*, the number of leaf nodes of *CPST(S, compre)* is equal to the number of corresponding valid suffixes. Hence, a contiguous memory block,

```
struct INTERNALNODE
{
    unsigned long edge_start;   //start location of the edge in the input string
    void * sons;                //pointer to son node
    void * right_sibling;       //pointer to right sibling node
    void * father;              //pointer to father node
    void * compre_suffix_link;  //compre suffix link
}
```

Figure 5.17. Data structure for CPST internal nodes.

let us say [$address_1$, $address_2$], for storing all leaf nodes can be allocated before the CPST construction process. During the CPST construction process, it can then be decided whether a node pointer points to a leaf node if its address is in the range [$address_1$, $address_2$].

5.4.3.4 Implementation Based on Master–Slave Paradigm

In Section 5.3.3, we evaluated three load-balancing strategies for mapping a dynamic programming matrix calculation for pairwise sequence alignment onto a hierarchical grid architecture. However, suffix tree construction and pairwise sequence alignment have different characteristics, such as the rate of free-dependent tasks, the data access pattern, and the task heterogeneity. In particular, each CPST can be constructed independently.

The time required to construct an individual CPST depends on the length of the input string, the number of valid suffixes, and the internal structure of the tree being constructed. Therefore, the use of a dynamic load-balancing strategy is advantageous. We employ a traditional master–slave technique in our implementation described in Section 5.3.3.3 (see Fig. 5.7). Assuming that all salves have access to the complete input string, the communication between *master* and *slaves* is minimal. Therefore, high efficiency can be achieved by having more tasks than number of *slaves*. The number of tasks in our suffix tree construction method can be easily varied by adjusting the length of the common prefixes to the number of *slaves*.

5.4.4 Performance Evaluation

We have used the hierarchical grid system described in Section 5.2 to evaluate the performance of our parallel implementation discussed in Section 5.4. We have measured the execution times for varying number of processors per cluster and varying

```
struct LEAFNODE
{
    unsigned long edge_start;  //start location of the edge in the input string
    void * right_sibling;      //pointer to right sibling node
}
```

Figure 5.18. Data structure for CPST leaf nodes.

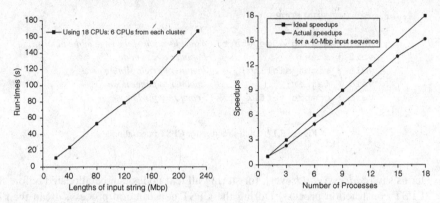

Figure 5.19. Execution times (left) and speedups (right) of our implementation on the hierarchical grid system. The used sequences are substrings of the human chromosome NC_000001.4.

DNA sequence lengths. In our experiments, the length of *compre* is set to 3; that is, the number of CPSTs is $4^3 = 64$. The individual tasks are mapped to processors using the dynamic load-balancing strategy described earlier. Figure 5.19 shows the corresponding execution times and speedups. The method used for computing speedup is identical to the one used in Section 5.3.4.1.

Figure 5.20 shows the runtimes while using different lengths of common prefixes: 1, 2, and 3. This is to investigate the overheads of constructing suffix trees using different number of CPSTs. The Figure 5.21 shows the effect of disturbance in terms of PDRD values using the same experimental setup as in Section 5.3.4.1.

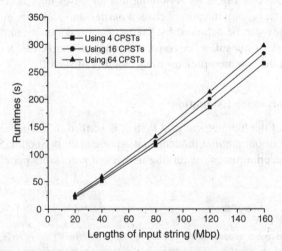

Figure 5.20. Execution times for using varying lengths of common prefixes. The used sequences are substrings of the human chromosome NC_000001.4. Five CPUs are used for four slaves (on four 2.60-GHz CPUs) and one master (on another cluster).

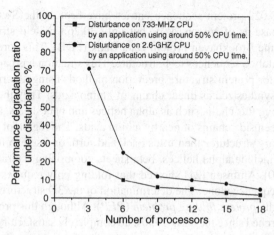

Figure 5.21. PDRDs (performance degradation ratio under disturbance) by an application running on one CPU that uses around 50% CPU time.

On the basis of these measurements, we can make the following observations:

(1) *Linear parallel speedups*: For constant sequence length and varying number of processors, our implementation achieves linear speedups.

(2) *Linear algorithmic complexity*: For constant number of processors and varying sequence length, the overall runtime grows linearly.

(3) *Low overhead for one CPST*: Similar runtimes for using different number of CPSTs.

(4) *Robustness*: By using a load-balancing approach based on master–slave paradigm, the application achieves robustness under disturbance.

(5) *Reduced memory consumption*: The measured average memory consumption of an individual CPST is $23 \times v(S, compre)$ for the human chromosome NC_000001.4, where $v(S, compre)$ denotes the number of valid suffixes for *compre* in S. The memory requirement would be $32 \times v(S, compre)$ without using the space optimization.

5.5 GENETIC ALGORITHMS FOR PROTEIN FOLDING ON A GRID

Knowing a protein's spatial structure is one of the foremost goals of molecular biology, because it is this structure that determines the protein's function. However, determining the three-dimensional structures of proteins using techniques such as X-ray crystallography and nuclear magnetic resonance has proved to be difficult, costly, and not always feasible. As a result, there currently exists a gap between the number of proteins with known sequences and the number of proteins with known three-dimensional structures. This gap has been widening every year. For example, 178,022 protein sequence entries have been in the SwissProt protein sequence database as of March 2005, but only 30,263 protein structures have been deposited in the Brookhaven Protein Data Bank (PDB). This corresponds to a ratio of approximately 6 sequences to 1 structure. This situation has caused much interest in searching for protein structure prediction methods using algorithmic techniques. Proteins are synthesized as linear chains of amino acids. They then form secondary structures along this chain, such as alpha helices and beta sheets, as a result of interactions between side chains of nearby amino acids. The region of the molecule with these secondary structures then folds back and forth on itself to form tertiary structures. These include alpha helices, beta sheets comprising interacting beta strands, and loops [20]. Anfinsen [21] showed that folding only requires knowledge of the amino acid sequence alone. The determination of the 3D structure from its sequence is known as the *protein folding problem* (*PFP*). Although this problem has been intensely researched since the early 1950s, no completely satisfactory solution has been found so far.

It has been shown that PFP is NP-hard [22]. Hence, exhaustive search of a protein's conformational space is not a feasible algorithmic strategy even for small protein sequences. Consequently, heuristic optimization methods seem the most reasonable algorithmic choice to solve PFP. In particular, a number of studies of the use of genetic algorithms (GAs) for PFP have been made in the past decade [23–27]. The fundamental nature of GAs relies on heuristics or randomization to quickly search large numbers of candidate results in order to achieve better solutions over time. Unfortunately, the more likely a good solution can be found, the more computational resources are needed by GAs [28]. This leads to high runtime on sequential architectures. Parallel processing is one approach to reduce this runtime significantly. In the following, we demonstrate how GAs for protein folding can be efficiently mapped onto computational grids.

5.5.1   Protein Folding Problems with HP Lattice Models

Lattice models have proven to be extremely useful tools for solving PFP. By sacrificing atomic details, lattice models can be used to extract essential principles, make predictions, and unify our understanding of many different properties of proteins [29]. One of the important approximations made by lattice models is the discretization of the space of conformations. While this discretization precludes a completely accurate model of protein structures, it preserves important features for computing the minimum energy conformations [30].

The hydrophobic–hydrophilic (HP) models on the 2D square and 3D cubic lattices were proposed by Lau and Dill [31]. HP models abstract the hydrophobic interaction process in protein folding by reducing a protein to a heteropolymer that represents a predetermined pattern of hydrophobicity in the protein. This is one of the most studied simple exact models, and despite its simplicity, the model is powerful enough to capture a variety of properties of actual proteins [30]. Although some amino acids are not hydrophilic or hydrophobic in all contexts, this model reduces a protein instance to a string of Hs and Ps that represents the pattern of hydrophobicity in the protein's amino acid sequence. Some extensions of the standard linear-chain HP model have been proposed in Reference 30.

Solving PFP with HP models is a good test problem for evaluating GAs because its complexity is well understood. There has been a lot of prior work developing GAs based on HP models for PFP. Unger and Moult have used a 2D HP model to demonstrate the usefulness of GAs in the search for minimal energy conformations [27]. In a 2D HP lattice model, each protein is a linear chain of a specific sequence of n amino acids. A chain conformation is represented as a self-avoiding walk on a two-dimensional square lattice. Thus, each amino acid is represented as simply occupying one lattice site, connected to its chain neighbor(s), and unable to occupy a site filled by any other residue. Bond angles are restricted to the values $90°$, $180°$, and $270°$. The force field to determine the inner energy of a fold is defined to be the sum of all hydrophobic interactions. A hydrophobic interaction contributes -1 energy units when two not directly connected hydrophobic residues are orthogonally adjacent to each other. Every other interaction among all other possible types of neighbor pairs has energy equal to 0.

The genetic algorithm for HP lattice models in Reference 27 starts with n extended conformations. In each generation all conformations are subject to a number of mutations. At the end of the mutation stage, a crossover operation is performed as follows: For a pair of selected conformations a random point is chosen along the sequence and the head part of the first conformation is connected to the tail part of the second conformation. If the resulting path is self-avoiding and fitter than its parent conformations, the conformation is then accepted. Figure 5.22 illustrates an example.

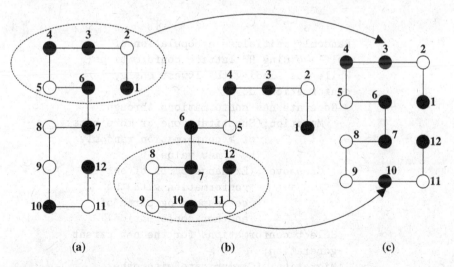

(a)   (b)   (c)

Figure 5.22. Illustration of the crossover procedure of the GA for HP lattice models. Black denotes a hydrophobic amino acid, and white denotes a hydrophilic amino acid. In this example the cut point is randomly chosen to be between residues 6 and 7. The first six residues of (**a**) are then joined with the last six residues of (**b**) to form the new conformation (**c**). The energy value of conformation (**c**) is -4, which is lower than the energies in conformations (**a**) (-3) and (**b**) (-2). Thus, the new conformation is accepted.

For a sequence chain, the conformation space is searched, and then the energy of each conformation is evaluated to find the native conformation(s), those with the minimum energy value.

5.5.2 Parallel Genetic Algorithms

Because of their inherent parallelism, GAs are suitable candidates for mapping onto parallel and distributed architectures. Generally, from the point of view of basic communication structures, parallel GAs can be categorized into three main types [32]: (1) global single-population master–slave GAs; (2) single-population fine-grained GAs; and (3) multiple-population coarse-grained GAs.

We mainly focus on the multiple-population coarse-grained GAs since it is the most popular GA used in computational biology. The basic outline of the multiple-population GA for PFP with HP lattice models is shown in Fig. 5.23.

The exchange of individuals is called migration. There are two popular approaches for modeling migration in multiple-population GAs: the island model and the stepping stone model. In the island model, individuals are allowed to be sent to any other subpopulations (see Fig. 5.24a). It places no restrictions on where an individual may migrate. In the stepping stone model, migration is limited by allowing emigrants to move only to neighboring subpopulations (see Fig. 5.24b) [33].

A few researchers have tried to combine two of the methods to parallelize GAs, producing hierarchical parallel GAs (HPGAs). HPGAs combine the benefits of its components, and it promises better performance than any of them alone [32]. Figure 5.25 shows two communication architectures for HPGAs.

```
Randomly initialize a population of
self-avoiding HP lattice conformations;
While not finding the lowest energy
conformation, do
   Generate new conformations through:
      Mutation;(Substitute one or more bits
               of a conformation randomly
               by a new value)
      Crossover;(Exchange parts of one
                conformation with the
                corresponding parts of
                another conformation)
   Select conformations for the new parent
   generation;
   Migration; (Communicate with other
               populations)
end while;
```

Figure 5.23. The outline of the multiple-population GA for PFP.

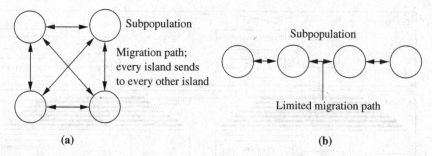

Figure 5.24. Migration models for multiple population GAs: (a) The island model (b) the stepping stone model.

5.5.3   Mapping onto the Hierarchical Grid Architecture

According to the characteristics of the parallel GA shown in Fig. 5.23, we divide the parallel GA into two parts: the sequential GA part and the communication part. The sequential GA part deals with the local behavior of a parallel GA, such as the mutation, variation, and crossover. The communication part processes the communication behavior between all populations participating in the parallel GA. By dividing parallel GAs in such a way, both parts of a parallel GA can evolve independently. This allows for the rapid prototyping of parallel programs and facilitates the mapping of parallel GAs onto parallel architectures. We propose a new way to map HPGAs onto computational grid architectures (see Fig. 5.26). The high-level part of an HPGA is mapped onto the grid layer and the low-level part is mapped onto the cluster layer. Two kinds of link functions, the link function within the cluster and the link function between clusters, are used to implement the intracluster and the intercluster communication within distributed populations.

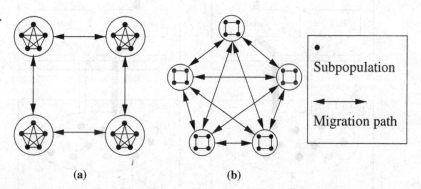

Figure 5.25. (a) Hierarchical parallel GAs with the stepping-stone model at the upper-level parts and the island model at the low-level parts. (b) Hierarchical parallel GAs with the island model at the upper-level parts and the stepping stone model at the low-level parts.

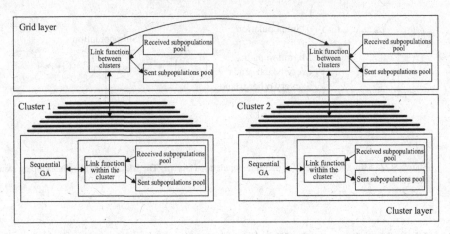

Figure 5.26. Our way to map HPGAs onto the computational grid environment.

In order to implement the mapping scheme in Fig. 5.26, different MPI libraries are used in the two layers. In the grid layer, MPICH-G2 [3] based processes run on the head node; it migrates the subpopulations in the local cluster to other clusters within the grid environment. Inside the cluster, MPICH-P4 [4] is used to transfer data between different nodes. Subpopulations can be exchanged between the grid layer and the cluster layer by reading and writing to two shared memory blocks on the head node of each cluster. Figure 5.27 shows the implementation detail of our two-layer architecture.

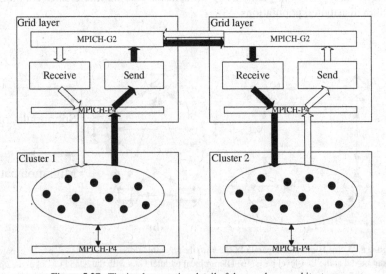

Figure 5.27. The implementation detail of the two-layer architecture.

In order to provide a better environment for code reuse and to make the implementation have good extensibility and flexibility, generic programming techniques are used. Generic programming techniques support static polymorphism through the use of templates. Compared with dynamic polymorphism using inheritance and virtual functions, there are many advantages of static polymorphism, such as type safe and efficiency. One of the most important advantages of generic programming is that the templates can be parameterized with user-defined classes. This advantage of generic programming techniques can facilitate the development of parallel programs [34]. For example, by using generic programming techniques, we can easily implement the separation of the communication part of a parallel GA from the sequential part. The code in Fig. 5.28 shows the structure of the class template `GenericPattern`.

The template parameters of `GenericPattern` are also defined as class templates. Thus, the user can extend the `GenericPattern` by specifying these application-independent templates. Different specialization will lead to different implementation strategies for a concrete parallel GA. Figure 5.29 shows how to use the `GenericPattern` to develop parallel GAs with different migration models. The user only needs to specify the relevant template parameters according to the characteristics of the parallel GA. In generic programming techniques, this extension is also

```
template<class datatype,
         class AlgorithmIni,
         class SequentialGA,
         class LinkFunction>
class GenericPattern{
    void HpComputing(){
        AlgorithmIni::PreProcess();
        SequentialGA::Launch();
        AlgorithmIni::PostProcess();
    }
};
...
template<class datatype>
class SequentialGA{
    static void Launch(){
        while the generation loop is
        not completed{
            ...
            LinkFunction::launch();
            ...
        }
    }
}
```

Figure 5.28. The structure of class template `GenericPattern`.

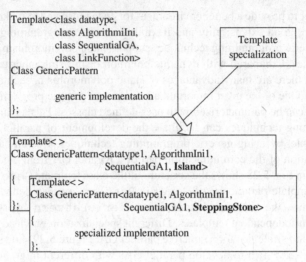

Figure 5.29. Using the `GenericPattern` to develop parallel GAs with different migration models.

called template specialization. From Fig. 5.29 we can also find that each template parameter is defined independently from other parameters. Yet different template parameters can interact with each other via standard interfaces. Consequently, this implementation has a good flexibility. For instance in Fig. 5.29, two algorithms share the same sequential characteristics. Thus, we can entirely reuse the overall design of `SequentialGA` to develop another algorithm with different migration models. The user can therefore reuse the existing components to develop new applications in a flexible way.

5.5.4 Experimental Results

Computing the speedup of a parallel algorithm is a well-accepted way of measuring its efficiency. According to the conventional definition, the speedup of a parallel GA can be defined as the ratio of the execution time of the best sequential algorithm, T_S, and the execution time of the parallel program, T_P [35]. T_P can be described as the sum of the time used by one subpopulation in the computation (T_{COMP}) and the time it used to communicate information to its neighbors (T_{COMM}); so we can compute the speedup as

$$S_P = \frac{T_S}{T_P} = \frac{T_S}{T_{COMP} + T_{COMM}} \tag{5.1}$$

Although speedup is very common in the deterministic parallel algorithms field, the topic of parallel speedups has raised significant controversy in the GA community. The main reason is that the execution time of the serial and parallel GAs are compared without considering the quality of the solutions found in each case. Because of the limited number of individuals and the inherited selection, the sequential GA has much more tendency to be trapped in a local minimum, without enough genetic diversity to help itself out. Communicating individuals between different evolutions in parallel GAs can help in keeping the genetic diversity of the population, thus greatly reducing the probability to be trapped into local minimum. Assuming that the GA is seeking the maximum of some fixed real-valued function, the parallel GA will have an unfair advantage to work out the result much faster. In fact, many researchers have achieved superlinear speedups when using a parallel GA. Shonkwiler [36] has proven this theoretically and provided the following formula to compute the speedup for parallel GAs:

$$S_P = P \times S^{P-1} \tag{5.2}$$

In Equation (5.2), he introduced an acceleration factor S that can explain the superlinear speedup ($S > 1$); P is the number of processors. It is also shown that for the "deceptive" problem where the time to reach the goal can be infinite, very large speedups are possible.

Equation (5.2) provides us a precise way to explain and predict the speedups for parallel GAs. However, the computation of the acceleration factor S is too complex. And because for any time T, there is a nonzero probability and the algorithm will take time T to work out the final result in order to get the expected speedups by Equation (5.2), the user may wait a very long time T [36]. This is not feasible in practice. During an experiment, if the time to reach the goal tends to be infinite, we think the algorithm is trapped into local minimum. We therefore define the *hit rate* of a running-parallel GA as the percentage of the number of outcomes achieved in finite time relative to the total number of experiments. With the concept of *hit rate*,

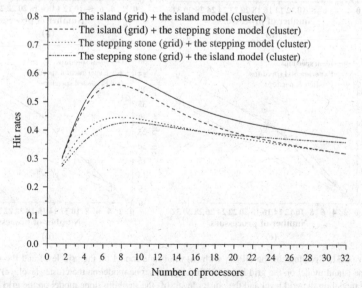

Figure 5.30. Hit rates of the HPGA on the computational grid environment.

we introduce an approximate way to compute the speedups for parallel GAs,

$$S_P = P \times \left(k \times \frac{H_P}{H_S} \right) \tag{5.3}$$

where H_S and H_P are the hit rates for the sequential and parallel GAs, respectively. k is an algorithm-dependent constant. In our experiments we have chosen the value of k to be 1.

The following sequence with the length 64 has been used in the experiments: *hhhh-hhhhhhhhphphpphhpphhpphpphhpphhpphpphhpphhpphphphhhhhhhhhhhh*. This sequence is based on the hydrophobic–hydrophilic (HP) model [29]. The HP model reduces a protein instance to a string of *h*s and *p*s that represents the pattern of hydrophobicity in the protein's amino acid sequence.

Figure 5.30 shows the hit rates of the HPGA with different migration models on the computational grid environment. Figure 5.31 shows the performance measurements

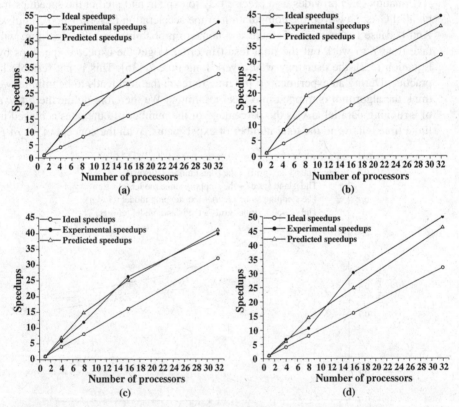

Figure 5.31. Speedups of the HPGA with (**a**) the island model on the grid level and the cluster level; (**b**) the island model on the grid level and the stepping stone model on the cluster level; (**c**) the stepping stone model on the grid level and the cluster level; (**d**) the stepping stone model on the grid level and the island model on the cluster level.

for the protein folding simulations using the HPGA on the computational grid environment. Because GAs are stochastic procedures, we have done more than twenty measurements for each configuration. The total population size is set to be 768. For the mutation stage and the crossover stage, the cooling scheme starts with $C = 2$ and is cooled by a factor of 0.99 for every four generations. The communication frequency is set to be every five generations, exchanging 10% subpopulations. The processors used are distributed evenly on the four clusters. The island model and the stepping stone model are used on the grid level and the cluster level, respectively. From these figures we can see that the hierarchical communication architecture in Fig. 5.26 for HPGAs can be efficiently applied to a computational grid environment. In our experiments, speedups of the HPGA with the island model on both the grid level and the cluster level are slightly higher. This is because the island model allows more freedom and brings more messages into subpopulations. Thus, the algorithm can work the result out faster. We can also find that the speedups predicted by Equation (5.3) are very close to the experimental speedups.

5.6 CONCLUSION

Computational biology is now faced with the burgeoning number of genome data. The rigorous postprocessing of this data requires an increased role for high-performance computing. In this chapter, we have investigated techniques and parallel algorithms for mapping three important bioinformatics applications onto hierarchical grid architectures: (1) large-scale DNA sequence alignment; (2) construction chromosome-size suffix trees; and (3) genetic algorithms for protein folding. In particular, we presented dynamic load-balancing and generic programming techniques that are tailored toward the architectural features of hierarchical grid systems. The application of these techniques in conjunction with efficient parallel algorithms has lead to significant runtime savings on our grid test-bed. Our future work will include evaluating the performance of our approaches on larger hierarchical systems such as the Grid5000 in France (www.grid5000.fr).

REFERENCES

1. I. Foster, C. Kesselman, *The Grid: Blueprint for a New Computing Infrastructure*, Morgan Kaufmann Publishers, San Francisco, 1998.

2. N. Karonis, B. Toonen, I. Foster, MPICH-G2: A grid-enabled implementation of the message passing interface, Journal of Parallel and Distributed Computing **63**(5), 551–563, 2003.

3. MPICH-G2 project, http://www3.niu.edu/mpi.

4. MPICH project, http://www-unix.mcs.anl.gov/mpi/mpich/.

5. Sun grid engine project, http://gridengine.sunsource.net/.

6. T.F. Smith, M.S. Waterman, Identification of common molecular subsequences, *Journal of Molecular Biology* **147**, 195–197, 1981.

7. D.S. Hirschberg, A linear space algorithm for computing longest common subsequences, *Communications of the ACM* **18**, 341–343, 1975.

8. E. Myers, W. Miller, Optimal alignments in linear space, *Computer Applications in the Biosciences* **4**, 11–17, 1988.

9. K.M. Chao, J. Zhang, J. Ostell, W. Miller, A local alignment tool for long DNA sequences, *Computer Applications in the Biosciences* **11**(2), 147–153, 1994.

10. A.L. Delcher, S. Kasif, R.D. Fleischmann, J. Peterson, O. White, S.L. Salzberg, Alignment of whole genomes, *Nucleic Acids Research* **27**(11), 2369–2376, 1999.

11. C.X. Chen, B. Schmidt, An adaptive grid implementation of DNA sequence alignment, *Future Generation Computer Systems - The International Journal of Grid Computing: Theory, Methods and Applications* **21**(7), 988–1003, 2005.

12. C.X. Chen, B. Schmidt, Constructing large suffix trees on a computational grid, *Journal of Parallel Distributed Computing*, **66**(12), 1512-1523, 2006, doi: 10.1016/j.jpdc.2006.08.004.

13. A. Plaat, H.E. Bal, R.H.F. Hofman, Sensitivity of parallel applications to large differences in bandwidth and latency in two-layer interconnects, in *Proceedings of 5th IEEE HPCA '99*, Orlando, Florida, January 9–13, pp. 244–253, 1999.

14. W.R. Zhu, Y.W. Niu, J.Z. Lu, C. Shen, G.R. Gao, A cluster-based solution for high performance hmmpfam using EARTH execution model, *Cluster 2003*, Hong Kong, 2003.

15. Ensembl Genome Browser, http://www.ensembl.org/index.html.

16. M. Li, B. Ma, D. Kisman, J. Tromp, PatternHunter II: highly sensitive and fast homology search, *Journal of Bioinformatics and Computational Biology* **2**(3), 417–440, 2004.

17. D. Gusfield, *Algorithms on Strings, Trees and Sequences: Computer Science and Computational Biology*, Cambridge University Press, New York, 1997.

18. S. Kurtz, Reducing space requirement of suffix trees, *Software Practice and Experience*, **29**(13), 1149–1171, 1999.

19. GenBank, http://www.ncbi.nlm.nih.gov/genbank/.

20. D.W. Mount, *Bioinformatics-Sequence and Genome Analysis*, Cold Spring Harbor Laboratory Press, Cold Spring Harbor, NY, 2001.

21. C.B. Anfinsen, Principles that govern the folding of proteins, *Science* **181**(96), 223–230, 1973.

22. W.E. Hart, S. Istrail, Robust proofs of NP-hardness for protein folding: General lattices and energy potentials, *Journal of Computational Biology*, **4**(1), 1–22, 1997.

23. T. Dandekar, P. Argos, Folding the main chain of small proteins with the genetic algorithm, *Journal of Molecular Biology* **236**, 844–861, 1994.

24. S.M. LeGrand, K.M. Merz, Jr, The genetic algorithm and the conformational search of polypeptides and proteins, *Molecular Simulation* **13**, 299–320, 1994.

25. J.T. Pedersen, J. Moult, *Ab initio* structure prediction for small polypeptides and protein fragments using genetic algorithms, *Proteins* **23**, 454–460, 1995.

26. S. Sun, Reduced representation of protein structure prediction: Statistical potential and genetic algorithms, *Protein Science* **2**, 762–785, 1993.

27. R. Unger, J. Moult, Genetic algorithms for protein folding simulations, *Journal of Molecular Biology* **231**, 75–81, 1993.

28. E.E. Santos, E. Santos, Jr., Reducing the computational load of energy evaluations for protein folding, in *4th IEEE Symposium on Bioinformatics and Bioengineering*, 2004.

29. K.A. Dill, S. Bromberg, K. Yue, K.M. Fiebig, D.P. Yee, P.D. Thomas, H.S. Chan, Principles of protein folding: A perspective from simple exact models, *Protein Science* **4**(4), 561–602, 1995.

30. W.E. Hart, A. Newman, *The Computational Complexity of Protein Structure Prediction in Simple Lattice Models*, CRC Press, Boca Raton, FL, 2003.

31. K.F. Lau, K.A. Dill, A lattice statistical mechanics model of the conformational and sequence spaces of proteins, *Macromelecules* **22**, 3986–3997, 1989.

32. E. Cantu-Paz, A survey of parallel genetic algorithms, *Calculateurs Paralleles, Reseaux et Systems Repartis* **10**(2), 141–171, 1998.

33. B. Wilkinson, M. Allen, *Parallel Programming-Techniques and Applications Using Networked Workstations and Parallel Computers*, Prentice-Hall, Upper Saddle River, NJ, 2005.

34. W. Liu, B. Schmidt, Parallel pattern-based systems for computational biology: A case study, *IEEE Transactions on Parallel and Distributed Systems* **17**(8), 750–763, 2006.

35. G. Almasi, A. Gottlieb, *Highly Parallel Computing*, Benjamin/Cummings Publishing Company, San Francisco, 1994.

36. R. Shonkwiler, Parallel genetic algorithms, 5th International Conference on Genetic Algorithms, 1992.

6

MULTIPLE SEQUENCE ALIGNMENT AND PHYLOGENETIC INFERENCE

Denis Trystram and Jaroslaw Zola

6.1 INTRODUCTION

Multiple sequence alignment (MSA) [1] is one of the most commonly performed tasks in computational biology. It appears as an essential component in areas such as database searching [2], identification of conserved motifs [3], and phylogenomic inference [4], just to name a few. At the same time, MSA is a hard optimization problem for two main reasons. First, it is very difficult to provide a formalization, for example, objective function, that would be satisfactory from the biological standpoint. Second, good modeling usually becomes very challenging algorithmically when the best (or optimal) alignment is desired.

Multiple sequence alignment and phylogenetic inference [5] are typically considered separately; however, both of these problems are closely linked. For instance, most character–based methods for phylogeny reconstruction (e.g., maximum parsimony or maximum likelihood) require an MSA as input data. Moreover, the quality of the results generated by these methods is strictly influenced by the quality of the input alignment [6]. On the contrary, when looking for similarities among related sequences, we should be aware of the fact that they are a result of some complex evolutionary process. Thus, in the optimal case, we should know their relationship described by some phylogenetic tree.

The reason for treating MSA and phylogeny separately is quite simple—each problem alone, even under simplified assumptions, belongs to either the class of *NP–Complete* or *NP–Hard* problems, which implies computational intractability [7–10]. In the last few years, many different heuristics that address both MSA and phylogeny have been proposed. Unfortunately, because some commonly used data sets consist of hundreds of long sequences, heuristic methods may require hours to days of compute time when executed on a commodity PC. A natural way of dealing with problems of that kind is to apply parallel and/or distributed processing.

Grid Computing for Bioinformatics and Computational Biology. Edited by E.-G. Talbi and A.Y. Zomaya.
Copyright © 2008 John Wiley & Sons, Inc.

In this chapter, we present *Parallel PhyloBuilder Server*, a generic approach that allows computing a multiple sequence alignment and its corresponding phylogenetic tree simultaneously. We show how parallel and distributed systems, enhanced by caching techniques, can be utilized to speedup multiple sequence alignment and phylogenetic inference, especially in the context of updating secondary biological databases. Further, the methods we present can be easily extended and combined with other MSA software.

The chapter is organized as follows: We start with a brief introduction to the multiple sequence alignment and phylogeny problems, followed by a short overview of parallel methods that address these problems. Then, we discuss in detail our method and its implementation, and provide some experimental results on actual biological sequence data. Finally, we describe a Grid environment designed to facilitate access to parallel MSA software.

6.2 MULTIPLE SEQUENCE ALIGNMENT AND PHYLOGENY

In this section, we introduce the problems of multiple sequence alignment and phylogenetic inference. We then show how these two problems are combined into the *Generalized Tree Alignment* problem [11], and how they can be solved using parallel and distributed computers.

6.2.1 Multiple Sequence Alignment

Multiple sequence alignment is a basic method that allows capturing the relationship between input sequences. To discover how sequences in a group are related to each other, we align them by introducing *gaps* (here denoted by special character "−") in such a way that the overall number of matching characters from each sequence is maximal. When aligning sequences, we assume that related sequences have diverged from a common ancestor by a process of mutation and selection. The basic mutational processes that we consider are *substitutions*, which change one letter into another, and *insertions* and *deletions*, which add or remove characters in sequences. Insertion and deletions, together referred as *indels*, are reflected in the alignment by gaps.

Formally, the multiple alignment of the set of input sequences $S = \{s_1, s_2, \ldots, s_n\}$, where $s_x \in \Sigma^*$, is a set $A = \{s'_1, s'_2, \ldots, s'_n\}$, where $s'_x \in (\Sigma \cup \{-\})^*$, and

- $|s'_1| = |s'_2| = \cdots = |s'_n|$,
- $\forall_{1 \leq i \leq |s'_1|} \exists_j \, s'_j[i] \neq \text{"−"}$,
- $s_x = (s'_x \text{ without "−"})$.

Σ is an alphabet consisting of four letters in the case of DNA ($\Sigma = \{A, C, G, T\}$) and RNA ($\Sigma = \{A, C, G, U\}$) and twenty letters (corresponding to amino acids) in the case of proteins. A multiple alignment A can be considered as a matrix with n rows and $|s_i|$ columns, where row i is represented by a sequence s'_i.

While the MSA idea appears to be a simple concept, there are a variety of problems remaining that must be solved—for instance, how to evaluate the quality of an alignment, how to find an optimal alignment under a given model of evolution, or how to decide if an alignment is statistically significant. Except for simple cases, it is extremely hard to define a single correct MSA. For example, we need to consider that related sequences are not independent but rather the result of some evolutionary process, and can be arranged into a phylogenetic tree (see next section). Obviously, this relationship should be somehow reflected during the alignment evaluation.

The scoring model is the most vital part of every MSA procedure. In theory, it should take into account everything that is known about the input sequences, for example, structure, function, and previously mentioned evolutionary relations. In most cases, however, this information is not available and some simplifications must be made. Historically, most of the MSA methods assumed that individual columns of an alignment were independent [12,13], and they defined the score of an alignment as a sum of scores for each column of the alignment,

$$\text{Score}(A) = \sum_{i=1}^{|s'_1|} \text{score}(A_i) - \Gamma$$

where A_i is the ith column of the multiple alignment A, $score(A_i)$ is a measure of similarity of the column (e.g., number of mismatches), and Γ is some general function penalizing gaps that occur in the alignment. The most standard method of this type is the *sum of pairs* (SP) function [12].

Because biological sequences may form complex higher-order structures, assuming column independence can be incorrect. As a result, several alternative scoring models have been devised. The most significant are consistency-based approaches [14,15] such as *Coffee* [16,17], ProbCons [18], the *Log Expectation* function implemented in MUSCLE [19], and methods based on *hidden Markov models* [18,20].

These approaches are a direct consequence of the observation that the most consistent alignments are often closest to the truth. Therefore, they create an MSA that agrees the most with all possible reference alignments represented by a "library" [16]. For instance, 3D-Coffee can use local and global pairwise alignments, as well as results from protein structure–structure and sequence–structure comparisons [17]. For comprehensive reviews of different MSA evaluation strategies, we refer the reader to References 1 and 21.

As previously mentioned, it is usually a hard optimization problem to construct the optimal alignment. Although the case of only two sequences can be solved using dynamic programming in $O\left(l^2\right)$ [22], where l is an average length of input sequences, dynamic programming turns out to be very impractical for more than a few sequences because it requires exponentially growing time and space [23]. For this reason, heuristic methods are in wide use, with progressive alignment being the most popular [24]. Strategies based on progressive alignment move toward the final solution step by step by following some predefined order. At the beginning, the most similar pairs of

Progressive		
ClustalW		
ProAlign	Stochastic	
ProbCons		
	SAGA HMMER	
Praline Prrn	Iterative	
MUSCLE		
POA		
MAFFT	DIALIGN	
3D/T-Coffee	Consistency	
PCMA		

Figure 6.1. Some of the popular MSA programs. Packages that have been parallelized are marked with italic font. Please note that ProbCons and SAGA also belong to the group of consistency-based methods, which is not indicated in the diagram.

sequences are aligned. Then, remaining sequences are added to the initial alignment one by one. Progressive alignment is heuristic as it does not separate the process of alignment scoring from the optimization algorithm. One of the most popular programs of that type is ClustalW [25]. Other alignment search methods include stochastic algorithms [20,26] or apply an iterative approach to improve the quality of solutions generated by other methods [27].

Figure 6.1 presents some popular MSA programs highlighting those that have been parallelized.

6.2.2 Phylogenetic Inference

The relationship between any set of species can be expressed by a phylogenetic tree. Here, we assume that the phylogenetic tree of a group of sequences reflects the phylogeny of their host species,[1] and that they share some common ancestor. The goal of phylogenetic analysis is to find the most accurate tree describing the evolution of given contemporary sequences. Each branch of such a tree describes an evolutionary divergence defined by some measure of distance between sequences. In most cases, this tree will be a weighted binary tree, which means that for n input sequences there are $B_r(n) = \Pi_{i=3}^{n}(2i - 3)$ rooted and $B_u(n) = \Pi_{i=3}^{n}(2i - 5)$ unrooted trees to consider. It is easy to see that the search space is quite large, making phylogeny a nontrivial task.

As in the case of MSA, there exists a plethora of different strategies to infer phylogenies (see References 5 and 29 for excellent reviews) that are based on different assumptions and use different search strategies. Here, we are interested in methods that infer trees from molecular sequences, unlike early methods based on morphological properties, and recent approaches based on gene order data [30]. In general, such

---

[1]This assumption is not necessarily true because of gene duplication and lateral gene transfer. See, for example, Reference 28 for detailed explanation.

sequence-based phylogenetic methods can be divided into two main groups: *distance-based methods* and *criteria-based methods*.

The distance-based approaches assume that similarity among analyzed sequences can be converted to convey sequence distances. Next, on the basis of these distances, a unique tree topology is rendered. Usually, this is achieved by iteratively joining sequences with minimum distance. The most popular algorithms in this category are *UPGMA* [31], *neighbor-joining* (NJ) [32], *BioNJ* [33], and *Weighbor* [34]. Although distance-based methods are very fast and are guaranteed to reproduce the correct tree when correct distances are given, they often appear to be inaccurate as a result of inevitable errors in the sequence distance estimation. First, it is hard to propose an accurate model to transform substitutions and indels into evolutionary distances. Second, errors propagate during tree construction. Even though attempts have been made to bypass these difficulties (e.g., in *Weighbor*) by combining a pure distance method with maximum likelihood distance estimation, distance-based methods are clearly less robust than criteria-based strategies.

Criteria-based methods differ substantially from distance-based approaches because they distinguish the tree evaluation stage from the tree searching procedure. In other words, they define phylogenetic inference as a pure optimization problem. There are two main advantages of this approach: Different tree evaluation criteria can be applied and various search strategies can be used. Unfortunately, two widely accepted optimization problems of that type, *maximum parsimony* (MP) [28] and *maximum likelihood* (ML) [5], are known to be *NP-Hard* [7,8].

Maximum parsimony methods work by selecting the tree that explains the observed input sequences (represented by their multiple sequence alignment) with a minimal number of substitutions. Each nucleotide change contributes to the parsimony score, and the main problem is to find a tree topology that minimizes the overall score. This involves another step, which is assignment of sequences to the internal nodes of the tree to guarantee that the score is minimal for a given topology. The MP approach has been implemented in several popular packages such as PAUP* [35] and PHYLIP [36].

Maximum likelihood approaches (including Bayesian methods [29]) are also widely used. ML methods try to find a tree that, under a given evolutionary model, has the highest probability to generate the input sequences. For each position in the input alignment, a likelihood of observed changes (given a tree topology) is computed, and the product of all the likelihoods induces the length of a tree's branches. Unlike MP, ML requires an evolutionary model to be explicitly stated. As a result, ML is the most accurate for phylogenetic inference, at the expense of highly CPU intensive computations. ML has been implemented in a number of computer programs, including fastDNAml [37], PHYLIP, RAxML [38], MrBayes [39], and PHYML [40].

As we already indicated, both MP and ML are optimization criteria. Hence, in each case some search strategy is required that finds an optimal (or near optimal) tree topology, staring from some initial tree, or constructing it iteratively. Obviously, since $B_r(50) = 2.75292 \times 76$ (which is close to the estimated number of atoms in the universe), exact enumeration cannot be considered unless the number of input sequences is relatively small. Therefore, heuristics and metaheuristics are usually used, for example, standard *hill climbing*, *Branch and Bound* [41], or stochastic methods such as simulated annealing [42] and genetic algorithms [43]. Unfortunately, in most cases the application of heuristics is not enough to make phylogenetic inference efficient, and other techniques like parallel processing are required.

6.2.3   Generalized Tree Alignment

Having defined two basic concepts, we turn now to the problem of combining them into one.

As previously explained, phylogeny is directly linked with multiple sequence alignment. This is because phylogenetic analysis of sequence data requires *positional homology* [28]. It means that the nucleotides observed at a given position in the sequence under study should appear in all ancestral sequences. To fulfill this requirement, insertions and deletions must be assumed, and in this way an alignment becomes a prerequisite of the phylogeny. Suppose we have a set of input sequences in which we are interested in their phylogeny as well as their best possible alignment. If the parsimony criterion is assumed, this problem can be expressed as a *minimal Steiner tree problem* [44] and is known as *generalized tree alignment* (GTA).

Let us consider a graph $G = (V, E)$ whose nodes are all possible sequences shorter than some large constants. A set S of input sequences, $S \subset V$, represents *terminal nodes*. The edge $e = (u, v)$ is inserted whenever sequence u can be obtained from sequence v by mutation (indel or substitution). The edge e receives weight equal to the score of the mutation. Finding the full Steiner tree with minimal length would obtain both the phylogenetic tree and the multiple alignment for S. The *Steiner points* of such tree would represent ancestral sequences for S. The above formalization has been shown to be *Max SNP-Hard* [10], which means that it cannot be approximated with arbitrary precision in polynomial time (unless $P = NP$).

The original GTA problem has been addressed by several researchers [45–48]. Hein [46,47] proposed an approach based on *sequence graphs* that uses an affine gap penalty, and this result has been improved by Schwikowski and Vingron in Reference 48. More general forms of the GTA, which are different than the parsimony criterion, have been studied as well [24,49–51]. Most of these methods first estimate phylogenetic tree using some distance-based algorithm, then progressively perform an alignment following the order induced by that tree. Recent solutions try to combine statistical MSA procedures (maximum-likelihood alignment) [52] with maximum-likelihood phylogeny inference [50,53]. Although very promising from the biological point of view (an explicit model for indels and a likelihood estimation of the model parameters), these methods cannot currently be applied for more than a few sequences because of excessive computational requirements.

6.2.4   Application of Parallel and Distributed Computing

Because of computational requirements, multiple sequence alignment and phylogenetic inference are very attractive problems for the parallel computing community [54]. In the case of MSA, parallel approaches may provide two main advantages. First, most existing MSA tools are coarse-grained and therefore can be easily parallelized using distributed memory systems (however, shared memory implementations are also common [55,56]). As a result, even very large MSA instances can be solved in a reasonable amount of time. Second, parallel environments (e.g., Grids) increase the throughput of MSA software by allowing several copies of the same application to be run simultaneously in either cooperative or unrelated manner. This may be crucial for institutions that provide online access to various biological tools.

In the last few years, several parallel MSA tools have been reported (see, for example, References 57 and 58). Even so, the most often parallelized package is ClustalW. The most time-consuming part of ClustalW is the construction of a distance matrix that is based on a pairwise global alignment of all pairs of input sequences. Because pairwise alignments are independent, this process can be easily parallelized by distributing matrix computations among a set of processors. Indeed, all published parallel versions of ClustalW take advantage of this observation. Currently, the only open source version of parallel ClustalW designed for distributed architectures is ClustalW-MPI. It is based on the MPI standard, and some attempts to run it using Grid–enabled MPI (mpich-g2 [59]) have been reported on the Internet.

Another interesting parallel implementation of the ClustalW algorithm is by Catalyurek et al. [60]. In this approach, the original ClustalW program is decomposed into a set of components, here called "filters," which take care of different operations (e.g., pairwise or progressive alignment). In addition, some "filters" are responsible for buffering alignment results. This approach benefits from both the parallel execution of a single task and the simultaneous processing of several different tasks. This is because "filters" are independent and a single "filter" can participate in several parallel executions.

As in the case of MSA, there are several distributed-memory parallel programs developed for phylogenetic inference. The majority of these tools are related to criteria-based approaches, which can be easily parallelized. This is because the time spent on evaluation of alternative tree topologies is predominant in these methods. In addition, evaluation of different topologies can be distributed among a set of workers that do not need to communicate with each other. Furthermore, parallel processing allows analyzing large bootstrap data sets to asses the quality of a reconstructed tree [5]. This process can be achieved by executing several copies of the same program but with resampled original input data.

Two parallel phylogeny tools are especially worth mentioning: fastDNAml [61] and the RAxML series of programs [38].

fastDNAml is one of the first maximum-likelihood phylogeny tools. Its parallel version has been ported to the Grid environment using the PACX-MPI framework [62], and it won first prize during the *SC 2003 HPC Challenge* as the most geographically distributed application [63]. In this experiment more than 600 CPUs provided by centers in eight countries, spread across six continents, were used to run fastD-NAml to analyze the evolution of 67 species of hexapods using 12 genes, and with 450 bootstraps. This project is very interesting from both the HPC (practical application of a large Grid) and the biological point of view (testing whether hexapods are single evolutionary group). At this point, however, we should mention that the algorithmic solutions provided by fastDNAml are currently considered to be obsolete, and fastDNAml has been outperformed by many newer programs (we refer the reader to Reference 64 for an interesting discussion on this subject).

The second tool, RAxML, is probably the most advanced parallel software for phylogenetic inference, in terms of both parallel solutions and algorithmic developments. RAxML implements a maximum-likelihood strategy and includes advanced search algorithms based on hill-climbing and simulated annealing heuristics. This system supports a variety of parallel architectures including shared memory systems (implementation on the basis of OpenMP standard), distributed memory clusters (MPI-based system), and geographically distributed systems (communication implemented via HTTP protocol). As in the case of fastDNAml, RAxML uses a master–worker approach with workers being responsible for evaluating topologies. Currently, RAxML can be used to infer trees consisting of thousands taxa with an alignment length of ∼50 Kbp (*Stamatakis, private communication*).

The purpose of this section was to give a general overview on how parallel and distributed systems are used to solve MSA and phylogeny problems. In the rest of this chapter, we describe how these techniques can easily be combined into a single system and enhanced by caching.

6.3 GENERIC SCHEME FOR GTA PROBLEM

In this section we describe the *PhylTree* method, which is a generic scheme for MSA with simultaneous phylogenetic inference. Then, we present its formalization that covers typical cases when updating secondary biological databases.[2]

6.3.1   The PhylTree Method

PhylTree (PT) has been first implemented by Parmentier and co-workers [65] and later extended by Zola and co-workers [51]. In general, its principle is to iteratively group optimal partial solutions that represent an MSA and phylogeny for small subsets of input data. To achieve this, PT introduces notions of a *neighborhood* and a *partial phylogenetic tree*.

Figure 6.2 provides an overview of the main *PhylTree* procedure. The method consists of two successive phases: a distance matrix computation and iterative sequence clustering.

The basic aim of the first phase is to provide a comparison measure that will be used to determine neighborhoods. To compute the distance matrix $D = \|d(i, j)\|$, all pairs (i, j) of input sequences are aligned and raw alignment scores are converted to approximate pairwise distances. The method for converting alignment scores to distances depends on the type of input data and can, for example, be based on the model of Kimura [66]. An important property of PT is its capacity to use various

---

[2]A secondary database is a database system that includes a variety of additional tools and methods to extract and represent data from a primary sequence databases such as GenBank.

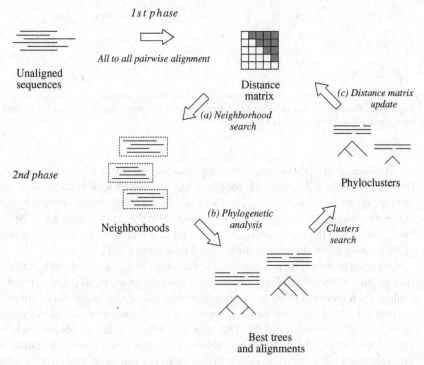

Figure 6.2. Overview of the PhylTree method. In (**a**) various definitions of neighborhood can be used, in (**b**) any phylogenetic method and scoring model can be applied, and in (**c**) any distance function can be used.

distance criteria in addition to sequence alignment. Such alternative criteria, for example, derived from structural comparisons, may be more evolutionarily accurate when rarely available. Other strategies, such as alignment-free methods [67] can also be applied, but they seem to be less precise. Thus, we consider the first phase as a process of $\Theta((n^2 - n)/2)$ pairwise alignments, where $n = |S|$ is the size of the input data set.

The second phase is an iterative procedure. Its purpose is to visit the search space of partial phylogenetic trees and simultaneously perform progressive alignment guided by those trees. A single iteration begins with establishing a set of neighborhoods, where a neighborhood is a set of sequences selected with respect to the distance matrix D. The exact neighborhood definition depends on the type of analysis performed and therefore is one of the input parameters, which we will discuss later. Having selected neighborhoods, the next step is to determine a set of new taxa. To achieve this, a phylogenetic analysis of neighborhoods is performed, resulting in *phyloclusters*.

Definition 6.3.1 *Phylocluster: A phylocluster is a set of sequences connected by the same partial phylogenetic tree in each neighborhood they appear.*

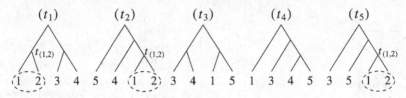

Figure 6.3. Example of five different neighborhoods with corresponding optimal partial phylogenetic trees. Group of sequences (1, 2) is a phylocluster.

To illustrate the above definition, suppose we are given five neighborhoods as presented in Fig. 6.3. Each neighborhood has associated with it an optimal partial phylogenetic tree, namely $t_1, \ldots, t_5$. Group (1, 2) is a phylocluster because it appears in the trees $\{t_1, t_2, t_5\}$ and each time is connected by the same subtree $t_{(1,2)}$. Note that taxa (3, 4) create the same subtree in $\{t_1, t_3\}$ but are connected by different subtree in t_4. According to the definition, these taxa do not form a phylocluster.

One issue that we have not explained so far is how to find a partial phylogenetic tree for a given neighborhood. For each neighborhood, we examine all possible topologies evaluated on the basis of an accompanying progressive alignment. More simply, we are looking for the tree with the best progressive alignment score guided by that tree to select a locally optimal topology. This approach, however, has an obvious drawback: To find the optimal tree for the neighborhood of size k, we have to evaluate $B_r(k)$ different topologies. As discussed in the previous section, such analysis of neighborhoods composed of more than four sequences becomes very time-consuming. The PT method is capable to incorporate different alignment scoring models. The current implementation provides functions based on the Sankoff's parsimony with an affine gap penalty as well as basic *Sum of Pairs* scores. Other investigated systems include *Coffee* and *Log Expectation* functions. While the ability to use different scoring models extends the possible applications of PT, it makes difficult to apply techniques other than exact enumeration. However, in some cases heuristics can be used, which we will demonstrate later.

As a result of the phylogenetic analysis, a set of phyloclusters is generated. From the evolutionary point of view, we expect that phylocluster is a group of closely related sequences with a common ancestor. Therefore, the partial guide tree associated with such a group should be preserved in the final tree. To achieve this, we consider each phylocluster as a single taxon represented by the associated multiple alignment. From that point, a new taxon replaces its component sequences in the input data set. Returning to the example in Fig. 6.3, sequences (1, 2) would be replaced by their alignment with respect to the tree $t_{(1,2)}$, and in the following iterations they would be considered as a single taxon.

The final task that we perform is computing the distance between newly created taxa and other sequences. This stage is called distance matrix update. The distances can be determined in various ways. For example, it can be a minimal or maximal distance between component sequences of the phylocluster and other taxa, and choice of a particular criterion depends on the type of analyzed data.

As we already indicated, the second phase of PT is an iterative process. Immediately after the distance matrix update, new neighborhoods are determined and another iteration begins. The entire procedure is repeated until all sequences are clustered. Finally, a single guide tree, which is the phylogenetic tree, as well as the corresponding multiple alignment is obtained.

We have not yet explained how to determine neighborhoods. The definition of neighborhood is probably the most vital part of PT for two reasons. First, it has a direct influence on the time complexity of the phylogenetic analysis. Second, it is responsible for the accuracy of PT. Intuitively, a neighborhood is a method to visit the search space of potential guide trees. Because larger neighborhoods require visiting a larger number of partial trees, this affects the time complexity of the method.

We have developed several different types of neighborhoods, of which two are in common use: *PhylTree* (or a fixed-size neighborhood) and *QuickTree*. Both are designed to analyze different types of data sets.

The *PhylTree* neighborhood is intended for high-precision analysis of relatively small sets of sequences. Here, the precision level can be tuned on the basis of neighborhood size.

Definition 6.3.2 *Fixed–size neighborhood: A neighborhood $N \subset S^i$ of sequence s is a set of k sequences, such that $s \in N$ and $\forall_{s_x \in N \setminus \{s\}} \forall_{s_y \in S^i \setminus N}\ d(s, s_x) \leq d(s, s_y)$. S^i is a set of input taxa at iteration i, and $k > 3$ is an integer parameter.*

According to the above definition, for each sequence we look for its $k - 1$ closest taxa to determine neighborhoods. In this case the precision of the analysis as well as its complexity clearly depends on the parameter k. Increasing k will have the effect of extending the search space, but at the same time it will significantly increase the time complexity of the phylogenetic analysis. For this reason, the *PhylTree* definition cannot be practically used for large input data sets. On the contrary, large data sets should be analyzed with increased precision because of the possibility of divers input sequences.

The *QuickTree* definition has been designed to reduce the complexity of the phylogenetic analysis. It can be applied to process very large sets of sequences; however, in such cases there is no guarantee about the quality of the multiple alignment and phylogenetic tree generated. In *QuickTree* we assume that neighborhoods are equivalent to phyloclusters. Thus, the only process performed is the determination of the neighborhoods of small size followed by their phylogenetic analysis. In each iteration, we first search a neighborhood of size 2.

Definition 6.3.3 *QuickTree neighborhood: A neighborhood of size 2 is a set $N = \{s_x, s_y\}$, where $s_x, s_y \in S^i$ and $\forall_{s_z \in S^i \setminus N}\ d(s_x, s_y) \leq d(s_x, s_z)\ \&\ d(s_x, s_y) \leq d(s_y, s_z)$.*

Next, we extend it by adding all sequences that satisfy the following condition. A sequence s is added to the neighborhood N if and only if

$$\forall_{s_x \in S^i \setminus (N \cup \{s\})}\ d(N, s) \leq d(s_x, s)\ \&\ d(N, s) \leq d(N, s_x)$$

where the distance between the neighborhood N and sequence s is defined as follows:

$$d(N, s) = \min_{s_i \in N} (d(s_i, s))$$

The *QuickTree* procedure allows finding disjoint groups of closely related sequences very rapidly. These groups are treated as clusters and processed to find optimal partial guide trees. In this way we strongly restrict the search space that is analyzed. Consequently, *QuickTree* is much faster when compared to *PhylTree* but also is more likely to produce less accurate results.

The last type of neighborhood attempts to combine properties of the *PhylTree* and *QuickTree* approaches.

Definition 6.3.4 *Dynamic-size neighborhood: A neighborhood $N \subset S^i$ of sequence s is a set of sequences, such that $s \in N$ and $\forall_{s_x \in N \setminus \{s\}} \forall_{s_y \in S^i \setminus N} d(s, s_x) \leq \epsilon \, \& \, d(s, s_x) \leq d(s, s_y)$ and $|N| \leq k$.*

A *dynamic-size* neighborhood is simply a subset of the neighborhood of size k such that elements more distant than some ϵ are excluded. In addition, please note that in the case when $\epsilon \to \infty$, Definition 6.3.4 is equivalent to the definition of *PhylTree* neighborhood variant. The ϵ parameter can be set in many different ways depending on the type of input data and the type of scoring function utilized to perform an alignment. This value can be changed dynamically upon execution or can be set for each taxon individually. For example, to exclude some sequences during the early stage of processing, we can set its $\epsilon = 0$.

6.3.2   PhylTree as a Generic Scheme

As previously mentioned, *PhylTree* has been designed to solve the GTA problem. In general, having a set of sequences S, we want to determine an optimal phylogenetic tree T and its corresponding alignment A.

This basic application of *PhylTree* is referred to as a *single execution*, which can be formalized as follows: *For a given tuple (S, F, a_F, k) find a relevant pair (T, A).* Here, S is the set of the sequences to be analyzed, T is a phylogenetic tree describing the relationship between sequences in the set S, and A is the corresponding multiple alignment. The three remaining input parameters (F, a_F, k) have special meanings: F characterizes the alignment method together with the scoring function, a_F is a set of scoring function arguments, and finally k is provided to allow precision of the alignment to be tuned. For instance, if we denote by F the *sum of pairs* score with a linear gap penalty, a_F represents the costs of gap opening and gap continuation, as well as the substitution matrix. In other words the pair (F, a_F) describes precisely the way in which we will evaluate a given alignment. The parameter k controls the trade-off between accuracy and the complexity of alignment computations. Please note that this is coherent with the definition of the parameter k given in the previous section.

The single execution case can be easily extended to cover the situation where family of sequences is updated periodically, as in the case of secondary biological databases: For a given (F, a_F, k) and $S_R = \{S_0, S_1, \ldots, S_l \mid S_i \subset S_j, i < j\}$ find $\{(T_0, A_0), (T_1, A_1), \ldots, (T_l, A_l)\}$.

Specifically, we treat an update of a sequence family as a series of single executions: S_0 describes an initial content of the family to be updated and $S_{ij} = S_j \backslash S_i, i < j$ is a set of sequences that we want to be add to the family S_i. The number of sequences that are added and stored in a single family varies greatly and can be as many as thousands of sequences, which of course strongly affects the time required to perform the database update.

In some cases a relation between sequence sets can be more general, such as $S_i \cap S_j \neq \emptyset$. This situation appears when only some of the sequences stored in the database are requested. Very often, when browsing a large family of sequences, we are interested in obtaining information about, for example, several primary species. In such a case, the set S_R may describe a stream of requests generated by users browsing the database.

The last possible scenario is to request alignments with a different level of precision. A series of single executions is performed for the same set of input sequences, which differs only by the parameter k: For a given (S, F, a_F) and $k_R = \{k_0, k_1, \ldots, k_l\}$, find $\{(T_0, A_0), (T_1, A_1), \ldots, (T_l, A_l)\}$.

Of course, it is possible that the parameter k will be changed along with a set of input sequences. Moreover, both sets S_R and k_R can be multisets corresponding to the situation when we assume that they describe dynamic requests generated by users accessing the database. This can be a common situation in a laboratory where different groups of scientists may work on the same family of sequences.

In the above formalization, we assume that all single executions share the same alignment procedure and the same scoring function arguments (F, a_F). This is a significant simplification, but it is reliable for many applications. In fact, we assume a single evolutionary model when analyzing a given family of sequences. This in turn has a very important consequence: If two single executions share some input data, then we may expect that they will require some common alignment computations. Consequently, we could apply caching to improve overall performance. We will explore this feature in the next section.

Now we closely consider the parameter k. In the case of the *PhylTree* method, k simply describes the size of the neighborhood that is used during the phylogenetic analysis step.

It is also possible to find a similar tuning parameter for many other packages. For instance, in the MUSCLE program we can change the number of iterations or the maximum time allotted to perform the refinement step of MUSCLE [19]. As with increasing k in *PhylTree*, higher numbers of iterations improve the final solution at the expense of increased processing time.

Another example is the 3D-Coffee package. Here, the factor that decides alignment precision and its time complexity is the size of the "library" composed of known protein structural information [17]. On this basis, classic sequence alignment information is extended with sequence-to-structure and structure-to-structure alignment information. Again, by increasing the number of utilized protein structures, we increase the quality of the final alignment and also the time required to compute it.

6.4 PARALLEL PHYLTREE AND ITS EXTENSIONS

On the basis of *PhylTree*, we created a parallel server that allows a series of *single executions*, submitted by one or several users, to be run. The server utilizes a decentralized cache of alignments to allow efficient execution of alignment computations, and it has been integrated with Grid portal supporting online job submission and results analysis.

6.4.1 Parallel PhylTree

To implement a parallel version of *PhylTree*, we chose a distributed master–worker architecture with a predefined master node. This choice was made on the basis of the following observations. (i) The first phase of *PhylTree* contains an independent task of $\Theta((n^2 - n)/2)$ pairwise alignments, which is easy to parallelize. Even so, parallelization should support heterogeneous architectures because, for example, two different pairwise alignments may require different computation times (depending on the lengths of the input sequences). Further, caching, which we will introduce later, may also affect the number of computations performed by a given worker. (ii) The second phase of *PhylTree* is an iterative process. During each iteration a set of neighborhoods is processed, and a single iteration is completed by the distance matrix update (single synchronization point). Because the number of neighborhoods per iteration is typically close to the number of available workers, assignment of neighborhoods to workers may result in large idle times even with master performing load balancing. (iii) A master–worker architecture provides an easy way to integrate supporting tools including web interfaces, and monitoring programs. In addition, it can be extended easily with decentralized caching system.

Figure 6.4 presents an overview of the *Parallel PhylTree* method. In the first step, the master node reads and preprocesses the input sequences that are subsequently broadcasted to all workers. Sequence data, which are necessary during *PhylTree* execution, require modest memory to be stored. Next, the distance matrix is generated. Because the time required to compute a single value of the distance matrix depends on the sequences' length, at this stage we use the *guided self-scheduling* (GSS) strategy to dynamically assign parts of the distance matrix to workers [68]. As a result, we can maintain reasonable load balancing for any sequence length and heterogeneity of processing units. Please note that this will be significant when we introduce cache support where the actual number of computations performed by a worker depends on cache efficiency. During distance matrix processing workers can analyze their performance by measuring the number of base pairs aligned per second. The master node can then rank all workers according to this statistic, which is useful for load balancing during neighborhoods processing.

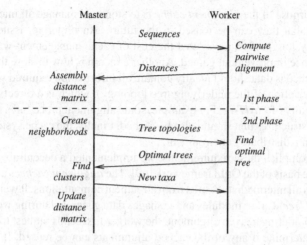

Figure 6.4. Generic scheme of parallel PhylTree.

Parallelization of the second stage is based on concurrent processing of tree topologies. The master determines neighborhood sets at the beginning of each iteration, and then starts to generate all possible trees for each neighborhood. Each worker receives its part of the generated topologies that are distributed on the basis of a modified GSS algorithm. At this stage the approximated efficiency of the processors is known, and it can be used to improve scheduling quality, especially to minimize the number of message exchanges between the master and its workers. Specifically, half of the total number of topologies is distributed proportionally on the basis of workers' priorities. Then, the other part is distributed using GSS. When a worker completes its part of the computations, it sends back the resulting best tree topology and the corresponding alignment to the master. To preserve locality of computations, the tree topologies are distributed such that topologies generated for the same neighborhood are assigned to the same processor when possible.

At the end of an iteration, the master computes the clusters and updates the distance matrix accordingly. This process is a synchronization point for the second phase. Finally, the master broadcasts newly created taxa to all workers, and new iteration begins.

Even though our parallel approach is rather simple, it explores effectively the inherent parallelism of *PhylTree* and, more importantly, allows further optimization by application of caching.

6.4.2   Cache of Alignments

In order to remove redundant computations, which are inherent for both series of *PhylTree* executions and overlapping neighborhoods during a *single execution*, we have designed and implemented an *alignment cache*.

The purpose of the *alignment cache* is to store and manage all intermediate alignments so that they can be reused in the future. An important issue is to design a caching system in such a way that the cost of cache management will not offset the performance improvement gained. Another concern is how to store the alignment results: Cachedas data should ideally contain all information required when it is reused (e.g., description of the underlying tree topology), which is a direct consequence of the generality of *PhylTree*. For example, some alignment procedures may use various auxiliary structures that should also be cached. Finally, the cache system must be able to work in a distributed environment.

To accomplish these requirements, we implemented a decentralized caching system on the basis of the CaLi framework [69]. The *alignment cache* is a two-tier system that stores all intermediate results from alignment computations. It works concurrently with *PhylTree* worker modules and manages data generated during worker execution. Before computing a given alignment, the worker first sends request to the cache manager to determine if any of the cached alignments can be reused. If not, the worker starts alignment.

Figure 6.5 shows the architecture of a single *alignment cache* node and how it interacts with a worker module of *Parallel PhylTree*. Each worker node runs one instance of the cache manager that is implemented using the CaLi library. The single cache manager is responsible for managing the local RAM memory as well as hard drive storage. It also handles communication with other cache managers.

The first level of the system (L1) is volatile, and its purpose is to keep the most frequently accessed alignments in the RAM memory. It is managed by each worker individually, but can be read by other workers remotely. Note that accessing RAM memory (even remote) is almost always significantly faster than accessing a hard drive. On the contrary, the capacity of RAM storage is limited, especially given that *PhylTree* session may consume a lot of memory by itself.

The second-level cache (L2) is persistent hard-drive storage. It is divided into two separate subsystems: one that keeps control of cached pairwise alignments and another that is responsible for multiple alignments. Because pairwise alignments are less costly to generate but are more frequently accessed, they require special

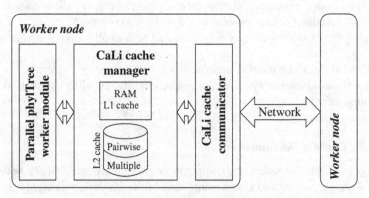

Figure 6.5. Overview of the alignment cache architecture.

treatment: In every single execution of the *PhylTree* pairwise alignment, cache is replicated among all workers. As a result, pairwise alignments that can be requested during a single execution are always served by a local cache manager. The multiple alignment cache is more complex. It is organized as a peer-to-peer cache with content addressing [70], where L2 cache storage of a single node can be accessed for both reading and writing by any other worker. The main reason to organize this caching system in a peer-to-peer manner is scalability: central cache server would not be able to provide the throughput required by *Parallel PhylTree*.

The document stored in the *alignment cache* is a sequence alignment with its score and all additional data. It is compressed using the zlib method and written to a binary file. Of course, all entries stored in the L1 cache are uncompressed to facilitate quick access. To describe a cache request uniquely, we use key generated as follows. First, identifiers of the sequences to be aligned and the guide tree topology are digested using some strong hashing function (e.g., SHA–256). Next, the resulting fingerprint is extended with the identifier of the alignment method F and its parameters a_F. In this way each worker can easily describe its request, and the cache manager can use such a key to label each cached object.

To obtain an alignment for a given set of sequences, a single worker generates an alignment identifier and checks the RAM memory cache (L1 cache). If it is not there, another cache level is checked using content addressing. Every key describing a multiple alignment cache record is mapped to one cache node, which becomes the *delegate node* for that particular key. If the requested multiple alignment is not stored locally, the request is forwarded to the delegate node cache. If a miss occurs, the worker computes the requested alignment and then inserts the result into the delegate node cache and into the local cache. On the contrary, if a remote hit occurs, the requested entry is inserted into local storage. In this way the multiple alignment cache is partially replicated, which in turn increases the number of local hits. Moreover, using a good hashing function further guarantees that cache entries are uniformly distributed. To detect possible collisions of keys, each time an alignment is loaded from the cache, identifiers of its component sequences are compared with identifiers of the input sequences.

The organization of the *alignment cache* described above has several important properties. First, replication of the pairwise alignment cache after the distance matrix computation (the first phase of the *PhylTree*) ensures that pairwise alignments are served locally. This eliminates remote pairwise alignment requests (and accompanying network traffic) and therefore improves scalability and cost savings ratio. Of course, we assume that all pairwise alignments generated by at least one single execution can be stored, which is easy to attain because pairwise alignment data usually are small in volume.

Second, the application of content addressing to perform request routing guarantees that if local miss occurs, only one remote request will be performed to check if data have been computed previously. Further, a partial replication of the cache allows the local hit ratio to be improved.

One important issue we have not yet considered is the maintenance of cache coherency between L1 and L2 caches. Because L1 cache is a working subset of the

L2 cache, we decided to use a weak coherency approach. In other words, every time a given entry is evicted from the L1 cache, appropriate information about this entry (e.g., number of references) is updated in the L2 cache. While this mechanism may cause the loss of some entries—that is, a document may be evicted from the L2 cache because of outdated information—it guarantees a high throughput of the cache manager.

The last and the most important element of the *alignment cache* is the choice of cache replacement policies. In the case of the L1 cache, we rely on the basic properties of the working set and use LFU policy that is sufficient to keep cache reloads. Management of the pairwise alignments cache is based on the observation that all alignments computed during the first phase of *PhylTree* will be reused some number of times in the second phase. This, together with an assumption that the cache is able to store all pairwise alignments generated in a single execution, is the rationale for using LRU policy.

The task of managing the multiple alignment cache is more complicated. This is because we must take into account two important factors: the cost of generating alignments and the location of the document in the peer-to-peer environment. Because there is no correlation between the size and the time of alignment, the replacement policy must be cost aware. The policy also must distinguish between documents that are local and replicated for a given cache node. Therefore, the multiple alignment cache is managed using a modified Greedy Dual Size (GDS) policy [71]. Our policy gives priority to the documents for which a given cache node is the delegate node. If two documents are equally useful with respect to the GDS policy and some level of precision Δu, which can be user defined or dynamically based on variance of the utility of cached documents, the document that is a local copy is removed first. As a result, the cache system may effectively utilize the entire storage of all participating nodes. This mechanism also allows the cache hit ratio to be increased because older copies are replaced by a more "useful" one.

The configuration of *alignment cache* described above is the basic one used in our parallel server. In addition, we have implemented mechanisms that allow for flexible modifications of caching strategies. For example, peer-to-peer storage can be replaced by a central caching system, or workers can run a decentralized cache but without peer-to-peer cooperation. This may be valuable in situations where worker nodes cannot handle caching or where the network interconnection is too slow for cache communication.

6.4.3   Simulated Annealing for Phylogenetic Analysis

The last extension that we have incorporated into our server is the well-known simulated annealing (SA) [72]. This option can be used to replace exact enumeration during *PhylTree* phylogenetic analysis [73]. Our solution is based on the observation that groups of closely related elements, which are recognized as phyloclusters, should be detectable even when suboptimal trees for analyzed neighborhoods are found. This is because partial trees that correspond to phyloclusters contribute strongly to the score of an optimal neighborhood tree, and similar observations have been reported, for example, in Reference 74. Given that SA is a stochastic search method, we have no guarantee on the quality of its solutions. As a result, SA is just an alternative and not a replacement for the exact search approach.

Simulated annealing is an easy-to-use metaheuristic approach. The search algorithm is analogous to physical process of annealing in which free energy of a solid is minimized. In general, there are four main components of the SA algorithm.

- A *configuration generator* that generates a candidate solution x_{i+1} on the basis of the current solution x_i.
- A *cooling scheme* that describes the procedure of decreasing the system temperature T. This parameter influences the probability of accepting backward steps (e.g., to escape local optima).
- A *metropolis step* in which the algorithm decides if a candidate solution x_{i+1} should be accepted. If x_{i+1} has a better cost than x_i, it is always accepted. If not, it is accepted with probability $P = e^{-(\Delta H/T)}$, where ΔH is the cost change.
- A *stopping criterion* that determines when to finish.

In *PhylTree* with SA, the desired solution is an optimal tree for a given neighborhood. The analysis of a neighborhood begins with a random guide tree. The configuration generator is implemented using a bijection between a rooted phylogenetic tree with k leaves and a perfect matching on $2k - 2$ points [75]. Here, a perfect matching on $2l$ points is defined as a partition of these points into l two-element subsets. Having such a perfect matching, we can render a corresponding phylogenetic tree as follows. First, we choose a matched pair that has both elements from the set $\{1, \ldots, k\}$, which is the set of leaves. If more than one such pair is available, we choose the one with the smallest element. Next, we assign to this pair a parent node that is the first available not-leaf label in the range $[k + 1, 2k - 2]$. From now on, this label is considered a leaf and we continue the process. Figure 6.6 shows an example of tree topology together with six configurations that can be generated based on it.

The matching provides a direct way to generate a random walk in the tree search space. To obtain a new topology, it is sufficient to make a transposition of two points in the matching. Obviously, such an operation can be easily implemented as a *configuration generator*.

Our implementation of simulated annealing also allows for different cooling schemes; for example, a simple model where temperature T is decreased with constant ratio $T_{i+1} = T_i - \Delta T$, or another one where $T_{i+1} = \alpha \cdot T_i, \alpha < 1$. Even so, our experiments suggest that there is no significant difference in the performance of various cooling schemes.

Also note that in our current implementation, SA computations can be stopped by the master to keep the workers' load balanced (see below), or, alternatively, they proceed for a fixed number of iterations, defined by the user. The initial temperature of the system is set on the basis of the sequence length and the substitution matrix, to guarantee proper values of the probability P in the *Metropolis step*. Finally, the number of iterations in the *Metropolis step* is equal to the size of neighborhood.

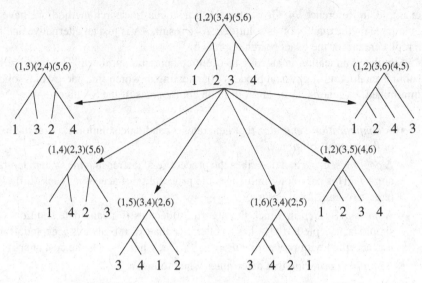

Figure 6.6. Example tree and its six neighbor topologies.

The search space decoded using a perfect matching can be described using a regular, undirected graph G with vertices of degree $k \cdot (k - 3) + 2$, where k is the size of the sequence neighborhood. Because graph G is regular, it is very likely that some vertices (i.e., search space points) will be visited more than once during a single search. Subsequent evaluations of the same vertex are handled by the *alignment cache*. Even so, they still generate some overhead when retrieved from cache storage. An unconstrained random walk in the graph G may also contain cycles. To address this concern, we have extended the SA algorithm with a naive tabu list. The list stores all points visited during a SA search, and each point is encoded using only a few bytes to achieve negligible memory consumption. When a candidate solution is generated, the tabu list is first checked and if the solution is not in this list, it is evaluated and inserted into it. On the contrary, if a given solution is found on the tabu list, it is rejected by SA and another solution is generated. In the case where there are no acceptable points to move to, the temperature parameter of our SA is restored to the value from the previous step of SA, and search is restarted from some random feasible solution. In this way we avoid possible deadlocks, as well as we improve the efficiency of the search algorithm. Please note that, even though our approach substantially differs from the typical tabu search algorithm [76] (especially, we do not restrict moves, but points, and we do not use an aspiration level mechanism), it performs similarly. This is because each point in our search space can be reached in several ways, and by restricting a point we do not restrict the reachability of its neighborhood.

To integrate our SA engine with the parallel version of *PhylTree*, we reimplemented the phylogenetic analysis step such that when SA is applied neighborhoods and not tree topologies are analyzed simultaneously.

In a single iteration of the second phase, each worker receives one neighborhood to analyze. If the number of neighborhoods to process is less than the number of available workers, then idle nodes are assigned to perform redundant neighborhood analysis. Note that this could result in some neighborhoods being processed by more than one worker. The assignment of neighborhoods to workers is performed in round-robin fashion. The obvious drawback of this approach is that load balancing is hard to maintain. To avoid load imbalance, redundant analysis of neighborhoods can be interrupted at any moment, and phylogenetic analysis is ended once all unique input neighborhoods have been processed. Resulting partial guide trees are the best trees found.

The above algorithm is very coarse grained. As a result, it may be more profitable to use exact enumeration search when the number of available processors is greater than the number of neighborhoods to process. Let P be the number of available workers. In the exact search approach, the expected time of completion of a single iteration can be expressed as follows:

$$T_e = \left\lceil \frac{n \cdot B_r(k)}{P} \right\rceil \cdot t_{avg}$$

where n is the number of input sequences in a given iteration and t_{avg} is the average time required to analyze a single tree. In the case of SA, we can assume that the complexity of the search method is $O(k^3)$; thus, the expected time of a single iteration completion is

$$T_{sa} = \left\lceil \frac{n}{P} \right\rceil \cdot k^3 \cdot t_{avg}$$

Using the above expressions, we have implemented a mechanism that dynamically changes the search strategy. In every iteration the master node verifies if $T_{sa} < T_e$. If the inequality is satisfied, the SA approach is utilized, otherwise, workers perform exact search. Figure 6.7 summarizes our implementation of *PhylTree* with SA.

```
Compute distance matrix in parallel;
repeat
    Determine neighborhoods;
    if T_sa < T_e then
        Distribute neighborhoods;
        Analyze neighborhoods using SA;
    else
        Distribute trees;
        Evaluate all trees;
    Find phyloclusters;
    Update distance matrix;
until All sequences clustered;
```

Figure 6.7. Design of *Parallel PhylTree* with simulated annealing.

6.5 EXPERIMENTAL RESULTS

To validate our server, we have performed a set of different experiments. Their detailed presentation can be found in References 51,73, and 77, and in this section we present only some of them.

The experiments were conducted on two different parallel systems: (i) *icluster2*, which consists of Itanium2 900 MHz nodes. Each node is equipped with 3GB of RAM memory, and runs Linux. Each node provides SCSI hard drive storage managed by a Ext3 file system. The cluster is connected by a Gbit-Ethernet network. (ii) *clusterix*, which consists of Itanium2 1300-MHz nodes. Each node is equipped with 4 GB of RAM memory and runs Linux. The system has been prepared to run *alignment cache*; therefore, each node provides SCSI hard-drive storage managed by a ReiserFS file system, which allows many small files to be handled efficiently. Similar to the *icluster2* system, *clusterix* is connected by a Gbit-Ethernet network.

In all experiments we utilized the mpich2-1.0.2, a well-known and efficient implementation of the MPI standard. All applications were compiled with the GCC set of compilers.

6.5.1 Database Update

The purpose of the first experiment was to verify the efficiency of our server when a family of sequences was periodically extended. In this case, a new alignment and corresponding phylogenetic tree are recomputed whenever new sequences are added to the family. To remove redundant computations, the *alignment cache* was used.

We performed experiment using seven nodes of the *clusterix* system. A single node of the *alignment cache* could use 32 MB of storage for a pairwise alignment of L2 cache, and 128 MB for a multiple alignment cache. The L1 cache was disabled. The cache capacity was limited, which allowed us to analyze performance of the cache replacement policy.

In the first run we used a set of $|S_0| = 32$ bacterial small subunit ribosomal RNA sequences (SSU rRNA) obtained from the European SSU rRNA database [78] that were longer than 1 Kbp (average length 1300 bp). Then, we doubled the number of sequences in each run: $S_i = S_{i-1} \cup S_x$, where S_x, $|S_x| = |S_{i-1}|$, is a group of new input sequences that should be added to the family S_{i-1}. In every execution we used $k = 5$ as a level of precision, and Sankoff's parsimony as a phylogeny and alignment criterion. Results of this experiment are presented in Table 6.1 and Fig. 6.8.

As expected, caching noticeably improved the performance of the server. Table 6.1 shows that the hit ratio Hr and cost hit ratio Cr (defined as the cost of alignments found in the cache divided by the total cost of alignments requested during the execution, where cost of alignment is the time required to compute it) increase at every execution. The cost-saving ratio Cs is dominated by the cost hit ratio of the multiple alignment cache. This confirms our claim that it is more profitable to cache multiple alignments. The cost savings generated by the pairwise alignment cache is less than we expected, but still significant. The cache hit ratio for the multiple sequence alignment cache stabilizes around 35% when 256 sequences are analyzed. At this point, the cache is

Table 6.1   Request Processing in the Database Update Experiment

$\|S\|$	$T_p[s]$	$T_c[s]$	Hr_p	Hr_m	Cr_p	Cr_m	C_s	$E\frac{T_p}{T_c}$
32	6747	3430	0.87	0.28	0.099	0.39	0.49	1.96
64	18182	9123	0.82	0.29	0.079	0.41	0.49	1.99
128	55300	24796	0.74	0.34	0.066	0.48	0.55	2.23
256	156831	63631	0.63	0.34	0.067	0.53	0.59	2.46
512	438539	144090	0.43	0.45	0.048	0.63	0.67	3.04

Note: T_p is the execution time for the parallel server and T_c is the execution time for the parallel server with cache support. Hr_p and Hr_m are the hit ratio for the pairwise and multiple alignment cache, respectively. Cr_p and Cr_m describe the cost hit ratio for the pairwise and multiple alignment cache, respectively, and $Cs = 1 - (T_c/T_p)$ is the cost-saving ratio for the whole cache system.

saturated and the cache replacement policy is used. Inspite of this, the cost saving ratio, and next cache hit ratio, increases. This is a result of the cost-aware replacement policy used. In fact, our trace-driven simulations have shown that GDS attains the highest hit ratio and cost-saving ratio as compared to other strategies such as, LRU, LFU, or other size-based policies.

6.5.2   Performance and Scalability Assessment

In many cases we may be interested in running the server on a larger number of machines. In addition, we may want to utilize *Parallel PhylTree* without cache support as a regular multiple sequence alignment tool. This may happen when, for example, no persistent cache storage is available and the *alignment cache* cannot be deployed.

To verify scalability of the *alignment cache*, we generated three data sets consisting of 32, 64, and 128 SSU rRNA sequences. Next, we processed each data set using our parallel server working with and without the *alignment cache*. The server has been run on 8 up to 64 nodes of the *icluster2* cluster. In the case when the *alignment cache* was

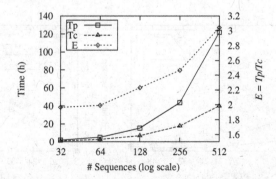

Figure 6.8. Request processing in the database update experiment.

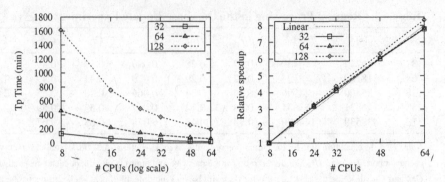

Figure 6.9. Parallel PT without cache support: processing time and speedup.

enabled, it could use 64 MB for pairwise alignment storage and 256 MB for multiple alignment storage. In these experiments, however, the L2 cache capacity was never exceeded. The L1 cache could occupy 64 MB of RAM memory. The average length of the analyzed sequences was 1100 bp. In every execution we have used $k = 5$ as a level of precision and used Sankoff's parsimony as a phylogeny and alignment criterion. Results of the experiment are presented in Figs. 6.9–6.11.

The above experiment shows that the *Parallel PhylTree* method scales well when working without cache support. The results depicted in Fig. 6.9 suggest that even for modestly sized data sets and large number of processing units, a linear speedup can be attained, which is not surprising given the properties of *PhylTree* described in previous sections. Specifically, inherent parallelism and the dynamic scheduling of computations allow for efficient utilization of CPUs, resulting in perfect speedups.

Slightly different results were observed when the *alignment cache* was enabled. Network traffic generated by our peer-to-peer cache system increased as a square function of the number of cache nodes. Consequently, we could expect that cache response time will increase with the number of cache nodes. Figure 6.10 shows that our server scales very well until 48 nodes. Then, cache performance decreases and

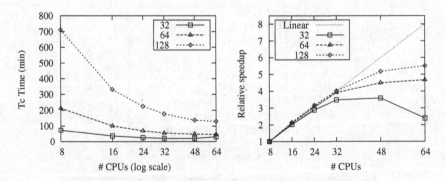

Figure 6.10. Parallel PT with cache support: processing time and speedup.

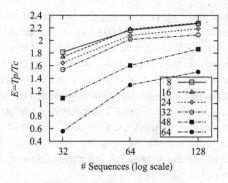

Figure 6.11. Alignment cache efficiency.

small data set runs become worse than the server without cache support. This can be explained by the fact that the cache system generates a large number of small messages at this point that cannot be efficiently handled by the TCP/IP protocol. Moreover, a Gbit-Ethernet protocol and the Gbit-Ethernet hardware utilized in the experiment are not able to provide satisfying scalability either. One of the possible solutions to this problem could be the application of different networks than interconnection networks such as Myrinet. On the contrary, the current MPI implementation provided by the Myrinet vendor does not support multithreading required by the CaLi library. Another source of performance degradation may be the very inefficient file system provided by the *icluster2*. The Ext3 FS is not able to handle efficiently small files, and I/O overheads decrease cache cost-saving ratio.

Despite scalability problems, the *alignment cache* increases performance of the server by factor of 2 when 32 cache nodes are used (Fig. 6.11).

In the last experiment we measured efficiency of the *Parallel PhylTree* when analyzing large data sets. We created several groups of 32–1024 bacterial 16S rRNA sequences obtained from the RDPII database [79]. The average length of the selected genes was 1600 bp. The *QuickTree* variant of the *PhylTree* was run on the *icluster2* system using 8 up to 32 nodes. Results of the experiment are presented in Fig. 6.12.

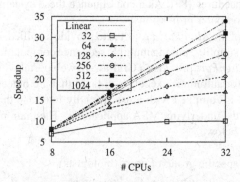

Figure 6.12. Parallel PT (*QuickTree variant*) speedup.

Parallelization of the *PhylTree* package was focused on the optimization of the phylogenetic analysis step when *PhylTree* or a similar neighborhood variant was used. Even so, *Parallel PhylTree* worked fine on very large data sets analyzed using the *QuickTree* variant. Figure 6.12 shows that for large enough data sets, *Parallel PhylTree* preserves a linear speedup. In the case of the *QuickTree* variant, the number of trees analyzed during a single iteration depended only on the number of input sequences. As a result, the number of computations performed for small data sets is lower than the number of workers. Obviously, this influences the efficiency of the system. Finally, the superlinear speedup observed for large numbers of input sequences is a result of the sequential implementation of *PhylTree* being slightly inferior to the parallel version.

6.6   ALIGNPORT—A GRID ENVIRONMENT FOR MSA

Today, web-oriented access to resources is a common standard. There is a wide range of available portals and services devoted to bioinformatics and computational biology. Most of these available solutions, however, do not provide direct and full support for Grid systems. To simplify the use of various parallel MSA programs, we have developed the *AlignPort* Grid portal [80] that allows using parallel server and other MSA packages (e.g., parallel T-Coffee [81]) from the Web browser level.

6.6.1   The AlignPort Portal Overview

Grids have become a popular way of organizing, sharing, and using geographically distributed resources. The way Grids are built may vary from spontaneous collaborations of thousands of workstations (e.g., the Folding@Home project [82]) to systematically organized infrastructures with a middle layer that provides access to different Grid components such as storage, processors, network, and others [83]. In the first case, participants of the Grid are usually provided with a simple-in-use client software that connects them to the Grid [84]. This is not so in the second case. Here, the user must be familiar with the basic tools provided by the specific middle layer including, for instance, authorization and authentication mechanisms, or job and data management procedures [83]. As a consequence these systems are seldom used by any other than computer professionals.

The purpose of the *AlignPort* project is to provide a unified, user-oriented environment that would simplify running multiple sequence computations in large distributed environments. *AlignPort* provides a Grid-aware web portal with a set of services that are responsible for automatic execution of tasks that are otherwise run manually. At the same time it is equipped with a user-friendly interface that maintains complete functionality of the underlying MSA applications. The main properties of *AlignPort* are summarized below:

- It targets a specific group of users (biologists).
- It offers access to distributed Grid resources.

Figure 6.13. Web browser window of the parallel PhyloBuilder task wizard.

- It fulfills all security requirements such as *authorization*, *authentication*, and *secure data transfer*.
- It offers wide functionality including MSA job creation and submission, monitoring of jobs' states, and online browsing of results.
- It provides a very intuitive graphical user interface.

In general, the *AlignPort* consists of three main subsystems. *Application Wizard* is responsible for choosing the MSA application, the configuration of its parameters, and the verification and upload of input data (see Fig. 6.13). *Results Manager* takes care of job monitoring; the user can inspect the state of all submitted jobs in this subsystem, and once the job is complete a user can download and analyze its results. The last subsystem is *Configuration Manager*. This system is used whenever a user needs to change the low-level configuration of the portal for reasons such as changing the type of compiler utilized to build an MSA application on the remote resource. In most cases, however, this functionality will not be used.

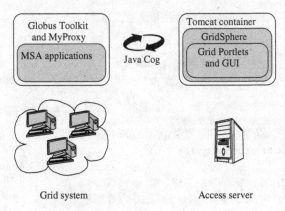

Figure 6.14. General scheme of the portal architecture.

6.6.2 Utilized Technologies

The core components of *AlignPort* are implemented on the basis of the *GridSphere* and *Grid Portlets* frameworks and the *Globus Toolkit* (GT). In Fig. 6.14, a general scheme of the portal is presented.

The main user interface is based on the *GridSphere* framework. This technology provides a portlet implementation, a portlet container, and a collection of core services and portlets, which are fully compliant with *Java Specification Request 168* standard [85]. Thanks to its XML-based layout configuration, *GridSphere* is very flexible and customizable. *Grid Portlets* provide a set of services and components responsible for communication with a Grid environment. A separate component is available for each MSA application, providing a simple way to configure specific options of the application as illustrated in Fig. 6.13. The main idea is to represent complete functionality of the application in an accessible way. Although our interface is currently clear and easy to use, it can be further improved, for example, by using ideas proposed in the *BioUse* project [86].

The Grid-related part of the *AlignPort* portal relies on the *Globus Toolkit* software, which is commonly used across the variety of Grid systems available. It provides robust and stable services that *de facto* have become standard in Grid environments. As mentioned above, it is crucial to ensure secure access to the Grid resources. Here, security covers a wide range of issues, such as secure data transfer, authorization of users, and/or control over access to particular resources. To address these concerns, GT software introduces the *grid security infrastructure* (GSI) concept. It provides a set of protocols, unifying the process of identification of system credentials with basic support for delegation and policy distribution [87]. In the case of *AlignPort*, we use two *X.509* credentials that take part in the process of authorisation: There is a *user credential* (password protected) used to operate on Grid resources on behalf of the user and a *host credential* used to obtain user credentials from the online *MyProxy* credential repository. *MyProxy* is a secure storage service for hosting long-term credentials of users as well as delegating short-term credentials (so-called proxy credentials) to grant authenticated operations on Grid resources [88]. It is also important to mention the *Grid Resource and Allocation Manager* or GRAM. This tool is responsible for processing and managing user jobs and also monitoring and allocating resources. In addition, a user can write specifications of his/her job in *Resource Specification Language* (RSL), which are processed by the GRAM as a part of a job request. Because RSL is scheduler-independent, scripts generated by *AlignPort* can be executed on any Grid managed by GT. Finally, transfer of files is driven by the *GridFTP* service, which is responsible for secure and efficient data operations [89].

One of the assumptions of the *AlignPort* project was to help users with portal and their Grid accounts configuration. As a result, we have created a set of scripts responsible for the configuration of a user's account (key creation, compiler configuration, cache deployment, etc.) and MSA applications, including setup and execution. Consequently, a user can simply choose an option from the portal interface (e.g., compiler setup), then the compiler archive is transferred to the Grid account prior to the execution of the appropriate script. This approach limits a user's contact with the console to one activity: delegating credentials to the online repository in the very beginning of the session. This requirement is a limitation of *MyProxy*.

6.7 CONCLUSION

Parallel and distributed computing, especially Grid environments, provide several advantages to the computational biology community. First of all, larger problem instances can be solved with a better precision. At the same time, well-designed Grid interfaces provide an easy and convenient way to access software and hardware that is otherwise reserved for small groups of specialists. Current MSA and phylogeny software, especially presented in this chapter, the *Parallel PhyloBuilder Server* and the *AlignPort* portal are good examples of how computational biology can benefit from high-performance computing.

The *AlignPort* portal as well as the software and hardware it provides can be accessed at the following URL: https://hal.icis.pcz.pl/PhyloServer/.

ACKNOWLEDGMENTS

We would like to express gratitude to our collaborators who greatly contributed to this work. We thank Gilles Parmentier who implemented the first version of the *PhylTree* method and to Piotr Dziubecki who designed and developed the *AlignPort* interface. We are grateful to Laboratory ID–IMAG, France and Institute of Computer Science of Czestochowa University of Technology, Poland, for access to their HPC facilities.

REFERENCES

1. C. Notredame, Recent progress in multiple sequence alignment: A survey, *Pharmacogenomics* **3**(1), 131–144, 2002.

2. L. Duret, D. Mouchiroud, M. Gouy, HOVERGEN, a database of homologous vertebrate genes, *Nucleic Acids Research* **22**, 2360–2365, 1994.

3. A. Krogh et al., Hidden Markov models in computational biology: Applications to protein modeling *Journal of Molecular Biology* **235**(5), 1501–1531, 1994.

4. D. Brown, K. Sjolander, Functional classification using phylogenomic inference, *PLoS Computers in Biology* **2**(6), e77, 2006.

5. J. Felsenstein, *Inferring Phylogenies*, Sinauer Association, Sunderland, MA, 2004.

6. D.A. Morrison, J.T. Ellis, Effects of nucleotide sequence alignment on phylogeny estimation: A case study of 18S rDNAs of Apicomplexa, *Molecular Biology and Evolution* **14**(4), 428–441, 1997.

7. B. Chor, T. Tuller, Maximum likelihood of evolutionary trees: Hardness and approximation, *Bioinformatics* (Suppl. 1), i97–i106, 2005.

8. W.H.E. Day, D.S. Johnson, D. Sankoff, The computational complexity of inferring rooted phylogenies by parsimony, *Mathematical Biosciences* **81**, 33–42, 1986.

9. I. Elias, Settling the intractability of multiple alignment, in: *Proceedings of ISAAC 2003 of LNCS*, Vol. 2906, pp. 352–363, 2003.

10. L. Wang, T. Jiang, On the complexity of multiple sequence alignment, *Journal of Computational Biology* **1**(4), 337–348, 1994.

11. T. Jiang, E.L. Lawler, L. Wang, Aligning sequences via an evolutionary tree: complexity and approximation, in: *Proceedings of 26th ACM Symposium on Theory of Computing*, pp. 760–769, 1994.

12. S.F. Altschul, D.J. Lipman, Trees, stars and multiple biological sequence alignment, *SIAM Journal on Applied Mathmatics* **49**, 197–209, 1989.

13. D. Sankoff, Minimal mutation trees of sequences, *SIAM Journal on Applied Mathematics* **28**, 35–42, 1975.

14. K. Katoh et al., MAFFT version 5: Improvement in accuracy of multiple sequence alignment, *Nucleic Acids Research* **33**(2), 511–518, 2005.

15. A.R. Subramanian et al., DIALIGN–T: An improved algorithm for segment–based multiple sequence alignment, *BMC Bioinformatics* **6**(66), 2005.

16. C. Notredame, D.G. Higgins, J. Heringa, T–Coffee: A novel method for fast and accurate multiple sequence alignment, *Journal of Molecular Biology* **302**(1), 205–217, 2000.

17. O. O'Sullivan et al., 3DCoffee: Combining protein sequences and structures within multiple sequence alignments, *Journal of Molecular Biology* **340**(2), 385–395, 2004.

18. C.B. Do et al., ProbCons: Probabilistic consistency–based multiple sequence alignment, *Genome Research* **15**(2), 330–340, 2005.

19. R.C. Edgar, MUSCLE: Multiple sequence alignment with high accuracy and high throughput, *Nucleic Acids Research* **32**(5), 1792–1797, 2004.

20. S.R. Eddy, Multiple alignment using hidden Markov models, in: *Proceedings of ISMB 1995*, pp. 114–120, 1995.

21. O. Gotoh, S. Yamada, T. Yada, *Handbook of Computational Molecular Biology, Multiple Sequence Alignment*, Chapman & Hall, New York, 2005.

22. S.B. Needleman, C.D. Wunsch, A general method applicable to the search for similarities in the amino acid sequence of two proteins, *Journal of Molecular Biology* **48**(3), 443–453, 1970.

23. H. Carrillo, D.J. Lipman, The multiple sequence alignment problem in biology, *SIAM Journal on Applied Mathmatics* **48**, 1073–1082, 1988.

24. P. Hogeweg, B. Hesper, The alignment of sets of sequences and the construction of phylogenetic trees: An integrated method, *Journal of Molecular Biology* **20**(2), 175–186, 1984.

25. R. Chenna et al., Multiple sequence alignment with the Clustal series of programs, *Nucleic Acids Research* **31**(13), 3497–3500, 2003.

26. C. Notredame, D.G. Higgins, SAGA: Sequence alignment by genetic algorithm, *Nucleic Acids Research* **24**(8), 1515–1524, 1996.

27. I.M. Wallace, O. O'Sullivan, D.G. Higgins, Evaluation of iterative alignment algorithms for multiple alignment, *Bioinformatics* **21**(8), 1408–1414, 2005.

28. D.L. Swofford et al., Phylogenetic inference, in: *Molecular Systematics*, Sinauer Association, Sunderland, MA, 1996.

29. M. Holder, P.O. Lewis, Phylogeny estimation: traditional and Bayesian approaches, *Nature Review of Genetics* **4**(4), 275–284, 2003.

30. B.M. Moret et al., A new implementation and detailed study of breakpoint analysis, *Proceedings 6th Pacific Symposium on Biocomputing*, pp. 583–594, 2001.

31. R.R. Sokal, C.D. Michener, A statistical method for evaluating systematic relationships, *University of Kansas Science Bulletin*, **38**, 1409–1438, 1958.

32. N. Saitou, M. Nei, The neighbor–joining method: a new method for reconstructing phylogenetic trees, *Molecular Biology and Evolution* **4**(4), 406–425, 1987.

33. O. Gascuel, BioNJ: An improved version of the NJ algorithm based on a simple model of sequence data, *Molecular Biology and Evolution* **14**(7), 685–695, 1997.

34. W.J. Bruno, N.D. Socci, A.L. Halpern, Weighted neighbor joining: likelihood–based approach to distance-based phylogeny reconstruction, *Molecular Biology and Evolution* **17**(1), 189–197, 2000.

35. D.L. Swofford, PAUP*. *Phylogenetic Analysis Using Parsimony (*and Other Methods)*, Sinauer Association, Sunderland, MA, 2003.

36. J. Felsenstein, PHYLIP (phylogeny inference package) 2006. http://evolution.genetics. washington. edu/phylip.html (last visited).

37. G.J. Olsen et al., fastDNAml: A tool for construction of phylogenetic trees of DNA sequences using maximum likelihood, *Computer Application in the Biosciences*, **10**, 41–48, 1994.

38. A. Stamatakis, RAxML-VI-HPC: Maximum likelihood–based phylogenetic analyses with thousands of taxa and mixed models, *Bioinformatics* **22**, 2688–2690, Nov 2006.

39. F. Ronquist, J. P. Huelsenbeck, MrBayes 3: Bayesian phylogenetic inference under mixed models, *Bioinformatics* **19**(12), 1572–1574, 2003.

40. S. Guindon, O. Gascuel, A simple, fast, and accurate algorithm to estimate large phylogenies by maximum likelihood, *Systematic Biology* **52**(5), 696–704, 2003.

41. D.A. Bader, M. Yan, High-performance algorithms for phylogeny reconstruction with maximum parsimony, in: *Handbook of Computational Molecular Biology*, Chapman & Hall, New York, 2005.

42. D. Barker, LVB: Parsimony and simulated annealing in the search for phylogenetic trees, *Bioinformatics* **20**(2), 274–275, 2004.

43. M.J. Brauer et al., Genetic algorithms and parallel processing in maximum–likelihood phylogeny inference, *Molecular Biology and Evolution* **19**(10), 1717–1726, 2002.

44. F. Hwang, D. Richards, P. Winter, *The Steiner Tree Problem, Annals of Discrete Mathematics*, Vol. 53, North–Holland, Amsterdam, 1992.

45. D. Gusfield, Efficient methods for multiple sequence alignment with guaranteed error bounds, *Bulletin of Mathematical Biology*, **55**(1), 141–154, 1993.

46. J. Hein, A new method that simultaneously aligns and reconstructs ancestral sequences for any number of homologous sequences, when the phylogeny is given, *Molecular Biology and Evolution* **6**(6), 649–668, 1989.

47. J. Hein, A tree reconstruction method that is economical in the number of pairwise comparisons used, *Molecular Biology and Evolution* **6**(6), 669–684, 1989.

48. B. Schwikowski, M. Vingron, The deferred path heuristic for the generalized tree alignment problem, *Journal of Computational Biology*, **4**(3), 415–431, 1997.

49. R.C. Edgar, K. Sjolander, SATCHMO: Sequence alignment and tree construction using hidden Markov models, *Bioinformatics*, **19**(11), 1404–1411, 2003.

50. R. Fleissner, D. Metzler, A. von Haeseler, Simultaneous statistical multiple alignment and phylogeny reconstruction, *Systematic Biology* **54**(4), 548–561, 2005.

51. G. Parmentier, D. Trystram, J. Zola, Large scale multiple sequence alignment with simultaneous phylogeny inference, *Journal of Parallel Distributed Computing*, **66**(12), 1534–1545, 2006.

52. J.L. Thorne, H. Kishino, J. Felsenstein, Inching toward reality: An improved likelihood model of sequence evolution, *Journal of Molecular Evolution*, **34**(1), 3–16, 1992.

53. G.A. Lunter et al., An efficient algorithm for statistical multiple alignment on arbitrary phylogenetic trees, *Journal of Computational Biology* **10**(6), 869–889, 2003.

54. A.Y. Zomaya, (Ed.), *Parallel Computing for Bioinformatics and Computational Biology*, John Wiley & Sons Hoboken, NJ, 2006.

55. X. Deng et al., Parallel implementation and performance characterization of MUSCLE, in: *Proceedings of IPDPS 2006*.

56. D. Mikhailov, H. Cofer, R. Gomperts, Performance optimization of ClustalW: Parallel ClustalW, HT Clustal, and MULTICLUSTAL, 2005 (last visited).

57. K.B. Li, ClustalW–MPI: ClustalW analysis using distributed and parallel computing, *Bioinformatics* **19**(12), 1585–1586, 2003.

58. J. Luo et al., Parallel multiple sequence alignment with dynamic scheduling, in: *Proceedings of ITCC*, 2005, pp. 8–13.

59. N.T. Karonis, B. Toonen, I. Foster, MPICH–G2: A grid–enabled implementation of the message passing interface, *Journal of Parallel Distributed Computing* **63**(5), 2003.

60. U. Catalyurek et al., A component–based implementation of multiple sequence alignment, in: *Proceedings of the 2003 ACM Symposium on Applied Computing*, 2003, pp. 122–126.

61. C.A. Stewart et al., Parallel implementation and performance of fastDNAml—a program for maximum likelihood phylogenetic inference, in: *Proceedings of SC*, 2001, pp. 32–42.

62. PACX–MPI, 2006. http://www.hlrs.de/organization/amt/projects/pacx-mpi/ (last visited).

63. C.A. Stewart et al., A global grid for analysis of arthropod evolution, in: *Proceedings of GRID*, 2004, pp. 328–337.

64. A. Stamatakis, Distributed and Parallel Algorithms and Systems for Inference of Huge Phylogenetic Trees Based on the Maximum Likelihood Method, PhD thesis, Technische Universitat, Munchen, Germany, 2004.

65. F. Guinand, G. Parmentier, D. Trystram. Integration of multiple alignment and phylogeny reconstruction, in: *Proceedings of ECCB 2002*, p. 78.

66. M. Kimura, *The Neutral Theory of Molecular Evolution*, Cambridge University Press, New York, 1983.

67. S. Vinga, J. Almeida, Alignment–free sequence comparison—A review, *Bioinformatics* **19**(4), 513–523, 2003.

68. C.D. Polychronopoulos, D.J. Kuck, Guided self–scheduling: A practical scheduling scheme for parallel supercomputers, *IEEE Transaction on Computers*, **36**(12), 1425–1439, 1997.

69. J. Zola, CaLi—Caching library, 2006. http://icis.pcz.pl/~zola/CaLi/, 2006 (last visited).

70. S. Ratnasamy et al., A scalable content–addressable network, in: *Proceedings of SIGCOMM 2001*, pp. 161–172.

71. S. Jin, A. Bestavros, GreedyDual* web caching algorithm, *International Journal of Computer Communications* **24**(2), 174–183, 2001.

72. S. Kirkpatrick, C.D. Gelatt, M.P. Vecchi, Optimization by simulated annealing, *Science* **220**, 671–680, 1983.

73. J. Zola et al., Parallel multiple sequence alignment with local phylogeny search by simulated annealing, in: *Proceedings of HiCOMB*, 2006.

74. T.L. Williams et al., The relationship between maximum parsimony scores and phylogenetic tree topologies, Technical Report TR–CS–2004–04, University of New Mexico, 2004.

75. P. Diaconis, S.P. Holmes, Random walk on trees and matchings, *Electronic Journal of Probability* **7**, 1–17, 2002.

76. F. Glover, Tabu search: A tutorial, *Interfaces* **20**(4), 74–94, 1990.

77. D. Trystram, J. Zola, Parallel multiple sequence alignment with decentralized cache support, in: *Proceedings of Euro-Par 2005 of LNCS*, Vol. 3648, pp. 1217–1226, 2005.

78. J. Wuyts et al., The European database of small subunit ribosomal RNA, *Nucleic Acids Research* **30**, 183–185, 2002.

79. J.R. Cole et al., The ribosomal database project (RDP–II): Previewing a new autoaligner that allows regular updates and the new prokaryotic taxonomy, *Nucleic Acids Research* **31**(1), 442–443, 2003.

80. P. Dziubecki, J. Zola, Grid portal for multiple sequence alignment, *Computing, Multimedia and Intelligent Techniques*, 2006, in press.

81. J. Zola, X. Yang, A. Rospondek, S. Alura, Parallel T-coffee: a parallel multiple sequence aligner, in: *Proceedings of the ISCA 20th International Conference on Parallel and Distributed Systems*, Las Vegas, pp. 248–253, 2007.

82. Folding@Home, 2006. http://folding.stanford.edu/ (last visited).

83. F. Berman, G. Fox, A.J.G. Hey (Eds.), *Grid Computing: Making the Global Infrastructure a Reality*, John Wiley & Sons, New York, 2003.

84. D.P. Anderson, G. Fedak, The computational and storage potential of volunteer computing, in: *Proceedings of IEEE/ACM International Symposium on Cluster Computing and the Grid*, 2006.

85. GridSphere project, 2006. http://www.gridsphere.org/ (last visited).

86. H. Javahery, A. Seffah, T. Radhakrishnan, Beyond power: Making bioinformatics tools user–centered, *Communication of the ACM*, **47**(11), 58–63, 2004.

87. F. Siebenlist, V. Welch, Grid security: The globus perspective, in: *Proceedings of GlobusWORLD 2005*.

88. J. Novotny, S. Tuecke, V. Welch, An online credential repository for the grid: MyProxy, in: *Proceedings of HPDC 2001*.

89. I. Foster, Globus toolkit version 4: Software for service–oriented systems, in: *Proceedings of IFIP 2005*, Vol. 3779 of LNCS, pp. 2–13, 2005.

7

DATA SYNDICATION TECHNIQUES FOR BIOINFORMATICS APPLICATIONS

Chen Wang, Albert Y. Zomaya, and Bing Bing Zhou

7.1 INTRODUCTION

In recent years, the vast amount of data produced from computers and other instruments challenge computer science and require novel algorithms to process and share them effectively. Web pages, Web logs (blogs), medical images, and scientific data are few examples of such types of data. In this chapter, we discuss the data syndication techniques for bioinformatics data.

The availability of molecular sequences is accelerated by high-throughput genome sequencing instruments. These sequences, particularly genome sequences are changing the practices in experimental biology and are unifying the biology in a world formed by genes and proteins. Knowledge has been accumulated around sequences rapidly. There is a growing need to integrate the data that represent this knowledge. However, data integration is a difficult problem. The main difficulties are as follows:

(1) The data sets produced from separate subfields in biology are heterogeneous and dynamic. Integration of heterogeneous and dynamic data challenges existing computer systems and requires new computational models and algorithms.

(2) The data sets are created by autonomous and heterogeneous sources, and distributed in nature as the research community grows. Data integration in a distributed environment presents a challenge to existing computing systems.

A typical workflow in bioinformatics involves at least data search and analysis stages. Some analysis results will turn into the data being searched by other analysis. In current

Grid Computing for Bioinformatics and Computational Biology. Edited by E.-G. Talbi and A.Y. Zomaya.
Copyright © 2008 John Wiley & Sons, Inc.

practice, data are downloaded from remote data sources or repositories, while analysis is done using local computer resources. Analysis results are normally stored locally. There are few data repositories such as *TreeBase* [1] that collect analysis results for a few subfields. In general, these stages are separately done due to the lack of effective data syndication mechanism that can glue data with diverse structures in a distributed environment together.

In this chapter, we review the technologies that can be used for handling heterogeneous bioinformatics data. We first review the efforts on regulating vocabularies and resource descriptions; second, we discuss how data with different structures are handled in a data integration system; third, we discuss technologies used for syndicating data in a distributed environment. Finally, we give an example to illustrate how the data syndication technologies can be used to provide genome sequence similarity search service on distributed genome databases.

7.2   CONTROLLED VOCABULARIES

In order to integrate a variety of biological data sets and the knowledge built around these data sets, defining standard vocabularies to describe data sets will greatly facilitate the communication between data producers and data consumers. In this section, we first use Gene Ontology (GO) as an example to describe the efforts in standardizing the vocabularies from bioinformatics community and then move forward to discuss how computer systems can integrate data described using controlled vocabularies.

Common conceptualization, referred to as ontology, is an important step for heterogeneous data integration. Gene Ontology [2] project aims to provide consistent descriptors for gene products in different databases and standardize the classification of sequences and sequence features. It started in 1998 as a joint project of three organism databases: FlyBase, Mouse Genome Informatics (MGI), and *Saccharomyces* Genome Database (SGD). GO project now includes many repositories for plant, animal, and microbial genomes.

GO provides ontologies to annotate gene products in four nonoverlapping domains:

- Molecular function (MF)—describes activities at the molecular level
- Biological process (BP)—describes a sequence of molecular functions in which a gene product is involved
- Cellular component (CC)—describes locations at which a gene product acts
- Sequence ontology (SO)—allows the classification and standard representation of sequence features

Every annotation attributes to a source, which may be a literature reference, another database, or an analysis; furthermore, the annotation must indicate the type of evidence the cited source provides to support the association between the gene product and the GO term. Benefit from this restriction is that the data sets in databases collaborated using GO are linked by GO vocabularies. GO has proven to be useful for the mining of significance from large data sets such as microarray results. It also facilitates the organization of data from fully annotated novel genomes and the comparison of biological information [3].

Currently, GO manages ontology changes through a central coordinator, *GO Editorial Office*. The curation of changes is done manually at this stage. However, the growing community and the increasing size of the vocabularies challenge the way ontologies are managed. One step for solving this problem is to describe these vocabularies clearly enough for a computer system to syndicate them automatically. By doing so, multiple coordinators can coexist with semantic linked between their data sets, so that given a term, an application can find its definition and relations to other terms using standard protocols.

In order to achieve this, there needs to be a platform in the Internet for uniquely identifying a term. Standard organizations such as like the Internet Engineering Task Force (IETF) and World Wide Web consortium (W3C) have put their major efforts on this in recent years with a focus on specifications that facilitate computer systems to share and process information.

The foundations of W3C effort in this direction are Uniform Resource Identifiers (URIs) and Resource Description Framework (RDF). URIs allow anything in the Web that can be uniquely identified. RDF provides a common framework for expressing information so that it can be exchanged between applications without loss of its meanings. The information includes those that cannot be directly retrieved in the Web. RDF identifies information using URIs. Figure 7.1 gives an example on how to describe a GO term called "reproduction" using RDF graph.

- Term "reproduction" is identified by "http://www.geneontology.org/go#GO: 0000003."

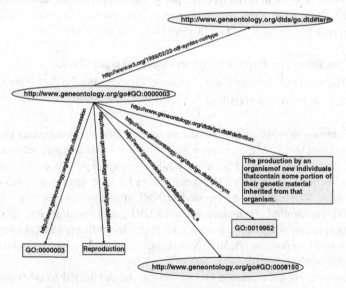

Figure 7.1. An RDF description of GO term "reproduction".

- Kind of things is identified by "http://www.geneontology.org/dtds/go.dtd# term."
- Properties of those things, for example, synonym are identified by "http://www. geneontology.org/dtds/go.dtd#synonym."
- Values of the properties, for example, the value of property "http://www. geneontology.org/dtds/go.dtd #is_a" is "http://www.geneontology.org/go#GO: 0008150."

RDF also provides XML-based syntax to store and exchange these graphs. The following is the XML corresponding to the graph in Fig. 7.1.

```
<go:go xmlns:go=''http://www.geneontology.org/dtds/go.dtd#''
       xmlns:rdf=''http://www.w3.org/1999/02/22-rdf-syntax-ns#''>
  <rdf:RDF>
    <go:term rdf:about=''http://www.geneontology.org/go#GO:0000003''
         n_associations=''0''>
    <go:accession>GO:0000003</go:accession>
    <go:name>reproduction</go:name>
    <go:synonym>GO:0019952</go:synonym>
    <go:definition>The production by an organism of new individuals
        that contain some portion of their genetic material
        inherited from that organism.
    </go:definition>
    <go:is_a rdf:resource=''http://www.geneontology.org/go#GO:0008150''/>
    </go:term>
  </rdf:RDF>
</go:go>
```

An RDF statement contains three parts: *subject*, *predicate*, and *object*; for example, the above RDF states that "http://www.geneontology.org/go#GO:0000003" has a synonym whose value is "GO:0019952." In this statement

- The subject is "http://www.geneontology.org/go#GO:0000003."
- The predicate is "http://www.geneontology.org/dtds/go.dtd#synonym."
- The object is "GO:0019952."

In addition to simple triple-based statement, RDF supports structure through aggregating things to describe a resource, for example, *term* is an aggregation of accession, name, and synonym. There are some built-in types and properties, such as containers and collections, defined in RDF specification for representing a group of resources and triples. RDF can also accommodate XML fragments as property values.

With a controlled vocabulary set and a URI-based resource description standard, finding necessary data becomes easier for applications that need to use them. The construction of computer applications also benefits from the reduced semantic ambiguity provided by the controlled vocabulary set.

However, even though the GO model can be duplicated to other subfields, it is unrealistic to assume that each subfield will come up with a similar consortium for coordinating its vocabularies and providing reference database schemas for data storage. There are lots of occasions where such an organization is impossible to establish; for example, it is impossible to define standard vocabularies to categorize online photos and other web contents. In these cases, users need to be given more flexibility to annotate their data using their own vocabularies and structures. This poses the challenge on how to manage and match similar vocabularies and structures so that applications can still find data described from different perspectives.

It is difficult to achieve accuracy in the similarity search of terms defined with uncontrolled vocabularies. However, relating data with a certain structure causes less ambiguity. Therefore, annotating data with a certain structure is helpful for matching data described in a different way. On the contrary, structures are essential for making computer systems process information effectively. Recently, XML formats that describe lists of related Web information called "feeds" in a structured manner have shown that adding simple structures to Web pages can greatly improve Web data syndication. These formats include Atom Syndication Format (Atom) [4] and RSS [5]. In biology area, although GO provides a few database schemas for storing gene product-related descriptions, there is no standard structures for grouping these vocabularies, which makes it difficult for a computer system to use data from a variety of data sources. We discuss below the techniques that are useful for addressing the problem of integrating data defined with different structures.

7.3 INTEGRATING STRUCTURED DATA

Metadata or data schema management has been studied for a long time in the database field. In this section, we review the related technologies in data integration systems.

Data integration system provides users with a uniform view of data residing at autonomous data sources. As Fig. 7.2 shows, in a data integration system, users do not pose queries in terms of the schema in which data are stored, but rather pose queries in terms of a *mediated schema* or *global schema*. The mediated schema is a set of *virtual relations* designed for specific data integration applications. These relations are virtual due to the fact that the corresponding data are not actually stored anywhere. A mediated schema can also have virtual relations among other mediated schemas.

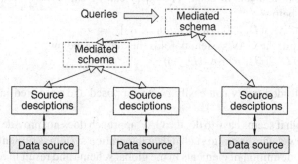

Figure 7.2. A typical architecture of data integration systems.

In order to answer queries composed using the mediated schema, the data integration system needs a set of source descriptions to specify the data source, including the attributes that can be found in the data source and the constraints on the data source [6]. In general, a data integration system needs to establish a mapping between the mediated schema and the data sources. How the mediated schemas and local schemas are related defines two commonly used mapping approaches called *global-as-view* (GAV)[6] and *local-as-view* (LAV)[7].

Global-as-view maps the elements in a global schema to a view of data sources. The queries in GAV are posed in terms of the global schema. In GAV, the mappings from the global schema to local schemas tell the data integration systems how to use data sources to retrieve data described in terms of the global schema. The queries can, therefore, be answered through unfolding the queries to local data sources.

Consider a data integration system for analysis records for some scientific data sets. An analysis record includes data sets, the year the analysis is done, and the reference to publications describing the analysis results. Some data sets are associated with annotations. The system defines the following global schema:

analysis (data set, year, reference)

usyd(reference)

data(data set, annotation)

Below are two data sources hosting data sets:

- Source s1 (*data set, year, reference*) contains analysis records that have been done at the University of Sydney(USYD) since 1999.
- Source s2 (*data set, annotation*) contains annotations of data collected since 2001.

In GAV, the global schema is expressed as views over data sources as below:

$analysis(D, Y, R) \supseteq \{(D, Y, R)|s1(D, Y, R)\}$,

$usyd(R) \supseteq \{(D)|s1(D, Y, R)\}$,

$data(D, A) \supseteq \{(D, A)|s2(D, A)\}$.

Suppose the following query is submitted to the system: select data set and annotation of analysis in 2003. The query can be expressed in terms of the global schema as below:

$\{(D, A)|analysis(D, 2003, R) \wedge data(D, A)\}$

Afterward, the GAV system unfolds the query as below:

$\{(D, A)|s1(D, 2003, R) \wedge s2(D, A)\}$

The unfolded query can easily be decomposed and answered in data sources s1 and s2.

Although it seems easy to do, the GAV approach does not provide good scalability. Adding new data sources to such a data integration system is difficult because it may change the definition of elements in the global schema and result in refining the views associated with the global schema.

Local-as-view, on the contrary, models each data source as a view defined in terms of the global schema. Since the data sources are the views over the global schema and these views do not provide direct information about which data source satisfies the global schema, the query answering is not as straightforward as in GAV scenario. Instead, it is done through *view-based query rewriting*.

For the example described above, a LAV system describes the data sources s1 and s2 in terms of the global schema as below:

$s1(D, Y, R) \subseteq \{(T, Y, D)|analysis(D, Y, R) \wedge usyd(R) \wedge Y > 1999\}$

$s2(D, A) \subseteq \{(D, A)|analysis(D, Y, R) \wedge data(D, A) \wedge Y > 2001\}$

Based on the mapping, the query

$\{(D, A)|analysis(D, 2003, R) \wedge data(D, A)\}$ is therefore rewritten as

$\{(D, A)|s2(D, A) \wedge s1(D, 2003, R)\}$

LAV respects the independence of the data sources. Adding a new data source means simply adding a set of virtual relations to the global schema without other changes to the existing mappings. However, query rewriting is a hard problem in LAV [8].

Both LAV and GAV assume that a stable and well-defined global schema subsumes all local schemas. However, it is difficult to satisfy this assumption in a large-scale distributed system due to the fact that the structure of information is dynamic and evolving. For instance, the annotation of a gene product evolves as new analysis methods appear or existing methods are improved. In a dynamic or highly scalable environment where data are distributed autonomously, such as Web and peer-to-peer (P2P) overlay networks, syndicating data together with flexible metadata structures is an essential step for constructing GAV/LAV-based data integration systems. In recent years, there have been lots of efforts attempting to address this problem. Many of them focus on semistructured data management in a decentralized environment.

7.4   SYNDICATING DISTRIBUTED DATA

Decentralized systems, particularly P2P systems, have drawn lots of attention in recent years due to their capability of content addressing, advantages in constructing systems in a self-organizing manner, and a potential high scalability they may offer. Meanwhile, XML has become more and more important in data exchange and syndication in recent years. One of the reasons is that it is adaptive to evolving structure. Semistructured data management in P2P environment provides additional benefits to scientific data syndication [9]:

(1) A P2P architecture offers truly distributed mechanism for sharing data. A data source can independently provide schema mappings to a set of neighbors it selects. A data integration system built on top of this mechanism can potentially answer queries along a path connecting related data sources. In this scenario, the burden of maintaining a global mediated schema is relieved, which is suitable for a loosely organized scientific research community.

(2) As mentioned above, traditional data integration systems normally assume that a single global schema can be developed. Considering that scientific activities are very dynamic and diverse, it is at least a nontrivial task to maintain the global schemas. With a P2P architecture, such kind of a single mediated schema is not necessary because an overlay network can accommodate multiple schemas in a flexible way.

In this section, we review data syndication technologies based on P2P architecture.

7.4.1   Data Indexing

There are two types of P2P overlay networks: *unstructured overlays* and *structured overlays*. Unstructured overlays, such as Gnutella [10], are widely used for file sharing in Internet environment. An unstructured overlay links nodes as a random graph. Search of a file is done through flooding the overlay or based on a certain randomized algorithm [11]. In the flooding scenario, one node sends query, normally a keyword, based to its overlay neighbors. These neighbors in turn forward the query to their neighbors recursively until the data are found or the maximum number of forwarding hops is reached. The maximum number of forwarding hops is defined as *"time-to-live"* of the query. For a large overlay network, flooding search can only reach a small fraction of nodes and may not find data that actually exist in the network. Some techniques have been developed for improving the search performance in unstructured overlays. One way is to cache the information of the data location on the flooding paths so that on average a query has better chance to find the target. *FreeNet* makes use of *small-world* model [11,12,13] to give an enhanced cache replacement algorithm. This approach associates a random number to each node in the overlay, and the cache replacement considers the distance between a random number and the hash key of a data file in the cache. In the ideal case, this improvement can achieve $O(log(n))$ query delivery time with $O(log(n^2))$ cache memory requirement in each node. This is a move toward structured overlay networks that achieve $O(log(n))$ query delivery time with $O(log(n))$ routing table size.

Structured overlays are normally based on *Distributed Hash Table* (DHT). A DHT algorithm associates data and nodes that store these data to a single key space. It defines rules for mapping data to nodes; typically data are stored in a node whose key is closest to that of the data [14–17]. Each node maintains a routing table to record the neighbors in the key space. A search for data is a routing process that approaches the target node step by step based on the distance between the key of the node and the key of the data in search.

Compared to unstructured overlays, structured overlays organize data and nodes as a structured graph, so that data search can make use of the structure information and find data more efficiently than in the unstructured overlays. However, due to the fact that the structure is described using simple relationships between keys, complex queries are difficult to pose and are also difficult to answer in a structured overlay network. In a typical DHT network, one has to know the key that associates with the data file in order to retrieve the file. To overcome this limitation, data-related information has to be associated with some keys. This is called *data indexing* technique. There are many *data indexing* techniques proposed attempting to enable database such as data management mechanism in DHT networks [18–23]. They can be classified into two categories based on the information used for generating the keys: attribute indexing and metadata structure indexing.

7.4.2   Indexing Unstructured Attributes Using Inverted List

A data source in PIER [22] describes its data using a set of attributes or keywords. These keywords are published separately to the underlying DHT networks using their hash IDs. In a DHT node that is responsible for a keyword, an inverted list is maintained to keep the keywords and their corresponding data information. When searching for a data file, one just need to supply the keywords. Since the node that is responsible for a keyword can be resolved using the underlying DHT routing algorithm, the query can be forwarded to that node and answer obtained there.

In many circumstances, the logical combination of keywords is used for accurately describing what a user needs. PIER supports distributed join on multiple keywords. The access plan for query about data with *key-2* = *A* AND *key-3* = *B* is as shown in Fig. 7.3. The search engine first routes the access plan to nodes that host *key-2* and *key-3*, and executes the distributed join of the matching inverted data entries. The join runs as follows: The host of key-2 sends selected *data-id*s to the host of key-3. The receiving node does a join on the *data-id*s selected from its local inverted list and sends back the data entries containing the pointers to data sources to the query node.

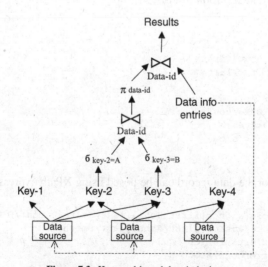

Figure 7.3. Keyword-based data indexing.

In the PIER system, each data source can choose any keywords to describe its data. However, the effectiveness of this mechanism depends on how well the query keywords match the publish keywords. It is not a trivial task and requires linguistic processing techniques or a clearly defined keyword set. GridVine [23] gives a data indexing mechanism for RDF triples that have clear definitions for attributes. As each subject, predicate, and object are defined using URIs, a search can be led to more accurate answers than in the completely unstructured indexing with free text attributes. A DHT insert operation of triple t in GridVine is in the following form:

$$insert(t) = insert(t_{subject}, t), insert(hash(t_{predicate}), t), insert(hash(t_{object}), t)$$

A query can, therefore, be posed in terms of the subject, predicate, or the object of the triple.

7.4.3 Indexing Data with Structures

Keyword or attribute-based data indexing enables distributed data search with known keywords. It is not enough for annotating data that are better to be described according to a certain structure. Structured data is convenient for processing with computer systems.

The work in Reference [19] describes a data indexing system for an XML bibliography database. In the system, a set of most-likely-to-be-asked XPath expressions is generated during the publishing phase of a database item. These XPath expressions are organized in a hierarchy so that a general query can be mapped to more specific queries. The most specific query contains the location information of the data item. When using incomplete information to query a data item, the query is recursively mapped to more specific queries till the most specific query is found. The query hierarchy reduces the possible computation and communication cost when a join operation is needed. For example, the following XML fragment describes the bibliographic data of "John Smith":

```
<article>
  <author>
    <first>John</first>
    <last>Smith</last>
  </author>
  <title>TCP</title>
  <conf>SIGCOMM</conf>
  <year>1989</year>
  <size>315635</size>
</article>
```

A search for the data record can be posed using XPath expressions as below:

```
q1 =/article[author[first/John][last/Smith]][conf/SIGCOMM]
q2 =/article/author[first/John][last/Smith]
q3 =/article/title/TCP
q4 =/article/conf/SIGCOMM
```

A query may cover another query if it is more general, for example, in the above example q2 covers q1. For an XML data item, a few XPath expressions can be constructed and published in the underlying DHT network. These published XPath expressions link to each other based on the *cover* relationship. A general expression contains a list of specific expressions. By doing so, a user query can be led to the node that host the data records through a path that links the published expressions that cover the user query.

As described in Section 7.3, *schema-match* is important for a data integration system that integrates heterogeneous data. It is also the case for indexing structured data in a decentralized environment.

Edutella [24,25] is one of the early systems attempting to address the metadata *schema-match* problem in a P2P environment. It enforces a common data model for accommodating different data schemas. Each data source has a wrapper to make its schema consistent to the common data model; therefore, queries posed in terms of the common data model can be answered directly in each data source that can transform the common data model to its local data schema. Mediators run as services in Edutella.

The *Piazza* [26] system tries to establish interlinked semantic mappings between peer's individual schemas in order to reduce the dependency to a centralized common data model. *Piazza* intends to provide both GAV and LAV features in a peer data management system (PDMS). It uses a set of *stored relations* to describe the local data source stored in a peer. Piazza contains two types of mappings, called *storage descriptions* and *peer mappings*. Storage descriptions specify data stored in a peer by relating its stored relations to peer relations. These descriptions can be seen as views from local data source to schemas shared by a group of peers. Different to LAV approach, there is no global schema in this case and storage descriptions can be related to multiple peer relations. *Peer mappings* provide semantic links between the different schemas of peers. The query answering is done through the *query reformulation* in which a rule–goal tree is built for transforming a query to use only stored relations. Paper [26] further proved that a conjunctive query can be answered in polynomial-time data complexity when the system includes only inclusion peer mappings and storage descriptions, and the peer mappings are acyclic.

The work in Reference 27 studies the answer quality problem of schema mapping. When a P2P network grows in size, inconsistencies and erroneous mappings can be big problems. The paper gives a probabilistic model for inconsistent mapping detection. The detection is based on mapping cycle and parallel path analysis. For example, in a P2P system consisting of four nodes $p1$, $p2$, $p3$, and $p4$, there may exist two schema mapping cycles as below:

$p1 \rightarrow p2 \rightarrow p4 \rightarrow p1$,

$p1 \rightarrow p2 \rightarrow p3 \rightarrow p4 \rightarrow p1$

and the following parallel mapping paths:

$p2 \rightarrow p4$,

$p2 \rightarrow p3 \rightarrow p4$.

A factor graph is built for computing the conditional probabilities that a mapping is correct (or incorrect) based on the feedback from probing cycles and parallel paths.

7.5 EXAMPLE: DISTRIBUTED GENOME DATABASE

In this section, we give an example to show how the data syndication technologies can be used to build a scalable genome sequence similarity search service. The search can be done on highly distributed dynamic data.

In recent years, high-throughput genome sequencing technologies have produced large amount of sequences that are collected in large public databases, such as GenBank [28] and the Swiss-Prot/TrEMBL [29,30], and many other specialized and private databases distributed worldwide. Biologists frequently search these databases to match the sequences they have. BLAST (Basic Local Alignment Search Tool) [31] is a sequence similarity search program that is widely used by life science researchers. There is also an enormous number of databases for gene functions, sequence annotations, and literatures derived from these sequences. Making use of these data in an efficient and timely manner is crucial for life science researchers to conduct their research and development more effectively. However, due to the constant increase of bioinformatics data as well as the size of the data provider community, the construction of applications that are capable of using data sets from diverse range of data sources remains a challenging task.

There are several approaches for integrating data from life science research. One of them is to move data to a centralized repository such as GenBank; however, the increase of sequences and the query requests coming to the central repository keep challenging the processing power and network bandwidth. The *nt* database in NCBI contained about 10 billion bases in February 2004, growing 20% or so from February 2003, and *nr* database contained about 540 million residues in February 2003, growing 25% from a year earlier. Meanwhile, the NCBI BLAST Web server received about 140,000 query requests per weekday in early 2004, growing from 100,000 in 2002 [32].

The data federation based on relational databases is another approach for data integration; for example, the IBM Discovery Link system uses wrappers to fit different bioinformatics data into a relational database and creates a data federation from these separated databases [33,34]. This approach ignores the difference of cost between string-match-based relational database search and the alignment-based sequence search. Sequence search is normally compute intensive and data intensive while the analysis of sequence relationships is often compute intensive. The data federation approach does not address the computation cost issue. It relegates the problem to the data provider alone and only offers optimization mechanisms at the SQL access plan level. Efficiently coordinating computing resources to match the sequence data search and/or analysis applications is crucial for alignment-based sequence search.

As the data locality is crucial for the performance of data-intensive BLAST search, it is important to keep track of the database fragments and organize them in a structured manner so that sequence searches can benefit from using computing nodes that own needed database fragments. The DHT-based structured overlay network is harnessed for this purpose in our system. We have built a multilevel data indexing mechanism to keep track of genome data source in the overlay network. It provides the capability of annotating and searching data. Moreover, a TTL (time to live)-based mechanism is used for data consistency control.

7.5.1 DataFile Schema

In the system, a genome data source information is exchanged using an XML message defined according to the following *DataFile* schema:

```
<complexType name=''DataFile''>
<element name=''fileName'' type=''string''/>
<element name=''dataID'' type=''string''/>
<!-- time to live of the data file -->
<element name=''TTL'' type=''string''/>
<element name=''data'' type=''hexBinary''/>
<element name=''encodingMethod'' type=''string''/>
<element name=''homeNode'' type=''string''/>
<element name=''whereClause'' type=''string''>
</complexType>
```

"dataID" is the hash ID of the file. There are five methods to feed the file content to the requestor.

(1) Encoding the data file as an array of hex binary and sending it along with the message. In this case, the sender has a copy of the data file and it populates the data field with the content of the file.

(2) Specifying the home node (the IP and the port number) and instructing the requestor to fetch the file from the specified locations. In this case, the sender does not have a copy of the file but knows where the file is and its identifier.

(3) Providing the hash ID of the data and instructing the requestor to search for it in the overlay network it belongs to. In this case, the sender does not have a copy of the file but knows the hash ID of the file.

(4) Filling up the where-clause based on a knows schema and instructing the requestor to query the data indexing system in the overlay network to find out the ID of the file. A schema defines the metadata that describe a data file. We will give an example of metadata in Section 7.5.2.1. In this case, the sender does not have a copy of the file but knows the metadata structure of the data file and some fields of the metadata of the file in search.

(5) Filling up the where-clause based on some attributes of the data file and instructing the requestor to query the RDF data indexing system in the overlay network to find out the ID of the file.

Methods 1 and 2 are straightforward. Method 3 makes use of the simple data indexing mechanism to find out the location of the data. Methods 4 and 5 need the support from a more complex data indexing system to be described in Section 7.5.2.

Once a data file is fetched to the local node, a message containing the dataID, local node ID, and address may be sent to the node that is responsible for the file's location (with node ID numerically closest to the file ID) depending on the TTL value of the data file. If the TTL value is larger than a threshold, an entry is added to the node responsible to keep track of the replica of the data file in the following format:

```
(dataID, hostNodeID, hostNodeAddress, replicaFlag, TTL)
```

The TTL field is also used to guard the currency of a data file. This field specifies a time interval indicating whether the data file is fresh enough to use, for example, when freshnessBound ="1 day," the local node first checks the time stamp of the data file in its local storage. If the time stamp is older than 1 day, the file needs to be fetched again from its home node if specified, or otherwise, the home node address is obtained from DHT lookup. The home node is responsible for tracking the changes of the data file versions. It gets the latest data file from its storage and distributes the file to the overlay network. The affected nodes then clean up the old data file and insert the new one to their storage.

7.5.2 Multilevel Data Indexing Mechanism

7.5.2.1 Schema-Based Data Indexing Mechanism

DHT relies on a known hash key to find a data file. However, in most cases, it is difficult for applications to gather these keys. Data indexing is thus introduced in our system to tackle this problem. A data file is annotated by its attributes based on predefined schemas when being published. Data indexing is a mechanism that maps the annotations of a data file to its key in DHT networks. The XML schema used for indexing BLAST data set is defined as given below:

```
<complexType name=''blastDataBase''>
  <element name =''dbName'' type=''string''/>
  <element name =''lastModifiedTime'' type=''string''/>
  <element name =''totalPartitionNumber'' type=''int''/>
  <element name =''partitionSize'' type=''int''/>
  <element name =''partitionNumber'' type=''int''/>
  <element name =''partitionTool''
          type=''typens:BlastDBPartitionTool''/>
  <element name =''dataFile'' type=''typens:DataFile''/>
  <element name =''TTL'' type=''string''/>
</complexType>
```

On the basis of the schema, the following infoset describes a partition of *nr* database:

```
<blastDataBase>
  <dbName>nr</dbName>
```

```
<lastModifiedTime>20050605101813.000</lastModifiedTime>
<totalPartitionNumber>17</totalPartitionNumber>
<partitionSize>52428800</partitionSize>
<partitionNumber>3</partitionNumber>
<partitionTool>
  <name>mpiformatdb</name>
  <version>1.3</name>
</partitonTool>
<DataFile>
  <id>BA74FE9D1AD5A96A158FD97866796A87</id>
  <homeNode>sogrid://129.78.8.70:9999</homeNode>
</DataFile>
<TTL>30 days</TTL>
</blastDataBase>
```

When publishing a data set, its annotation is also published to a node that is numerically closest to the hash ID of the schema used to annotate it. The message of publishing the annotation is in the following format:

```
(hash(schema(``blastDataBase'')), the-infoset,
  host-DHT-key, (host_ip, host_port));
```

If there are multiple schemas used to annotate the data set, multiple messages are sent out to different nodes. The DHT node that is closest to the hash ID of the schema is therefore responsible for maintaining a table of all infosets derived from the schema.

Applications use a query engine to obtain data file locations from the knowledge about the annotations of these files. A query is in the following format:

```
(schema_hash_id, where-clause, additional descriptions)
```

The where-clause is composed as XPath expression as below:

```
/blastDataBase[dbName=``nr'' & totalPartitionNumber=17
  & partitionNumber=3]/
```

When receiving a query, the query engine forwards the query to the node that hosts the schema node.

7.5.2.2 RDF-based Data Indexing Mechanism

Compared to the schema-based data annotation, RDF is more flexible as it relaxes the requirements about knowledge of the metadata. One needs to only know the *subject* and *predicate* in order to find the location where the RDF annotation is stored. Below is a simplified example of RDF annotation of the output of a BLAST query to the *nr* database.

```
<rdf:RDF xmlns:rdf=``http://www.w3.org/1999/02/22-rdf-syntax-ns#''
         xmlns:blast=``http://blast.sogrid.org/2.0/''>
<rdf:Description rdf:about=``http://sogrid.org/blast''>
```

```
<blast:blast_output>
  <blast:blast_output_program>
    <blast:program_name>blastp</blast:program_name>
    <blast:parameters>
      <blast:matrix>BLOSUM62</blast:matrix>
      <blast:evalue>2e-05</blast:evalue>
    </blast:parameters>
  </blast:blast_output_program>
  <blast:blast_db>
    <blast:db_name>nr</blast:db_name>
    <blast:db_date>2005-11-08</blast:db_date>
  </blast:blast_db>
  <blast:query_sequence>MACLHETRTPSSTR</blast:query_sequence>
  <blast:output_detail>
    <blast:file_id>DF83CA4F1A931426CFF1917972856CED</blast:file_id>
  </blast:output_detail>
</blast:blast_output>
</rdf:Description>
</rdf:RDF>
```

The annotation can be published using multiple paths, for example.

```
(hash(``http://sogrid.org/blast/blast_output/query_sequence''),
  object, rdf-infoset, host node);
(hash(``http://sogrid.org/blast/blast_output/blast_db/db_name''),
  object, rdf-infoset, host-node);
```

This is equivalent to a DHT *insert* operation that uses the hash ID of (subject and predicate) as key and (object and RDF infoset) as value.

In order to find a RDF annotation, one needs to know a path that leads to some properties of the corresponding data set and the values of these properties. Once receiving these queries, the system reaches the node that is responsible for the hash ID of the XPath and returns the RDF infosets that satisfy the criteria.

The system architecture with data indexing and a search engine is shown in Fig. 7.4.

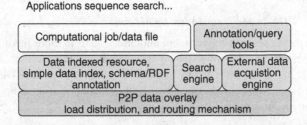

Figure 7.4. System architecture.

7.5.3   Locate a Data File

Below is a list of messages used for retrieving a data file:

Message Name	Parameters
DataRequest	(DataID, RequestNode, CheckUpdateFlag)
DataRequestResponse	DataFile | "not found" | "not changed"
DataLookup	(DataID, RequestNode)
DataLookupResponse	HostNode | "not found"
DataIDQuery	(SchemaID, Where-Clause, RequestNode),
	(RDFID, Where-Clause, RequestNode)
DataIDQueryResponse	(DataID, HostNode) | "not found"

DataRequest and *DataRequestResponse* are used for Scenario 1. *DataLookup* and *DataLookupResponse* are used for simple data indexing scenario. *DataIDQuery* and *DataIDQueryResponse* are used for querying data ID of a known schema or RDF subject and predicate ID. Once the data ID is known, the file can be obtained using DataRequest message.

When a data file is retrieved and saved into a node's local data store, whether the data file is indexed is determined by the TTL carried with the file. If the data file has a TTL greater than a certain threshold, a data index message is sent to the node that is responsible for the location of the data file and an entry for the file is inserted into the data index table on the node. In response to a *DataLookup* message for a data ID that has multiple entries registered in the node, it returns the location of the file in a *round-robin* manner to the requesters so that data requests will less likely overwhelm the node that hosts the data.

7.5.4   Scheduling Search Requests

A BLAST service is built on top of these distributed data sources and some computing resources. Computing resources and data resources can be overlapped nodes in the overlay. Each computing node maintains a job queue for processing genome search requests to the data it hosts. A scheduler dispatches these requests to multiple job queues that are grouped based on the data they serve. The scheduling is based on the imbalance ratio between queues. Its detail can be found in Reference 35. In the case that data are missing or stale in a node to which a job is dispatched, the data are fetched from one of the nodes that hosts the data.

7.5.5   Data Diffusion with Data Indexing Support

We measure the data propagation speed in the system. As mentioned above, the currency guard of a data file has an impact on the average job processing time, as the data need to be fetched again from the original data source. The total time used by a computing node for processing a job is shown as below:

$$C^s = pC^s_{\text{GetData}} + C^s_{\text{Search}} + C^s_{\text{TransResults}} \tag{1}$$

in which

$$p = \begin{cases} 1 & \text{TTL} = 0 \text{ \&\& QueryIncomingRate} \\ \min(1, \frac{1}{\text{TTL} \cdot \text{QueryIncomingRate}}) & \text{TTL} > 0 \text{ \&\& QueryIncomingRate} \neq 0 \\ 0 & \text{QueryIncomingRate} = 0 \end{cases} \tag{2}$$

is the probability that a data set needs to be fetched from a remote node. The total cost of fetching data sets is

$$C^{s-\text{all}}_{\text{GetData}} = \sum_{si \text{ has data set } s} pC^{si}_{\text{GetData}}$$

The more the data sets are distributed, the higher the data fetching cost is. DISTRIBU-TION_DEGREE defines the maximum number of replicas of a data file in the system. When p and DISTRIBUTION_DEGREE are high, the data source node could be overwhelmed and degrade the performance of query processing. We plot processing time of a computing node changes with the TTL value in Fig. 7.6 using the average remote data fetching time, search time, and result transfer time gathered from running the 25 queries on 17 nr database fragments, each with 50 MB. Figure 7.6 shows that the cost of managing data consistency is assimilated as the incoming query request rate increases and currency requirement is relaxed. However, when data consistency requirement and DISTRIBUTION_DEGREE are high, the processing time will be dominated by how fast the data set is distributed.

The data indexing mechanism can effectively reduce the data distribution cost by allowing data to be fetched from multiple nodes that host the data. We measure the data diffusion speed in Fig.7.5. The data diffusion speed is obtained under DIS-TRIBUTION_DEGREE 2. Initially, all data sets are put into one data provider and the location is indexed, and afterward each subscriber node fetches a data set when assigned a job. The subscriber node may publish the data set it just obtained to the overlay depending on the TTL value of each data set. When TTL is less than a thresh-old, no index is published as the data is transient; otherwise, the data set location is published to a node that is responsible for the ID of the data. Therefore, the following requests to the data set could be scheduled to this node. As mentioned previously, when there are multiple nodes that host the same data set, the scheduling of data set requests is done in a round-robin manner. Figure 7.5 shows that the data diffusion mechanism significantly reduces the data diffusion cost as it automatically provides a content delivery system for requested data sets.

With a data indexing system that can effectively diffuse data to computing re-sources, a genome similarity search can easily scale with the increase of computing nodes.

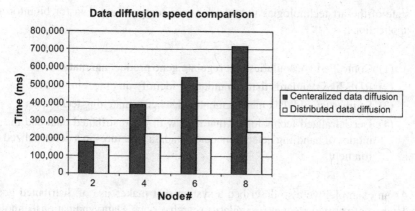

Figure 7.5. Data diffusion speed for the second copy of data sets: Each data set contains seven files and the total size is about 150 MB. There are nine data sets in total.

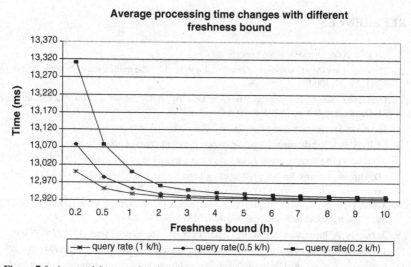

Figure 7.6. Average job processing time changes with freshness bound and query incoming rate.

7.6 SUMMARY

The rapidly growing biology research communities have produced vast amount of data in recent years. Syndicating related data is not only important for constructing effective bioinformatics systems, but also essential to provide bioinformatics applications sufficient information to make correct decisions while exploiting the unknown world. The distributed, dynamic, and heterogeneous nature of these data makes efficient data syndication a difficult problem. In this chapter, we reviewed the following state-of-the-art technologies that can be used to syndicate data for bioinformatics applications:

(1) Controlled vocabularies that regulate gene product annotations
(2) RDF-like standards that can uniquely identify an object in the Web
(3) Semistructured data management and schema matching techniques
(4) Decentralized technologies that deal with the distributed data and the techniques of handling heterogeneous metadata structures in a decentralized environment.

As an example, we also described a system that makes use of distributed genome databases to provide sequence similarity search service. Data syndication technologies are still in their "teenage years" [9]. However, they have already shown their potentials to leverage the research in the fast-growing bioinformatics area.

REFERENCES

1. CIPRES 2006. http://www.phylo.org.
2. The Gene Ontology Consortium, Gene ontology: Tool for the unification of biology, *Nature Genetics* **25**(1), 25–29, 2000.
3. The Gene Ontology Consortium, The Gene Ontology (GO) project in 2006, *Nucleic Acids Research* **34** (Database issue), pp. D322–6, 2006.
4. The Atom Syndication Format, IETF RFC4287, 2005.
5. Really Simple Syndication, 2006. http://www.rssboard.org/rss-specification.
6. A.Y. Halevy, Answering queries using views: A survey, the *VLDB Journal* **10**, 270–294, 2001.
7. J.D. Ullman, Information integration using logical views, in: *Proceedings of the 6th International Conference on Database Theory* (ICDT '97), Springer, Berlin, 1997.
8. A. Halevy, Logic-based techniques in data integration, in: *Logic Based Artificial Intelligence*, J. Minker Ed., Kluwer Academic Publishers, Norwell, MA, 575–595, 2000.
9. A. Halevy, A. Rajaraman, J. Ordille, Data integration: The teenage years, In: *VLDB*, 2006.
10. The Gnutella protocol specification, 2000. http://dss.clip2.com/GnutellaProtocol04.pdf.
11. H. Zhang, A. Goel, R. Govindan, Using the small-world model to improve Freenet performance, in: *Proceedings IEEE Infocom*, 2002.
12. J. Kleinberg, The small-world phenomenon: An algorithmic perspective, in: *Proceedings of the 32nd ACM Symposium on Theory of Computing*, 2000.
13. S. Milgram, The small world problem, *Psychology Today* **1**, 61, 1967.
14. A. Rowstron, P. Druschel, Pastry: Scalable, distributed object location and routing for large-scale peer-to-peer systems, in: *IFIP/ACM International Conference on Distributed Systems Platforms (Middleware)*, Heidelberg, Germany, November 2001, pp. 329–350.
15. S. Ratnasamy, P. Francis, M. Handley, R. Karp, S. Shenker, A scalable content-addressable network, in: *Proceedings of ACM SIGCOMM*, August 2001.
16. N. Harvey, M. Jones, S. Saroiu, M. Theimer, A. Wolman, SkipNet: A scalable overlay network with practical locality properties, in: *Fourth USENIX Symposium on Internet Technologies and Systems (USITS '03)*, Seattle, WA, March 2003.

17. I. Stoica, Robert Morris, David Karger, M. Frans Kaashoek, Hari Balakrishnan, Chord: A scalable peer-to-peer lookup service for internet applications, in: *Proceedings of ACM SIGCOMM*, 2001.

18. K. Aberer, A. Datta, M. Hauswirth, R. Schmidt, Indexing data-oriented overlay networks, in: *Proceedings of the 31st VLDB Conference*, Trondheim, Norway, 2005.

19. L. Garces-Erice, P. A. Felber, E.W. Biersack, G. Urvoy-Keller, K.W. Ross, Data Indexing in Peer-to-Peer DHT Networks, in: *Proceedings of 2004 ICDCS Conference*, pp. 200–208, 2004.

20. C. Tang, Z Xu, M Mahalingam, pSearch: Information retrieval in structured overlays, *ACM SIGCOMM Computer Communications Review* 33(1), 2003.

21. S. Abiteboul, I. Manolescu, N. Preda, *Constructing and Querying Peer-to-Peer Warehouses of XML Resources*, SWDB 2004, LNCS 3372, 2005. pp 219–225.

22. B.T. Loo, J.M. Hellerstein, R. Huebsch, S. Shenker, I. Stoica, Enhancing P2P file-sharing with an Internet-scale query processor, in: *Proceedings of VLDB*, 2004.

23. K. Aberer, P. Cudré-Mauroux, M. Hauswirth, T. V. Pelt, GridVine: Building Internet-Scale Semantic Overlay Networks, in: *Proceedings of the 3rd International Semantic Web Conference*, 2004.

24. W. Nejdl, B. Wolf, C. Qu, S. Decker, M. Sintek, A. Naeve, M. Nilsson, M. Palmér, T. Risch, EDUTELLA: A P2P networking infrastructure based on RDF, in: *International World Wide Web Conference (WWW)*, 2002.

25. W. Nejdl, M. Wolpers, W. Siberski, C. Schmitz, M. Schlosser, I. Brunkhorst, A. Löser, Super-peer-based routing and clustering strategies for RDF-based peer-to-peer networks, in: *International World Wide Web Conference (WWW)*, 2003.

26. A.Y. Halevy, Z.G. Ives, J. Madhavan, P. Mork, D. Suciu, I. Tatarinov, The Piazza peer data management system, *IEEE Transactions on Knowledge and Data Engineering* 16(7), 787–798, 2004.

27. P. Cudre-Mauroux, K. Aberer, A. Feher, Probabilistic message passing in peer data management system, in: *22nd International Conference on Data Engineering (ICDE)*, 2006.

28. D.L. Wheeler, D.M. Church, R. Edgar, S. Federhen, W. Helmberg, T. Madden, J.U. Pontius, G.D. Schuler, L.M. Schriml, E. Sequeira, T. Suzek, T.A. Tatusova, L. Wagner, Database resources of the National Center for Biotechnical Information, Update, *Nucleic Acids Research* 32, D35–D40, 2004.

29. A. Bairoch, B. Boeckmann, S. Ferro, E. Gasteiger, Swiss-Prot: Juggling between evolution and stability, *Briefing Bioinformatics* 5(1), 39–55, 2004.

30. E. Gasteiger, A. Gattiker, C. Hoogland, I. Ivanyi, R.D. Appel, A. Bairoch, ExPASy: The proteomics server for in-depth protein knowledge and analysis, *Nucleic Acids Research* 31(13), 3784–3788, 2003.

31. S. Altschul, W. Gish, W. Miller, E. Myers, D. Lipman, Basic local alignment search tool, *Journal of Molecular Biology* 215(3), 403–410, 1990.

32. S. McGinnis, T.L. Madden, BLAST: At the core of a powerful and diverse set of sequence analysis tools, *Nucleic Acids Research*, 32(web server issue), W20–W25, 2004.

33. L.M. Haas, J.E. Rice, P.M. Schwarz, W.C. Swope, P. Kodali, E. Kotlar, DiscoveryLink: A system for integrated access to life sciences data sources, *IBM Systems Journal* 40(2), 489–511, 2001.

34. B.A. Eckman, A. Kaufmann, Querying BLAST within a data federation. *Bulletin of the IEEE Computer Society Technical Committee on Data Engineering* 27(3), 12–19, 2004.

35. C. Wang, B. Alqaralleh, B.B. Zhou, M. Till, A.Y. Zomaya, A BLAST service built on data indexed overlay network, *IEEE e-Science*, 2005.

8

MOLECULAR DOCKING USING GRID COMPUTING

Alexandru-Adrian Tantar, Nouredine Melab, and
El-Ghazali Talbi

8.1 INTRODUCTION

With the evolution of distributed high-performance and high-throughput computing and with the support of nuclear magnetic resonance (NMR) data, we are at the dawns of a new era in molecular research and pharmaceutical drug design. Having been studied for more than a decade, protein–protein[1] docking is fundamental in understanding biomolecular processes, interactions between antibodies and antigens, intracellular signaling modulation mechanisms, inhibitor design, and macromolecular interactions and assemblies, among others.

The importance of the protein–protein docking problem is reinforced by the ubiquitousness of proteins in the living organisms, applications of computational molecular docking directing to computer-assisted drug design and computer-assisted molecular design. From a structural point of view, proteins are complex organic compounds composed of amino acid residue chains joined by peptide bonds— please refer to Fig. 8.1 for a schematic example. Proteins are involved in immune response mechanisms, enzymatic activity, signal transduction, and other such activities.

In conceptual terms, the molecular docking describes the complexed macro-molecule resulting from the binding of two separate folded molecules, exerting geometrical and chemical complementarity. From a computational standpoint, *in silico* docking simulates molecular recognition, although relating not to the molecular pathways of the process but to the final complexed result.

As an abstract and general definition, molecular docking may be described as the prediction of the optimal bound conformation of two molecular complexes— exclusively the atomic coordinates are assumed to be known as initial information.

---

[1] Proteins were discovered in 1838 by Jöns Jakob Berzelius, a Swedish chemist; the term was derived from the Greek *protas*, standing for "of primary importance."

Grid Computing for Bioinformatics and Computational Biology. Edited by E.-G. Talbi and A.Y. Zomaya.
Copyright © 2008 John Wiley & Sons, Inc.

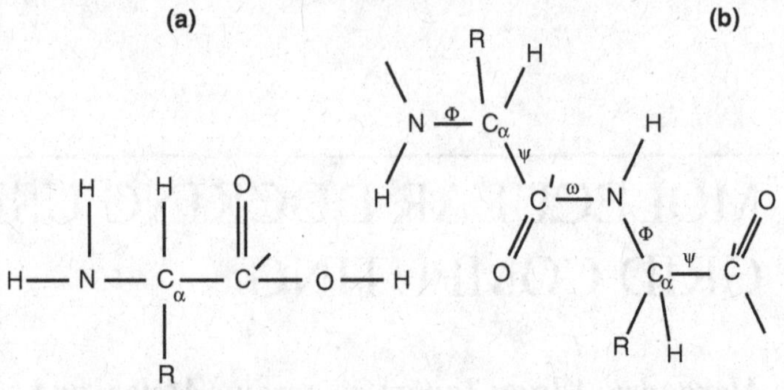

(a)

(b)

Figure 8.1. Amino acid: (a) $NC_{\alpha}C$ backbone structure; (b) polymeric structure; ω, Φ, and Ψ relate to dihedral angles; R designates the specific amino acid's *side chain* characteristic.

In this context, the optimal bound is defined as the conformation of the final macro-molecular result having the minimum binding free energy. Nevertheless, although in practice additional information is employed, offering *pharmacophore*[2] details, the *a priori* knowledge may be erroneous or misleading as multiple potential binding sites may exist, and reduced flexibility, while focusing on a specific region, may not correctly define the *in vivo* molecular conformations.

The docking problem combines three interrelated principal algorithmic components: a model for representing the molecular complexes, algorithmic mechanisms for performing conformational space search, and a scoring modulus for evaluating the potential solutions. Considering the perspective of the underlying physical principles governing the different aspects of the molecular-related processes, docking and folding are similar in nature. As a consequence, analogous algorithmic techniques are employed for docking and folding, relating to conformational space search and conformation scoring. As in folding, the binding energy landscape has a funnel-like shape, thus the search for an optimal conformation aiming for a global-minimum energy configuration.

The existing approaches may be differentiated in *bound* and *unbound* docking. Bound docking initiates having the receptor and the ligand molecules in a binded conformation, the computational approach being an attempt in reconstructing the originating complex. In this case the component parts of the process are obtained from an initial X-ray/NMR crystal structure, enclosing both the ligand and the receptor in a bound form. At a higher level of complexity, predictive computational schemes involve unbound structures for the ligand and the receptor, which, in this case, may originate from crystallographic native-structure data, *ab initio* calculations, and so on. Algorithmic resolution schemes extend over different optimization methods, ranging from energy minimization approaches to geometric complementarity-based

---

[2] An ensemble of structural features that comport a specific three-dimensional distribution, that is, describing the active binding site conformation, common to most of the ligands, exhibiting an analogous biological activity. The term was defined in 1909 by Paul Ehrlich, a German scientist, being derived from the Greek words *pharmacon*, meaning drug, and *phoros*, meaning bearer, or carrier.

techniques and including elements of electrostatics, van der Waals energy terms, surface contact and overlap criteria, nonpolar surface area, and number of hydrogen bonds, among others.

Due to the intrinsic relation between the structure of a molecule and its functionality, the problem implies important consequences in medicine- and biology-related fields. An extended referential resource for protein structural data may be accessed through the Brookhaven Protein Data Bank[3] 1. For a comprehensive introductory article on the structure of proteins, consult Reference 2. Also, for a glossary of terms, see Reference 3.

8.1.1 Complexity Considerations

The accuracy of the computational docking is inherently determined by the flexibility level used in modeling the ligand and the receptor molecules. Simulating flexibility is computationally expensive, hence a bias is mandatory at the price of the accuracy of the results—to be mentioned for accuracy the methods based on binding free-energy calculations as in Reference 4. A classification of the existing approaches by considering the flexibility as a criterion conducts a classification consisting of three classes of docking.

- Rigid docking—An extreme simplification of the docking process by considering both the ligand and the receptor as rigid entities, no flexibility being allowed at any point, neither the ligand nor the binding site in the receptor.
- Partially flexible docking—To some extent flexibility is modeled in the process by focusing on the smaller molecule—typically the ligand—or by defining comprehensive regions of significance.
- Flexible docking—Both the ligand and the receptor are modeled as flexible molecules, although, to some extent, limitations may be imposed in order to reduce the computational complexity. An example of molecular docking of a highly flexible ligand to a highly flexible macromolecule is described in Reference 5.

The docking problem is computationally difficult, since the number of possible binding combinations exponentially increases in correlation with the magnitude of the involved molecular complexes. The corresponding degrees of freedom are determined by the three translational and the three rotational axes. As a consequence, ligand and binding-site flexibility is computationally expensive to model, increasing the number of possible conformations (resulting as a power of the number of rotatable bonds). As an example [6], note that for a molecular complex with 10 rotatable bonds and with six minima allowed per bond, the number of possible conformations rises at 3.48×10^9. As a direct implication, no extensive conformational space exploration is possible, unless *a priori* information is provided. Different approaches

[3] http://www.rcsb.org—Brookhaven Protein Data Bank offers geometrical structural data for a large number of proteins.

may be considered for attaining complexity reduction, by assuming and employing knowledge of the binding site as well as by performing rigid-body docking. The main drawbacks incurred in such approaches are the fact that there might exist multiple potential binding sites and that extensive simplification may lead to inaccurate models and predictions of the native molecular complexes.

8.1.2 Historical Remarks

The first approaches for molecular docking and related aspects were developed at the beginning of the 1980s, the initial principles being based on geometric criteria—one of the first geometrical resolution schemes was developed by Kuntz et al. [7]. Considering the geometric surface and structural complementarity, the alignment of the ligand and the receptor is achievable by computing a rigid transformation, thus performing a geometric fit of the two molecules. Mathematical models were constructed for describing the van der Waals surface, along with techniques for molecular surface analysis—one important landmark was set by Connolly [8]. Another important contribution to be mentioned is the one of Crick [9] who remarked that the side chains of the coiled coils (structural motifs consisting of two to five α-helixes) exhibit complementarity and, hence, can be modeled as knobs fitting into holes.

The basis for domain rearrangement studies in large proteins were set in the late 1950s by Koshland [10], as noted by Halperin et al. [11], after more than two decades, further studies being conducted by Janin and Wodak [12] and Bennett and Huber [13]; domain movements were later classified in *shear* and *hinge binding* movements by Lesk et al. [14].

Addressing the molecular docking by quantifying the binding energy of the receptor and the ligand involves as a fundamental component a force field model. The construction of an energetic model is based on the atomic coordinates of the two molecules, approximating the Born–Oppenheimer ground-state energy surface. As it is not computationally feasible to employ quantum mechanics structure calculations, classical approaches make use of molecular dynamics on the basis of experimentally derived parameters. Initial formulations for molecular force field models date back to the beginning of the 1980s, originating in organic chemistry studies.

For an extensive introduction enumerating the principles of docking and encompassing the results obtained over the last decades, please refer to Reference 11. Also, for a detailed description of classical force fields designed for protein simulations, refer to Reference 15.

Outline of the following sections
A brief introduction to the large-scale grid computing domain is offered in Section 8.2, continued with presenting several standard approaches, the most widely used resolution schemes being enumerated along with a minimalistic description in Section 8.3. Furthermore, results presented in comparative studies are included, with several works in the domain offering an overview of the molecular docking domain. Of interest for the herein addressed segment of the docking research field, evolutionary algorithms and genetic algorithms are initially defined from a stand-alone, problem-independent

point of view, to be later detailed as a part of grid-enabled implementations. Also, as an important component of the protein–protein docking approaches, a number of consecrated force fields are presented in general terms. In Section 8.4 a few remarkable docking on grid experiments are presented; the final section, Section 8.5, offers examples of docking software.

8.2   INTRODUCTION TO LARGE-SCALE GRID COMPUTING

The proliferation of research and industrial projects on grid computing is leading to the proposition of several, sometimes confusing, definitions of the grid concept. As a consequence, a number of articles [16,17] especially address an attentive analysis of these definitions. A computational grid is a scalable pool of heterogeneous dynamic resources, geographically distributed across multiple administrative domains and owned by different organizations. Discussing the afferent-defining characteristics, a summarizing description might be formulated as follows:

- *The grid includes multiple autonomous administrative domains*—The users and providers of resources are clearly identified. This allows to reduce the complexity of the security issue; however, the firewall traversal remains a critical problem to deal with. In global computing middlewares based on large-scale cycle stealing, such as XtremWeb [18], the problem is solved in a natural way as communications are initiated within the boundaries of the domains, "inside the domains."
- *The grid is heterogeneous*—The heterogeneity in a grid is intensified by its large number of resources belonging to different administrative domains. The emergence of data exchange standards and platform-independent technologies such as Java RMI allows to deal with the heterogeneity issue.
- *The grid has a large scale*—The grid has a large number of resources growing from hundreds of integrated resources to millions of PCs. The design of performant and scalable grid applications has to take into account the communication delays.
- *The grid is dynamic*—The dynamic temporal and spatial availability of resources is not an exception but a rule in a grid. Due to the large-scale nature of the grid, the probability of a number of resources failing is high. Such characteristic highlights issues such as dynamic resource discovery, fault tolerance, and so on.

Furthermore, on an algorithmic scale, computational performance is achieved through parallel hybrid cooperative metaheuristics—the gridification of such an approach requires taking into account the characteristics and underlined issues of the computational grids and the parallel cooperative models at the same time. Some of the issues related to grids may be solved by middlewares allowing to hide their inherent complexity to users. The number of issues that could be solved in a transparent way for the users depends on the middleware at hand. The choice of this later mentioned is crucial for performance and ease of use. Maintaining a logical communication topology in a volatile environment may be complex and inefficient because of the high cost of the dynamic reconfiguration of the topology. For example, for an island-based model, one of the approaches allowing to deal with such issue is based on a shared space for storing the emigrant solutions between the islands. The island that initiates a migration operation sends the emigrants to the shared space, and these later are stored together with the identity of their source islands. Islands can also initiate immigration operations by sending requests to the shared space, and immigrants are randomly chosen from this later. In Reference 19, it has been experimentally proven that random topologies (random selection of the target islands) could be as efficient as the common topologies (ring, mesh, etc.). Grid middlewares that support such approaches are Dispatch–Worker ones such as XtremWeb. In such systems, clients can submit their jobs to the dispatcher. A computational pool of volatile workers requests for the jobs from the dispatcher according to the large cycle stealing model. Then, they execute the jobs and return back the results to the dispatcher to be collected later by the clients. The islands could be deployed as workers and the dispatcher could serve to provide the global space.

One of the major limitations of such middlewares is that they are well suited for embarrassingly parallel (e.g., multiparameter) applications with independent tasks. In this case, no communication is required between the tasks and, thus, workers. The deployment of parallel cooperative metaheuristics that need cross-worker/task communication is not straightforward. The developer has the burden to manage and control the complex coordination between the workers. To deal with such problems existing middlewares must be extended with a software layer that implements a coordination model. Several examples of interesting coordination models may be found in the works of Gelernter and Carriero [20] and Papadopoulos and Arbab [21].

8.3   MOLECULAR DOCKING

8.3.1   Molecular Docking Results and Directions

An interesting comparison study is presented in Reference 22, the authors evaluating a random search procedure for flexible molecular docking and four heuristic search algorithms, namely, genetic algorithms, evolutionary programming, simulated annealing, and tabu search. The study is performed on five test cases, using basic implementations of the mentioned heuristics, allowing for flexibility of active site residues of the ligand and receptor, on a user-defined basis or by automatic assignment. The employed energy function includes penalizing factors for internal clashes of ligand and for solutions that are not within the boundaries of a box enclosing the active site—defined by allowing a 2.0-Å deviation, along each axis, as compared with the crystallographic location, resulting in a 64-Å^3 box. The nonbonded interaction term is extracted from four 0.2-Å-resolution pre-calculated grids. The results obtained for the genetic algorithm, as reported by the authors, are presented in Table 8.1.

Table 8.1   Results Obtained for the Genetic Algorithm

Enzyme	Ligand	PDB ID	Success Rate
Dihydrofolate reductase	Methotrexate	3DFR	76%
Influenza virus neuraminidase	DANA	1NSD	57%
HIV-1 protease	XK263	1HVR	59%
Thrombin	NAPAP	1ETS	11%
Thrombin	Argatroban	1ETR	13%

In Fig. 8.2, a schematic representation is offered, for the dihydrofolate reductase methotrexate complex (PDB ID 3DFR)—the first column—and for the HIV-1 protease with the XK263 inhibitor (PDB ID 1HVR)—the second column. In addition, the structure of the ligands is depicted—the methotrexate and the XK263 inhibitor, respectively. The presented molecular graphic images were produced using the UCSF Chimera package from the Resource for Biocomputing, Visualization, and Informatics at the University of California, San Francisco (supported by NIH P41 RR-01081) [23].

The presented test cases, as the authors mention, were selected on criteria relating to their importance for the molecular docking domain, the inhibitors being used as therapeutical agents in clinical trial drugs or already on the market. Moreover, dihydrofolate reductase methotrexate is evidentiated as being the standard benchmark employed in recent research. The algorithms under study were compared considering the characteristics of the energy distribution, that is, the average energy of a conformation, and the distribution width (having as center the average energy point). In addition, the root mean square deviation (RMSD) is computed, having as reference the crystallographic complexed conformation. A standard RMSD definition considers the Cartesian deviations as follows:

$$\sqrt{\frac{\sum_{i=1}^{n_{At}}(x^2_{dev,i} + y^2_{dev,i} + z^2_{dev,i})}{n_{At}}}$$

where n_{At} stands for the number of atoms considered, and $x_{dev,i}$, $y_{dev,i}$, and $z_{dev,i}$ denote the deviation of the ith atom on each of the Cartesian axes, respectively, as compared to the crystallographic coordinates.

The success rate is defined as the percent of solutions having an RMSD within 1.5 Å as opposed to the crystallographic structure. The authors conclude that, considering the median energies as evaluation criterion, the genetic algorithm ranked first in three of the five test cases. Hence, as a conclusion, it may be stated that genetic algorithms stand as candidate methods for conformational sampling. For the detailed results of the study and for a more in-depth description of the algorithms, as well as for the context of the performed experiments, consult the previously cited paper. A pseudocode outline is offered for each of the algorithms along with a schematic chemical representation of the employed ligands.

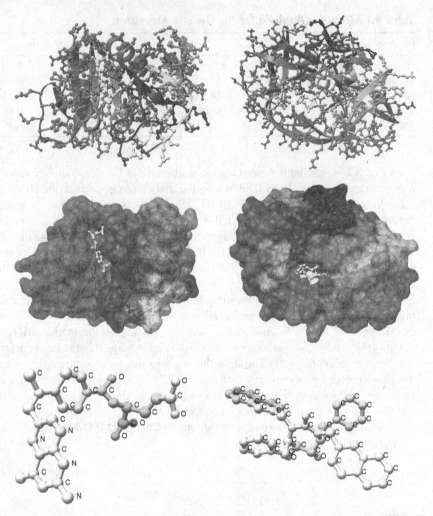

Figure 8.2. The first column depicts the 3DFR complex, the second column corresponds to 1HVR. The images in the first line display structural patterns, in addition, in the second line, the surface of the receptors being drawn. The third line outlines the structure of the ligands.

Addressing the various parametric elements modeling the behavior of conformation sampling methods, the work of Thomsen [24] discusses the impact of variation operators and local search hybrids employed for flexible ligand docking evolutionary algorithms. The performance of the evolutionary algorithms is evaluated by varying different algorithm specific settings, for example, population size, mutation, recombination, and local search operators. The presented results lead to an interesting conclusion, indicating that local search operators determine the EAs to be more prone to getting trapped in local minima, hence being unable to sample an extensive conformational domain. As a counterpart, an annealing scheme for variance control in the mutation operator is identified as being an important efficiency determinant component. In this context, the search for different annealing schemes is underlined as an interesting area for further research.

Another comprehensive study was conducted by Morris et al. [25], comparing a Monte Carlo simulated annealing, a common genetic algorithm, and a Lamarckian genetic algorithm. The article discusses the various aspects related to the compared algorithms, problem concepts, empirical free energy function definition, among others. Overall, it is concluded with the efficiency of the Lamarckian genetic algorithm under study, indicating it as the candidate for the case of ligands with an increased number of degrees of freedom.

8.3.2   Force Field Models for Protein Docking

In order to accurately address the docking problem, by analytical and computational means, a mathematical model that describes interatomic interactions must be constructed. The interactions to be considered are a resultant of electrostatic forces, entropy, hydrophobic characteristics, hydrogen bonding, and so on. In practice, a trade-off is accepted, opposing accuracy against the approximation level, the existing models varying from exact, physically correct mathematical formalisms, to purely empirical approaches. The main categories to be mentioned are *de novo, ab initio* electronic structure calculations, semiempirical methods, and molecular mechanics based models.

An introductory study discussing different force field theoretical notions may be found in Reference 26, the article proposing a general perspective, with a focus on quantum mechanics calculations. Additionally, an extensive discussion on force fields designed for protein simulations, with in-depth details, is offered in the article of Reference 15. The first part of the mentioned work covers the evolution of the force fields, starting from the 1980s and discussing various formulations that include the Amber, CHARMM, and OPLS force fields. Further, the authors complete the study by including details on charge distribution flexible models, polarizable force fields, models including environment effects, and so on. Neumaier [2] represents another important referential work, encompassing a variate range of protein-related aspects, from the structure of proteins to algorithmic approaches and mathematical modeling. In addition, a CHARMM potential formulation is exemplified in the mentioned article, as described in Table 8.2.

In the exposed CHARMM potential, Q_i represents partial charges, determined in order to approximate the potential of the electron cloud, while D represents a dielectric constant. φ stands for the interatomic pair potential, in simplistic forms being expressed as a *Lennard–Jones* potential:

$$\varphi \left(\frac{R_0}{r} \right) = \left(\frac{R_0}{r} \right)^{12} - 2 \left(\frac{R_0}{r} \right)^{6}$$

The values assigned for the constants present in the expression are determined in concordance with the atoms type and, moreover, in correlation with the location of

Table 8.2 A CHARMM Potential Example Presented in the Work of Arnold Neumaier

$V(x) =$	$\displaystyle\sum_{\text{bonds}}$	$c_l(b - b_0)^2$	(b—bond length)
$+$	$\displaystyle\sum_{\text{bond angles}}$	$c_a(\theta - \theta_0)^2$	(θ—bond angle)
$+$	$\displaystyle\sum_{\text{improper torsion angles}}$	$c_i(\tau - \tau_0)^2$	(τ—improper torsion angle)
$+$	$\displaystyle\sum_{\text{dihedral angles}}$	$trig(\omega)$	(ω—dihedral angle)
$+$	$\displaystyle\sum_{\text{charged pairs}}$	$\dfrac{Q_i Q_j}{D r_{ij}}$	(r_{ij}—Euclidean dist. from i to j)
$+$	$\displaystyle\sum_{\text{unbonded pairs}}$	$c_w \varphi(\frac{R_i + R_j}{r_{ij}})$	(R_i—the radius of the atom i)

the atoms in the functional group. The constants b_0, θ_0, and τ_0 represent equilibrium constants corresponding to reference bond length, reference bond angle, and reference improper torsion angle, respectively.

The exact mathematical model describing molecular systems is formulated upon the Schrödinger equation, which makes use of molecular wavefunctions for modeling the spatiotemporal probability distribution of constituent particles—an introductory section may be found in Reference 26. It should be noted that, though offering the most accurate approximation, the *Schrödinger* equation cannot be solved in exact manner for more than two interacting particles. Extended explanations for the herein exposed directions are available via References 2, 26, and 27.

Ab initio (first principles) calculations rely on quantum mechanics for determining different molecular characteristics, comprising no approximations and with no *a priori* required experimental data. Molecular orbital methods make use of *basis functions* for solving the *Schrödinger* equation. The high computational complexity of the formalism restricts their appliance area to systems composed of tens of atoms.

Semiempirical methods substitute computationally expensive segments by *ab initio* technique approximations. A decrease in the time required for calculus is obtained by employing simplified models for electron–electron interactions: *extended Hückel model, neglect of differential overlap, neglect of diatomic differential overlap*, and so on.

Empirical methods rely upon molecular dynamics (classical mechanics based methods), and were introduced by Alder and Wainwright [28,29]. After more than a decade, protein simulations were initiated on bovine pancreatic trypsin inhibitor—BPTI [30]. Empirical methods often represent the only applicable methods for large molecular systems, namely, proteins and polymers. Empirical methods do not make use of the quantum mechanics formalism, relying solely upon classical Newtonian mechanics, that is, Newton's second law—the equation of motion. Conceptually, molecular dynamics models do not dissociate atoms into electrons and nuclei but regard them as indivisible entities.

8.3.3   Resolution Schemes for Molecular Docking

As no exploration method is applicable for performing an exhaustive conformational space search due to computational complexity matters, approximation schemes are employed as resolution patterns for molecular docking. The related exploration algorithms, in basic form, can be classified in geometric complementarity methods, molecular dynamics based algorithms, Monte Carlo methods, evolutionary approaches, among other. In the following, a few standard approaches are sketched, referential work being cited as the starting point for further study—to no extent and by no means exhaustive in description, serving for no more than a basic outline.

8.3.3.1   Geometric Matching

Molecular complementarity, on a geometrical and biochemical basis, may be computationally simulated by using geometric primitives for defining the molecular constituent entities, that is, atoms, and other entries. Different geometrical attributes may be used at this point in order to define an optimal conformation as, for example, surface normals, molecular overlap, and so on. Matching techniques utilize geometric hashing and indexing schemes, grid-based Fast Fourier Transformation (FFT) docking correlation, rigid three-dimensional geometric transformations (as affine and projective transformations), and so on.

For a more in-detail, geometry-oriented discussion of the aforementioned concepts, please refer to Reference 31. For an induced-fit, geometry-based docking exemplification, refer to Reference 32, in which a computer vision inspired, hinge-bending docking approach is illustrated. As the authors remark, domain movements, at different structural levels, represent an essential element to consider when constructing a molecular docking resolution pattern. Conformational modifications were allowed for both the ligand and the receptor, thus providing an induced-fit docking procedure— although inside-domain conformational rigidity is maintained, molecular flexibility is simulated by allowing for domain movements.

The algorithm, as the authors note, has been tested on five complexes, using a flexible docking approach, allowing hinge-bending movements in the ligand molecules: (1) the HIV-1 protease with the U-75875 inhibitor, (2) the dihydrofolate reductase complexed with methotrexate and (3) separately with NADPH, (4) lactate dehydrogenase complexed with NAD-lactate, and (5) a Fab fragment of an IgG antibody complexed with a peptide antigen. The obtained average RMS of the correct solutions is reported to be at 1.4 Å with a 1-min average execution time for each complex—the experiments were conducted on a SGI-Challenge R8000 machine.

8.3.3.2 Monte Carlo Techniques

Monte Carlo methods, or, *in extenso*, importance sampling and Markov chain Monte Carlo, perform random conformational space exploration, discriminating the selected conformations by following a Boltzman probability distribution model. Monte Carlo methods are commonly employed as refinement components in multistage molecular docking, in correlation with terms for quantifying solvation and electrostatic effects, among others. A multistage molecular docking approach usually consists of (a) an initial, fast, conformational sampling phase, relying upon soft-docking techniques, geometric matching, and so on, and (b) a final phase accounting for the refinement of the resulting conformations—achieved by performing accurate energy calculations, increased flexibility, and so on.

In Reference 33, an approach including Monte Carlo algorithmic components is exposed, a more detailed study of the initial method being published in Reference 34. The authors analyzed several protein–protein complexes: For all the reported cases, the obtained conformations fall within 3.0-Å RMSD as compared to the crystal structure. As a first step, automated rigid-body Monte Carlo docking simulations are conducted on a nonredundant data set of protein–protein complexes, with soft interaction energy potentials being precomputed over a grid enclosing the potential active site. The sampling phase is carried by a pseudo-Brownian Monte Carlo algorithm, with the Metropolis criterion being used as a conformational filter. For the initial phase, a complete simulation cycle consists of 20,000 energy evaluations at the end of each random step, with a local optimization being performed. The second phase, the refinement step, is focused on further optimizing the interface side chains by using a Biased Probability Monte Carlo algorithm—the induced fit of the association is thus simulated, allowing for near-native conformation solutions. The energy terms accommodate the van der Waals and the Coulomb electrostatic energy, hydrogen bonding, and torsion energy, describing also the internal energy for the ligand interface side chains:

$$E = E_{H\text{vw}} + E_{C\text{vw}} + E_{\text{el}} + E_{\text{hb}} + E_{\text{hp}}$$

where, as the authors note, $E_{H\text{vw}}$ represents the van der Waals potential for a hydrogen atom probe, $E_{C\text{vw}}$ the van der Waals potential for a heavy atom probe (that is, a generic carbon of 1.7-Å radius), E_{el} the electrostatic potential generated from the receptor (considering a distance-dependent dielectric constant), E_{hb} the hydrogen-bonding potential, and E_{hp} a hydrophobicity potential.

8.3.3.3 Evolutionary Algorithms

Evolutionary algorithms are stochastic search iterative techniques, inspired from the Darwinian evolutionary theory, having a large area of appliance—epistatic, multimodal, multicriterion, and highly constrained problems [35]. Stochastic operators are applied for evolving an initial randomly generated population, in an iterative manner, that is, in generations. Each of the individuals composing the population contains genotype information encoding its defining features—the phenotype. Each generation undergoes a selection process, with the individuals being evaluated by employing a problem-specific fitness function.

Algorithm 1 EA pseudocode.

```
Generate(P(0));
t := 0;
while not Termination_Criterion(P(t)) do
   Evaluate(P(t)) ;
   P'(t)      := Selection(P(t)) ;
   P'(t)      := Apply_Reproduction_Ops(P'(t)) ;
   P(t + 1)   := Replace(P(t), P'(t)) ;
   t := t + 1;

endwhile
```

The pseudocode above exposes the generic components of an EA. The main sub-classes of EAs are the genetic algorithms, evolutionary programming, and evolution strategies, among others.

Due to nontrivial addressed problems, requiring extensive processing time, different approaches were designed in order to reduce the computational costs. Complexity is also addressed by developing specialized operators or hybrid and parallel algorithms. We have to note that the parallel affinity of the EAs represents a feature determined by their intrinsic population-based nature. In Reference 36, three main parallel models are identified: the island synchronous cooperative model, the parallel evaluation of the population, and the distributed evaluation of a single solution.

Genetic algorithms (GAs) are population-based metaheuristics that allow a powerful exploration of the conformational space. However, they have limited search intensification capabilities, which are essential for neighborhood-based improvement (the neighborhood of a solution refers to part of the problem's landscape). Therefore, different approaches combine GAs with local search methods, in order to improve both the exploration and the intensification capabilities of the two techniques.

For a complete overview on parallel and grid specific metaheuristics, please refer to References 35, 36, 37, and 38.

8.4   MOLECULAR DOCKING ON GRIDS

The main computational challenge of molecular docking consists in screening a large number of compounds against a protein target, in the search for a potential inhibitor to be further used in drug design. Considering a real-life approach, several problematic elements have to be overcome—screening chemical databases consisting of millions of compounds rises data transfer and storage difficulties as well as computational time problems. As specified in Reference 39, considering a few minutes to hours as the expense for screening a compound on a standard desktop computer, depending on structural complexity, results in years for screening the entire database. The authors extrapolate offering a more specific example for edifying the computational complexity: For a screening involving 180,000 compounds, and with a per-compound execution time expected to take about three hours on a desktop computer, the amount of required processing time raises to 540,000 hours, more than 60 years. Moreover, as the authors indicate, a cluster-based supercomputer with 64 nodes might reduce the computation time to about one year, or, further, to be solved by a grid of hundreds of computers within a day.

As an outline for the molecular docking on grids, it may be stated that the process is largely biased toward the computational aspect, a reduced fraction of time being allocated for data transfer. Nevertheless, data transfer imposes a problem because it is impractical to replicate an entire database of compounds over the nodes of a distributed environment. Alleviating the problem is possible by selective replication of the database over a reduced number of coordinating nodes, as well as by dynamic data distribution, inquiring remote databases as the computation advances.

Although extensively platform and grid-environment oriented and not offering relevant information regarding the details of the employed docking protocol, the work of Buyya et al. [39] represents a starting point in understanding the principles of a grid-enabled approach. The docking code enclosed in the environment, DOCK, represents a research result of the University of California in San Francisco (UCSF)—a comprehensive insight of the algorithm is given in Reference 40.

The paper is concerned with offering the development details of a *Virtual Laboratory*, as the authors entitled the developed computing system, constructed on top of several existing Grid technologies. The environment is defined as a layered architecture as depicted below:

- **DOCK**—the central molecular docking algorithmic element
- **Nimrod Parameter Modeling Tools**—allows for the DOCK software to be enabled as a parameter sweep application
- **Nimrod-G Grid Resource Broker**—responsible for scheduling the DOCK jobs on the grid
- **Chemical database (CDB) management and intelligent access tools**
  - CDB database lookup/index table generation
  - CDB and associated index table replication
  - CDB replica catalogue for CDB resource discovery
  - CDB servers for providing CDB services
  - CDB broker for selecting a suitable CDB service (replica selection)
  - CDB clients for fetching molecular records (data movement)
- **GrACE**—resource trading toolkit software
- **Globus middleware**—secure and uniform access to distributed resources

The above-presented details are extracted from the previously mentioned article; for further details or references regarding the components, consult the cited paper. As an outline, it is straightforward to observe the complexity of a distributed approach, as determined by several combined factors.

The execution pattern followed for completing a screening experiment consists in first formulating the query as a time and resource constrained problem. Further, the broker is responsible for discovering the available resources and for establishing the associated costs, with a scheduling being constructed for mapping the docking tasks—for each task, a list of operations to be performed is specified. Finally, the broker dispatcher deploys an agent on each of the identified resources, the agent being responsible for executing the enlisted operations. A data broker component is responsible for performing a transaction with a CDB service provider, in order to obtain a molecule record.

Scheduling experimentations are reported to have been conducted on a grid resource in Australia (one Sun: Ultra-1 node) with the additional support of four resources in Japan (three sites regrouping twelve Sun: Ultra-4 nodes and two Sun: Ultra-2 nodes) and one in the United States of America (eight Sun: Ultra-8 nodes). The experimentation consisted of a 200-molecule screening trial, on an endothelin-converting enzyme (ECE) receptor.

Another impressive large-scale docking on grids is reported in Reference 41, the article reporting on the effort of developing new drugs for fighting malaria—part of the WISDOM project (*World-wide In Silico Docking on Malaria*, a European initiative initially reuniting the Fraunhofer Institute for Algorithms and Scientific Computing, in Germany, and the Corpuscular Physics Laboratory, CNRS/IN2P3, in France). The goal of the project aimed at proposing new potential inhibitors for a family of proteins produced by *Plasmodium falciparium*, as drug resistance reduced the efficiency of classical pharmaceutics. The demonstration took place starting from the 11th of July until the 19th of August, 2005, enumerating over 46-million docked ligands and simultaneously gathering 1700 computers from 15 countries around the world. Another closely related report is offered in Reference 42, an outcome of the first mentioned article, fighting against avian flu. Authors mention the work to be based on docking tools such as AutoDock. The performed experiments made use of more than 2000 CPUs, performing virtual screening over the extent of six weeks. Authors report to have screened eight protein targets against 308,585 compounds, each target simulating a possible mutation of the avian flu virus. The estimated equivalent sequential computation time was estimated to be more than 16 years, with an overall speedup of 203, while having a distribution efficiency of 84%. The corroborated results for the two experiments are presented in Table 8.3, as exposed by the authors in the papers cited above.

Table 8.3   Corroborated Results for Two Experiments

Compl. Dockings[a]	Duration	1CPU exec.[b]	Speedup	Distr. Eff.[c]
2×10^6	6 weeks	88.3 years	767.37	38.4%
308585	30 days	16.7 years	203	84%

The first line of the table corresponds to the WISDOM experiment.
[a]Total number of completed dockings.
[b]Equivalent execution time on 1 CPU.
[c]Distribution efficiency—defined as the approximation of the ratio between the overall speedup and the maximum number of concurrent CPUs.

The experiment resulted in more than two million docking complexes, cumulating 123,440 files with a total amount of 600 GB of data, stored for further study and in-depth biological analysis to be performed in several research laboratories.

In the same line of ideas, in Reference 43 a Grid-enabled conformational space approach is presented, CONFLEX-G, the exposed method being derived from CON-FLEX, a sequential exhaustive conformational space search of low-energy regions. The implementation is based on a grid RPC system, called OmniRPC, a thread safe implementation of Ninf RPC. The original CONFLEX algorithm, as defined by the authors, consists of four distinct stages:

- An initial conformation is extracted from a previously discovered database of conformers.
- Perturbations are applied on the initial selected structure, in order to generate trial structures.
- The previously generated trial structures are optimized on a geometrical basis.
- The optimized structures are compared with other conformers stored in a database, preserving the newly discovered structures.

Trial structures, as mentioned in the paper, are obtained by corner flapping and edge flipping for the ring atoms and stepwise rotation for side chains or backbone chains. Because the geometry optimization phase takes as much as 95% of the spent computational time, the method has been parallelized using a master–worker technique.

8.5   MOLECULAR DOCKING SOFTWARE

Considering the numerous techniques and applications developed in order to address the molecular docking problem, it is not possible to enumerate even an infinitesimal fraction of the existing software applications. As a consequence, in the following a resume is presented, enclosing a reduced number of the most representative developed applications. An ample review discussing the characteristics of different existing molecular docking software is presented in Reference 44, offering a categorized approach and discussing scoring function aspects and multiple method algorithms. The final part of the article offers bibliographic references regarding techniques of comparison studies.

8.5.1   AutoDock

AutoDock,[4] *Automated Docking of Flexible Ligands to Macromolecules* is a collection of components with aims ranging from the interactive definition of the torsion angles to automatic docking. The software is distributed free of charge for academic

---

[4] http://www.scripps.edu/mb/olson/doc/autodock

and noncommercial use, and a commercial version is also available. AutoDock represented the basis of several large-scale experiments on grids, as mentioned in the previous section, being also employed behind the *FightAIDS@Home*[5] project—reported to have cumulated over 2×10^{15} of energy evaluations for HIV-1 protease candidate inhibitors. In addition, *AutoDockTools* or *ADT* completes the application by offering a visual interface. From an algorithmic point of view, AutoDock employs several evolutionary techniques, also including Monte Carlo simulated annealing and Lamarckian Genetic Algorithm. The AMBER-derived force field model is based on linear regression analysis, using empirical weighting factors determined from protein–ligand complexes for which the binding constants are known. A detailed description is available in Reference 25.

8.5.2 DOCK

DOCK represents one of the pioneering programs in molecular docking, at its origins, approximating the process by considering both the ligand and the receptor as rigid molecules. The docking algorithm consists of a conformational search method and a scoring function, relying on graph theoretical techniques for superimposing ligand atoms onto predefined sets of points in the active site. The algorithm presumes the chemical and geometrical complementarity of the molecules, hence inaccurately modeling docking processes involving conformational modifications. Furthermore, the algorithm is directed by considering *a priori* important regions of the designated potential thus alleviating the computational complexity incurred by the conformational sampling process. Newer versions of DOCK offer the possibility of modeling the ligand in a flexible manner, as well as simulating protein flexibility by using multiple conformations. Details may be found in the work of Ewing and Kuntz [40], which offers an insight into the graph techniques enclosed in the algorithm, presenting the final part of a number of experiment-extracted results.

8.5.3 FlexX and FlexE

FlexX[6] is a fragment-based incremental construction algorithm, with FlexE being derived from the aforementioned; essentially, it makes use of ensemble approach adapted concepts: scoring function, interaction scheme, and incremental construction algorithm, among others. The molecular docking process in FlexX considers multiple stages, initiated by selecting a base ligand fragment, a determinant for the rest of the process; a geometry interaction database is used for the selection. Further, a geometry-based alignment is performed, including hydrophobic interaction elements and geometric constraints; finally the ligand is built into the active site, in incremental fashion. A comparison test case of FlexX and FlexE is presented in Reference 45, with the experimentations being performed on 10 protein structures ensembles—an

[5]http://fightaidsathome.scripps.edu
[6]http://www.biosolveit.de/FlexX

overall of 105 crystal structures. FlexE is reported to find conformations with a 2.0-Å RMSD for 67% of the cases, while, in the same context, FlexX amounts for 63%.

References

1. F.C. Bernstein, T.F. Koetzle, G.J.B. Williams, E.F. Meyer, Jr., M.D. Brice, J.R. Rodgers, O. Kennard, T. Shimanouchi, M. Tasumi, The protein data bank: A computer-based archival file for macromolecular structures, *Journal of Molecular Biology* **112**, 535–542, 1977.

2. A. Neumaier, Molecular modeling of proteins and mathematical prediction of protein structure, *SIAM Review* **39**(3), 407–460, 1997.

3. G. Grassy, H. Kubinyi, Y.C. Martin, M.S. Tute, P. Willett, H. Van de Wasterbeemd, R.E. Carter, Glossary of terms used in computational drug design, *Pure and Applied Chemistry* **69**(5), 1137–1152, 1997.

4. M.L. Lamb, W.L. Jorgensen, Computational approaches to molecular recognition, *Current Opinion in Chemical Biology* **1**, 449–457, 1997.

5. M. Teodoro, G.N.J. Phillips, L.E. Kavraki, Molecular docking: A problem with thousands of degrees of freedom. In IEEE International Conference on Robotics and Automation, IEEE Press, Seoul, Korea, 2001.

6. D. M. Lorber, B. K. Shoichet, Flexible ligand docking using conformational ensembles, *Protein Science* **7**(4), 938–950, 1998.

7. I.D. Kuntz, J.M. Blaney, S.J. Oatley, R. Langridge, T.E. Ferrin, A geometric approach to macromolecule–ligand interactions, *Journal of Molecular Biology*, **161**(2), 269–288, 1982.

8. M. Connolly, Analytical molecular surface calculation, *Journal of Applied Crystallography* **16**(5), 548–558, 1983.

9. F.H.C. Crick, The packing of α-helices: Simple coiled-coils, *Acta Crystallographica* **6**(8–9), 689–697, 1953.

10. D.E. Koshland, Jr. Application of a theory of enzyme specificity to protein synthesis, *Proceedings of the National Academy of Sciences of the United States of America*, **44**, 98–123, 1958.

11. I. Halperin, B. Ma, H. Wolfson, R. Nussinov, Principles of docking: An overview of search algorithms and a guide to scoring functions, *Proteins* **47**(4), 409–443, 2002.

12. J. Janin, S.J. Wodak, Structural domains in proteins and their role in the dynamics of protein function, *Progress in Biophysics and Molecular Biology* **42**(1), 21–78, 1983.

13. R. Bennett, W.S. Huber, Structural and functional aspects of domain motion in proteins, *Critical Review in Biochemistry* **15**, 291–384, 1984.

14. A.M. Lesk, M. Gerstein, C. Chothia, Structural mechanism for domain movements in proteins, *Critical Reviews in Biochemistry* **33**, 6739–6749, 1994.

15. J.W. Ponder, D.A. Case, Force fields for protein simulations, *Advances in Protein Chemistry* **66**, 27–85, 2003.

16. I. Foster, C. Kesselman, S. Tuecke, The anatomy of the Grid: Enabling scalable virtual organizations, *International Journal of High Performance Computing Application*, **15**(3), 200–222, 2001.

17. K. Krauter, R. Buyya, M. Maheswaran, A taxonomy and survey of grid resource management systems for distributed computing, *Software Practice and Experience* **32**(2), 135–164, 2002.

18. C. Germain, V. Neri, G. Fedak, F. Cappello, Xtremweb: Building an experimental platform for global computing, *GRID*, pp. 91–101, 2000.

19. T.C. Belding, The distributed genetic algorithm revisited, in: Lary Eshelman (Ed.), *Proceedings of the Sixth International Conference on Genetic Algorithms*, Morgan Kaufmann, San Francisco, CA, 1995, pp. 114–121.

20. D. Gelernter, N. Carriero, Coordination languages and their significance, *Communications of the ACM* **35**(2), 96, 1992.

21. G.A. Papadopoulos, F. Arbab, Coordination Models and Languages, Centrum voor Wiskunde en Informatica (CWI), ISSN 1386-369X, 31, 761, 55, 1998.

22. D.R. Westhead, D.E. Clark, C.W. Murray, A comparison of heuristic search algorithms for molecular docking, *Journal of Computer-Aided Molecular Design* **11**(3), 209–228, 1997.

23. T.D. Goddard, C.C. Huang, G.S. Couch, D.M. Greenblatt, E.C. Meng, E.F. Pettersen, T.E. Ferrin, Ucsf chimera - a visualization system for exploratory research and analysis, *Journal of Computational Chemistry* **25**(13), 1605–1612, 2004.

24. R. Thomsen, Flexible ligand docking using evolutionary algorithms: investigating the effects of variation operators and local search hybrids, *Biosystems* **72**(1–2), 57–73, 2003.

25. G.M. Morris, D.S. Goodsell, R.S. Halliday, R. Huey, W.E. Hart, R.K. Belew, A.J. Olson, Automated docking using a lamarckian genetic algorithm and an empirical binding free energy function, *Journal of Computational Chemistry* **19**(14), 1639–1662, 1999.

26. H. Dorsett, A. White, Overview of molecular modelling and *ab initio* molecular orbital methods suitable for use with energetic materials, Technical Report, DSTO-GD-0253, Weapons Systems Division, Australia, Sept 2000.

27. A. White, F.J. Zerilli, H.D. Jones, *Ab initio* calculation of intermolecular potential parameters for gaseous decomposition products of energetic materials, Technical Report, DSTO-TR-1016, Weapons Systems Division, Australia, Aug 2000.

28. B.J. Alder, T.E. Wainwright, Phase transition for a hard sphere system, *Journal of Chemical Physics* **27**, 1208–1209, 1957.

29. B. J. Alder, T. E. Wainwright, Studies in molecular dynamics. i. general method, *Journal of Chemical Physics* **31**, 459–466, 1959.

30. B.R. Gelin, J.A. McCammon, M. Karplus, Dynamics of folded proteins, *Nature* **267**, 585–590, 1997.

31. H.J. Wolfson, I. Rigoutsos, Geometric hashing: An overview, *IEEE Computing in Science and Engineering* **4**(4), 10–21, 1997.

32. B. Sandak, H.J. Wolfson, R. Nussinov, Flexible docking allowing induced fit in proteins: Insights from an open to closed conformational isomers, *Proteins* **32**(2), 159–174, 1998.

33. J. Fernandez-Recio, M. Totrov, R. Abagyan, Screened charge electrostatic model in protein–protein docking simulations, in: *Pacific Symposium on Biocomputing*, pp. 552–563, 2002.

34. J. Fernandez-Recio, M. Totrov, R. Abagyan, Soft protein–protein docking in internal coordinates, *Protein Science* **11**(2), 280–291, 2002.

35. S. Cahon, N. Melab, and E.-G. Talbi, An enabling framework for parallel optimization on the computational grid, *CCGRID*, IEEE Computer Society, Los Alamitos, CA, pp. 702–709, 2005.

36. S. Cahon, N. Melab, E.-G. Talbi, Paradiseo: A framework for the reusable design of parallel and distributed metaheuristics, *Journal of Heuristics* **10**(3), 357–380, 2004.

37. E.-G. Talbi, A taxonomy of hybrid metaheuristics, *Journal of Heuristics* **8**(5), 541–564, 2002.

38. E. Alba, E.-G. Talbi, G. Luque, N. Melab, Metaheuristics and parallelism, in: E. Alba, (Ed.), *Parallel Metaheuristics*, Wiley Series on Parallel and Distributed Computing, John Wiley & Sons, Hoboken, NJ, 2005.

39. R. Buyya, K. Branson, J. Giddy, D. Abramson, The virtual laboratory: A toolset to enable distributed molecular modelling for drug design on the world-wide grid, *Concurrency and Computation: Practice and Experience* **15**(1), 1–25, 2003.

40. T.J.A. Ewing, I. D. Kuntz, Critical evaluation of search algorithms for automated molecular docking and database screening, *Journal of Computational Chemistry* **18**(9), 1175–1189, 1998.

41. Y. Legr, M. Reichstadt, F. Jacq, M. Zimmermann, A. Maaß, M. Sridhar, K. Vinod-Kusam, H. Schwichtenberg, M. Hofmann, V. Breton, N. Jacq, J. Salzemann, Demonstration of *in silico* docking at a large

scale on grid infrastructure, in: *Challenges and Opportunities of HealthGrids, Proceedings of Health-Grid 2006*, Studies in Health Technology and Informatics, Ios Press, Amsterdam, 2006.

42. N. Jacq, L.-Y. Ho, H.-Y. Chen, V. Breton, I. Merelli, L. Milanesi, S.C. Lin, H.-C. Lee, J. Salzemann, Y.-T. Wu, Grid-enabled high throughput *in-silico* screening against influenza a neuraminidase, NETTAB 2006, Santa Margherita, Italy, 2006.

43. Y. Nakajima, M. Sato, H. Goto, T. Boku, D. Takahashi, Implementation and performance evaluation of conflex-g: Grid-enabled molecular conformational space search program with omnirpc ICS '04, in: *Proceedings of the 18th Annual International Conference on Supercomputing*, ACM Press, New York, pp. 154–163, 2004.

44. P. J. Jewsbury, R. D. Taylor, J. W. Essex, A review of protein–small molecule docking methods, *Journal of Computer-Aided Molecular Design* **16**, 151–166, 2002.

45. M.R.H. Claußen, C. Buning, T. Lengauer, Flexe: Efficient molecular docking considering protein structure variations, *Journal of Molecular Biology* **308**, 377–395, 2001.

9

DEPLOYMENT OF GRID LIFE SCIENCES APPLICATIONS

Vincent Breton, Nicolas Jacq, Vinod Kasam, and Jean Salzemann

9.1 INTRODUCTION

9.1.1 Context

The availability of massive volumes of data in molecular biology has completely changed the landscape of life sciences. In genomics, several hundreds of genomes are now sequenced. In transcriptomics, the development of microarray technology provides a wealth of information on gene expression. In proteomics, hundreds of thousands of proteins are now fully sequenced. All these data are much harder to interpret than it was initially foreseen. Human genome sequencing did not open an era of discoveries but rather has highlighted the complexity of life. Modeling of living systems is just emerging with the onset of theoretical biology. In addition, one can wonder how long it will take biology to achieve modeling the living organisms with their multiple expression levels when it took physics more than 20 years to build a standard model to describe the world of particles.

In front of the challenges raised by molecular biology, a new scientific discipline has emerged at the interface between computer and life sciences: bioinformatics. Bioinformatics aims at developing software tools to help biologists in the analysis of their data. Research in bioinformatics is therefore about new algorithms and new services with improved performances. Twenty years of research in bioinformatics has brought a wealth of new software tools, databases, and portals. A major challenge specific to molecular biology is that researchers need to have a constant access to the state of the art in order to compare their results to the existing information. Molecular biologists need an on-demand access to a constantly actualized representation of all the knowledge accumulated in their field. This requirement is not at all expressed in other fields of sciences like physics or chemistry, where the evolution of the knowledge corpus is much slower.

Grid Computing for Bioinformatics and Computational Biology. Edited by E.-G. Talbi and A.Y. Zomaya. Copyright © 2008 John Wiley & Sons, Inc.

Scientists now depend on databases to access the avalanche of information that they produce. For example, geneticists are now trawling through the human genome for genes that are involved in diseases. Data providers put a huge amount of effort into providing data resources that are comprehensive, user-friendly, and cross-linked to other databases; but different data providers use different methods. This means that a researcher might have to search 10 or more different databases to find all the information pertaining to a particular set of candidate genes. If they are doing these kinds of searches on a regular basis, they will want their own local copies of all these databases. Maintaining up-to-date and fully functioning versions of all these databases and the tools to search them is a huge and complex task.

There is therefore a need to offer to the biologists access to an up-to-date view of the molecular biology data relevant to their research. This requires integrating a large variety of databases filled with information relevant to the different expression levels of living systems. With the explosion of high-throughput data production systems, the databases are exponentially growing.

In summary, the main challenge for data analysis in life sciences is to offer to the molecular biologists an integrated and up-to-date view of an exponentially growing volume of data in a multiplicity of formats.

9.1.2   The Grid Impact

Grids propose environments where new approaches to science can be envisaged. These new approaches are described under the concept of e-Science, which is about inventing and exploiting new advanced computational methods:

- To generate, curate, and analyze data coming from experiments, observations, and simulations in order to demonstrate and preserve reliable proofs
- To develop and explore models and simulations combining computation and data at an unprecedented scale to achieve quick, reliable, and relevant results
- To help the setup of distributed virtual organizations to ease collaboration and sharing of resources and information with guaranteed conditions of security, reliability, responsibility, and flexibility

Today, grids offer to biologists and bioinformaticians on demand computing and storage resources. Several grid projects oriented toward the life sciences are underway, such as the North Carolina BioGrid [1], the Canadian BioGrid [2], the EuroGrid BioGrid [3], the Asia Pacific BioGrid [4], the GenoGrid [5], the cancer Biomedical informatics grid [6–8], the Simdat project [9], and the Biomedical Informatics Research Network [10]. All these projects involve the sharing of computational resources and the large-scale movement of data. One example is OpenMolGRID [11], an extensible, grid-enabled environment using UNICORE for the molecular science and engineering system that is effectively used in molecular design [12,13]. There are an increasing number of life sciences applications that employ cluster/grid technologies [14–24,25]. grids allow offering services like database replication or automatic database update to reduce the load of the groups offering bioinformatics services to the scientific community. Grids also offer an environment to achieve integration of the molecular biology data through standardized access to bioinformatics resources throughout Europe and beyond. Standardization should allow to turn the relationship between user and provider on its head by enabling data providers to provide well-defined interfaces to their databases that will conform to the same standards, essentially creating a grid that will allow users to make the most of dispersed data resources.

To achieve this vision, research and development are needed at several levels:

- The grid technology must provide the services needed by data providers to develop the interfaces to their databases. Once standards are agreed upon, bioinformatics resources need to be properly interfaced in agreement to these standards.
- A grid infrastructure must be deployed "underneath" the bioinformatics services to provide the resources enabling the services and to provide the security framework defining the access to these resources.
- User interfaces are needed for the biologist to pursue the analysis work. Such interfaces can become workbenches or virtual laboratories where semantic Web technologies are deployed to manipulate the biological objects and concepts while hiding all the underlying technicalities. The development of these high-level environments is eased by the development of standard interfaces to the bioinformatics tools and databases.

All current efforts in the field of grid development for life sciences in Europe address one of these three lines of developments:

- Some efforts like EMBRACE [26] focus on the promotion, development, and implementation of standards for the interoperability of resources in the life sciences community.
- Other efforts like EGEE [27] aim at deploying a secured grid infrastructure offering resources for research communities.
- Other efforts like BioinfoGRID [28] aim at exploiting the existing infrastructures for data production or analysis in relation to molecular biology.
- Other initiatives like myGRID [29] or VLe [30] aim at developing *in silico* workbenches for biologists.

These different initiatives share the use of biological applications as pilots to drive their developments. The definition of these pilot applications depends on the approaches: If the applications are used to drive the deployment of grid infrastructures, they need to take into account the services currently available on these grids and are often a piece of a more complete biological analysis workflow. On the contrary, applications used to drive the deployment of *in silico* workbenches address all the dimensions of a specific workflow but generally do not require significant resources. This illustrates the long way to set up an environment in which hetero-geneous and dispersed life sciences data can be accessed by all users as a tailored information providing system according to their authorization and without loss of information.

There is still a gap between the services made available on the grid infrastructures and the services needed by *in silico* workbenches. This gap is slowly being filled, and the goal of this chapter is to present projects and initiatives that aim at bridging this gap.

9.1.3   Content of This Chapter

In the previous section, we have explained the potential impact of grids to help ana-lyze the avalanche of data generated by high-throughput molecular biology facilities. In this chapter, we are going to provide an overview of the results obtained within the framework of the different projects we are involved. Indeed, significant progress is being made in parallel with the different fronts described previously of standardiza-tion, deployment of grid infrastructures, and development of *in silico* workbenches for biologists. In this chapter, we will not discuss further this last point but refer readers to myGRID [29] and VLe [30] initiatives for further details.

Section 9.2 is going to focus on the issue of developing standardized interfaces that is addressed within the framework of the EMBRACE network of excellence. In Section 9.3, we will describe an attempt to use Web service technology to expose bioinformatics services within the framework of the RUGBI project. In Section 9.4, we will present the WISDOM initiative in the field of *in silico* virtual screening, which is our first successful attempt to deploy a life sciences application at a large scale on the grid.

9.2   INTEROPERABILITY OF BIOINFORMATICS RESOURCES: THE EMBRACE PROJECT

The classical way of enabling bioscientists to use bioinformatics services is to collect a series of databases and software packages on one single location and to augment this system with a hotlist pointing at them. Maintenance of local databases and software is time consuming so that budget limitations often translate directly into service limita-tions. The global introduction of the World Wide Web (WWW) has removed the need for the existence of local bioinformatics service centers because bioscientists can find the same services on the Internet, often even more up to date than is locally possible. Experiments on genomics, transcriptomics, proteomics, metabolomics, and so on, are producing massive amounts of data. Conversion of these data into useful knowledge requires robust and extended access to a large series of bioinformatics facilities. To-day, the Internet allows access to thousands of bioinformatics facilities. Nevertheless, the situation is far from ideal for bioscientists because they need to learn about (and *in silico* visit) all those sites to gather the desired results. Each database has its own id-iosyncratic data schema and nomenclature. Each server uses a different expert-friendly user interface. Most WWW servers can be used only to analyze data one by one.

9.2.1   Goals

The EMBRACE project suggests a solution for this "omics era bioinformatics bottleneck." The goal of EMBRACE is to initiate a grid-based infrastructure that can be used by bioinformatics groups to present to bioscientists an integrated set of bioinformatics databases and software packages, without the need to download data or install software. This grid-based solution should take advantage of the existing national and European infrastructures for security, access, authentication, authorization, data, and information exchange. It should take away the need for bioinformaticians to maintain local copies of databases and software, and should allow them to concentrate fully on homogeneous, bioscientist-friendly interfaces. As a consequence, bioscientists could shift emphasis from technical database and software maintenance issues to scientific data and information integration issues.

In other words, the goal of EMBRACE is to define standards to build a knowledge grid for the European bioinformatics community. This means that the goal of EMBRACE is to enable the integration of bioinformatics services and to make these services available to the community. This is a rather different concept than the idea of building a computing grid because EMBRACE should not only provide support to deploy applications but also offer services specific to the bioinformatics domain and try to cover this domain as much as possible. The main issue is that EMBRACE needs to integrate services and allow humans and machines to understand and use these services in a transparent way. This objective will surely be achieved if EMBRACE can successfully provide common interfaces and rules to make all these services interoperable. For this purpose, manipulated data need to have common definitions using concepts from the scientific domain and interfaces should provide a common way to manipulate these data, which means defining a common protocol to make all these services communicate with each other.

9.2.2   Strategy

A grid is only as useful as the services that are made available on it. Therefore, the EMBRACE strategy is to progressively integrate on its infrastructure the major databases and software tools in bioinformatics, which explicitly says how flexible it has to be. The integration efforts will be driven by an expanding set of test problems representing key issues for bioinformatics service providers and end-user biologists. As a result, groups throughout Europe should be able to use the EMBRACE service interfaces for their own local or proprietary data and tools.

It is envisaged that by the time the EMBRACE grid enables access to most of the popular bioinformatics services, bioinformatics groups from all over Europe will want to join and bring in their own databases and services, thereby generating a bioinformatics facility avalanche that can cope with the postgenomics era data avalanches.

The goal is to achieve integration, and the integration is almost all about interfaces and ontologies. So it means that EMBRACE needs a high-level technology enabling integrating heterogeneous data and systems in a service-oriented architecture (SOA). Major information technology companies have agreed to develop Web services as the technology to enable the deployment of services on Internet. It has also been adopted by the Global grid Forum [31], which is the acknowledged body to propose and develop standards for grid technology. Moreover, the Web service technology provides the bridge between the grid world and the Semantic Web, which is about common formats for interchanging of data and about language for recording how the data relate to real-world objects. It must be understood, however, that most of the existing grid infrastructures presently deployed in the world do not offer a Web service interface to their services and, moreover, none of these infrastructures are truly interoperable.

9.2.3   Status of Web Services

The initial idea behind Web services was to enable the WWW to become more and more the support for real applications and a means of communication among them. The Web services specifications recommended by the World Wide Web Consortium [32] propose a set of standards and protocols allowing the interactions between distant machines over a network. These interactions are made possible through the use of standardized interfaces that basically describe what are the available operations in a service, what are the messages exchanged (requests and responses), and where the service is physically located on the network and through which support. This interface, which is just a conceptual representation of an application written in a given programming language, is written in Web Service Description Language (WSDL) [33]. The typical file extension is wsdl.

The glue between the services, or between a server exposing a Web service and a client (any piece of software that will communicate with the Web services), which enable them to communicate are these request and response messages. They can be described in a standardized way on the network and be exchanged with a standard protocol over basic http or SMTP or any common Internet protocol. All the messages and description languages are based on XML.

The main language used to make Web services communicate with each other is Simple Object Application Protocol (SOAP). SOAP has the advantage of being implemented in several languages and toolkits [2].

9.2.3.1   WSDL

Web Service Description Language is used in Web services to describe the service interface. It includes descriptions of the operations available at the service, the data formats used by the operations, and how and where the service can be accessed. WSDL files can be autogenerated but sometimes tools are not mature enough, which might require manual editing of the WSDL file.

The data formats used by a Web service are expressed using XML schema definitions. These definitions can be combined into a single file that can easily be imported into a WSDL file. This also simplifies the task of updating the data formats at a later stage.

WSDL is rich, resulting in many possible ways to describe interfaces and still be interoperable. The WS-Interoperability Basic Profile [3] provides a mechanism for restricting the WSDL language, and interfaces that are compliant with the profile are therefore more interoperable. A further restriction of WSDL design is the Document/Literal Wrapped style [4]. This is not a specification but is to be considered as a best practice in WSDL design.

9.2.3.2 Web Service Specifications

The Web service specifications can be divided into first-generation and second-generation specifications. The first generation of specifications includes those mentioned above. These specifications are widely adopted and are fairly stable (WSDL will soon come in a new version). The second generation of Web service specifications are often called WS-* because their name usually starts with WS-, such as WS-Addressing and WS-Security. This set of specifications provides functionality for state, workflow composition, security, policies, attachments, and more. The WS-* specifications take advantage of various "utility services" to perform the tasks they are designed for. Another feature of WS-* specifications is that they can require that a client also needs to have a Web service available. Specifications are currently becoming more standardized and stable, but in some areas there are still rapid developments. The main advantages of Web services are as follows:

- They offer great interoperability (mainly because of standardized specifications).
- They enable the communication of processes and the transfers of data independently of the programming language of the underlying applications. Therefore, by extension, virtually almost any piece of software can be exposed as a Web service.
- They can be considered as firewall friendly because they are based on standard Internet protocols.

The main weaknesses of Web services are as follows:

- They are not adapted for transferring huge quantities of data.
- The performance can be worse with respect to other remote procedure call-based communication methods due to the overhead of sending XML messages and multiple encapsulations.
- There is no permanent state.

9.2.3.3 Web Services Resource Framework

Web Services Resource Framework (WSRF) is a set of five specifications [5 REF] that defines conventions for modeling and accessing stateful resources using Web services. The five specifications are WS-Resource, WS-ResourceProperties, WS-ResourceLifetime, WS-ServiceGroup, and WS-BaseFaults. WS-Notification is often related but not part of WSRF. WSRF 1.2 was approved as OASIS standard in April 2006, and WSRF is also part of the future WS roadmap [REF] backed up by HP, IBM, Intel, and Microsoft.

Traditionally, Web services have been either stateless or state handling, which has been implemented in a case-specific way. A common solution is to add state-handling-specific parameters for the operation calls. WSRF separates operations and state by introducing the concept of WS-Resource that maintains the state information during several operation calls.

Simple services could be implemented as stateless services, thus avoiding the complexity of state handling altogether. However, with many services state becomes an issue that has to be dealt with. These include, for example, services with long-lasting operations and large input or output data. In addition to complexity, state handling can also make a Web service substantially more flexible to use and monitor.

In March 2006, the major industry leaders within the field of Web services agreed together with the Globus Alliance that the WSRF specifications would be merged with the WS-Transfer set of specifications. This process is expected to be completed within 18–24 months.

The WSRF specification is already used in the grid world and has several widely used implementations. The industry partners recognize this and will work to simplify the process of merging with WS-Transfer. It should also be noted that the final WS-Transfer specification will semantically be very similar to WSRF and will operate with the same concept of resources, so the difference will mostly be in syntax. The main advantages of WSRF are the following ones:

- Standard and interoperable ways for implementing state in Web services;
- WSRF separates state information from the operations.

The main drawbacks of WSRF are as follows:

- WSRF is still a fairly new specification.
- Tool support for WSRF is not very good yet.
- WSRF will be merged with WS-Transfer.

The WSRF Primer [11] is a good source for further information on WSRF technology. The WSRF specification version 1.2 as standardized by OASIS is compliant with WS-I Basic Profile 1.1, which proposes a set of rules to achieve interoperability of web services between different platforms. However, the existing tools to produce WSRF services are not yet WS-I compliant.

9.3   REPLICATION AND UPDATE OF MOLECULAR BIOLOGY DATABASES

In the previous section, we have described the efforts deployed within EMBRACE to develop standard interfaces to the existing databases and tools using Web service technology. A grid for bioinformatics needs to provide access to these resources, but it also needs to provide additional services. As stressed in the introduction, biologists require access to updated databases for a comparative analysis. Update of molecular biology databases is a growing burden on the biomedical research community. The grid allows us to share and replicate data. In this section, we present a service to automatically update the biology databases from a single changing reference using web services. This service was deployed on the French RUGBI grid infrastructure.

9.3.1 Introduction

A large fraction of the biological data produced are publicly available on Web sites or available by FTP protocols. These public databases are internationally known and play a key role in the majority of the public and private researches. The frequent and regular update of the databases is a recurrent issue for all host or mirror centers, and also for scientists using locally the databases for confidentiality reasons. Grid is an opportunity to reduce human cost for distributing updated data. An update can be propagated automatically in the different centers with the grid replication and information services. Deploying a service for automatic database update is a requirement within a grid for bioinformatics.

The goal is to give the most up-to-date version of each database for a job in a grid environment. Hence there is a need for a service that will update each site storing the databases through the grid with their last modifications. Here, the real challenges are to optimize the use of network bandwidth and to have a scalable system that can easily support a large number of grid storage elements. The system must also be light and transparent enough so as not to disrupt job execution and to automate the procedure to achieve a minimum of human intervention. At the end the service should be a black box delivering up-to-date databases on the grid that should prevent users from wondering which is the version deployed. In this section, after defining the components and the architecture of the service, we will describe its deployment on the RUGBI grid.

9.3.2 Related Work

The biological database providers [34,35] make database publicly available on FTP servers. Each bioinformatics center or laboratory [36] needs to download the updated database to give access to its users. There are update services, but they can be integrated in a specific commercial tool, such as the SRS-Prisma module of SRS [37], a Web-based retrieval system for biological data. There is an update server development [25], but the aim of this package is to download the update of several public databases in a unique local database, instead of distributing the databases on many nodes. Scientists working on a grid infrastructure such as EGEE need to have the ability to deploy the database they are interested in on the grid nodes they select. A large number of research papers and development projects focus on file replication, but there is not much literature about database update services in a grid environment. A review is carried out in Reference 38. In this paper, the authors proposed a replica consistency service conceived for data grids, allowing asynchronously replica updates in a single-master scenario. This method is close to the methods described in this document, but their service is designed for relational databases whereas the RUGBI service has especially been developed to handle bioinformatics databases that are mostly flat-files databases. We will also mention xNDT that redistributes databases from the Swedish EMBnet node to a number of national EMBnet subnodes [39]. It is being adapted for a grid environment, but it is limited for the moment to MySQL relational database and is still in the development stage. The service proposed here is based on the same process as [38], but it is specialized for flat files.

9.3.3 Service Components

RUGBI [40] is a French project financed by the GenHomme network whose goal is to build a computing grid infrastructure on the basis of the existing middleware technologies for the community of scientists in bioinformatics. A set of applications has been selected to define the requirements for the RUGBI grid. Most of the applications are fed with third-party databases. The databases used by the biologists are constituted of several flat files organized in directories. They are just handled as file systems: Files can be added, removed, or modified and are available directly on FTP servers anonymously. The users have shown interest in the update of SWISSPROT [41], TREMBL [42], EMBL [43] , PDB [44], KEGG [45], and NCI [46], which all fall into this category of file system databases.

The RUGBI grid considers databases as resources that are all registered in the information system of the grid, such as applications, computing elements, and storage elements. This information system is based on XML (Extensible Markup Language) native databases, and all the resources are described in XML sheets stored into it. XML is well-adapted to store textual information and metadata on the databases such as information on their FTP repositories, their version, their size, or the date of the last update. While the description sheets are held on a central service, the databases are stored physically on the grid on storage elements (SE). Among these storage elements, there are some storage elements of reference (SER) (one per database) that are the central repositories of the databases on the grid. These grid repositories should be synchronized with the FTP servers. The RUGBI architecture also includes a grid service called the database finder used mainly to find the best location of a given database on the grid for a given user. The service manages locks put on the databases by the running jobs to prevent its modification while the job is being executed. Moreover, it can forbid a job to use a given database location, hence allowing the update service to perform its operations without disrupting job execution. Locks are needed to ensure the safety of jobs and the integrity of the database replica. For security issues, locks are automatically removed after a given period of time. The service is intended to be a direct interface between the databases FTP servers and the grid storage elements. Its operations are governed by the information in XML sheets. The whole service is designed to work as a stand-alone tool that we can adapt easily to any middleware architecture and with any database.

The update service as a client/server application is conceived in two parts communicating with each other. The server, deployed on the storage elements of reference, just regularly compares the versions available on the FTP with the ones deployed on the grid using the XML description sheet of the databases given by the information system. If necessary, it rebuilds the databases by downloading the necessary files or directory on repository spaces on the storage element. After this first step, it queries the information system to know which are the SEs that host the database and notifies the SE clients to update the database. When an update notification is received by a client, it pulls the data from the SER. To do so, it simply downloads the differences on the SER in a new local working space, closed for jobs, using the specified transfer protocol. As soon as the number of SEs (clients) that successfully deployed the updates reaches a given threshold, the RUGBI Database Finder service is notified to register the new database, and this implies that the working space will open and accept new jobs. If a database version is already on the SE (in a working space), the same service is notified to unregister the old version. New jobs are not allowed to run on the old version since it is unregistered, but they are allowed to use the new registered version. When the grid has registered the new deployed database, the XML description sheet of the database is updated on the information system and the old one deleted. As soon as no more jobs are using the old version, the server is notified by the Database Finder Service about it, and the server deletes the old version. This notification is propagated through the grid so that any SE hosting this version will delete it. The whole process can be repeated through time to keep the databases updated.

9.3.4 Service Development and Deployment

Developments were made in Java for portability and modularity. A raw version, including the client/server subservices was developed using basic IP socket programming for communication. This development enables simple networks to host databases and synchronize them with FTP servers. The internal data transfers between SEs can be achieved through GridFTP (FTP protocol implementing secured and reliable multichanneled transfers using Globus Security Infrastructure (GSI)) and Rsync (a protocol that optimizes transfer by comparing the sources with the destinations and copies just the differing parts). As the RUGBI grid is based on Globus Toolkit 4 [47], the subservices were also implemented as web services, messaging with SOAP protocol, and simply deployed under the Globus Toolkit 4 services container. This deployment also allows to embed the service into the GSI, which allows secured invocation of the service through authentication and authorization of the users with their personal certificate. The use of a secured environment is mandatory whenever the service has to handle licensed or confidential databases. The web services interfaces also enable better connectivity with the other services and avoid grid sites to handle exotic firewall configurations: they should just allow inbound and outbound connectivities for web services (8080 for Apache tomcat) and GridFTP (2811 most of the time). The developments were done under an Apache Axis environment, with the GridFTP and GSI API provided by the Globus Commodity grid Kits. The RUGBI grid has currently height sites in Clermont-Ferrand, Lyon, and Grenoble. The client update service is deployed on each SE of the grid. Moreover, the Clermont-Ferrand and Grenoble sites host the SER of the grid, so the master service is deployed there. The following bases are deployed and updated regularly: SWISSPROT (700 MB),

TREMBL (2.4 GB), EMBL (release without annotations: 180 GB), KEGG (13 GB), PDB (2.9 GB), NCI (900 MB), representing a total of 200 GB. Once the update of a database is initiated from the portal by the database administrator, its reference site runs the update process each time it is configured. The volume of transfers required by each update varies from several kilobytes to several gigabytes, which depends on the databases and their activity. Performance of the complete update process depends of the network bandwidth.

9.4   *IN SILICO* DRUG DISCOVERY ON THE GRID: THE WISDOM INITIATIVE

So far, we have described in this chapter a strategy to address the integration of bioinformatics resources using grids and a first grid service to replicate and update biological databases. We are now going to describe the first successful attempt to produce biological data *in silico* using grid infrastructures.

In *silico* drug discovery is one of the most promising strategies to speed up the drug development process. Large-scale grids open opportunities of particular interest to neglected and emerging diseases. In 2005, for the first time, we had been able to deploy large-scale virtual docking within the framework of the WISDOM initiative [48] against malaria: More than 41 million ligands were docked in less than 6 weeks using about 80 years of CPU on the EGEE infrastructure. This success led to a second computing challenge targeting avian flu neuraminidase N1 that required more than 100 CPU years on the EGEE, Auvergrid, and TWGrid infrastructures in April and May 2006. These achievements demonstrated the relevance of large-scale grids for the drug discovery process, especially for the virtual screening by molecular docking, while addressing neglected and emerging diseases.

9.4.1   Introduction

In silico drug discovery is one of the most promising strategies to speed up the drug development process [49]. Virtual screening is about selecting *in silico* the best candidate drugs acting on a given target protein [50]. Screening can be done *in vitro*, but it is very expensive as there are now millions of chemicals that can be synthesized [51]. A reliable way of *in silico* screening could reduce the number of molecules required for *in vitro* and then *in vivo* testing from a few millions to a few hundreds [52]. *In silico* drug discovery should foster collaboration between public and private laboratories. It should also have an important societal impact by lowering the barrier to develop new drugs for rare and neglected diseases [53]. New drugs are needed for neglected diseases such as malaria where parasites keep developing resistance to the existing drugs, or sleeping sickness for which no new drug has been developed for years. New drugs against tuberculosis are also needed as the treatment now takes several months and is therefore hard to manage in least developed countries. However, *in silico* virtual screening requires intensive computing, on the order of a few teraflops per day to compute 1 million docking probabilities or for the molecular modeling of 1000 ligands on one target protein. Access to very large computing resources is therefore needed for a successful high-throughput virtual screening [54]. Grids now provide such resources. A grid infrastructure such as EGEE [27] today provides access to more than 30,000 computers and is particularly suited to compute docking probabilities for millions of compounds. Docking is only the first step of virtual screening since the docking output data have to be processed further [55].

The section will present our experience in grid-enabled drug discovery. We will also propose some perspectives for the coming years.

9.4.2 Related Works

Recently, high-throughput virtual screening projects on grids have emerged with the perspective to reduce costs and time. The Virtual Laboratory project [56] was the pioneer in enabling molecular modeling for drug design on geographically distributed resources. It optimizes for time or cost the use of grid resource. The Nimrod-G [57,58] resource broker, based on Globus, is used for scheduling and on-demand processing of docking jobs on the World-Wide grid resources. The Virtual Laboratory is used by the Australian BioGrid Portal to submit easily docking jobs [58]. The test case reported in Reference 58 was deployed on seven nodes with about 450 CPUs in only few hours. The purpose of the Drug Discovery grid [60] is to set up a desktop and a cluster grid environment with aggregated computing and data resources to provide drug virtual screening services and pharmaceutical chemistry information services. BOINC is the desktop grid middleware and Nimrod-G is the cluster grid middleware. The drug discovery grid composed of five sites with 336 CPUs was used to screen 120,000 compounds against an interesting target for the treatment of hyperlipidemia, cholelithiasis, and cholestasis. GROCK [61] is a portal that facilitates mass screening of potential molecular interactions in the Life Sciences. It aims to facilitate for users the performance of huge amounts of computational tasks using EGEE. They use LCG-submitter, a tool developed by the Experiment Integration and Support team, as an interface with the EGEE middleware for job submission and monitoring. The GROCK portal is not yet available and no deployment has been reported. The Grid-based Virtual Screening of Dengue Virus Target Proteins project, supported on the national Swiss grid SwissBioGrid, aims to find new compounds against dengue [62]. The first massive deployment was made on four heterogeneous nodes (desktops and clusters) with 360 CPUs using the in-house middleware ProtoGrid. They docked 500,000 compounds and consumed about 4 CPU years. First results are promising but the technology choice for the middleware on SwissBioGrid is not yet confirmed. These four initiatives aim to provide full virtual screening environments on large grids, but there are no reports of virtual screening deployment on thousands of processors for many weeks such as is required for high-throughput virtual screening. Access to the grid infrastructures used by these applications (except Grock) is not possible for external initiatives such as WISDOM.

9.4.3   Large-Scale *In Silico* Docking Against Malaria

9.4.3.1   Introduction

The number of cases of deaths from malaria has increased in many parts of the world. There are about 300–500 million new infections, 1–3 million new deaths, and a 1–4% loss of gross domestic product (at least $12 billion) annually in Africa caused by malaria. The main causes for the comeback of malaria are that the most widely used drug against malaria, chloroquine, has been rendered useless by drug resistance in most part of the world [63,64] and that anopheles mosquitoes, the disease vector, have become resistant to some of the insecticides used to control the mosquito population. Genomics research has opened up new ways to find novel drugs to cure malaria, vaccines to prevent malaria, insecticides to kill infectious mosquitoes, and strategies to prevent the development of infectious sporozoites in the mosquito [65]. These studies require more and more *in silico* biology: from the first steps of gene annotation via target identification to the modeling of pathways and the identification of proteins mediating the pathogenic potential of the parasite. Grid computing supports all of these steps and, moreover, can also contribute significantly to the monitoring of ground studies to control malaria and to the clinical tests in plagued areas.

A particularly computing intensive step in the drug discovery process is virtual screening, which is about selecting *in silico* the best candidate drugs acting on a given target protein. Screening can be done *in vitro* using real chemical compounds, but this is a very expensive and not necessarily an error-free undertaking. A reliable way of *in silico* screening could reduce the number of molecules required for *in vitro* and then *in vivo* testing from a few millions to a few hundreds. Advancement in combinatorial chemistry has paved the way for synthesizing millions of different chemical compounds. Thus, there are millions of chemical compounds available in pharmaceutical laboratories and also in a very limited number of publicly accessible databases.

9.4.3.2   WISDOM Objectives

Biological Objectives. Malaria is a dreadful disease caused by a protozoan parasite plasmodium. There are several antimalarial drugs presently available. But the constant emergence of resistance and the costs of the present drugs are worsening the disease condition [64]; therefore, it is important to keep exploring new strategies to fight malaria. The one strategy investigated within WISDOM aims at the hemoglobin metabolism, which is one of the key metabolic processes for the survival of the parasite. There are several proteases involved in the degradation of human hemoglobin inside the food vacuole of the parasite inside the erythrocytes. Plasmepsin, the aspartic protease of Plasmodium, is responsible for the initial cleavage of human hemoglobin and is later followed by other proteases [66]. There are 10 different plasmepsins coded by 10 different genes in *Plasmodium falciparum* (Plm I, II, IV, V, VI, VII, VIII, IX, X, and HAP) [63]. High levels of sequence homology are observed between different plasmepsins (65–70%). Simultaneously, they share only 35% of sequence homology with their nearest human aspartic protease cathepsin D4 [67]. This and the presence of accurate X crystallographic data make plasmepsin an ideal target for rational drug design against malaria. Docking is the first step for *in silico* virtual screening.

Basically, protein-compound docking is about computing the binding energy of a protein target to a library of potential drugs using a scoring algorithm. The target is typically a protein that plays a pivotal role in a pathological process, for example, the biological cycles of a given pathogen (parasite, virus, and bacteria). The goal is to identify which molecules could dock on the active sites of the protein in order to inhibit its action and, therefore, interfere with the molecular processes essential for the pathogen. Libraries of compound 3D structures are made openly available by chemical companies that can produce them. Many docking software products are available either through open source or through a proprietary license.

Grid Objective. A large number of applications are already running on grid infrastructures. Even if many have passed the proof of concept level [68], only few are ready for large-scale production with experimental data. Large hadron collider experiments at CERN, like the ATLAS collaboration [69], have been the first to test a large data production system on grid infrastructures [70]. In a similar way, WISDOM [71] aimed at deploying a scalable, CPU-consuming application generating large data flows to test the grid infrastructure, operation, and services in very stressing conditions. Docking along with BLAST [72] homology searches and some folding algorithms is one of the most prominent applications that have successfully been demonstrated on grid test beds. It is typically an embarrassingly parallel application, with repetitive and independent calculations. Large resources are needed in order to test a family of targets, a significant amount of possible drug candidates, and different virtual screening tools with different parameter/scoring settings. This is both a computational and data challenge problem to distribute millions of docking comparisons with millions of small compound files. Moreover, docking is the only application for distributed computing that has prompted the uptake of grid technology in the pharmaceutical industry [73]. The WISDOM scientific results are also a means of making a demonstration of the EGEE grid computing infrastructure for the end-user community, of illustrating the usefulness of a scientifically targeted virtual organization, and of fostering an uptake of grid technologies in this scientific area [74].

The EGEE project [27] (enabling Grid for e-Science) brings together experts from over 27 countries with the common aim of building on recent advances in grid technology and developing a service grid infrastructure that is available to scientists 24 hours a day. The project aims to provide researchers in academia and industry with access to major computing resources, independent of their geographic location. The EGEE infrastructure is now a production grid with a large number of applications installed and used on the available resources. The infrastructure involves more than 180 sites spread out in Europe, America, and Asia.

The WISDOM application was deployed within the framework of the biomedical virtual organization that scaled up to 3000 CPUs and 21 TB disk space in 15 countries.

9.4.4 *In Silico* Docking Against Avian flu

9.4.4.1 *Introduction*

The first large-scale docking experiment focused on virtual screening for neglected diseases, but new perspectives have also appeared for using grids to address emerging diseases. While the grid added value for neglected diseases is related to their cost effectiveness as compared to *in vitro* testing, grids are also extremely relevant when time becomes a critical factor. A collaboration between Asian and European laboratories has resulted in the analysis of 300,000 possible drug components against the avian flu virus H5N1 using the EGEE grid infrastructure in April and May 2006 [75]. The goal was to find potential compounds that could inhibit the activities of an enzyme on the surface of the influenza virus, the so-called neuraminidase, subtype N1. Using the grid to identify the most promising leads for biological tests could speed up the development process for drugs against the influenza virus.

9.4.4.2 *Objectives*

Biological Objectives. The potential for reemergence of influenza pandemics has been a great threat since the report that avian influenza A virus (H5N1) could acquire the ability to be transmitted to humans. Indeed, an increase of transmission incidents suggests a risk of human-to-human transmission [76]. In addition, the report of the development of drug-resistant variants [77] is another potential concern. Two of the present drugs (oseltamivir and zanamivir) were discovered through structure-based drug design targeting influenza neuraminidase (NA), a viral enzyme that cleaves terminal sialic acid residues from glycoconjugates. The action of NA is essential for virus proliferation and infectivity; therefore, blocking its activity generates antivirus effects. To minimize nonproductive trial-and-error approaches and to accelerate the discovery of novel potent inhibitors, medical chemists take advantage of modeled NA variant structures and structure-based design. A key task in structure-based design is to model complexes of candidate compounds to the structures of receptor binding sites. The computational tools for the work are based on molecular docking engines, such as AutoDock [78], to carry out a quick conformation search for small compounds in the binding sites, fast calculation of binding energies of possible binding poses, prompt selection for the probable binding modes, and precise ranking and filtering for good binders. Although docking engines can be run automatically, one should control the dynamic conformation of the macromolecular binding site (rigid or flexible) and the spectrum of the screening small organics. This process is characterized by computational and storage loads, which pose a great challenge to resources that a single institute can afford.

Grid Objective. Besides the biological goal of reducing time and the cost of the initial investment on structure-based drug design, there are two grid technology objectives for this activity: One is to improve the performance of the *in silico* high-throughput screening environment on the basis of what has been learnt in the previous challenge against malaria; the other is to test another environment that would enable users to have efficient and interactive control of the massive molecular dockings on the grid. Therefore, two grid tools were used in parallel in the second large-scale deployment. An enhanced version of WISDOM high-throughput workflow was designed to achieve the first goal, and a lightweight framework called DIANE [79,80] was introduced to carry a significant fraction of the deployment for implementing and testing the new scenario.

9.4.5   The Grid Tools

9.4.5.1   The WISDOM Production Environment

A large-scale deployment requires the development of an environment for job submission and output data collection. A number of issues need to be addressed to achieve significant acceleration from the grid deployment:

- Grid performances are impacted by the amount of data moved around at job submission. As a consequence, the files providing the 3D structure of targets and compounds should preferably be stored on grid storage elements in preparation for the large-scale deployment.
- The rate at which jobs are submitted to the grid resource brokers must be carefully monitored in order to avoid their overload. The job submission scheme must take into account this present limitation of the EGEE brokering system.
- Grid submission process introduces significant delays, for instance, at the level of resource brokering. The jobs submitted to the grid computing nodes must be sufficiently long in order to reduce the impact of this middleware overhead.

The WISDOM production environment was designed to achieve production of a large amount of data in a limited time using EGEE, Auvergrid, and TWGrid middleware services. Three packages were developed in Perl and Java. Their entry points are a simple command-line tool. The first package installs the application components (software, compounds database) on the grid computing nodes. The second package tests these components. The third package monitors the submission and the execution of the WISDOM jobs. The environment was improved to address the limitations and bottlenecks identified during the first large-scale deployment against malaria deployed in the summer of 2005 on the EGEE infrastructure. For instance, the number of resource broker machines and the rate at which the jobs were submitted on them were reduced to avoid their overload. Another improvement concerned the resubmission process after a job failure that was redesigned to avoid sinkhole effect on a failing grid computing node. Automatic resubmission was replaced by the manual intervention of the WISDOM production user.

9.4.5.2   The DIANE Framework

DIANE is a lightweight distributed framework for parallel scientific applications in master–worker model. It assumes that a job may be split into a number of independent tasks, which is a typical case in many scientific applications. It has been successfully applied to a number of applications ranging from image rendering to data analysis in high-energy physics. A detailed description can be found in Reference 75.

9.4.6   Results

9.4.6.1   WISDOM Results

General Statistics. The WISDOM experiment ran on the EGEE grid production service from July 11, 2005, until August 19, 2005. It saw over 41 million docked ligands, the equivalent of 80 years on a single PC, in about 6 weeks. Up to 1700 computers were simultaneously used in 15 countries around the world. FlexX [81], a commercial software with a license server, was successfully deployed on more than 1000 machines at the same time. WISDOM demonstrated how grid computing could help drug discovery research by speeding up the whole process and by reducing the cost to develop new drugs to treat diseases such as malaria. This deployment was the opportunity to highlight several issues:

- The overall grid efficiency was on average about 50%. This means that a large fraction of the jobs had to be resubmitted. This generated a significant extra workload on the users.
- About 1 TB of data were produced by the 72,000 jobs submitted. Collection and registration of these output data turned out to be a heavy task.
- The grid data management services allowed replicating all the output files for backup. However, they did not allow storing all the results directly in a database.
- Postprocessing of the huge amount of data generated was also a very demanding task as millions of docking scores had to be compared.

Several of these issues were improved for the second large-scale docking targeted on avian flu, which is described in the next subsection.

Biological Results. Besides demonstrating large-scale docking on computational grid, several inhibitors for Plasmepsin were identified. The best 1000 compounds based on scoring were selected thanks to postprocessing ranking jobs deployed on the grid. They were inspected individually. Several strategies were employed to reduce the number of false positives. A further 100 compounds were selected for postprocessing. These compounds had been selected on the basis of the docking score, the binding mode of the compound inside the binding pocket, and the interactions of the compounds to the key residues of the protein. There are several scaffolds in the 100 compounds selected for postprocessing. The scaffolds urea, thiourea, and guanidino analogues are most repeatedly identified in the top 1000 compounds. Some of the compounds identified were similar to already known plasmepsin inhibitors, such as the urea analogues that were already established as micromolar inhibitors for plasmepsins (Walter Reed compounds) [67]. This indicates that the overall approach is sensible and that large-scale docking on computational grids has the potential to identify new inhibitors. The guanidino analogues can become a novel class of plasmepsin inhibitors.

9.4.6.2   Results from Large-scale Deployment Against Avian Flu

General Statistics. Table 9.1 summarizes the deployments achieved using WISDOM and DIANE environments, respectively. During the data challenge, the WISDOM activity distributed 54,000 jobs on 60 grid CEs. The 6-week activity covered the computing power of about 88 CPU years and docked about 2 million pairs of target and chemical compounds. Due to the fact that the grid resources were used by other VOs during the data challenge, a maximum of 2000 CPUs were concurrently running at the same time. For the DIANE part, we were able to complete 308,585 docking runs (i.e., 1/8 of the whole challenge) in 30 days using the computing resources of 36 grid CEs. A total number of 2580 DIANE worker agents were running as grid jobs during this period and 240 of them were concurrently maintained by the DIANE master. About 600 GB of data have been produced on the grid during the data challenge.

Efficiency and Throughput. Since a grid is a dynamic system in which the status of resources may change without central control, transient problems occur which cause job failures. In the WISDOM activity, about 83% of the jobs were reported as success-fully finished, according to the status logged in the grid Logging and Bookkeeping system; the observed failures were mainly due to errors at job scheduling time be-cause of the misconfiguration of grid Computing Elements. However, the success rate went down to 70% after checking the content of the data output file. The main cause for these failures was frequent last-minute errors in the transfer of results to the grid Storage Elements. Compared to the previous large-scale deployment, im-provement was significant as the observed success rates were, respectively, 77% and 63%. The last-minute error in output data transfer is particularly expensive since the results are no longer available on the grid Worker Node, although they might have been successfully produced. In DIANE, a similar job failure rate was also observed; nevertheless, the failure recovery mechanism in DIANE automated the resubmission and guaranteed a fully complete job. On the contrary, the feature of interactively returning part of the computing efforts during the runtime (e.g., the output of each docking) also introduces a more economical way of using the grid resources. For the instances submitted using WISDOM production environment, the overall crunching factor was about 912. The corresponding distribution efficiency defined as the ratio between the overall crunching factor and the maximum number of concurrently run-ning CPUs was estimated 47%. This is due to the known issue of long job waiting time in the current EGEE production system. The task pull model adopted by DIANE allows isolating the scheduling overhead of the grid jobs and is, therefore, expected to achieve a better distribution efficiency. During the data challenge, DIANE was able to push the efficiency to higher than 80%. Because of the highly scalable nature of the WISDOM framework, high-throughput docking could be achieved at a rate of 1.7 s

Table 9.1   Statistical Summary of the WISDOM and DIANE Activities

Total number of completed dockings	2×10^6	308,585
Estimated duration on 1 CPU	88.3 years	16.7 years
Duration of the experience	6 weeks	4 weeks
Cumulative number of grid jobs	54,000	2585
Maximum number of concurrent CPUs	2000	240
Number of used computing elements	60	36
Crunching factor	912	203
Approximated distribution efficiency	46%	84%

per docking. As DIANE was handling not more than a few hundred concurrent jobs, its throughput was limited to about one docking every 8.4 s.

Biological Results. Two sets of reranked data for each target were made (QM–MM method and the selection by the study of the interactions between the compound and the target active site). The top 15% is about 45,000 compounds for each target. This set will be publicly available for the scientific community working on the avian influenza neuraminidase. The top 5% is about 2250 compounds for each target. This set will be refined by different methods (molecular modeling, molecular dynamics). The analysis will indicate which residue mutation is critical, which chemical fragments are preferred in the mutation subsites, and other information for lead optimization to chemists. Finally, at least 25 compounds will be assayed experimentally at the Genomic Research Center, Academia Sinica.

9.4.7   Perspective: From Virtual Docking to Virtual Screening

Virtual screening involves a significant number of subsequent treatments after the initial docking step. Indeed, the best hits coming out of the docking step need to be further analyzed in terms of molecular dynamics (MD) [82].

For the same number of compounds, MD analysis requires much heavier computing than docking: indeed, compared to docking, molecular modeling adds time and therefore movement as an additional degree of freedom. As a consequence, molecular modeling can only be applied to a restricted number of compounds, usually the best hits coming out of the docking step. MD analysis most often changes significantly the scoring of the best compounds and it is therefore very important to apply it to as many compounds as possible. As a consequence, grids appear very promising in improving the virtual screening process by increasing the number of compounds that will be processed using MD. For instance, running MD analysis with Amber 9 software [83] on one protein target and 10,000 compounds requires about 50 CPU years for a model with a few thousand atoms and a few tens of thousands of steps. This process produces only 10 GB of data. One run with only one compound takes 44 h (computing time heavily depends on the choice of conditions). Both grids of clusters such as EGEE and grids of supercomputers such as DEISA [84] are relevant for MD computing. MD computations of large molecules are significantly faster on a supercomputer. Within the framework of the BioinfoGRID European project, focus will be put on the reranking of the best scoring compounds coming out of WISDOM. The goal will be to deploy at least one of the European grid infrastructures on MD software to rerank the best compounds before *in vitro*testing.

9.5   CONCLUSION

We have attempted to review the issues related to the deployment of life sciences applications on grid environments. We have highlighted the challenges related to the analysis of the avalanche of data coming from molecular biology high-throughput devices. Data and tool integration is the first challenge: We have explained how initiatives such as the EMBRACE project developed standard interfaces to the existing resources using the Web service technology. A second challenge is the deployment of bioinformatics services on the grid. The services related to the replication and the update of biological databases are particularly important as biologists need frequent access to these resources for data analysis. We have presented the efforts undertaken within the French RUGBI project to develop such a service on top of an existing grid. All these developments are still at a prototype level, and there is not yet a bioinformatics service to help biological data analysis with a demonstrated grid added value.

In parallel to these efforts to integrate existing biological resources and to develop bioinformatics services, groups are presently attempting to use directly the existing grids with the services they offer. As of today, our main success stories are related to the production of new data in the area of drug discovery. We have presented the WISDOM initiative to study *in silico* drug discovery against emerging and neglected diseases on grid infrastructures.

There is still a long road to an environment created through the sharing of resources in which heterogeneous and dispersed biological data as well as applications can be accessed by all users as a tailored information providing system according to their authorization and without the loss of information. To achieve this goal, R&D activities are still needed along three lines: development of life sciences grid services using OGSA compliant grid toolkits and e-Science environments, deployment of biomedical grid applications on the existing infrastructures, and development of life sciences infrastructures. Indeed, there is no dedicated grid environment for life sciences so far, and there are no OGSA compliant grid toolkits and e-Science environments available on the existing infrastructures. The R&D lines are now actively pursued around the world as biomedical applications are deployed on almost all grid infrastructures and many projects are now under development that use Web services toolkits or e-Science environments. A convergence of these research axes should be achieved in about 2 to 3 years when the middleware deployed on the grid infrastructures will offer Web service interfaces to their grid services so that the grid toolkits and e-Science environments will be available to all grid users.

ACKNOWLEDGMENTS

EGEE-II is a project funded by the European Union under contract number INFSO-RI-031688. The EMBRACE network of excellence is funded by the European Commission within its FP6 Programme, under the thematic area "Life sciences, genomics and biotechnology for health," contract number LHSG-CT-2004-512092. The BioinfoGRID project is funded by the European Union within the framework of the Sixth Framework Programme for Research and Technological Development (FP6). Auvergrid is a project funded by Conseil Régional d'Auvergne. The authors thank particularly the RUGBI (Réseau Gen'Homme) and GLOP (ACI GRID) projects funded by the French Ministry of Research.

REFERENCES

1. http://www.ncbiogrid.org

2. http://www.cbr.nrc.ca

3. http://biogrid.icm.edu.pl/

4. http://www.apbionet.org/grid/

5. D. Lavenier, H. Leroy, M. Hurfin, R. Andonov, L. Mouchard, F. Guinard, Le projet GénoGRID: Une grille expérimentale pour la génomique, *Journées Ouvertes Biologie, Informatique et Mathématique*, 27–31, 2002.

6. P.A. Covitz, F. Hartel, C. Schaefer, S. De Coronado, G. Fragoso, H. Sahni, S. Gustafson, K. H. Buetow, caCORE: a common infrastructure for cancer informatics, *Bioinformatics* **19**, 2404–2412, 2003.

7. W. Sanchez, B. Gilman, M. Kher, S. Lagou, P. Covitz, caGRID White Paper, National Cancer Institute Center for Bioinformatics, 2004.

8. K.H. Buetow, Cyberinfrastructure: Empowering a "third way" in biomedical research, *Science* **308**, 821–824, 2005.

9. http://www.simdat.org

10. J.S. Grethe, C. Baru, A. Gupta, M. James, B. Ludaescher, M. E. Martone, P. M. Papadopoulos, S. T. Peltier, A. Rajasekar, S. Santini, I. N. Zaslavsky, M. H. Ellisman, Biomedical Informatics Research Network: Building a national collaboratory to hasten the derivation of new understanding and treatment of disease, *Studies in Health and Technology Informatics* **112**, 100–109, 2005.

11. S. Sild, U. Maran, A. Lomaka, M. Karelson, Open computing grid for molecular science and engineering, *Journal of Chemical Inforamtion and Modeling* **46**, 953–959, 2006.

12. W. Dubitzky, D. McCourt, M. Galushka, M. Romberg, B. Schuller, Grid-enabled data warehousing for molecular engineering, *Parallel Computing* **30**, 1019–1035, 2004.

13. P. Mazzatorta, E. Benfenati, B. Schuller, M. Romberg, D. McCourt, W. Dubitzky, S. Sild, M. Karelson, A. Papp, I. Bagyi, F. Darvas, OpenMolGRID: molecular science and engineering in a grid context, in: *Proceedings of the International Conference on Parallel and Distributed Processing Techniques and Applications*, pp. 775–779, 2004.

14. C. Goble, The grid: From concept to reality in distributed computing, *Scientific Computing World* May/June, *Bioinformatics World*, **2**, 811, 2002.

15. A. Solomonides, R. McClatchey, M. Odeh, M. Brady, M. Mulet-Parada, D. Schottlander, S.R Amendolia., MammoGrid and eDiamond: Grids applications in mammogram analysis, in: *Proceedings of the IADIS International Conference: e-Society*, pp. 1032–1033, 2003.

16. T. Tweed, S. Miguet, Medical image database on the grid: Strategies for data distribution, in: *Proceedings of HealthGrid '03*, pp. 152–162, 2003.

17. M.E. Martone, A. Gupta, M. H. Ellisman, E-neuroscience: Challenges and triumphs in integrating distributed data from molecules to brains, *Nature Neuroscience* **7**, 467–472, 2004.

18. C. Goble, Review: The low down on e-science and grids for biology, *Comparative and Functional Genomics* **2**, 365–370, 2001.

19. F. Harris, M. Lamanna (Eds.), *EGEE User Forum Book of Abstracts*, 2006.

20. Y.-M. Teo, X. Wang, Y.-K. Ng, GLAD: A system for developing and deploying large-scale bioinformatics grid, *Bioinformatics* **21**, 794–802, 2005.

21. M. Cannataro, C. Comito, F. Lo Schiavo, P. Veltri, Proteus, a grid based problem solving environment for bioinformatics: Architecture and experiments, *IEEE Computational Intelligence Bulletin*, 2003.

22. G. Aloisio, M. Cafaro, S. Fiore, M. Mirto, ProGenGrid: A workflow service infrastructure for composing and executing bioinformatics grid services, in: *18th IEEE Symposium on Computer-Based Medical Systems*, pp. 555–560, 2005.

23. D. Hull, K. Wolstencroft, R. Stevens, C. Goble, M. Pocock, P. Li, T. Oinn, Taverna: A tool for building and running workflows of services, *Nucleic Acids Research* **34**, W729–W732, 2006.

24. C. Blanchet, Grid deployment of legacy bioinformatics applications with transparent data access, in: *IEEE Conference on Grid Computing*, 2006.

25. D. Sulakhe, A. Rodriguez, M. D'Souza, M. Wilde, V. Nefedova, I. Foster, N. Maltsev, GNARE: An environment for grid-based high-throughput genome analysis, CCGrid 2005 BioGrid Workshop, 2005.

26. http://www.embracegrid.info/

27. F. Gagliardi, B. Jones, F. Grey, M.-E. Bégin, M. Heikkurinen, Building an infrastructure for scientific grid computing: Status and goals of the EGEE project, *Philosophical Transactions: Mathematical, Physical and Engineering Sciences*, **363**, 1729–1742, 2005. Available at http://public.euegee.org

28. http://www.bioinfogrid.eu/

29. R.D. Stevens, A. J. Robinson, C. A. Goble, myGrid: Personalised bioinformatics on the information grid, *Bioinformatics* **191**(1), i302–i304, 2003.

30. H. Rauwerda, M. Roos, B. Hertzberger, T. Breit, The Promise of a virtual lab, *Drug Discovery Today* **11**(5–6), 228–36, 2006.

31. http://www.globalgridforum.org/

32. http://www.w3.org/

33. Web Services Description Language. Available at http://www.w3.org/TR/wsdl

34. http://www.ebi.ac.uk/

35. http://www.ncbi.nlm.nih.gov/

36. C. Combet, C. Blanchet, C. Geourjon, G. Deléage, NPS@: Network protein sequence analysis, *TIBS* **25**, 147–150, 2000.

37. http://www.lionbioscience.com/

38. A. Domenici, F. Donno, G. Pucciani, H. Stockinger, Relaxed data consistency with CONStanza, in: *6th IEEE International Symposium on Cluster Computing and the grid*, IEEE Computer Society Press, Los Alamitos, pp. 16–19, 2006.

39. www.uppmax.uu.se/Members/lottab/xndt-on-swegrid/

40. RUGBI project. http://rugbi.in2p3.fr

41. A. Bairoch, R. Apweiler, The SWISS-PROT protein sequence data bank and its supplement TrEMBL in 1999, *Nucleic Acids Research* **27**, 49–54, 1999.

42. The European Bioinformatics Institute. http://www.ebi.ac.uk

43. G. Stoesser, M.A. Tuli, R. Lopez, P. Sterk, The EMBL nucleotide sequence database, *Nucleic Acids Research* **27**, 18–24, 1999.

44. H.M. Berman, J. Westbrook, Z. Feng, G. Gilliland, T.N. Bhat, H. Weissig, I.N. Shindyalov, P.E. Bourne, The protein data bank, *Nucleic Acids Research* **28**, 235–242, 2000.

45. M. Kanehisa, S. Goto, KEGG: Kyoto encyclopedia of genes and genomes, *Nucleic Acids Research* **28**, 27–30, 2000.

46. NCI and NCBI's SKY/M-FISH and CGH Database, 2001. Available at http://www.ncbi.nlm.nih.gov/sky/skyweb.cgi

47. I. Foster, Globus toolkit version 4: Software for service-oriented systems, *IFIP International Conference on Network and Parallel Computing*, New York, LNCS 3779, Springer-Verlag, pp. 2–13, 2005.

48. N. Jacq, J. Salzemann, Y. Legré, M. Reichstadt, F. Jacq, E. Medernach, M. Zimmermann, A. Maass, M. Sridhar, K. Kasam, J. Montagnat, H. Schwichtenberg, M. Hofmann, V. Breton, Grid enabled virtual screening against malaria, accepted for publication in *Journal of Grid Computing*, 2007.

49. BCG Estimate, *A Revolution in R&D, The Impact of Genomics*, 2001.

50. P.D. Lyne, Structure-based virtual screening: An overview, *Drug Discovery Today* **7**, 1047–1055, 2002.

51. M. Congreve, C. W. Murray, T. L. Blundell, Structural biology and drug discovery, *Drug Discovery Today* **10**, 895–907, 2005.

52. R.W. Spencer, High throughput virtual screening of historic collections on the file size, biological targets, and file diversity, *Biotechnology and Bioengineering* **61**, 61–67, 1998.

53. S. Nwaka, R.G. Ridley, Virtual drug discovery and development for neglected diseases through public–private partnerships, *Nature Review. Drug Discovery* **2**, 919–928, 2003.

54. A. Chien, I. Foster, D. Goddette, Grid technologies empowering drug discovery, *Drug Discovery Today* **7**, 176–180, 2002.

55. S. Ghosh, A. Nie, J. An, Z. Huang, Structure-based virtual screening of chemical libraries for drug discovery, *Current Opinion in Chemical Biology* **10**, 194–202, 2006.

56. R. Buyya, K. Branson, J. Giddy, D. Abramson, The virtual laboratory: A toolset to enable distributed molecular modelling for drug design on the world-wide grid, *Journal of Concurrency and Computation: Practice and Experience* **15**, 1–25, 2002.

57. D. Abramson, J. Giddy, L. Kotler, High-performance parametric modeling with nimrod-G: Killer application for the global grid? in: *Proceedings of the International Parallel and Distributed Processing Symposium*, IEEE CS Press, New York, 2000.

58. R. Buyya, D. Abramson, J. Giddy, Nimrod/G: An architecture for a resource management and scheduling system in a global computational grid, in: *Proceedings of the 4th International Conference on High Performance Computing in Asia Pacific Region*, 2000.

59. H. Gibbins, K. Nadiminti, B. Beeson, R. Chhabra, B. Smith, R. Buyya, The Australian BioGrid portal: Empowering the molecular docking research community, in: *Proceedings of the 3rd APAC Conference and Exhibition on Advanced Computing, Grid Applications and eResearch*, 2005.

60. W. Zhang, J. Zhang, Y. Chang, S. Chen, X. Du, F. Liu, F. Ma, J. Shen, Drug discovery grid, in: *Proceedings of the UK e-Science All Hands Meeting*, 2005.

61. D.J. Garcia Aristegui, P. Mendez Lorenzo, J.R. Valverde, GROCK: High-throughput docking using LCG grid tools, in: *The 6th IEEE/ACM International Workshop on Grid Computing*, pp. 85–90, 2005.

62. M. Podvinec, S. Maffioletti, P. Kunszt, K. Arnold, L. Cerutti, B. Nyffeler, R. Schlapbach, C. Türker, H. Stockinger, A. J. Thomas, M. C. Peitsch, T. Schwede, The SwissBioGrid Project: Objectives, preliminary results and lessons learned, *2nd IEEE International Conference on e-Science and Grid Technologies and Applications—Workshop on Production Grids*, IEEE Computer Society Press, Los Alamitos, CA, 148, 2006.

63. G.H. Coombs, D.E. Goldberg, M. Klemba, C. Berry, J. Kay, J.C. Mottram, Aspartic proteases of plasmodium falciparum and other protozoa as drug targets, *Trends in Parasitology* **17**, 532–537, 2001.

64. J. Weisner, R. Ortmann, H. Jomaa, M. Schlitzer, New Antimalarial drugs, *Angewandte Chemic International* **42**, 5274–5293, 2003.

65. C.F. Curtis, S.L. Hoffman, *Science* **290**, 1508–1509, 2000.

66. S.E. Francis, D.J. Sullivan, D.E. Goldberg, Hemoglobin metabolism in the malaria parasite plasmodium falciparum, *Annual Review of Microbioly* **51**, 97–123, 1997.

67. A.M. Silva, A.Y. Lee, S.V. Gulnik, P. Majer, J. Collins, T.N. Bhat, P.J. Collins, R.E. Cachau, K.E. Luker, I.Y. Gluzman, S.E. Francis, A. Oksman, D.E. Goldberg, J.W. Erickson, Structure and inhibition of plasmepsin II, a haemoglobin degrading enzyme from Plasmodium falciparum, in: *Proceedings of the National Academy of Science of the United States of America* **93**, 10034–10039, 1996.

68. N. Jacq, C. Blanchet, C. Combet, E. Cornillot, L. Duret, K. Kurata, H. Nakamura, T. Silvestre, V. Breton, Grid as a bioinformatics tool, *Parallel Computing* **30**, 1093–1107, 2003.

69. S. Campana, D. Barberis, F. Brochu, A. De Salvo, F. Donno, L. Goossens, S. Gonzalez de la Hoz, T. Lari, D. Liko, J. Lozano, G. Negri, L. Perini, G. Poulard, S. Resconi, D. Rebatto, L. Vaccarossa, Analysis of the ATLAS Rome Production Experience on the LHC Computing Grid, in: *IEEE International Conference on e-Science and Grid Computing*, 2005.

70. I. Bird, Operating the LCG and EGEE production Grids for HEP, in: *Proceedings of the CHEP'04 Conference*, 2004.

71. V. Breton, N. Jacq, V. Kasam, M. Hofmann-Apitius, Grid added value to address malaria, in: *Proceedings of the 6th IEEE International Symposium on Cluster Computing and the Grid 40, 2006*. Available at http://wisdom.healthgrid.org/.

72. S.F. Altschul, W. Gish, W. Miller, E. W. Myers, D. J. Lipman, Basic local alignment search tool, *Journal of Molecular Biology* **215**, 403–410, 1990.

73. R. Ziegler, Pharma GRIDs: Key to pharmaceutical innovation? in: *Proceedings of the HealthGrid Conference* 2004.

74. N. Jacq, J. Salzemann, Y. Legré, M. Reichstadt, F. Jacq, M. Zimmermann, A. Maaß, M. Sridhar, V. Kasam, H. Schwichtenberg, M. Hofmann, V. Breton, Demonstration of *in silico* docking at a large scale on grid infrastructure, *Studies in Health Technology and Informatics* **120**, 155–157, 2006.

75. H.-C. Lee, J. Salzemann, N. Jacq, H.-Y. Chen, L.-Y. Ho, I. Merelli, L. Milanesi, V. Breton, S.C. Lin, Y.-T. Wu, Grid-enabled high-throughput *in silico* screening against influenza A Neuraminidase, *IEEE Transactions on Nanobioscience*, **5**, 288–295, 2006.

76. K.S. Li, Y. Guan, J. Wang, G. J. Smith, K. M. Xu, L. Duan, A. P. Rahardjo, P. Puthavathana, C. Buranathai, T. D. Nguyen, A. T. Estoepangestie, A. Chaisingh, P. Auewarakul, H. T. Long, N. T. Hanh, R. J. Webby, L. L Poon, H. Chen, K. F. Shortridge, K. Y. Yuen, R. G. Webster, J. S. Peiris, Genesis of a highly pathogenic and potentially pandemic H5N1 influenza virus in eastern Asia, *Nature* **430**, 209–213, 2004.

77. M.D. de Jong, T. T. Thanh, T. H. Khanh, V. M. Hien, G. J.D. Smith, N. V. Chau, B. Van Cam, P. T. Qui, D. Q. Ha, Y. Guan, J.S. M. Peiris, T. T. Hien, J. Farrar, Oseltamivir resistance during treatment of influenza a (H5N1) infection, *The New England Journal of Medicine* **353**, 2667–2672, 2005.

78. G.M. Morris, D.S. Goodsell, R.S. Halliday, R. Huey, W.E. Hart, R.K. Belew, A.J. Olson, Automated docking using a lamarckian genetic algorithm and empirical binding free energy function, *Journal of Computational Chemistry* **19**, 1639–1662, 1998.

79. J.T. Moscicki, DIANE—Distributed analysis environment for GRID-enabled simulation and analysis of physics data, NSS IEEE 2004.

80. J.T. Moscicki, H.C. Lee, S. Guatelli, S.C. Lin, M.G. Pia *Biomedical applications on the gRID: Efficient management of parallel jobs*, NSS IEEE, New York, 2003.

81. M. Rarey, B. Kramer, T. Lengauer, G.A. Klebe, A fast flexible docking method using an incremental construction algorithm, *Journal of Molecular Biology* **261**, 470–489, 1996.

82. M.L. Lamb, W.L. Jorgensen, Computational approaches to molecular recognition, *Current Opinion in Chemical Biology* **1**, 449, 1997.

83. .A. Case, T.E. Cheatham, T. Darden, H. Gohlke, R. Luo, K.M. Merz, A. Onufriev, C. Simmerling, B. Wang, R.J. Woods, The Amber biomolecular simulation programs, *Journal of Computational Chemistry* **26**, 1668–1688, 2005.

84. http:// www.deisa.org

10

GRID-BASED INTERACTIVE DECISION SUPPORT IN BIOMEDICINE

Alfredo Tirado-Ramos, Peter M.A. Sloot, and Marian Bubak

A huge gap exists between what we know is possible with today's machines and what we have so far been able to finish.

Donald Knuth

10.1 INTRODUCTION

The challenges discovered when studying humans as complex systems, from a biomedical viewpoint (from cells to interacting individuals), cover the whole spectrum from genome to health and cross-temporal and spatial scales [1]. This includes studying biomedical issues using multiscale and multiscience models and techniques all the way from genomics to the macroscopic medical scale. This is also aggravated by the continuous increase in the amount of digital data produced by modern high-throughput biomedical detection and analysis systems. As reported by Hey et al., it is expected that larger amounts of digital data will be generated by next generations of large-scale, collaborative e-Science experiments [2]. New experiments in science and engineering will cover the whole spectrum, from the simulation of complete biological systems, to cutting-edge research in bioinformatics.

At the macroscopic scale, for instance, there are research efforts in biomedical informatics that are gradually pushing the boundaries of the state of the art, moving from monolithic software architectures to building more generic components. Such efforts normally leverage object-oriented and distributed component architectures to encapsulate or wrap legacy data in order to improve application interoperability and scalability [3,4]. This allows for enhanced data and process flow at the macroscopic level, where models such as DICOM provide support for data access from work stations to archiving and communications systems and back to hospitals' information systems.

Grid Computing for Bioinformatics and Computational Biology. Edited by E.-G. Talbi and A.Y. Zomaya.
Copyright © 2008 John Wiley & Sons, Inc.

Current distributed computing technologies address communication among tightly coupled systems very well, they though they may fail when addressing loosely coupled resources. Such resources may belong to sites within large distributed virtual organizations that use distributed computing models like the Common Object Resource Broker Architecture (CORBA) [5]. These technologies allow seamless and secure data access *within a single organization*. Large amounts of data can be distributed across domains, with distributed applications forming federations that may be scaled but that assume architecturally invariant systems. Relational data representation and access, modular component, and object-oriented models have clearly advanced the state of the art. New sets of conditions and requirements for software architectures for biomedical applications are emerging in the field, particularly in systems biology, where

- a high degree of user interaction is required,
- digitalized biomedical resource usage spaces become increasingly distributed,
- inaccessibility and lack of interoperability among modeling, simulation, and analysis tools should be leveraged for multidisciplinary biomedical informatics research to be possible.

In this chapter we discuss interactive decision support environments, from the perspective of both health informatics and bioinformatics, for a system-level approach to distributed collaborative laboratories for biomedicine. In the first case we present a problem-solving environment (PSE) for decision support through virtual bypass surgery. In the second case we focus on a more complex system centered around a decision support engine for drug ranking in human immunodeficiency virus (HIV) drug resistance. Our reasons to use this bioinformatics application as the main case study in this chapter are twofold: HIV drug resistance is becoming an increasing problem worldwide, with combination therapy with antiretroviral drugs failing to completely suppress the virus in a considerable number of HIV-infected patients. On the contrary, HIV drug resistance is one of the few areas in medicine where genetic information is widely available and has been used for many years. This has resulted in large numbers of data available, not only on complex genetic sequences but also on all levels up to populations. The sheer complexity of the disease, the distribution of the data, the required automatic updates to the knowledge base, and the efficient use and integration of advanced statistical and numerical techniques necessary to assist the physician motivate our research. We discuss here some of the possibilities for individualized e-Science that can be supported by virtual collaborative environments based on grid technology [6].

This chapter is divided as follows: In Section 10.2 we will discuss a problem-solving environment for biomedical applications on the grid, focusing on interactive simulation scenarios. In Section 10.3 we will present research on a collaborative virtual laboratory for e-Science that fulfills the requirements presented by decision support-centric applications. We will conclude in Section, 10.4, where we present a discussion and future work in the field.

10.2   A GRID FOR INTERACTIVE APPLICATIONS

Processing, visualization, and integration of information from various sources play an increasingly important role in modern health care [7]. Information sources may be widely distributed, and the data processing requirements can be highly variable, both in the type of resources required and the processing demands put upon these systems. Grid technology is one of the cornerstones of today's computational science and engineering; it offers a unified means of access to different and distant computational and instrumental resources; unprecedented possibilities and benefits are expected. Connectivity between distant locations, interoperability between different kinds of systems and resources, and high levels of computational performance are some of the most promising features of the grid. In the case of biomedical applications, issues such as remote access to patient data, medical knowledge bases, advanced visualization technologies, and specialized medical instruments are of the most importance [8]. For these applications, grid technology provides dedicated support such as strong security, distributed storage capacity, and high throughput over long-distance networks [9]. Besides these immediate benefits, the computational resources of the grid provide the required performance for large-scale simulations, complex visualization, and collaborative environments, which are expected to become of major importance to many areas of medicine in order to study the possibilities and limitations of interactive and collaborative problem-solving environments.

We propose an architecture for interactive biomedical applications running on a grid [10], focusing on a simulation-centric application and on production-type grid infrastructure requirements. We map this architecture to an interactive problem-solving environment [11,12] for computer simulation of preoperative planning of vascular reconstruction being developed by the University of Amsterdam [13,14], and we define a model for representing it that reflects the loosely coupled and concurrent nature of grid computing.

Our grid architecture allows us to build an interactive PSE that offers an integrative approach for constructing and running complex interactive systems on the grid: Highly distributed computational, storage, and grid service resources are used for access to medical image repositories for the simulation and visualization of blood flow. We deployed this interactive PSE within the European CrossGrid framework [15] (Fig. 10.1), exploiting available achievements from other European grid projects such as European DataGrid (EDG) [16] and the Large Hadron Collider Computing grid (LCG) [17]. For additional background, motivation, and the latest grid-based results, we refer the reader to Reference 18.

10.2.1   Interactive Simulation on the Grid

Scalability and seamless resource sharing are at the heart of the grid-based architectural design, which we base on requirements by a simulation-centric interactive biomedical application and a production grid infrastructure and services. We use the Virtual Radiology Explorer (VRE) environment, developed at the University of Amsterdam, which is part of a PSE that puts a user at the center of an experimental cycle

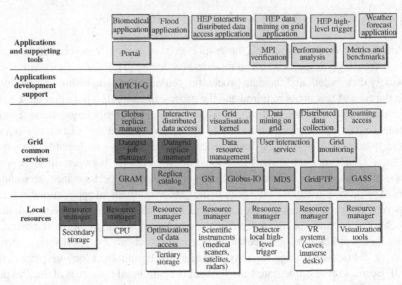

	Biomedical application	Flood application	HEP interactive distributed data access application	HEP data mining on grid application	HEP high-level trigger	Weather forecast application
Applications and supporting tools	Portal			MPI verification	Performance analysis	Metrics and benchmarks
Applications development support	MPICH-G					
Grid common services	Globus replica manager	Interactive distributed data access	Grid visualisation kernel	Data mining on grid	Distributed data collection	Roaming access
	Datagrid job manager	Datagrid replica manager	Data resource management	User interaction service	Grid monitoring	
	GRAM	Replica catalog	GSI	Globus-IO	MDS	GridFTP	GASS
Local resources	Resource manager	Resource manager	Resource manager	Resource manager	Resource manager	Resource manager	Resource manager
	Secondary storage	CPU	Optimization of data access	Scientific instruments (medical scaners, satelites, radars)	Detector local high-level trigger	VR systems (caves, immerse desks)	Visualization tools
			Tertiary storage				

Figure 10.1. The CrossGrid test bed: Layered architectural view with local resources at the bottom fabric layer, a set of common grid services and middleware from Globus, datagrid, and CrossGrid, application development support for cross-site job submission, and a set of interactive applications such as the biomedical VRE.

controlled by a computer and allows him to apply his expertise *in silico* to find better solutions for treatment of vascular diseases. The aim of the VRE is to provide an end user with an intuitive virtual simulated environment to access medical image data, visualize it, and explore patient vascular condition.

Naturally, since this kind of medical image processing is usually a complicated and resource intensive task, additional computational resources are needed. The VRE contains an efficient parallel computational hemodynamics solver [19] that computes pressure, velocities, and shear stresses during a full systolic period. The simulator is based on the Lattice–Boltzmann method (LBM), a mesoscopic approach for simulating fluid flow based on the kinetic Boltzmann equation [20]. To convert the medical scans into LBM meshes, the raw medical data are first segmented such that only the arterial structures of interest remain in the data. The segmented data are then converted into a mesh that can be used by the LBM solver; boundary nodes, inlet, and outlet nodes are added to the grid using a variety of image processing techniques. The simulator generates the blood flow parameters of the patient using grid resources. In order to allow for parallel execution, the simulation volume is divided into several subvolumes and each subvolume is processed concurrently [21]. For visualization the VRE uses a semi-immersive two-dimensional wall as a projection environment [22–24].

The VRE system uses a virtual reality environment where the patient's data obtained from the imaging modality is visualized as a 3D stereoscopic image, together with the graphical interpretation of the simulation results [25]. A user can then manipulate the 3D images of arteries, patient's body, and blood flow structures in virtual reality, an environment where users interact freely in a 3D space with entities within it. The working prototype of the VRE is provided with a multimodal interface described in Reference 26.

10.2.2   Usage Scenario

Once we designed and specified the grid architecture, we consider the following scenario (Fig. 10.2): A patient walks into a Medical Center scanning room somewhere in Europe to get his blood flow measured; the technician scans the abdominal aorta area, and the resulting image is stored in the radiology information system repository or Picture Archiving and Communications System (PACS), to be pre-examined and segmented. Later, a physician (user) somewhere else (e.g., in Amsterdam) logs into the CrossGrid Migrating Desktop (MD) grid portal using his grid certificate and private key. The user checks if there are segmented or nonsegmented medical data sets ready for analysis and simulation in one of the virtual nodes to work with them locally, and securely transfers a few. The user then starts the DesktopVRE from within the portal, loads the segmented medical data, selects a region of interest, crops image, adds a bypass, and creates an LBM mesh. The user selects the biomedical application icon within the portal (parameters and files are taken from user's profile) and submits the

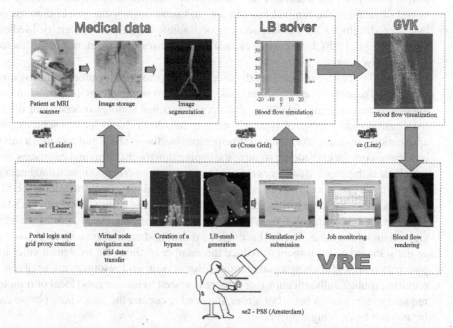

Figure 10.2. Data and process flow in the VRE environment, where a Grid-based virtual simulated environment is used to access medical image data, visualize it, and explore patient vascular condition; here, the Grid-based process flow allows for natural mapping to the user process flow.

job to the CrossGrid, to the nearest/most adequate CE in the grid, using a replica manager service. The user may then check job submission or simulation progress via the portal. After the job has been completed, the velocities, pressure, and shear stress are transferred to the local SE or to the appropriate visualization engine to be rendered and reviewed by the user. This scenario implies downloading the portal from Poznan Supercomputing and Networking Center to a local roaming storage element; secure access to the test bed; virtual exploration of available SEs throughout the grid; secure data transfer from an image repository SE (Leiden Medical Center); the preparation of the data for the blood flow simulation within the DesktopVRE version of the biomedical application; job submission to the LBM solver via the RB, at Lisbon Instrumentation and Experimental Particle Physics Laboratory; and visualization of the simulation results using the visualization tools from Johannes Kepler University, Linz. All processes are transparent to the user. For more details on integration of the visualization service into the test bed, we refer the reader to Reference 27.

10.2.2.1 Medical Image Segmentation

Once medical images are acquired, for example, by magnetic resonance angiography (MRA), the data are stored in a medical image repository for further analysis. Next, advanced image segmentation techniques are applied: The accurate assessment of the presence and extent of vascular disease requires the Determination of vessel dimensions. For this, a method for automatically determining the trajectory of the vessel of interest, the luminal boundaries, and subsequently the vessel dimensions has been developed by the Department of Radiology, Leiden University Medical Center (LUMC) [28]. In this way, relevant 3D structures such as arteries are extracted from the raw data.

The grid portal we use enables the user to access the grid resources from roaming machines like stand-alone PCs, notebooks, or desktop workstations. It allows running applications, managing data files, and storing personal settings independent of the localization or the terminal type. Users may handle grid and local resources, run applications, manage data files, and store personal settings. The portal provides a front-end framework for embedding some of the application mechanisms and interfaces, and it facilitates the user virtual access to grid resources from other computational nodes. Access to the CrossGrid test bed is based on globus grid security infrastructure (GSI). GSI uses public key encryption, X.509 certificates, and the secure sockets layer (SSL) communications protocol. Extensions to these standards have been added for single sign-on and delegation. The GSI provides a delegation capability, with an extension of the standard SSL protocol to reduce the number of times the user must enter his pass phrase. If a grid computation requires that several grid resources are used (each requiring mutual authentication), or if there is a need to have agents (local or remote) requesting services on behalf of a user, the need to reenter the user's pass phrase can be avoided by creating a proxy.

Average transfer times for the medical image data, once taking into account the Globus caching mechanism, did not vary much above 400 ms for the smaller size files and no more than 850 ms for the larger size files.

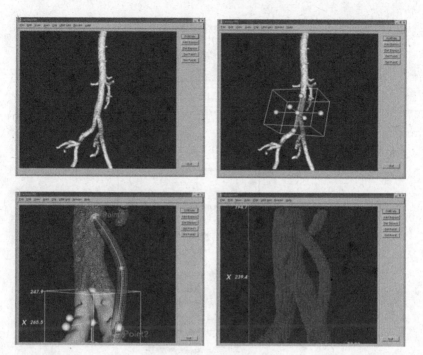

Figure 10.3. Segmented data rendering, bypass creation, and Lattice–Boltzmann mesh creation in the 2D Desktop Virtual Radiology Explorer; the LBM mesh editing also allows indicating boundary conditions.

The segmentation step is connected to the DesktopVRE-based reconstruction of a 3D model of an artery. A geometrical modeling tool allows the interactive manipulation with 3D geometry and procedures, such as the clipping operation, editing of LBM mesh, handling of problematic areas, and interactive placement of a bypass (Fig. 10.3).

10.2.2.2   Simulation Job Submission

Within the portal, application-specific information can be described using extensible markup language (XML) schema. In order to integrate visualization libraries into the computational grid test bed, we created and posted application XML schemata for job submission, to be dynamically linked to the portal via a job submission wizard. Then XML style sheet transformations (XSLT) is used in order to transform the schemas into appropriate XHTML. The portal sends the job request to the RAS, which then is sent to a job submission service, which then sends the job to a RB and logs all operations. The RB starts a job on the target CE. Before the job is started, a job submission script downloads all necessary files for simulation from a virtual node. Within the portal, we use the EDG replica manager for replication services, which allows one to copy files into grid storage, register files, replicate files between SEs, delete individual replicas, and delete all replicas of a particular file.

Figure 10.4. Simulation monitoring via the CrossGrid lightweight portal, based on an Enterprise Information Portal, using Java and XML, and interfacing with a lightweight Personal Digital Assistant (PDA).

Grid monitoring in CrossGrid includes services for application monitoring, as well as services for monitoring instruments and infrastructure. Application monitoring is substantially different from monitoring infrastructure and instruments, so separate approaches are offered, with application monitoring aimed at observing a particular execution of an application. The collected data are useful for tools for application development support, which are used to detect bugs and bottlenecks or just visualize the application's behavior, in the context of a particular execution. For our purposes, we use the MD portal and CrossGrid lightweight portal capabilities for monitoring job submission (Fig. 10.4).

We integrated more advanced application monitoring and performance prediction tools, as well as fine-grain infrastructure monitoring to allow for more interactive usage of collected information. The application monitoring infrastructure developed in the CrossGrid is the Grid-based OMIS-compliant Monitoring (OCM-G) [29], a distributed decentralized, autonomous system that runs as a permanent grid service. It provides monitoring services accesible via a standardized interface, to be used by visual tools such as Grid-Performance Monitoring (GPM)[30]. We use GPM extensively (Fig. 10.5) to define our own performance metrics and also to access a set of fixed ones, as well as to handle the process of measuring the performance properties.

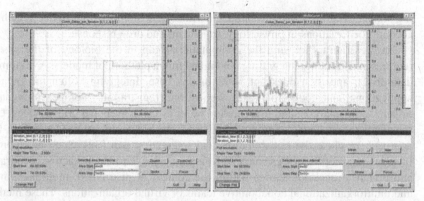

Figure 10.5. Simulation monitoring of the blood flow simulation in the CrossGrid, via OCM-G/G-PM: graphs showing communication delay per iteration or percentage of time that the solver spends in communication routines in one iteration, at two different timescales of simulation within 5 and 7 min of running time (x-axis) and delay (y-axis). The figure identifies a twofold jump in the amount of time in communication at 5.4 min on the shorter timescale, which continues on the larger timescale and points out to possible bottlenecks on kernel performance.

We also use GridBench [31], a tool developed to administer benchmarking experiments, publish their results, and produce graphical representations of their results.

After jobs have been completed, the user can then submit the results of visualization on the grid using grid visualization tools, either anywhere in the network or to a specific CE where the simulation has run, to avoid large data transfers. Finally, visualization results are transferred to the VRE to be rendered and reviewed by the user.

We address the combination of grid applications and corresponding visualization clients on the grid. While grids offer a means to process large amounts of data across distant resources, visualization aids in understanding the meaning of data. For this reason, visualization capabilities use Globus services, thereby providing grid visualization services via dedicated interfaces and protocols while at the same time exploiting the performance of the grid for visualization purposes. A resource intensive module of the visualization pipeline is instantiated on a high-performance computer. Then, the visualization pipeline on a graphics workstation connects (via redirection through the portal service) to this module, uses the power of the high-performance computer to generate the visual results, and downloads them to the visualization device. We created links within the MD portal for initialization of the visualization client application, and experimented with rendering the flow both remotely and locally in the access storage element. In this way, remote visualization and local rendering are fully linked via the portal for final rendering.

10.3 INDIVIDUALIZED BIOMEDICAL E-SCIENCE

Computer science provides the language needed to study and understand complex biomedical systems. Computer system architectures reflect the same laws and organizing principles used to build individualized biomedical systems, which can account for variations in physiology, treatment, and drug response.

On the contrary, closing the computational gap in the biology of the systems requires constructing, integrating, and managing a plethora of models. A bottom-up, data-driven approach does not work in this case. Integrating often incompatible applications and tools for data acquisition, registration, storage, provenance, organization, analysis, and presentation requires using Web and grid services. Once the computational and integration challenges are addressed, we need a system-level approach to close the collaboration and interaction gap [32]. Such an approach involves sharing processes, data, information, and knowledge across geographic and organizational boundaries within the context of distributed, multidisciplinary, and multiorganizational collaborative teams or virtual organizations. These methods dynamically streamline and, most importantly, *individualize* scientific data flow processes depending on their availability, reliability, and the specific interests of medical doctors, surgeons, clinical experts, researchers, and other end users We call this a *molecule-to-man* approach (Fig. 10.6).

10.3.1   The ViroLab Collaboratory

During the past decade, researchers have made significant progress in treating patients with viral diseases. Effective antiretroviral therapy has lead to sustained HIV viral suppression and immunological recovery in patients who have been infected with the virus. Adherence to antiretroviral treatment, therefore, remains the cornerstone of effective treatment, and failure to adhere is the strongest predictor of virological failure. Long-term therapy can lead to metabolic complications. Other treatment options are now available, with the recent introduction to clinical practice of fusion inhibitors, second-generation nonnucleoside reverse transcriptase inhibitors, and nucleotide reverse transcriptase inhibitors. However, in order to completely suppress the virus, patients must take a combination of at least two of the four different classes of antiretroviral drugs [33]. Nevertheless, in a significant proportion of patients, the drugs fail to completely suppress the viral disease, resulting in the rapid selection of drug-resistant viruses and loss of drug effectiveness. This complicates the clinician's decision process, since clinical interpretation is based on data sets relating mutations to changes in drug sensitivity and relating mutations present in the virus to clinical responses of specific treatment regimens.

In recent years, researchers have developed several genotypic resistance-interpretation tools that help clinicians and virologists choose effective therapeutic alternatives to address, for example, genotypic resistance interpretation. Furthermore, applying artificial intelligence and computational techniques has resulted in the development of specialized computer-based decision Support Systems (DSSs). Recent developments in distributed computing further allow the virtualization of the deluge of available data and computational and software resources required by complex e-Science. ViroLab [34] is an international collaborative laboratory, the goal of which is to provide such virtual laboratory where researchers and medical doctors have easy access to distributed simulations and can share, process, and

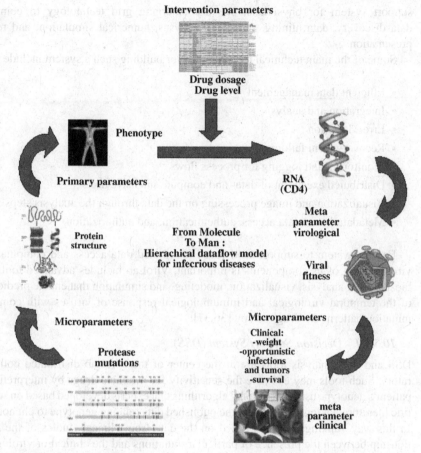

Figure 10.6. Data flow model in ViroLab showing the model for the prediction of the temporal behavior of the immune system to drug therapy that aims to qualitatively correspond to clinical data. The multiscale approach from microparameters such as protease mutations to macro results at the clinical level go through primary, interventional, and meta virological parameters, as supported by the Virtual Laboratory.

analyze virological, immunological, clinical, and experimental infectious disease data [35]. Currently, virologists browse journals, select results, compile them for discussion, and derive rules for ranking and making decisions.

ViroLab's grid-based DSS for infectious diseases consists of modules for individualized drug ranking in human immunodeficiency disease. It offers clinicians a distributed virtual laboratory securely accessible from their hospitals and institutes throughout Europe.

10.3.2   System Requirements

ViroLab's research goal is to investigate novel computational methods and techniques that support the development of a secure and user-friendly integrated decision support system for physicians. We use emerging grid technology to combine data discovery, data mining, statistical analyses, numerical simulation, and result presentation.

Some of the main technical requirements for building such a system include

- Efficient data management
- Integration and analysis
- Error detection
- Recovery from failures
- Monitoring and logging for process flows
- Distributed execution of data- and compute-intensive tasks
- Visualization and image processing on the data through the analysis steps
- Metadata-based data access, authentication, and authorization

For the system to support Grid-based distributed data access and computation, virtualization of its components is important. ViroLab includes advanced tools for biostatistical analysis, visualization, modeling, and simulation that enable prediction of the temporal virological and immunological response of viruses with complex mutation patterns for drug therapy [36,37].

10.3.2.1 Decision Support System (DSS)

DSS and data analysis tools are at the center of the ViroLab distributed collaboratory. Such tools may estimate the sensitivity for available drugs by interpreting a patient's genotype using mutational algorithms that experts developed based on scientific literature, taking into account the published data relating genotype to phenotype. In this way, rankings are also based on the data from clinical studies of the relationship between the presence of particular mutations and the clinical or virological outcome.

A number of bioinformatics software programs have been developed in the last few years to support bioinformatics decision-making in clinical environments. A couple of examples of such systems are the Virtual Phenotype (developed by Virco NV)[1] and Retrogram (developed by Virology Networks BV[2]). The output of these programs consists of a prediction of the drug sensitivity of the virus, generated by comparing the viral genotype to a relational database containing a large number of phenotype–genotype pairs. The Retrogram[3] decision software, in particular, interprets the genotype of a patient by using rules developed by experts on the basis of the literature, taking into account the relationship of the genotype and phenotype [38]. In addition, it is based on (limited) available data from clinical studies and on the relationship between the presence of genotype directly to clinical outcome. It is important to note, however, that these systems focus on biological relationships and are

---

[1] http://www.vircolab.com/
[2] http://www.vironet.com/
[3] Registered Trademark University of Amsterdam: no. 713908

limited to the role of resistance. The next step is to use clinical databases and investigate the relationships between the viral resistance profile (mutational profile and/or phenotypic data) and therapy outcome measures such as amount of virus (HIV-RNA) and CD4+ cells.

In DSSs like the Retrogram, the primary goal of the data analysis is to identify patterns of mutations (or naturally occurring polymorphisms) associated with resistance to antiviral drugs and to predict the degree of *in vitro* or *in vivo* sensitivity to available drugs from an HIV genetic sequence. The statistical challenges in doing such analyses arise from the high dimensionality of these data. A variety of approaches have been developed to handle this type of data, including clustering, recursive partitioning, and neural informatics. Neural informatics is used for synthesis of heuristic models received by methods of knowledge engineering, as well as for results of the formal multivariate statistical analysis in uniform systems. Clustering methods have been used to group sequences that are near each other according to some measure of genetic distance: Once clusters have been identified, recursive partitioning can be used to determine the important predictors of drug resistance, as measured by *in vitro* assays or by patient's response to antiviral drugs.

10.3.2.2   Interactivity and Process Flow

The availability of grid infrastructures and tools for interactive applications presents an important research opportunity. For bioinformatics collaboratory work, we build the previous efforts where we developed a unified approach for running interactive distributed applications on the grid by providing solutions to the following issues:

- Automatic porting of applications to grid environments
- User interaction services for interactive startup of applications, online output control, parameter study, and runtime steering
- Advanced user interfaces that enable easy plug-in of applications and tools, like interactive performance analysis combined with online monitoring
- Scheduling of distributed interactive applications
- Benchmarking and performance prediction
- Optimization of data access to different storage systems

In ViroLab, an important issue is for users to be able to register and publish derived data and processes and to keep track of the provenance of information flowing through the generated pipelines, as well as accessing existing (patient and scientific literature) data and acquiring new data from scientific instruments. These domain-independent features can then be customized by adding domain-specific components and semantic annotation of the components and data being used. In order to automate the construction of process flow applications, the system needs to generate ontological descriptions of services, system components, and their infrastructure [39,40]. Semantic data are usually stored as a registry that contains Web Ontology Language (OWL) descriptions of service class functionality, instance properties, and performance records. The user provides a set of initial requirements about the process flow use; then the system builds an abstract process flow using the knowledge about services' functionality that service providers have supplied to the registry. Subsequently, the system must apply semantic information on service properties, which results from analyzing the monitoring data of services and resources, to steer running process flows that still have multiple possibilities of concrete Web service operations.

The system can select the preferable service class by comparing semantic descriptions of the available service classes and matching the features of the classes to the actual requirements. ViroLab users can therefore verify and identify the data's origin and rerun experiments when required. ViroLab extends this feature by categorizing the level of information, including the data and process flows. The collected data-provenance information is archived in ViroLab's portal and accessible through search and discovery methods.

10.3.2.3   Virtual Organization (VO)

Grid computing is based on the central concept of distributed *Virtual Organizations* that span multiple trust domains. Trust in grids is commonly established via a Public Key Infrastructure (PKI): Every entity in the system is issued with a "certificate" that links an identifier to a piece of unique cryptographic data.

In ViroLab we developed a distributed virtual organization that binds the various components of the distributed VO. This binding layer spans a number of geographically separated physical institutions across Europe, including five hospitals. ViroLab's VO-based security infrastructure is based on grid middleware and a set of interfaces providing user-friendly and transparent access to the ViroLab applications, within a grid portal.

Security is, naturally, an important concern. The sensitive nature of clinical patient data, together with concerns that data and resources be made available in a timely fashion to just those who are authorized to access them, is supported by grid authentication and authorization components that span all aspects of the infrastructure. It is important to note, though, that in ViroLab grid security policy definition is left to the local owner's trust policy. VO members with access to the VOs resources can therefore use and share distributed resources securely, leveraging single sign-on.

Maintaining confidentiality is important in the development of monitoring protocols and procedures. Therefore, in order to guarantee patient confidentiality, database access is limited and anonymized, especially in the case of overview in which HIV results can be linked to individuals. In this case such overviews are destroyed as soon as relevant data have been retrieved.

10.3.3   System Architecture

The ViroLab system's design guarantees the interaction between a user and running applications, similar to methods used in real experiments, so the user can change a selected set of input data or parameters at runtime. For instance, under a typical usage scenario in ViroLab,

- A scientist from a clinical and epidemiological virology laboratory in Utrecht, Netherlands, securely accesses virus sequence, amino acid, or mutations data from a hospital AIDS lab in Rome using grid technology components running in Stuttgart, Germany.
- The scientist applies quality indicators needed for data-provenance tracking using provenance-server components running in Krakow, Poland.
- Researchers use these data as an input to (molecular dynamics) simulations and immune system simulations running on grid nodes that reside at University College London and the University of Amsterdam.
- The virtualized DSS automatically derives meta rules.
- Intelligent system components from Amsterdam use first-order logic to clean rules, identify conflicts and redundancy, and check logical consistency.
- The scientist validates new rules that the system automatically uploads into the virtualized DSS.
- The system presents a new ranking.

We next elaborate on ViroLab's Grid-based architecture design, in terms of the system's virtual laboratory, presentation, and virtualization viewpoints (Fig. 10.7).

Our system's architecture is based on the grid concept of distributed virtual organizations (VOs), which has a virtualized decision support system at its core, and a pervasive grid infrastructure that provides PKI security access. We distinguish a base *Grid Resource* layer, where computational (computing elements within hospitals or research centers) and data resources (storage elements—individual patient data, medical knowledge data, intermediate experimental data, and so forth) are archived. On top of this layer, a virtual laboratory component encapsulates the runtime system that interacts with the collaboration and data access components via a session manager that handles the provenance components as well. Finally, the application and presentation layers contain the user interfaces and individual application interfaces for either the core rule-based system used for initial decision support and ranking or the scientific tools for the enhancement of such rankings. We next elaborate on the different components and their functionalities.

10.3.3.1   *Virtual Laboratory*

In order to cover the temporal and spatial scales required to infer information from a molecular level up to patient medical data, multiscale methods are applied in ViroLab, where distributed simulation, statistical analysis and data mining are combined and used to enhance the base rule-based decision process. In this scenario, resources are widely distributed, and the data processing requirements are highly variable, both in the type of resources required and computational processing demands. Experiment design, integration of information from various sources, as well as transparent scheduling and execution of experiments is initially supported by the DAS2 test bed in The Netherlands, providing additional computational power for computational intensive jobs. We reuse grid middleware from successful European projects to provide basic

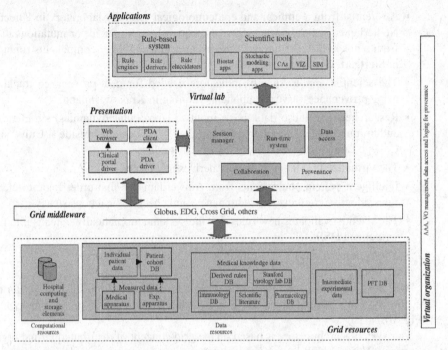

Figure 10.7. ViroLab system architecture; distributed resources (computing elements, data, and storage) that the biomedical applications use are coordinated with the grid middleware and a virtualized runtime system. Resources are automated and virtualized, and the resulting data are fed to anonymizing components, as well as directly to the Decision Support System.

grid services for data management, resource management, and information services on top of Globus middleware.

In order to support such a distributed decision support infrastructure, we start with VO support for a DSS-centered prototype. Here, users are assisted by rules developed by experts on the basis of the available literature, taking into account the relationship between relevant genotype and phenotype data. We extend this monolithic base DSS by virtualizing its basic building blocks, and distributing the relevant components and data from clinical studies across the VO.

10.3.3.2   Presentation

In the initial design phases we aim to maintain the same level of usability and readability as the original Web version of the DSS interface. This is accomplished by maintaining the same structure, but with some modifications. A Proxy method is implemented for accessing the Web-based software from mobile devices as well, where the Proxy server acts between the remote server (the DSS) and a mobile device. Here, a navigation script in the Proxy is responsible for the following:

- Take the patient data from the mobile user (i.e., patient detail, laboratory information).

- Create an HTTP communication with the remote server.
- Submit data to the remote server.
- Take the result from the remote server.
- Parse HTML code and retrieve only relevant information (i.e., drug ranking, error messages, drug references, etc.).
- Send the wireless pages to the mobile device.

In the initial Web version, the Proxy is implemented using a hypertext preprocessor as a server-site scripting language running on the Web server (Fig. 10.8). Two versions are developed using the Proxy method: WAP version and Web clipping. If a user wants to enter the patient details fields, he has to move from one screen to the other and come back again. The fields already filled in the previous screens should not be lost.

For ViroLab, an extra layer of grid services is implemented in order to allow access to both applications and resources via a grid portal. The portal serves as the central access point where users are authenticated using single sign-on, and it provides direct access to the virtual laboratory infrastructure, runtime system and collaboration support. Our aim is that the portal is based on standard portlet technologies, using a set of portlet Web applications that collaborate within the framework and support of standard grid security. We initially leverage the support for grid integration of the GridSphere portal framework. In GridSphere, a collection of grid portlets provided as add-on modules form a cohesive end-user environment for managing

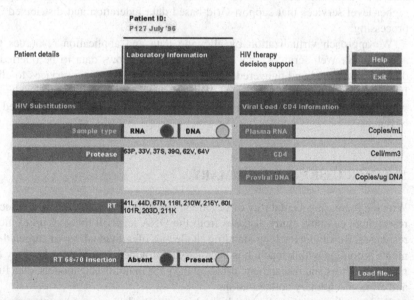

Figure 10.8. Web Retrogram: User enters patient substitutions in order to get drug ranking results by logging into the interface, accessing patient detail and laboratory information, and accessing the DSS for drug ranking and interpretation. Courtesy Sloot et al. [35].

users and groups, supporting remote job execution and file staging, and providing access to information services. GridSphere provides two portlet implementations; one is the JSR 168 *de facto* portlet API standard and the other is based on the IBM WebSphere Portlet API. GridSphere supports the development of reusable portlets and portlet services. It includes a set of core portlets and portlet services that provide the basic infrastructure required for developing and administering Web portals.

10.3.3.3   *Application and Resource Virtualization*

ViroLab infrastructure provides virologists with an advanced environment to study trends on an individual, population, and epidemiological level. That is, by virtualizing the hardware, compute infrastructure, and databases, the virtual laboratory offers a user-friendly environment, with tailored process flow templates to harness and automate such diverse tasks as data archiving, integration, mining, and analysis; modeling and simulation; and integrating biomedical information from viruses (proteins and mutations), patients (viral load), and the literature (drug-resistance experiments).

In ViroLab we need access to different types of data resources via grids. In order to achieve this goal, we provide a way of querying, updating, transforming and delivering data via Web services in a consistent, independent way. In order to automate archiving, integration, mining, as well as transparent access to applications, we work with metadata and the data resources in which these data are stored and accessed via Web services that can be combined to provide higher-level services that support Grid-based data federation and distributed query processing.

We approach virtualization by allowing data and application resources to be accessed via Web services; that is, a Web service allows data to be queried, updated, transformed and delivered, while integrating the data via services to clients. In ViroLab we use the OGSA-DAI Web services model, which can be deployed within a grid environment. This allows us to Grid-enable the distributed data resources.

10.4   DISCUSSION AND SUMMARY

With the increasing availability of genetic information and extensive patient records, researchers can now study diseases from the DNA level all the way up to medical responses. Resolving the long-standing challenges of individual-based, targeted treatments is coming within reach. It is necessary to provide integrating technology to the medical doctors and researchers, bridging the gaps in multiscale models, data fusion, and cross-disciplinary collaboration.

With the first case study, we showed a framework for rapid prototyping of exploration environments that permits users to explore interactively the visualized results of a simulation and manipulate the simulation parameters in near real time. We introduced generic architectural requirements, defined a generic component-based software architecture and its abstract interactions, and identified a specific-use case for validation of the architecture.

The second and main case study presented here consists of a decision support system that compares patients' viral genotype to a distributed relational database containing a large number of phenotype–genotype pairs. The decision software interprets a patient's genotype by using rules developed by experts on the basis of the literature, taking into account the relationship of the genotype and phenotype. In addition, the output is based on the available data from clinical studies and on the relationship between the presence of genotype and the clinical outcome.

We have showed how in the understanding of processes from bioinformatics to heath informatics, from molecule to man, distributed computing in general and grid technology in particular can play a crucial role. We found that in order to cover the huge time and spatial scales required to infer information from a molecular (genomic) level up to patient medical data, we need to apply multiscale methods where simulation, statistical analysis, and data mining are combined in an efficient way. Moreover, such required integrative approach requires distributed data collection (e.g., HIV mutation databases, patient data, literature reports, among others) and a virtual organization (physicians, hospital administration, computational resources, etc.) to support it. The access to and use of large-scale computation (both high performance as well as distributed) is essential since many of the computations involved require near real-time response and are too complex to run on a personal computer or personal digital assistant. Furthermore, data presentation is crucial in order to lower the barrier of actual usage by the physicians; here the grid technology (server–client approach) can play an important role.

For future work, we will work on enhancements to the current test bed like scientific collaboration support, as required to process the variety of data and information generated from a number of ViroLab applications as well as data providers and hospitals. For instance, in addition to the basic requirements of voice and video support between scientists, we will work on scientific collaboration support for the sharing of drug rankings (current rankings and new rankings resulting from the new applications), collaborative validation of drug rankings (once validation of a new ranking has been performed, users may want to discuss and share their findings with relevant stakeholders), and feedback from experts via links to the workflow engine (collaboration tools may allow the direct and instant communication with experts during and at all steps of scientific workflow execution).

ACKNOWLEDGMENTS

The authors wish to thank the members of the CrossGrid and ViroLab consortia. This research is partly funded by the EU IST CrossGrid (IST200132243) and ViroLab (IST027446), and the Bsik Virtual Laboratory for e-Science (VL-e) projects.

REFERENCES

1. A. Finkelstein, J. Hetherington, L. Li, O. Margoninski, P. Saffrey, R. Seymour, A. Warner, Computational challenges of system biology, *IEEE Computer* **37**(5), pp. 26–33, 2004.

2. A.J.G. Hey, A.E. Trefethen, The data deluge: An e-science perspective, in: F. Berman, G.C. Fox, and A.J.G. Hey (Eds.), *Grid Computing Making the Global Infrastructure a Reality*, John Wiley & Sons, Hoboken, NJ, pp. 809–824, 2003.

3. R. Martinez, J.F. Cook, A. Tirado-Ramos, Java CORBA DICOM Adapter Service for DICOM-compliant datasets in: *First Latin American Conference on Biomedical Engineering*, Sociedad Mexicana de Ingenieria Biomedica IEEE-EMBS, Mazatlan, Mexico, pp. 621–622, November 1998, ISBN 968-5063-03-6.

4. A. Tirado-Ramos, J. Hu, K.P. Lee, Information object definition-based unified modeling language representation of DICOM structured reporting: a case study of transcoding DICOM to XML, *Journal of the American Medical Informatics Association* **9**, 63–72. 2002.

5. Object Management Group, *The Common Object Request Broker: Architecture and Specification*, second edition, July 1995.

6. I. Foster, C. Kesselman, S. Tuecke, The anatomy of the grid: Enabling scalable virtual organizations, *International Journal of High Performance Computing Applications* **15**(3), 200–222, 2001.

7. S. Martin, D.C. Yen, J. K. Tan, E-health: Impacts of internet technologies on various healthcare and services sectors, *International Journal of Healthcare Technology and Management* **4**, 71–86, 2002.

8. P.M.A. Sloot, Simulation and visualization in medical diagnosis: Perspectives and computational requirements, in: A. Marsh, L. Grandinetti, T. Kauranne (Eds.), *Advanced Infrastructures for Future Healthcare*, IOS Press, Amsterdam, pp. 275–282, 2000.

9. M. Cannataro, C. Comito, A. Congiusta, G. Folino, C. Mastroianni, A. Pugliese, G. Spezzano, D. Talia, P. Veltri, Grid-based PSE toolkits for multidisciplinary applications, FIRB grid.it WP8 Working Paper 2003-10, ICAR-CNR, December 2003.

10. A. Tirado-Ramos, P.M.A. Sloot, A.G. Hoekstra, M. Bubak, An integrative approach to high-performance biomedical problem solving environments on the grid, in: Chun-Hsi Huang and Sanguthevar Rajasekaran (Eds.), *Parallel Computing*, special issue on High-Performance Parallel Bio-computing, **30**(9–10), 1037–1055, 2004.

11. E.N. Houstis, J.R. Rice, S. Weerwarna, P. Papachio, Wang K. Yang, M. Gaitatzes, *Enabling Technologies for Computational Science Frameworks Middleware and Environments*, Kluwer Academic Publishers, Dordrecht, Chapter 14, pp. 171–185, 2000.

12. E. Gallopoulos, E. Houstis, J.R. Rice, Computer as thinker/doer: problem-solving environments for computational science, *IEEE Computational Science Engineering* **1**(2), 11–23, 1994.

13. K.A. Iskra, R.G. Belleman, G.D. van Albada, J. Santoso, P.M.A. Sloot, H.E. Bal, H.J.W. Spoelder, M. Bubak, The polder computing environment, a system for interactive distributed simulation, in: *Concurrency and Computation: Practice and Experience* (special Issue on Grid Computing Environments), Vol. 14, John Wiley & Sons, Hoboken, NJ, pp. 1313–1335, 2002.

14. R.G. Belleman, P.M.A. Sloot, Simulated vascular reconstruction in a virtual operating theatre, CARS 2001 Conference, Berlin, Germany, June 2001.

15. M. Bubak, M. Malawski, K. Zajac, Architecture of the grid for interactive applications, in: *Proceedings of the International Conference on Computational Science*, LNCS 2657, Springer, Berlin, pp. 207–213, 2003, www.crossGrid.org.

16. EU DataGrid Project, http://eu-datagrid.web.cern.ch/eu-datagrid/

17. http://lcg.web.cern.ch/LCG/Documents/default.htm

18. http://www.science.uva.nl/research/scs/HotResults/

19. A.M. Artoli, A.G. Hoekstra, P.M.A. Sloot, 3D pulsatile flow with the lattice Boltzmann BGK method, *International Journal of Modern Physics C* **13**(08), 1119–1134, 2002.

20. S. Succi, *The Lattice Boltzmann Equation for Fluid Dynamics and Beyond*, Oxford Science Publications, Clarendon Press, New York, 2001.

21. A.M. Artoli, A.G. Hoekstra, P.M.A. Sloot, Mesoscopic simulations of systolic flow in the human abdominal aorta, *Journal of Biomechanics* **39**, 873–884, 2006.

22. R.G. Belleman, B. Stolk, R. de Vries, Immersive virtual reality on commodity hardware, in: *Proceedings of the Seventh Annual Conference of the Advanced School for Computing and Imaging*, pp. 297–304, May 2001.

23. The University of Amsterdam Distributed Real-time Interactive Virtual Environment, UvA-DRIVE. http://www.science.uva.nl/ robbel/DRIVE/

24. E.V. Zudilova, P.M.A. Sloot, R.G. Belleman, A multi-modal interface for an interactive simulated vascular reconstruction system, in: *Proceedings of the IEEE International Conference on Multimodal Interfaces*, Pittsburgh, Pennsylvania, pp. 313–319, October 2002.

25. R.G. Belleman, J.A. Kaandorp, D. Dijkman, P.M.A. Sloot, *GEOPROVE: Geometric Probes for Virtual Environments*, Lecture Notes in Computer Science, No. 1593, Springer-Verlag, Berlin, pp. 817–827, April 1999.

26. E.V. Zudilova, P.M.A. Sloot, Virtual reality and desktop as a combined interaction–visualisation medium for a problem-solving environment, in: *Proceedings of International Conference on Computational Science-ICCS 2003, Melbourne, Australia*, Series Lecture Notes in Computer Science, Springer-Verlag, Berlin, pp. 1025–1035, June 2003.

27. A. Tirado-Ramos, H. Ragas, D. Shamonin, H. Rosmanith, D. Kranzlmueller, Integration of blood flow biomedical application grid visualization Kernel via a grid portal, in: *Second European Across grids Conference,* Nicosia, Cyprus, January 2004, pp. 28–30.

28. P.F. Lelieveldt, S.C. Mitchell, J.G. Bosch, R.J. vander Geest, M. Sonka, J.H.C. Reiber, Time continuous segmentation of cardiac image sequences using active appearance motion models, proceedings of IPMI, *Lecture Notes in Computer Science 2082*, 446–452, 2001.

29. B. Balis, M. Bubak, W. Funika, T. Szepieniec, R. Wismueler, An infrastructure for grid application monitoring, in: D. Kranzlmueller, P. Kacsuk, J. Dongarra, and J. Volker (Eds.), *Recent Advances in Parallel Virtual Machine and Message Passing Interface, Proceedings of the Ninth European PVM/MPI Users Group Meeting*, Linz, Austria, September/October 2002, LNCS 2474, pp. 41–49, 2002.

30. M. Bubak, W. Funika, R. Wismueller, T. Arodz, M. Kurdziel, The G-PM tool for grid-oriented performance analysis, in: *Lecture Notes in Computer Science*, Vol. 2970, pp. 240–248, Jan 2004.

31. G. Tsouloupas, M.D. Dikaiakos, GridBench: a tool for benchmarking grids, in: *Proceedings of the Fourth International Workshop on Grid Computing*, pp. 60–67, 2003.

32. P.M.A. Sloot, A. Tirado-Ramos, I. Altintas, M.T. Bubak, C.A. Boucher, From molecule to man: Decision support in individualized e-health, *IEEE Computer* **39**(11), 40–46, 2006.

33. S.G. Deeks, Treatment of antiretroviral-drug-resistant HIV-1 infection, *Lancet*, **362**, 2002–2011, 2003.

34. http://www.virolab.org/

35. P.M.A. Sloot, A.V. Boukhanovsky, W. Keulen, A. Tirado-Ramos, C.A. Boucher, A grid-based HIV expert system, *Journal of Clinical Monitoring and Computing* **19**(4–5), 263–278, 2005.

36. P.M.A. Sloot, F. Chen, C.A. Boucher, Cellular automata model of drug therapy for HIV infection, in: S. Bandini, B. Chopard, and M. Tomassini (Eds.), in: *Proceedings of the 5th International Conference on Cellular Automata for Research and Industry (ACRI 02)*, LNCS 2493, Springer, Berlin, **2493**, pp. 282–293, 2002.

37. T.E. Scheetz et al., Gene transcript clustering: A comparison of parallel approaches, *Future Generation Computer Systems*, 731–735, 2005.

38. A. Been-Tiktak, K. Korn, W. Keulen, E. Schwingel, H. Walter, B. Schmidt, et al., Evaluation of an open expert-based genotype interpretation program: RetroGram, 41st Interscience Conference on Antimicrobial Agents and Chemotherapy, 2001.

39. B. Ludascher, I. Altintas, C. Berkley, D. Higgins, E. Jaeger, M. Jones, E.A. Lee, J. Tao, Y. Zhao, Scientific workflow management and the Kepler system, *Concurrency and Computation: Practice and Experience* **18**(10), 1039–1065, 2006.

40. M. Bubak, T. Gubala, M. Kapalka, M. Malawski, K. Rycerz, Workflow composer and service registry for grid applications, *Future Generation Computer Systems* **21**(1), 79–86, 2005.

11

DATABASE-DRIVEN GRID COMPUTING AND DISTRIBUTED WEB APPLICATIONS: A COMPARISON

Hans De Sterck, Aleks Papo, Chen Zhang, Micah Hamady, and Rob Knight

Two approaches for unleashing the power of distributed computing for large bioinformatics problems are compared, namely, an approach based on database-driven grid computing and an approach that uses distributed Web applications. In the first approach, users can upload their own application programs and data to the grid system for processing, while the second approach targets users who wish to employ a standard set of available bioinformatics programs in workflows with user-specific data. The first approach is realized in the GridBASE framework for database-driven grid computing. The design and a prototype implementation of the framework are discussed. All tasks are task farmed to distributed worker nodes independently. Industry-strength database technology plays a key role in the design of the framework. The database is used as a scalable, reliable, and remotely accessible component both for storing and organizing the configuration information of the grid and for managing information related to (a) the grid users, and the jobs and (b) the tasks they submit for execution. Other system components are worker nodes, a simple resource broker, a grid operator console, and application clients. No extra scheduling component is needed in the system. Application code can be written in any language, and simple workflow support is provided. In our prototype implementation, we experiment with code delivery and input and output file deliveries via the database component. Our approach is based on decentralization and implemented in Java, leading to a lightweight, portable, and scalable grid computing solution. The approach is then compared with web applications that access dedicated clusters, on which a standard suite of application programs with large input data files is preinstalled. A Web application system that utilizes dedicated clusters for processing is described in some detail, with description of typical workflows. A case study is presented. Advantages and disadvantages of both concepts are discussed.

Grid Computing for Bioinformatics and Computational Biology. Edited by E.-G. Talbi and A.Y. Zomaya.
Copyright © 2008 John Wiley & Sons, Inc.

11.1 INTRODUCTION

There is a clear need for transparent, user-friendly, and efficient distributed computing systems for bioinformatics. Indeed, many bioinformatics problems require extensive computational resources. This may be due to either the large size of data sets to be analyzed or the high computational complexity of analysis algorithms, or both. Parallel and distributed computing approaches are, therefore, steadily gaining interest in the bioinformatics field. Especially for loosely coupled problems, grid computing approaches [1] may be attractive. The computational grid metaphor is illustrated in Fig. 11.1: Jobs submitted by grid users are executed transparently on any of the computers that are made available to the grid users by the grid operator. Computing power is thus treated as an exchangeable commodity in analogy with the electrical power distributed on a power grid. Web applications that give users access to distributed computing power for a predefined suite of bioinformatics programs installed on dedicated clusters are another way to offer distributed computing power to bioinformatics researchers. This chapter will describe an implementation of each of these two different approaches and will discuss our experience with each.

While the grid computing idea is attractive for certain applications and substantial effort has been dedicated to working out this concept by various research groups around the world, it has also turned out that this idea is not easy to realize in practice. Among the stumbling blocks encountered, we can mention security and privacy concerns, lack of hardware or software compatibility between heterogeneous computing equipment, complexity of new solution environments proposed, and the general inertia of legacy computing environments that the grid may attempt to use. Grid solutions are now being used for applications in many forms, both in research and industry environments, but due to difficulties such as the ones mentioned above, many issues remain unresolved, and consequently no satisfactory grid computing solution has emerged as a standard yet. Driven by the ever-increasing need for computational power, research on grid computing concepts is therefore still active.

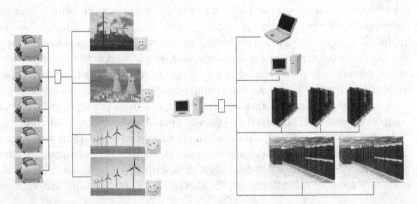

Figure 11.1. Analogy between a power grid (left) and a computational grid (right). Both exhibit scalability from the user's and the producer's sides.

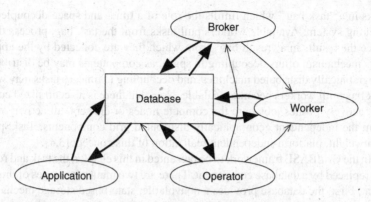

Figure 11.2. Conceptual diagram for database-driven grid computing system. The thick lines represent information transfer through database access. The thin lines represent direct control interactions between system components.

This chapter first presents the GridBASE framework for grid computing [2]. The purpose of GridBASE is to make it easy to grid enable a certain class of (task-farmable) applications. GridBASE is based on a few simple ideas (Fig. 11.2): All exchange of information in the grid occurs through an SQL database, which may be distributed. The only central component of the system is this passive database. All grid activities originate from the geographically distributed grid components that include worker, broker, and application components. The workers pull jobs from the database superqueue. The use of industry-strength databases allows to leverage the tremendous developments in database technology that have been made in recent years, especially with respect to scalability, performance, and reliability.

Just like its predecessor TaskSpaces [3,4], GridBASE employs the "bag-of-tasks" paradigm for distributed computing [5] (Fig. 11.3) in which applications deposit

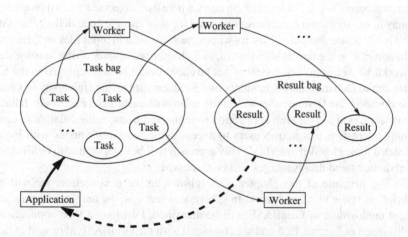

Figure 11.3. The bag-of-tasks paradigm for distributed computing.

tasks in a "task bag," which fulfills the role of a time- and space-decoupled passive queuing system. Available workers pull tasks from the task bag, process them, and place the results in a "result bag" from which they are collected by the application. This mechanism offers decoupling in space, as components may be distributed over geographically distributed machines, and decoupling in time, as tasks may wait in the task bag until workers become available. Note that there is no centralized component that actively pushes jobs onto the compute nodes or clusters; all activity originates from the independent geographically distributed grid components. TaskSpaces is a lightweight, platform-independent realization of this concept [3,4].

In the GridBASE framework to be presented in this chapter, the task and result bags are replaced by a database component. There are two main advantages of this replacement. First, the database provides a nonvolatile, state-based storage mechanism that makes the system much more stable and reliable. Second, the use of industry-strength databases allows to leverage the tremendous developments in database technology that have been made in recent years, especially with respect to scalability, performance, and fault tolerance.

In the simple prototype implementation of GridBASE that we present in this chapter, we took the database idea to its limit and also decided to implement, in addition to job management, all other aspects of the grid computing system via the database, including code delivery and job input and output. While this may be an approach that is too radical for some applications (for instance, applications requiring very large input or output files), it turns out to work very well for other applications. When files are large, it would be easy to provide alternative file serving mechanisms, for instance, using by servers. In fact, the idea of having all data-related entities in the grid computing system pass through the database may not be that radical, given the fact that in the Internet economy entire multibillion dollar enterprises are constructed around central databases.

The grid computing environment offered by systems such as GridBASE may not always be the most desirable way to allow users to execute bioinformatics jobs remotely in transparent ways. For instance, in cases where users execute standard programs that may have large input files, there is no need for user-specific code delivery, and it may be better to use dedicated clusters where the software and input files are preinstalled. In addition to the GridBASE system, this chapter will also describe in some detail a workflow web application system that has been designed and deployed in the Knight lab of the Department of Chemistry and Biochemistry of the University of Colorado at Boulder. The DivergentSet web application is discussed as a case study. It has been made accessible as a Web application to registered users, using a database-centered implementation that allows users to access dedicated cluster nodes with input uploaded through a Web interface. This approach will be compared with GridBASE and advantages and disadvantages will be discussed.

The structure of this chapter is as follows. In the next section, we will give a brief overview of related work. In subsequent sections, the design, implementation, and deployment of GridBASE will be described. Distributed Web applications are discussed in Section 11.6 and are compared with the GridBASE approach in Section 11.7. The chapter closes with sections about future work and conclusions.

11.2 RELATED WORK

The field of grid computing [1] is enjoying increasing attention in research projects all around the world [6], and, in recent years it has also been getting more and more attention in commercial and corporate settings [7–10]. Some of the goals of grid computing systems are also related to high-throughput computing systems such as Condor [11,12] and volunteer computing systems such as Berkeley Open Infrastructure for Network Computing (BOINC) [13].

Worker-driven grid computing systems where workers pull jobs from passive bag-of-tasks superqueues have been considered in experimental grid computing systems [14], including our TaskSpaces system [3,4]. Most grid computing projects that target large-scale scientific computing, however, employ the orthogonal approach of trying to integrate legacy queuing systems using sophisticated resource managers and cluster schedulers that push tasks to suitable clusters. See, for example, the open source TORQUE resource manager and Maui cluster scheduler projects [15]. Databases are being used as the central components of grid-like computing systems in the particular context of several volunteer computing projects, for instance, BOINC [16]. An overview of many workflow solutions for grid computing that have been proposed is given in [17], and [18] and [19] contain online discussions on grid workflows.

11.3 GRIDBASE DESIGN

11.3.1 Target Applications and Design Goals

GridBASE in its present form targets compute jobs that can easily be divided into many independent tasks (or sets of many independent jobs). The second assumption in the present implementation of GridBASE is that each task has small input/output (I/O) requirements. GridBASE can thus also be described as a task-farming system. It aims at improving throughput for these types of applications by giving users transparent access to heterogeneous computing networks. Design goals are to produce a lightweight platform-independent grid computing framework for taskfarming applications that is easy to deploy and install.

11.3.2 System Components and Roles

The major GridBASE design concepts are reflected in the conceptual diagram shown in Fig. 11.2.

The GridBASE system has five major types of components: a database, an operator, a broker, and one or more worker and application processes. Application processes submit jobs to the database. Each job consists of a number of tasks. Workers register with the database when they are available. The broker periodically queries the database and matches available tasks with available workers. After the matching, the broker notifies the workers who have been assigned to tasks. Workers then download tasks from the database, execute them, and upon task completion place the results back into the database. The conceptual role of "operator" is the responsibility for starting and maintaining the workers, the broker, and the database. Maintenance operations may include adding new users of the grid system, adding new workers or worker clusters, cleaning up residual information in the database when needed, and so on. During normal grid operation, the operator remains idle.

An important observation is that the GridBASE design makes a clear distinction between the role played by grid users on the one hand, who develop and submit application code but are otherwise mostly isolated from resource deployment and selection, and the conceptual role played by the grid operator on the other hand, who is responsible for providing computing resources and assuring system availability and maintenance. Some of the duties of the conceptual operator have been implemented in an operator console program (see below), but other tasks remain to be executed manually by the physical operator in the present implementation of GridBASE.

11.4   GRIDBASE IMPLEMENTATION

11.4.1   System Components

In our prototype implementation, the components of the conceptual diagram in Fig. 11.2 are implemented as follows. The operator, worker, broker, and application components are four stand-alone Java programs. The use of Java allows for seamless platform independence and easy installation. We use the standard Oracle database. We use the Java Database Connectivity (JDBC) API for database access from Java. JDBC is a standard SQL database access interface. This allows in principle to substitute the Oracle database with another database of SQL type. Files are stored within the database as binary large objects.

All data transfers between system components occur via the database. System components interact with the database in a classic client–server way. As will be detailed further below, the database stores all information that is related to the operation of the computational grid. This includes user information, grid configuration information, job and task information, task code files and task commands, task input files, and task output files.

In our simple prototype implementation of the GridBASE design, process execution by tasks is command-line based. For example, C code can be uploaded to the database as task input, and task commands may then compile the code and execute it. This approach is, of course, rudimentary and only as platform independent as the heterogeneity of the worker systems allows. Alternatively, Java bytecode can be uploaded, which allows for more platform independence. It is clear that this initial approach may be complemented by scripting approaches providing more platform independence that are used in other grid computing systems, but for our purpose of demonstration and testing this initial approach has shown sufficient result.

The application component is a simple interactive program that allows users to define jobs by specifying tasks and associated input files and command lines. In addition to job specification, the application program allows the user to interactively submit jobs, monitor job progression, and retrieve job results from the database.

The broker component periodically queries the database at short intervals of, for instance, 5 s and matches available tasks with available workers. Workers are notified by the broker when they are assigned to a task. The broker uses simple socket connections to notify a listening server that runs in a separate thread in each worker.

Upon startup, the workers register their availability with the database. Upon notification by the broker, they download task code and input files for the task they are assigned to. Command-line execution of the task commands is then invoked. After completion of the task commands, the output files are compressed and stored in the database as a single output file per task.

The operator component is another interactive Java program that accesses the database for various tasks such as adding users, clearing residual information, resetting tables, and so on. In addition, the physical operator also needs direct SSH access to the machines on which the workers, the database, and the broker reside. This allows the operator to start, restart, or shut down these components.

11.4.2   Data Model

Figure 11.4 shows a simplified logical data structure (LDS) for our prototype implementation of the GridBASE design. Our LDS diagram convention is based on Reference 20. All the data presented in the LDS are stored in the database.

There are seven main data entities in our system. Each entity has one or more attributes. For example, every user has a userID, userName, and userPassword and is associated with one or more jobs. Every job is associated with one user and is composed of one or more tasks. Similarly, workers can be associated with one or more tasks (all the tasks they execute over time), while every task may be associated with just one worker. WorkerStatus can be available or busy. WorkerIP and workerPort are used by the broker to notify workers when tasks are assigned to them. TaskStatus can be unassigned, assigned, in execution, or completed.

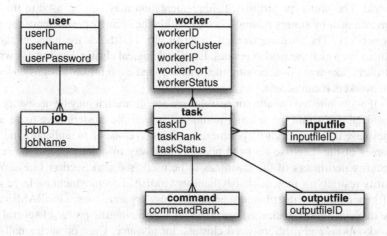

Figure 11.4. Simplified logical data structure for GridBASE.

Every task has one or more task commands. The order of commands within a given task is determined by the commandRank attribute. This enables rudimentary workflow control. The taskRank attribute gives the rank of the task within the job and is available on the command line in order to allow for rank-determined action within a given task program that may be common to all tasks within a job. Every task can have multiple input files, and every input file can be associated with multiple tasks. This allows files to be used by several tasks while being stored in the database only once. Finally, for simplicity we assign to every task at most one output file (a compressed file that holds the actual task output files). Users have access to only the jobs they own and do not have access to worker information. Some unessential details of the actual implementation have been omitted in this description for simplicity.

11.5   GRIDBASE DEPLOYMENT

11.5.1   Deployment Diagram

Figure 11.5 shows a typical deployment diagram for GridBASE in which several workers on individual workstations are combined with workers on a cluster.

11.5.2   Access Requirements

The deployment of the prototype implementation of GridBASE has several require-ments on the accessibility of some of the system components, which may be limiting in some environments due to firewalls or other security mechanisms that may exist. All workers need to be able to contact the database machine and need to be acces-sible to their associated broker. This may be difficult to achieve on certain Intranets or clusters. In many cases, clusters or Intranets do allow node-initiated connections to the outside world, but nodes may not be visible and reachable from the outside world. The prototype GridBASE implementation may still be used in this kind of environment by simply adding a broker within the security perimeter of the machine or network. The attribute workerCluster in Fig. 11.4 holds the name of the logical cluster on which the worker resides. Each such logical cluster then has its own broker. Brokers take turns in accessing the database, and each broker assigns tasks to only the workers it can access.

If node-initiated outside connections are not allowed, it may be necessary to place the database within the security perimeter. If multiple clusters have to be used that may have their own security perimeters, a solution could be to replicate synchronized copies of the database on head nodes or gateway machines within the respective security perimeters of the machines to be used (see also Section 11.8). While se-curity restrictions may obviously hamper GridBASE deployment on large numbers of geographically distributed machines across organizations, GridBASE can often be deployed easily within an organization, combining the power of several desktop workstations and medium-sized clusters, for instance. Even on such small-scale ad hoc grids, it turns out that it is a great advantage to have job submission and result

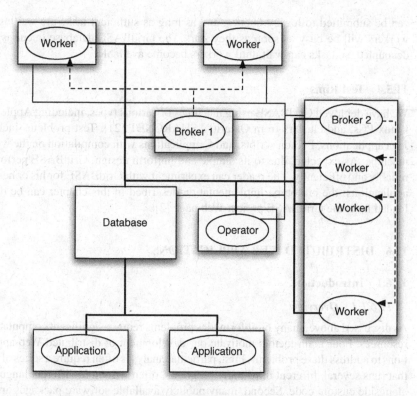

Figure 11.5. Gridbase deployment diagram. Rectangular boxes represent different machines. The thick solid lines represent connections to the database. The thin solid lines represent direct control interactions initiated by the operator component. The dashed lines represent notification of workers by their associated brokers.

retrieval centralized via a central database because this significantly facilitates in keeping track of job progress and, for instance, also removes the need for manual or script-based file transmissions.

11.5.3   Interaction with Legacy Queuing Systems

Ideally, once worker machines are engaged in a GridBASE system that works at full capacity, the workers should require no jobs other than the ones provided by the Grid-BASE system, so queuing systems should be superfluous. (In fact, GridBASE acts as a space-decoupled passive superqueue.) In reality, however, dedicated GridBASE machines may not be available, and one may want to use existing systems. Unfortunately, however, existing systems will have their own individual queuing systems, and it is well known that combining grid computing approaches with these legacy queuing systems is difficult. For task-farming applications that do not require synchronization between tasks, the situation is not too bad, however. Workers processes can be submitted to legacy queues; and as long as sufficient tasks are waiting, the workers will be busy as soon as they start. The GridBASE database queue is time decoupled, so tasks can wait until workers become available.

11.5.4   Test Runs

We have deployed GridBASE using machines of various types, including Apple PCs, Linux PCs, and clusters from Ontario's SHARCNET [21]. Test problems included Java applications, Python scripts, and C applications with compilation on the worker machine. As expected, due to its simple and uniform design, GridBASE performed reliably and efficiently. The reader can experiment with GridBASE for his or her own applications: the prototype implementation described in this chapter can be downloaded from the GridBASE project Web page [2].

11.6   DISTRIBUTED WEB APPLICATIONS

11.6.1   Introduction

11.6.1.1   Overview

As discussed above, many bioinformatics problems require significant computational resources. Four main factors motivate our development of distributed Web applications to address these problems. First, particular analyses often require a series of steps that runs several different third-party programs, often written in different languages, alongside custom code. Second, many publicly available software packages are difficult to use in practice (in terms of compiling, installing, and running the program, and parsing and interpreting the results) and are computationally intensive. Third, the same workflow is often needed by several people within a research group, and it is both difficult and a poor use of resources to have each researcher reimplement the same workflow. Fourth, as a workfloecomes more widely accepted, it is often desirable to open it up to less technical users who may be able to access an existing installation through a GUI but who would not be capable of setting up an installation from scratch or run the analysis through command-line tools.

11.6.1.2   Motivation

We will focus on two specific examples of web applications we have developed recently. The first application, DivergentSet, allows users to find groups of diverse but related sequences using additional sequences related to their query from public databases such as GenBank. This has traditionally been an extremely laborious manual process, often taking an experienced researcher days to weeks. The second application, UniFrac, allows users to compare a set of environmental samples of bacteria in terms of the amount of sequence evolution that is unique to each environment. UniFrac moves away from the paradigm of significance tests that reveal whether two communities are identical or not, instead allowing hundreds of microbial communities to be related to one another. These types of analyses often take months to perform with ad hoc tools. Our Web applications allow each of these tasks to be completed in minutes.

We have three main goals in developing Web applications such as UniFrac [22,23] and DivergentSet [24]. First, we want to minimize the perceived amount of time taken to perform the analyses and to allocate resources equitably among multiple users. Typically, this means minimizing wall clock time by distributing tasks, but factors such as breaking up time-consuming tasks with steps that require user input can also be important. Second, we need to manage access and resources centrally to reduce administrative overhead and to track usage of the different tools so that their development can be justified in funding agencies and so that effort can be allocated to benefit users the most. Third, we strive for modularity and simplicity, using off-the-shelf, free software where appropriate and developing simplified interfaces that allow users to perform the most common workflows easily without being distracted by large numbers of irrelevant options.

11.6.1.3 Advantages and Disadvantages of Web Applications

Web applications have many advantages over other possible ways of allowing users to access workflows. These can be broadly divided into ease-to-use, administration, and scalability advantages.

One key ease-of-use advantage is that most users are familiar with web interfaces, thus minimizing the effort required to get useful results. Hyperlinked graphical displays increase the ability of users to correctly interpret complex data sets. The user does not need to write new code, compile it, or interact explicitly with the queuing system. It is also easy to implement portability so that the user can upload, analyze, and store data and results on the server and access them from any computer with a Web browser.

There are three main advantages related to system administration. First, the shared authentication and logging mechanism allows for the central managing and monitoring of users. This allows rapid deployment of new applications and provides security because the per-user access prevents users from accidentally or intentionally disrupting the work of other users. Second, resources are centrally managed so that users can always use the latest version and do not need to download and install their own bug fixes. Third, the only requirement from the users' perspective is a Web browser, allowing them to use powerful but often difficult to install open-source packages on the server without supporting installation and maintenance of these packages on users' systems. Some of the key components we use are TORQUE/Maui, Apache, Python, and Oracle, which can take substantial effort to configure.

Web applications have many features that promote scalability. First, additional hardware can be added to handle increased usage in a way that is invisible to end users. If shared on a single system, they can also maximize hardware ROI by adjusting the balance of server resources between outside users and internal need, thus translating into higher mean usage of resources without negatively affecting internal research efforts. One key scalability issue for bioinformatics tasks is I/O, especially with tools such as BLAST [25] that must read large sequence databases. I/O can be distributed and localized by replicating data-intensive resources such as sequence and pathway databases across multiple nodes, where they can be accessed on local disks. This is a major advantage over models such as GridBASE, which currently requires the data to be bundled together with the code and distributed over the network.

In contrast, the disadvantages are relatively minor. First, custom code typically needs to be written for each Web application we want to add. Second, the system is less flexible than generic systems such as GridBASE.

Overall, however, our Web application framework is especially well-suited for bioinformatics research because of the large amount of data and the limited time and resources to analyze them, because of the fact that there are many related analyses that can share components and data, and because of the wide range of technical ability among researchers who may be experts in their field but not in the open-source tools required to perform this research efficiently.

11.6.2   Components of a Typical Workflow

11.6.2.1   Overview

A typical workflow can be broken down into several high-level components. These are authentication, logging, reporting, polling, dynamic callbacks, and resource management (including queue control and management).

11.6.2.2   Authentication

Users are required to register before using the shared resources of the Web application. When users first register, they are assigned default privileges for one or more Web applications and entries are saved to the appropriate authentication tables (Fig. 11.6). Each user and session is assigned a unique identifier that along with other information, such as the IP address used to access the system, are stored in a shared database and used for resource tracking and allocation.

When registered users wish to access a Web application, they are presented with a standard login screen. The username and password are sent encrypted over https to the authentication module that checks the username and encrypted password against those stored in the database. If successful, the resource limits for the current user and for the current Web application are loaded into the session, and the user is redirected to the main screen. Each login attempt, whether successful or not, is logged to the database.

11.6.2.3   Logging and Reporting

Activity and resource usage are tracked via a central database. This centralization allows reports to be generated easily using SQL. Users and administrators can be notified when resource limits are close to being reached, and accounts can be automatically locked or made to expire when resource limits are exceeded. Access is also tracked by IP address, which can be used for assisting user validation or for detecting violations of usage agreements.

11.6.2.4   Polling

The current implementation of job management is driven by polling. When the user initiates an analysis, the server assigns the request a unique ID that is then used to

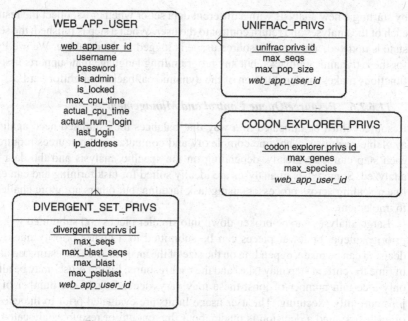

Figure 11.6. Simplified example of authentication tables.

track the state of the analysis. The user is presented with a dynamic "status" page that is automatically refreshed while the analysis is running. Each time the page is refreshed, the server checks the status of the current step of the analysis, and it either (1) initiates the next step and updates the status page and next refresh time or (2) collects the results of the analysis and returns them to the user. The server stores a stateful session that tracks user-driven requests and the progress of each job. If multiple steps are required for a particular analysis, the session information will determine the resource allocation and the callback execution path.

11.6.2.5 Dynamic Callbacks

When a specific step in an analysis is finished, a decision must be made about which action to take. Dynamic callbacks are a straightforward way to implement these decisions and to allow a flexible execution path. Before each step is executed, a default callback is assigned to handle the expected results of the current step. If during the execution of the step it needs to alter the execution path of the step, it can assign an arbitrary function as the callback. After the step is complete, the callback can decide whether to enter execution or to pass control to a different function, depending on the state of the current analysis. For example, if the result of a previous step is large and the next step has a high estimated time complexity, more resources will be allocated than if the result is small. Another example of a dynamic callback is when running in batch mode. If a user wishes to perform the same analysis on multiple data sets, a decision must be made after processing each data set whether to reenter execution by starting a new analysis with a different data set or whether to collect the results of each of the analyses and return control to the user. When a step is finished, the session state is updated, and actual resource usage is logged to the database. We use Python for these dynamic callbacks, but any programming language that supports first-class functions makes implementation of the dynamic callbacks straightforward.

11.6.2.6   Resource/Queue Control and Management

Resources must be allocated in a way that balances the estimated need against the available resources. The time complexity and computational resources required for each step can vary greatly, depending on the specific analysis and the data being analyzed. Some types of analyses are ideally suited for task farming and can exhibit linear scaling across processors using task farming, but others are more challenging to implement.

Large analyses can be broken down into smaller pieces and submitted to a lower priority queue, or fewer pieces can be submitted to a higher priority queue. This decision can be made, depending on the size of the analysis (i.e., the estimated amount of time the current step may take) and the user resource limits. A user may be allowed only a certain number of jobs; these may vary, depending on the number of other jobs currently executing. The user usage limits are evaluated prior to the execution of each step, and a decision is made about the amount of resources allocated, their priority, and whether the user has exceeded his on her resource limit. An extension we plan to add when merging this system with the enhanced GridBASE framwork would augment the polling-driven model with a database-driven model. This relatively simple modification would allow users to submit a series of jobs but would eliminate the current requirement that the users be online for the duration of execution. Results could be generated and stored on disk and in the database for later retrieval, and tasks could be submitted to both local and remote clusters for true grid computing.

11.6.2.7   I/O Considerations

As we outlined above, I/O consideration can be a major problem for bioinformatics tasks. GenBank [26], the major sequence repository, has been growing exponentially for over 20 years, and individual mammalian genomes contain several gigabytes of data. BLAST searches [25] (to find homologs of a given gene) typically run against databases containing hundreds of megabytes to hundreds of gigabytes of indexing information. Similarly, input and output files for specific analyses can be very large. It is often essential to distribute this information across the available nodes and to make it persistent so that the time taken to distribute it is amortized across many analyses.

For example, the best estimate of the function of a gene is the functions of its close relatives. A typical bacterial genome consists of about 4500 genes, but because the rates of gene loss and gene transfer between different kinds of organisms are high, these genes need to be searched against all the genes available, not just the genes in close relatives. For example, the three strains of *E. coli* that were first completely sequenced shared only 40% of the genes in their genomes [27]. Each of these genes must thus be matched to a BLAST database containing approximately 100 GB of

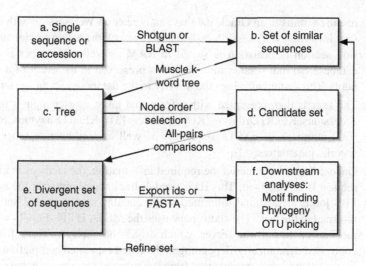

Figure 11.7. DivergentSet interactive workflow.

sequence data and indices. Distributing this database across the network for each query, or requiring each node to access it from a shared filesystem via NFS, saturates I/O on the cluster and is not feasible. Fitting this type of workflow into the GridBASE model remains an important area of future research.

11.6.3 DivergentSet Case Study

For a concrete example of how a distributed Web application works, we will describe our DivergentSet software [24]. DivergentSet is a workflow that is designed to solve the problem of picking a representative divergent set of sequences from a larger collection (Fig. 11.7). This task is critical for several key bioinformatics analyses. DivergentSet integrates the process of (1) finding additional homologous sequences, (2) building and refining the divergent set, for example, including sequences that have crystal structures, (3) producing different random divergent sets from the same sequences and (4) exporting IDs and sequences for other bioinformatics analyses. DivergentSet can be run in an "interactive mode" where the user can manipulate and view a specific set of sequences in the context of a phylogenetic tree. The system uses custom code written in Python and C, which access an Oracle database. In addition, the system runs the freely available FASTACMD, BLAST [25], PSI-BLAST [28], MUS-CLE [29], and MEME [30] programs. Parallelization is achieved via TORQUE/Maui [15]. We use Apache as the web server, using mod_python to handle the session management, and have deployed the system across multiple Linux/Opteron clusters.

The steps in the interactive workflow are as follows:

1. The first step is to authenticate the user and initialize a Web session. The system checks the user information, application-specific permissions, and current

resource limits in an Oracle database and creates a Web session with the necessary information. A session cookie is set to track the active session and server-side session information is stored in RAM as well as in a persistent DBM database (so that session information is preserved in the event of a server reboot). The system also logs the activity to the database and the system logs.

2. The user is then presented with a form that takes as user input a list of GIs, accessions, KEGG Ortholog (KO) identifiers [31], KEGG Enzyme Commission (EC) numbers, or FASTA sequences as well as a number of other analysis-specific parameters.

3. Once the user has entered the required information, the analysis is initiated. A request ID is assigned. This ID is used to track the progress of the analysis. A PBS job is created and submitted to the queuing system, and a status page is returned to the user. The status page uses the META HTTP-EQUIV="Refresh" mechanism to poll the server, which drives the analysis. The refresh rate is controlled dynamically, depending on load and estimated completion time. The first step is to retrieve sequences from the selected sequence database (typically the nt or the nr databases available from the National Center for Biotechnology Information (NCBI), which contain the bulk of fully annotated sequences that have been characterized to date) using the NCBI FASTACMD program.

4. Depending on the parameters specified by the user, the execution path may change to search for additional related sequences. If this option has been set for each input sequence, the system will generate a set of BLAST or PSI-BLAST jobs (depending on the number of sequences, user resource limits, and current server activity) and submit the jobs to the PBS queue to run in parallel. The BLAST databases are very large (tens of gigabytes), so the database files have been replicated on all of the worker nodes. The disks on each worker node are 10k striped disks to minimize the I/O access times.

5. While the BLAST or PSI-BLAST jobs are still running, the system updates the status page as well as the session state of running jobs and the amount of time the jobs have been running on the cluster.

6. Once the BLAST or PSI-BLAST jobs have finished running, the system collects the results using the Shotgun algorithm [32]. The system then passes execution to a function that creates a set of new jobs that build a MUSCLE tree with the resulting sequences, resubmits these jobs to the queuing system, and updates the status page.

7. Once the MUSCLE tree has been built, a new set of jobs is created to pick a set of candidate divergent sequences using the tree as a guide. Since all pairwise combinations of sequences must be checked, the number of jobs created can vary greatly (this step is quadratic in the number of candidate sequences). During this step, an upper triangular matrix is built and all pairwise combinations are split up such that no processor is assigned more than some maximum number of comparisons. This maximum number is controlled on the basis of user resource limits and server load. While these jobs are still running, the system updates the status of running jobs and amount of time jobs have been running on the cluster.

These updates take place on the status page, in the "resources used" area of the database, and in the active session.

8. Once all pairs of candidate sequences have been analyzed, the final set of divergent sequences is picked using either the maximal set or the tree order method (see "Experimental Procedures" in Reference 24).

9. Finally, control is passed to a function that generates a text representation of the final phylogenetic tree. For the convenience of the user, this function highlights in gray the original input sequences and highlights in yellow all preferentially kept sequences (e.g., those with crystal structures available). If the user has requested a keyword search, the display also indicates which sequences are annotated with labels that contain these keywords. The results of this search are cached in the session to allow the user to rapidly refine the results of the search by manually adding or deleting sequences from the divergent set or by changing the BLAST thresholds.

10. If the user wants to refine the set or search for additional sequences, a new request id is assigned to the user and the workflow is restarted, bypassing the FASTACMD step and instead using the cached session information.

11.7 COMPARISON AND DISCUSSION

Grid computing approaches and distributed web application approaches for distributed bioinformatics are clearly complementary. In some situations, the flexibility offered by the grid computing approach is a deciding advantage, while for specific predetermined tasks with possibly less experienced users the web application approach is preferable.

In general, we can observe that grid-type solutions may be desirable for experienced users who have a need to develop substantial parts of processing code themselves when the amount of computational resources required may at times be very large, and for jobs that are highly compute intensive when not requiring substantial I/O.

Web application approaches are suitable for data-intensive applications that require large input or output files, for applications that need to be made accessible to unexperienced users, and for making a suite of specific predetermined applications available to end users.

While the grid computing and web application systems described in this chapter are currently not integrated, combining the two approaches may lead to a unified system that can serve the two types of needs transparently and use shared resources. This idea will be discussed in more detail in the next section on future work.

11.8 FUTURE WORK

11.8.1 Integration of GridBASE with Existing Grid Computing Tools

It is clear that the current prototype implementation of GridBASE can be enhanced significantly at a low cost by integrating it with various grid computing tools that have been developed by other researchers. For instance, the GridBASE grid operator can take advantage of remote job submission services offered by, for example, the Globus Toolkit for starting worker and broker processes. Similarly, quality of service (QoS) support, user accounting, and general grid organization procedures can be leveraged as well. Platform independence can be increased by using existing approaches for harmonizing scripting and compilation specifications across platforms. Advanced policy-based brokering that is based on task requirements and machine properties can be used, thus trying to find a good match between tasks and machines. We also plan to investigate deployment of large systems such as SHARCNET [21].

11.8.2   Enhancing the GridBASE Prototype Implementation

The GridBASE prototype implementation needs to be enhanced in terms of security. For instance, access to the database has to be controlled through an access layer (both for performance and security reasons). Application code has to be authenticated through a digital certificate mechanism. Fault tolerance has to be enhanced using database mechanisms, and fault recovery has to be automated.

It also seems a good idea to have users submit jobs from their own user database in which they would store job descriptions and job results. Each user's personal project database would act as a center for further result processing and for long-term storage of results. In the present implementation of GridBASE, we chose to put the burden of setting up and maintaining an SQL database only onto the shoulders of the grid operator, but it is clear that storing some types of results in a database may also have substantial advantages for end users.

Parallel databases for scalability are another topic of further interest, as well as the replicated databases to deal with firewall issues across several organizations.

Using a grid computing system as a high-performance compute engine at the back end of large biology databases would allow to use grid resources for distributed calculations on the basis of data in database. Guaranteed QoS would be an important requirement for GridBASE as a back-end system for Web applications, and QoS policies and mechanisms should be added to GridBASE.

Finally, interprocess communication is needed for many of the most demanding bioinformatics applications, which poses additional challenges to a grid computing system (see also Reference 3).

11.8.3   Integration of Grid System and Web Application System

In an integrated grid and Web application system, one could let Web applications submit jobs to the database-driven grid computing system. This calls for a mechanism that would allow grid jobs to specify required resources that are preinstalled on specific hosts, including large data files or specific application programs. In such an environment, dynamic allocation of appropriate amounts of resources for separate elements of workflows has to be provided as well, possibly using callback mechanisms as described for the Web application system or using approaches as in Condor's DAGMan metascheduler [11].

11.9 CONCLUSION

Two approaches for unleashing the power of distributed computing for large bioinformastics problems were compared, namely, an approach based on database-driven grid computing and an approach that uses distributed Web applications. The GridBASE system for database-driven grid computing was described and was compared with a web application approach.

Our approach to software for distributed bioinformatics processing is application driven. One target application is the study of RNA folding statistics on computational grids [4,33]. In general, we find that there is no general-purpose distributed computing software available that suits our needs. Therefore, we pursue simple but comprehensive home-built solutions for our applications: Our guiding principles are platform independence, easy maintenance and installation, and overall simplicity. We realize that this application-driven approach may be of somewhat limited generality and may not always be useful for other types of applications or environments. However, we believe that some of what we try and learn in this process may turn out to be useful for systems that target general applicability.

ACKNOWLEDGMENTS

This work was made possible in part by the facilities of the Shared Hierarchical Academic Research Computing Network [21].

REFERENCES

1. I. Foster, C. Kesselman, S. Tuecke, The anatomy of the grid: enabling scalable virtual organizations, *Lecture Notes in Computer Science*, 2001, 2150.

2. The GridBASE prototype implementation discussed in this chapter can be downloaded from www.math.uwaterloo.ca/~hdesterc/GridBASE.

3. H.D. Sterck, R. Markel, T. Pohl, U. Rüde, A lightweight Java TaskSpaces framework for scientific computing on computational grids, in: *Proceedings of the ACM Symposium on Applied Computing, Track on Parallel and Distributed Systems and Networking*, pp. 1024–1030, 2003.

4. Hans De Sterck, Rob Markel, Rob Knight, TaskSpaces: A software framework for parallel bioinformatics on computational grids, in: A. Zomaya (Ed.), *Parallel Computing for Bioinformatics and Computational Biology*, John Wiley & Sons, Hoboken, NJ, pp. 651–669, 2006.

5. G.R. Andrews, *Foundations of Multithreaded, Parallel, and Distributed Programming*, Addison-Wesley, Boston, 2000.

6. International scientific projects related to grid workflows as described in http://www.gridworkflow.org/snips/gridworkflow/space/Projects.

7. Apple's Xgrid system. http://www.apple.com/server/macosx/features/xgrid.html.

8. Sun's Grid Engine project. http://gridengine.sunsource.net.

9. Globus Alliance homepage. http://www.globus.org.

10. Cluster Resources Inc. http://www.clusterresources.com.

11. Condor project homepage. http://www.cs.wisc.edu/condor.

12. T. Tannenbaum, D. Wright, K. Miller, M. Livny, Condor—a distributed job scheduler, in: *Beowulf Cluster Computing with Linux*. MIT Press, Cambridge, MA, 2002.

13. D.P. Anderson: BOINC: A system for public-resource computing and storage, 5th IEEE/ACM International Workshop on Grid Computing, 2004.

14. M. Noble, S. Slateva, Scientific computation with JavaSpaces, Technical report, Harvard-Smithsonian Center for Astrophysics, Boston University, Boston, 2001.

15. TORQUE Resource Manager and Maui Cluster Scheduler. http://www.clusterresources.com.

16. D.P. Anderson, E. Korpela, R. Walton, High-performance task distribution for volunteer computing, in: *First IEEE International Conference on e-Science and Grid Technologies*, 2005.

17. J. Yu, R. Buyya, A taxonomy of workflow management systems for grid computing, *SIGMOD Record* **34**(3), 44–49, 2005.

18. Grid Workflow Forum. http://www.gridworkflow.org.

19. Scientific Workflows Survey. http://www.extreme.indiana.edu/swf-survey.

20. J. Carliss, J. Maguire, *Mastering Data Modeling*, Addison-Wesley, Boston, 2001.

21. Shared Hierarchical Academic Computing Network, Ontario, Canada. http://www.sharcnet.ca.

22. C. Lozupone, M. Hamady, R. Knight, UniFrac–an online tool for comparing microbial community diversity in a phylogenetic context, *BMC Bioinformatics* **7**, 371, 2006.

23. C. Lozupone, R. Knight, UniFrac: A new phylogenetic method for comparing microbial communities, *Applied and Environment Microbiology* **71**(12), 8228–8235, 2005.

24. J. Widmann, M. Hamady, R. Knight, DivergentSet, a tool for picking non-redundant sequences from large sequence collections, *Molecular and Cellular Proteomics* **5**(8), 1520–1532, 2006.

25. S.F. Altschul, W. Gish, W. Miller, E.W. Myers, D.J. Lipman, Basic local alignment search tool, *Journal of Molecular Biology* **215**, 403–10, 1990.

26. D.A. Benson, I. Karsch-Mizrachi, D.J. Lipman, J. Ostell, D.L. Wheeler, GenBank, *Nucleic Acids Research* **34**(Database issue), 16–20, 2006.

27. R.A. Welch, V. Burland, G. Plunkett 3rd, P. Redford, P. Roesch, D. Rasko, E.L. Buckles, S.-R. Liou, A. Boutin, J. Hackett, D. Stroud, G.F. Mayhew, D.J. Rose, S. Zhou, D.C. Schwartz, N.T. Perna, H.L.T. Mobley, M.S. Donnenberg, F.R. Blattner, Extensive mosaic structure revealed by the complete genome sequence of uropathogenic *Escherichia coli*, *Proceedings of the National Academy Sciences of the United States of America* **99**(26), 17020–17024, 2002.

28. S.F. Altschul, T.L. Madden, A.A. Schaffer, J. Zhang, Z. Zhang, W. Miller, D.L. Lipman, Gapped BLAST and PSI-BLAST: a new generation of protein database search programs, *Nucleic Acids Research* **25**, 3389–3402, 1997.

29. R.C. Edgar, MUSCLE: multiple sequence alignment with high accuracy and high throughput, *Nucleic Acids Research* **32**, 1792–1797, 2004.

30. T.L. Bailey, C. Elkan, Fitting a mixture model by expectation maximization to discover motifs in biopolymers, in: *Second International Conference on Intelligent Systems for Molecular Biology*, Menlo Park, CA, 1994. AAAI Press, pp. 28–36.

31. M. Kanehisa, S. Goto, KEGG: Kyoto encyclopedia of genes and genomes, *Nucleic Acids Research* **28**(1), 27–30, 2000.

32. S.C. Pegg, P.C. Babbitt, Shotgun: Getting more from sequence similarity searches, *Bioinformatics* **15**, 729–40, 1999.

33. R. Knight, H. De Sterck, R.S. Markel, S. Smit, A. Oshmyansky, M. Yarus, Abundance of correctly folded RNA motifs in sequence space, calculated on computational grids, *Nucleic Acids Research* **33**, 5924–5935, 2005.

12

A SEMANTIC MEDIATION ARCHITECTURE FOR A CLINICAL DATA GRID

Kai Kumpf, Alexander Wöhrer, Siegfried Benkner, G. Engelbrecht, and Jochen Fingberg

Life is a hospital in which every patient is possessed by the desire to change his bed.

Charles Baudelaire

12.1 INTRODUCTION

Clinical Information Systems (CISs) play an outstanding role in integrated systems with respect to their requirements in stability, accuracy, reliability, performance, and security. While advances in data storage and exchange standards (e.g., DICOM, HL7 [1]) and the use of controlled vocabularies (SNOMED, MeSH, UMLS [2]) have significantly changed the information flow efficiency within hospitals, complete integrated information systems that enable hands-on access to all relevant accessory data for one single information item at hand remains a remote goal. Potential survivors of the race for ever better systems will allow the general practitioner, the specialized surgeon, as well the clinical researcher within one virtual organization accessing all patient-related information along with general and epidemiological information with dynamically adjustable scope on one or the other aspect. The shift from paper-based to computer-based processing and storage, as well as the steady increase of data in healthcare settings has not yet resulted in best standards.

Hospital Informations Systems (HIS) and patient admission systems (PAS) are systems whose main concern is in administration, whereas a CIS in the narrow sense is involved in everything related to the electronic patient record (EPR). EPRs are usually seen as a subset of an electronic health record (EHR) that should be more comprehensive in terms of anamnesis (medical history). CISs are sometimes split

[1] http://umlsks.nlm.nih.gov/

Grid Computing for Bioinformatics and Computational Biology. Edited by E.-G. Talbi and A.Y. Zomaya.
Copyright © 2008 John Wiley & Sons, Inc.

into other supporting systems like RIS (radiology information system), LIS (laboratory information system), and PACS (picture archiving and communication system), and sometimes they remain confined to the patient-specific data. For the purpose of this chapter, a CIS shall embrace *all* data that can be associated with a patient record or a clinical condition.

CISs are said to be designed to bring the management of patient data into the information age. It is intended to replace the the acquisition, storage, manipulation, and distribution of clinical information on paper by flexible and secure electronic equivalents that capture and support the complete clinical organization. With the advent of universally available data, however, the concerns for patient privacy and anonymity and data security increase rapidly [3]. Attempts to keep up data security at the same rate as information management system possibilities usually counteract the latter's development rate. Advances in grid technologies have sparked a new round of development for ensuring patient record security and patient privacy using basic features of grid security layers [4–6].

As the emphasis in CIS slowly progresses from the management of billing records and patient tracking to a more comprehensive view comprising clinical, epidemiological, digital image, molecular, and other laboratory data, we also witness a shift from institution-centered departmental and, later, hospital information systems toward regional and global information networks.

End users of a CIS will probably eventually not only be found amongst health care professionals and administrators but also include patients and health consumers [7]. Patients carrying sensors for continuous monitoring for nonacute states can profit from the expert knowledge systems retransmitting feedback in real time—one of the big goals in —as well as from appropriately filtered access to their own electronic record. When a critical mass in exchangeable case records is transcended, CIS data will serve not only for patient care and administrative purposes but also for healthcare planning as well as clinical and epidemiological research [8].

Given those visions, it becomes immediately clear that the core challenges for a successful CIS from a data-centric point of view are twofold:

1. As complete as possible data integration
2. Data analysis and filtering adapted to the end user

Data integration requires mapping of data models onto each other and in general will also rest on mediation—the transformation of typed data to make data models match. Complete integration of all clinically relevant data would of course result in a huge data schema that would be unwieldy for most practical purposes; thus, integration will invariably have to be accompanied by the definition of application-specific views on the complete structure for filtering.

Clinical researcher will by far be the most demanding customer for CISs because of their need to transparently access and combine public domain biomedical, epidemiological, and literature data with patient-specific genetic, anatomic, and patient-history data. The second challenge is in careful selection of the potential data flood for the specific needs of a clinical practitioner, the surgeon preparing for an operation, a comprehensive risk analysis, and so on.

12.1.1 Previous CIS projects

Complete CISs and—in particular—Grid-based CISs are a field of research that so far has not produced more than prototypes. The GEMSS system, discussed in Section 12.2.5.2, focuses on the provision of advanced medical simulation applications as grid services. The e-Science project CLEF (Cooperative Clinical e-Science Framework) [9][2] focuses on distributed electronic health record repositories for research access. MobileMed [10] integrates distributed and fragmented patient data across heterogeneous sources and makes them accessible through a webserver on mobile devices. Web interfaces to integrated clinical data were already explored in WebCIS [11,12], a system that allows secure reviewing and entering of data into the electronic medical record. Various biological grid research projects share marked traits in their data integration strategies with the @neurIST approach introduced below, although not with a similar emphasis on security and privacy. The North Carolina BioGrid[3] is one example of a large-scale data grid on the basis of the Globus Toolkit that emphasizes the convergence of compute and data grid parts. Matsuda [13] presents an OGSA-DAI-based architecture that makes explicit use of metadata for binding together heterogeneous databases. Geissbühler et al. [14–16] report their experience with an XML/HTTP-based federative approach to develop a hospital-wide CIS.

The trend in biomedical data grids is outlined clearly by many researchers. The seminal White Paper [8] is a huge work on the perspectives of and requirements on the grid in the clinical environment. On the medical research side, the BIOINFOMED project [17][4] highlighted the synergies between "classical" and well-evolved bioinformatics and medical informatics with respect to correlation between essential genotypic information and expressed phenotypic information. An up-to-date overview of grid-enabled health-care systems can be found in Reference 18.

12.1.2 @neurIST

The European Integrated Project @neurIST[5] aims at providing an integrated infrastructure for clinicians and researchers in the field of brain surgery and risk control. Aneurysms are localized dilations or balloonings of a blood vessel by more than 50% of the diameter of the vessel carrying the risk of rupture and . Unruptured aneurysms have a 4% chance of bursting per year and mortality rate varies from 30% to 90% . The incidence rate of cerebral aneurysms has been estimated to be about 1 in 15 people once in a lifetime. @neurIST set out to develop an IT infrastructure for the management and processing of heterogeneous data associated with the diagnosis and treatment of

---

[2]http://www.clinical-escience.org/
[3]http://www.thebiogrid.org/
[4]http://bioinfomed.isciii.es/
[5]http://www.aneurist.org

cerebral aneurysm and subarachnoid hemorrhage. The data span all length scales, from molecular, through cellular to tissue, organ, and patient representations. These data are increasingly heterogeneous in form, including textual, image, and other symbolic structures, and are also diverse in context, from global guidelines based on the broadest epidemiological studies, through knowledge gained from disease-specific scientific studies, to patient-specific data from electronic health records. New methods are required to manage, integrate, and interrogate the breadth of data and to present it in a form that is accessible to the end user. @neurIST seeks to provide channels for the integration of all data sources on cerebral aneurysms. It has three work packages dedicated respectively to the collection, processing, and integration of these data. Another work package is dedicated to the development of four integrated exploitation suites of software for clinical and industrial use. Two platforms will be developed that will exploit directly the IT infrastructure and will provide immediate application to other disease processes.

This chapter will give a goal-centric view on the technologies required for the @neurIST approach and the strategy for their combination, both of which are kept as generic as possible to allow their adaptation to other clinical application fields.

12.2 TECHNOLOGIES

This section introduces the technology basis required to achieve the semantic vision of the @neurIST infrastructure.

12.2.1 Data Integration

The problem of combining data residing at different sources and providing the user with a unified view of these data [19] has been the most tenacious problem for database researchers ever since the advent of computer networks. The straightforward solution of data warehousing—that is, setting up a new database and importing all heterogeneous data for centralized storage—is not practical as a rule, because the required mechanisms for keeping changing source data updated is counterproductive. Only "inert" data that obey the "write once, read many" (WORM) principle lend themselves to warehousing. Keeping the data sources separate, the naive approach of setting up pairwise connections will of course result in a combinatoric explosion with $K_n = n(n-1)/2$ connections for n sources. For changing data, adopting database views for integration has become a favorite strategy. Given a hypothetical global data model or database schema, depending on whether the sources are defined in terms of the global schema or vice versa, the strategy is called *local-* or *global-as-view* (LAV, GAV) 19, respectively. All kinds of intermediate solutions are conceivable and will often be found in realistic settings. The rationale behind choosing views, of course, is to allow for all source data changes to be reflected in the (virtual) global data store.

12.2.2   Data Mediation

In contrast to data-model mapping, data mediation is about the transformations between mapped, semantically related resources. As a simple example, imagine a table A that contains a column T_F temperature with unit in Celsius and a mapped column T_F that contains temperature data in Fahrenheit. Thus, mediation, depends on schema matching but requires additional manipulations for joining the related resources (in this case a numerical transformation: $T_C = (T_F - 32)/1.8$).

12.2.2.1   The GDMS system

The grid Data Mediation Service (GDMS) has been described in detail elsewhere [20,21]. It is following a wrapper-mediator approach, introduced in Reference 22. A data mediation service is capable of presenting multiple heterogeneous data sources as a single virtual data source providing a virtual schema. Two or more heterogeneous data sources can be provided as a virtual data source on the basis of flexible data mediation mechanisms. To access the heterogeneous data sources, a mediator needs wrappers (for each kind of data source a different one) that hide the technical and data model heterogeneities of the various sources.

The GDMS currently provides wrappers for relational database management systems accessible via JDBC, native XML databases, comma-separated value (CSV) files, and other data services. By providing means to access other data services via wrappers during the mediation process, a distributed hierarchical approach is supported. This allows us to split the maintenance effort and workload for a data service into smaller, manageable pieces. For example, each participating organization can maintain its own data sources and the combination of them, where the origin and particularities of the data are known and understood. It becomes even more desirable if rich semantic descriptions, as discussed in Section 12.2.3.3, are provided for virtual data sources.

The mediation mechanisms need the information on how the virtual data source should be built (what data sources are participating, which wrapper to use for it, and how they are combined) and how it should be presented to the user (the mediated schema). This is defined via an XML mapping schema that specifies the virtual schema over the mediated data sources as well as the instructions on how to decompose queries against the virtual schema into queries against the target data sources. In addition, all kinds of heterogeneities can be resolved by applying user-defined functions (written in Java) on the intermediate data during the mediation. Internally a data mediation service relies on OGSA-DAI (see Section 12.2.5.4), the *de facto* standard for data access on service-based grids, with an integrated mediation component. The objective was a seamless integration of our mediation component into OGSA-DAI, from the available metadata for a virtual data source (table name, columns, and their types) to a query interface supporting a subset of SQL. By this, from a client's point of view, the data mediation is fully transparent, and as a consequence the same interface and access mechanisms as for single data sources accessible over OGSA-DAI can be used. Note, however, that GDMS currently only supports read access.

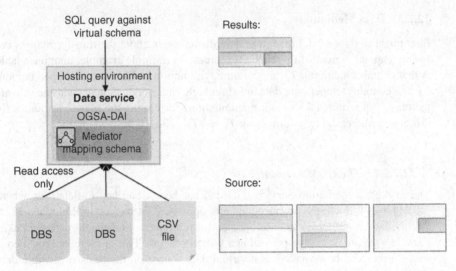

Figure 12.1. Grid Data Mediation Service structural view on the left and corresponding data view on the right.

In Fig. 12.1 a structural view of data mediation services is shown. It uses two kind of wrappers to access the target data sources, one for the relational database management system and one for the CSV file. The mediation component is responsible for decomposing queries against the virtual schema into a set of target queries on the basis of the rules described in the mapping schema. Moreover, it provides composition of the individual results from the target data sources into a single result. The virtual schema comprises a set of relations, specifying how the individual schemas are mapped into the mediated global schema. Providing a global schema means tight federation, which offers schema, language, and interface transparency. The data mediation service follows the virtual integration approach, ensuring to always query up-to-date data. The mapping schema, however, does not necessarily contain all the relations and attributes modeled in each of the sources.

12.2.3 Semantic Web

The Semantic Web is an ongoing effort to use the semantically descriptive Resource Description Framework (RDF) and derived XML languages like the Web Ontology Language (OWL) to provide machine-readable (and interpretable!) descriptions that supplement or replace the HTML markup content of Web documents that was designed for humans only. Semantic annotations can be inlined as RDF markup that remains invisible to the reader during rendering and only shows up on demand or it can be stored in specialized metadata repositories that allow linking of controlled vocabulary terms with pointers to Web resources or parts thereof. Because the bulk of static Web pages remains read-only to most of the world except for its author owner, the in-lining of auxiliary information is generally out of the question and so, in today's experimental proof-of-principle settings like FOAF or Annotea/Annozilla [23],[6] the second possibility reigns. In self-organizing open systems like Wikipedia, semantic markup has come in the form of hierarchically organized categories that can be used in an n : m manner for categorizing Wikipedia pages with generally agreed concepts.[7]

12.2.3.1   RDF and RDF-Based Ontologies

A central hypothesis underlying communication in medicine and healthcare holds that the methodology and the conceptual rigor of a philosophically inspired formal ontology can bring significant benefits in the development and maintenance of application ontologies [24].

RDF (Resource Description Framework)[8] and derived languages are W3C-coordinated metadata language efforts invented for semantic enhancement of Web resources. RDF allows the formation of statement triples (subject, predicate, object) forming directed graphs. Subjects, objects, and predicates are concepts identified by URIs; objects can be literals. Owing to the triple form of an atomic RDF statement, the persistence stores are often called triple stores of which several implementations exist. One of the most active projects in the field is the Jena RDF toolkit that also features an RDF persistence layer.

OWL, the Web Ontology Language. OWL, a W3C Candidate recommendation, is actually a complete family of languages built on the basis of RDF with different expressivity: OWL Lite, OWL DL, and OWL Full. OWL DL is equivalent to DAML+OIL [25] and thus incorporates syntax structures for description logics. All three of them allow describing concepts, relationships, constraints, and axioms in a sound, complete, and efficient way. OWL provides means for reasoning over expressions to infer relationships between concepts rather than simply asserting them (including the hierarchy). An excellent feature comparison of current representative ontology languages can be found in Reference 26.

12.2.3.2   Query Languages

RDF knowledge bases lend themselves in extracting information in the form of URIs, blank nodes, plain and typed literals, extracting RDF subgraphs, or constructing new RDF graphs on the basis of information in the queried graphs. A comparison of a number of query languages, mostly SQL-inspired, has been given by Haase et al. [27]. (SPARQL RDF Querying Language)[9] that has received the status of a W3C recommendation in 2006 is one of the latest attempts. A SPARQL query is a tuple (GP, DS, SM, R) where

- GP is a graph pattern,
- DS is an RDF Dataset,

[6]http://www.w3.org/2001/Annotea/
[7]http://en.wikipedia.org/wiki/Wikipedia:Categorical_index
[8]http://www.w3.org/RDF
[9]http://www.w3.org/TR/2006/CR-rdf-sparql-query-20060406/

- SM is a set of solution modifiers, and
- R is a result form.

In particular, a result form can be a SQL-type SELECT clause acting on a DS. A basic type of graph pattern is a triple pattern, constraining subjects, predicates, and objects and acting as the constraint part in a WHERE clause. The graph nature of triple stores makes SPARQL a superset of SQL although the basic query patterns are largely isomorphic. An implementation of the SPARQL language by the name of ARQ is provided for the Jena RDF toolkit. It is expected that with maturity of a language like SPARQL, RDF triplestores could make a viable alternative to relational databases. First steps in this direction, like Oracle's support for RDF including querying via graph patterns in its latest release [28], are already under way.

12.2.3.3 Semantic Annotation

Given a set of distributed resources within a cooperative infrastructure such as Web pages in the World Wide Web, a long-standing goal has been the unified access to and retrieval of these resources. This should be possible using a standardized terminology for content-related search instead of substring search that attempts to stumble upon keywords that adequately describe the content. Semantic annotations on scattered resources on the basis of a common machine-readable knowledge model should provide the semantic "glue" that dispenses with trial-and-error retrieval. According to the W3C SAWSDL[10] working group, a semantic annotation is *additional information in a document that identifies or defines a concept in a semantic model in order to describe a part of that document*. It is clear that most Web resources that await annotation are effectively read-only for the annotator, and thus a common strategy of most current annotation toolkits is to store annotations nonintrusively in a dedicated repository as has been mentioned above. Some annotation systems like KIM [29] come with their own ontology, whereas others like Simile's Piggy-Bank [30] from the MIT as well as Annozilla count on the evolution of folksonomies from free tagging. It has been remarked that there is a dual meaning to semantic annotations, referring both to the concept identifiers used or mappings from the annotated document parts to the concepts and thus the implicit generation of metadata. We use here the second definition, because it allows us to use the term annotation as an RDF triple of subject–predicate–object, where the subject would be substituted by a resource, the object by a concept identifier, and the predicate by an appropriate relationship.

Annotation Systems. Annotation systems exist in large variety mostly for Semantic Web purposes. Ontomat Annotizer from the University of Karlsruhe[11] has been one of the first efforts [31,32]. A more powerful system from the same group that also

---

[10]http://www.w3.org/TR/sawsdl/
[11]http://annotation.semanticweb.org/ontomat

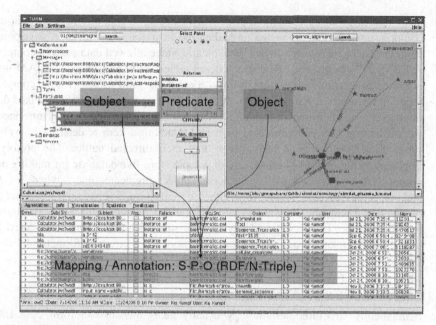

Figure 12.2. TUAM tool for universal annotation and mediation. An arbitrary number of data sources of different types can be loaded into the top panels (here: WSDL document, left, and domain ontology graph, right). Data items can be mapped onto each other using a relationship type defined in the top middle panel. Together, these three make up an RDF subject–predicate–object-type statement.

includes full-fledged ontology authoring is KAON [33].[12] iAnnotate, a plug-in for the popular ontology editor Protege-2000,[13] is a small tool for Web page annotation from within an RDF/OWL environment. AnnotateIt[14] and DELT/A (Document Exploration and Linking Tool)[15] follow slightly different notions—the former intended for general information annotation of documents, and the latter designed to support structured knowledge acquisition of clinical guidelines in their HTML textual format to a formal representation—specifically, it allows linking of unstructured text passages via common annotations.

TUAM. There is a considerable gap extending beyond those annotation systems that allow formalized (ontology-based) or free tagging of Web resources. The Fraunhofer SCAI software project called TUAM (Tool for Universal Annotation and Mapping)[16] (see Fig. 12.2) goes beyond current annotation systems, in that it allows establishing and persisting arbitrary relationships between any number and kind of

---

[12]http://kaon.semanticweb.org/
[13]http://www.dbmi.columbia.edu/ cop7001/iAnnotateTab/iannotate.htm,http://protege.stanford.edu/
[14]http://freshmeat.net/projects/annotateit/
[15]http://ieg.ifs.tuwien.ac.at/projects/delta/
[16]http://www.scai.fraunhofer.de/tuam0.html

data sources in an n:m fashion, effectively building a semantic network that can comprise unstructured or prestructured data and terminologies with expressive power from thesauri to OWL ontologies. Specifically, since allowed data sources comprise ASCII-files, spreadsheets, database schema tables, RDF and images, TUAM does not bring annotation information in-line—a generally valid strategy for the complete range of resources is hardly conceivable—but stores pointers to the interlinked data items. Since no additional information except for the relationship types is introduced, the distinction between annotated item and annotation item is determined by the relationship type between both, because of their directed nature. The prototype implementation of TUAM makes use of a triple store-like database for making persistent RDF-analogous triples of the form: subject–predicate–object, where subject and object are data item indexes from either the same or different data sources and the predicate is a semantically well-defined relationship between both. While the default persistence store is logically and physically distinct from the data sources used for annotation, annotations or mappings can be exported in a variety of formats, including OWL.

12.2.3.4 Semantic Navigation

Semantically structured terminology usually takes the abstract form of a DAG (directed acyclic graph) structure, where keyword terms form the nodes and the directed relationships between them are linking edges. In the simplest case of a flat term list, the DAG becomes completely disconnected and no paths between the nodes exist that could be exploited for navigating from one concept to another. Sinha et al. [34] have defined what they deem natural modes of navigation through an RDF graph on the basis of the notion of implicit similarity of concepts:

Object summary: Given an item, navigate to other items that share a particular attribute.

Collection summary: Given a collection, expand to include other items that are similar to some of those in the collection.

Refine collection: Given a collection, narrow down to the subset of items that share a common value on a given attribute.

Obviously, this is a mode of navigation that utilizes graph structure as well as constraints on attributes (even though these might not be defined explicitly in the navigation process). The author's description is restricted to an RDF-model only. How do we go about RDF-annotated data that resides in different repositories and possibly does not share the data model structure?

We note that semantic navigation is the basis for semantic querying in the sense that the structure of the knowledge model has to be exploited as far as possible, with a special emphasis on the user-side presentation. Even purely manual navigation in a semantic network can be a fascinating and aesthetically pleasing procedure, as is demonstrated, for example, in the commercial Visual Thesaurus[17] application that zooms in on natural words and their nearest semantic neighbors, employing a hyperbolic graph view. Similar showcases include the WikiBrowser built upon Touch-Graph's nonproprietary technology.[18] We discern a five-step process for querying semantically annotated data based on RDF knowledge graphs:

1. Graph navigation in a semantic network
2. Optional selection of concept or class node attributes
3. Setting constraints on selected attributes
4. Translation of the RDF query into the appropriate target query language (SQL for annotated databases)
5. Display of results and optional feedback of result set choice on the selection of the annotation concepts

The critical step here is of course the Meta-QL translation into SQL. Semantics-preserving mapping of SPARQL or other RDF-query languages to isomorphic SQL is still a widely empirical field of research [35,36].

12.2.4 Service-Oriented Architectures

Service-oriented architectures (SOAs) are sometimes identified as the gist of grid architectures and sometimes set aside. This might partly be due to the considerably fuzzy definitions that one can find for both aspects of distributed information architectures. If we define services as "virtualized resources," then every architecture that allows a user or client to handle those resources just like local resources available on your workplace computer is an SOA in the broadest sense. A handy definition is as follows[19]:

> A service-oriented architecture is a collection of services that communicate with each other. The services are self-contained and do not depend on the context or state of the other service. They work within a distributed systems architecture.

In a more confined sense, an SOA is any type of architecture where virtualized resources are first published to a service registry plus an optional broker that negotiates service requests from a client and on finding matches passes back the according service handles to him (see left-hand side of Fig. 12.3). The service broker is thus an intervening unit that allows structured and filtered access to all virtualized resources in the network. Where the "desktop" and "explorers" or "finders" of today's workstations provide a view on virtualized local resources—control panels,

[17] http://www.visualthesaurus.com/
[18] http://www.touchgraph.com/
[19] http://www.service-architecture.com/web-services/articles/service-oriented_architecture_soa_definition.html

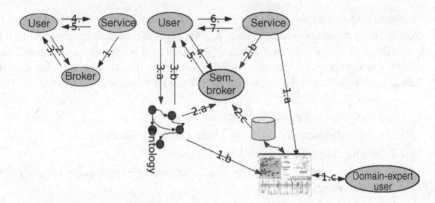

Figure 12.3. A Semantic grid SOA (sgSOA) based upon the semantic annotation of services. The original SOA is supplemented and enhanced by external semantics that can be put to use by a specifically enhanced brokering instance. LHS: 1.service registration; 2.service query; 3.service access data; 4.service access; 5. data retrieval. RHS: 1. semantic service annotation (using TUAM); 2. annotated service registration; 3. ontology query; 4. semantic service query; 5. service access data; 6. service access; 7. data retrieval.

user applications, disks—the SOA promises a simple navigation through generalized, platform-independent, distributed resources.

12.2.4.1   Web Services

The W3C defines a Web Service (WS) as

> a software system designed to support interoperable machine-to-machine interaction over a network.

This definition by itself is not really useful, but a few quasistandards have emerged over the course of time. Nowadays every well-behaved WS is expected to exchange data via SOAP (Simple Object Access Protocol)[20] messages and presents a WSDL-compliant service description. WSDL (Web Service Description Language)[21] is an XML dialect that essentially describes the input and output specifications of a service. WSDL defines services as collections of network endpoints or ports. In WSDL the abstract definition of endpoints and messages is separated from their concrete network deployment or data format bindings. A port is defined by associating a network address with a binding; a collection of ports defines a service. The six elements of WSDL specification 1.1 are as follows:

Types provides data-type definitions used to describe the messages exchanged.

---

[20]http://www.w3.org/TR/soap12-part0/
[21]http://www.w3.org/TR/wsdl/

Message represents an abstract definition of the data being transmitted. A message consists of logical parts, each of which is associated with a definition within some type of system.

PortType is a set of abstract operations (a combination of input message and output messages). PortTypes are the actual interface of the WSDL description.

Binding specifies concrete protocol and data format specifications for the operations and messages defined by a particular PortType.

Port specifies an address for a binding, thus defining a single communication end point.

Service is used to aggregate a set of related ports.

A wordy introduction can be found, for example, in Reference 37.

Services as Virtualized Resources. For the sake of a common terminology with the grid domain, it is best to view services as virtualized resources, that is, compute the data resources that receive a platform and operating-system-independent wrapper for universal transparent access.

WSRF. The Web Service Resource Framework (WSRF) is a family of OASIS-published[22] specifications for WSs. The statelessness of WSs severely limits their usefulness, although workarounds like database back ends can be envisioned. WSRF supports the management of stateful resources that have been associated with WSs; WSs are forced to communicate with so-called resource services that allow data to be stored and retrieved. When clients talk to a WS, they also include the URI and key of the resource service that should be used.

12.2.4.2 Service Annotation and Semantic Services

Services, irrespective of their origin, come with a basic set of descriptors, sometimes generated dynamically (e.g., Apache AXIS[23]) sometimes more or less handwritten by the service provider. A minimum requirement for service descriptions comprises the specification of their input and their output data (type, format) as well as—optionally—the method taken for transforming one into the other. Beyond that, the additional descriptions range from user-side free-text documentation text (e.g., within the WSDL documentation tag) to semistructured information required for SLA (service level agreement) negotiation and QoS (quality of service) support.

We note that the basic problems of semantic annotation as described in Section 12.2.3.3 propagate to the world of services and from here to a Semantic grid.

The sgSOA (Semantic Grid SOA) as shown in Fig. 12.3 was first informally introduced by one of the authors [38] and extends conventional SOA by semantic annotations on the service description level that extend and complement the "raw" descriptions. The appeal of the semantic add-on information is that while the original SOA implementation is left in working order, the clients are enabled to extensively

---

[22]http://www.oasis-open.org/
[23]http://ws.apache.org/axis/

make use of the well-defined and interlinked semantic descriptions that can be enriched throughout the life cycle of the service in question. Significant constraints are—of course—imposed by the level of expressivity and consistency of the ontology as well as the semantic querying and reasoning capabilities of the service broker. sgSOA is at the heart of the semantic architecture of the @neuInfo module, discussed in Section 12.4.2.

Given service description languages in XML format, an extension to existing descriptions is straightforward and will usually involve the introduction of additional tags and tag contents for more fine-grained specification. The basic problem of introduction of new information is equivalent to the problem encountered in the Semantic Web scenario: In lining, added information into existing markup is usually ruled out for any institution different from the original publishing source or author. Standard WSDL, as we have seen, lacks semantic descriptions of the input and output and is for most purposes accessible as read-only code. Following the standard strategy of nonintrusive annotation via storage of data pointers, however, semantics can easily be introduced in a cumulative fashion. TUAM, described in Section 12.2.3.3, is a tool that was conceived for annotation of arbitrary data sources, including Web Services. Services can be semantically described exhaustively by complete specification of their input, their output, and—optionally—the type of algorithm that transform the one into the other. The PortType section in WSDL documents contains the summary of operations offered by the Web Service along with their input and output message reference that in turn refer to message data types. Together those three form the abstract definition of the service as opposed to the remaining sections that deal with the service implementation. Semantic annotation of services—for client-side use—should therefore take place in the Types, Message, and PortType sections. For a summary description, it can be sufficient to annotate only the PortType part, provided that the knowledge model includes rich concepts for complex input and output types. An alternative bottom-up approach would concentrate on semantically specifying the data types involved in messages and PortTypes. The SAWSDL draft (Semantic Annotations for WSDL)[24] describes annotation on all three levels. A partially complementary approach to WSDL is also taken by OWL-S, the OWL-based Web Service Ontology[25] that, while distinguishing between the presentation and implementation parts of a service, maintains the input–output specification of a service.

Exploitation of Service Annotations. We already remarked on the need to extend the brokering module according to the type of annotation used. It is mandatory that the broker reasoning and querying capabilities match the expressivity of the annotation knowledge model. In the case of RDF/OWL, the broker should be able to make use of the graph structure behind the entities used for classification and the specific qualities of the relationship that connect the knowledge classes (transitivity, symmetry, etc.). In particular, it should be "aware" of inheritance relationships for generalization for the resolution of queries that are too specific. The broker requires access to

---

[24] http://www.w3.org/2002/ws/sawsdl/
[25] http://www.daml.org/services/owl-s/

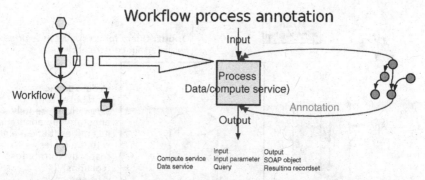

Figure 12.4. Workflow process annotation: Input and output parameters can be semantically enhanced by attributing ontology classes to them. The output of one service in the process has to match the input of the successor service. Data and compute services can be treated alike as a first approximation in that they both possess input and output parameters. Semantic enhancements for compute services must be in-line. RDF in WSDL or similar Data services must be annotated not on the WSDL side but on either the the data model metalevel (table attributes/columns) or the data level itself (records/record attribute values) instead (see Fig. 12.5).

the service annotations plus the complete knowledge model that implies a centralized storage of both within dedicated repositories. For the sake of conciseness and interface simplicity, a common representation should be endeavored. This requirement can be achieved when the annotation subjects (service parts) are defined as instances of the annotation objects (knowledge model classes). In the bioinformatics field, there are several semantics-enabled service registries including Feta [39] and GRIMOIRES[26] in myGrid, and Semantic MOBY[27] in BioMoby [40]. Feta and Semantic MOBY have ontology support but do not support the service matchmaking. UDDI (Universal Description Discovery and Integration[28]) based GRIMOIRES is very much lightweight and currently has no ontology support.

The Special Case of Data Service Annotation. A far-reaching but generally stated goal of semantics in the grid context is the exploitation of one or several common knowledge models for binding together service modules of ad-hoc-defined workflows. A prerequisite for the unrestrained flow of data within a workflow is the matching of data types as well as semantic types from one stage within the workflow to the succeeding one. Good hands-on examples can be found in the e-Science workflow software Taverna.[29] To be more precise, the output of one module has to match the input of the next. This is exemplified in Fig. 12.4. Workflow modules (individual grid services) have to match up in order to be connected to a sensible workflow. On top of the matching of output–input basic data types, the semantic categories of the inputs and outputs have to match. This goal can be achieved using semantic annotation of the service description with an external common knowledge model represented as an ontology.

[26]http://www.grimoires.org/
[27]http://semanticmoby.org/
[28]http://uddi.org/
[29]http://taverna.sourceforge.net/

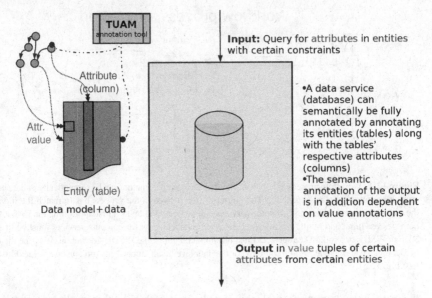

Figure 12.5. The mode of semantic annotation for data services (virtualized data stores). A full semantic description of both input and output is given implicitly by complete annotation of the data schema on the two levels: table and attribute (column). Record (row) annotation optionally provides information for constraint formulation in a semantic data query.

Since prestructured data repositories like RDBs constitute the most common data sources in workflows, a common data model is required to ensure the interchange-ability in a distributed data environment. Semantic annotation of data sources using a common knowledge model in ontology representation is the semantic equivalent of using a global view on several separate databases. In a SOA-conformant grid environment, it is essential to have a common framework for the description of diverse kinds of services, especially with respect to the commonly found subdivision into data and compute services. In Fig. 12.5 we show how data services can be treated alike to compute services provided the semantic annotation takes place at the level of the data model or database schema(s), rather than the level of the input–output description.

12.2.5   Grid

As mentioned above, the terms "Grid" and "SOA" are today often used interchange-ably and sometimes as complementing parts. One of the more tangible impressions of the grid is the extension of previous HPC-architectures by fine-grained and flexible dynamic security layers. According to CERN's GridCafe,[30] the broader view is that

> ...whereas the Web is a service for sharing information over the Internet, the grid is a service for sharing computer power and data storage capacity over the Internet.

---

[30] http://gridcafe.web.cern.ch

The grid goes well beyond simple communication between computers, and aims ultimately to turn the global network of computers into one vast computational resource.

This, of course, is nothing short of an ambitious goal and still a field of active research. The one aspect that the grid shares with the SOA vision is the virtualization of resources without making explicit how they should be published, as is the case for SOA.

12.2.5.1   Virtual Organizations

Virtual Organizations (VO) are a kind of dynamically varying user groups working on the same project and using the same application software on the grid. Access and authorization rights are homogeneous for all users in one VO. A VO as such is always a temporary network of users that need not correspond to individual persons only but can comprise complete companies, suppliers, customers, or employees both as individuals and groups. All information and data within one VO can be passed around freely according to the given VO authorization policy. Being linked only by appropriate telecommunication tools, a VO can be geographically widely scattered. The individuals making up the VO can be legally independent collaborators striving for a common temporary goal. In grid computing in particular, the VOs are gathered around virtualized grid resources or services that represent anything from data records to computational software programs or electronic instruments that can be monitored or controlled remotely.

12.2.5.2   Middlewares

Middlewares are loosely defined to be a software that connects software components or applications. Middleware is used most often to support complex, distributed applications. It includes Web servers, application servers, content management systems, and similar tools that support application development and delivery. Modern information systems based on SOAP, Web services, and service-oriented architectures usually require a middleware component. In particular, "Grid software" is often said to be a kind of middleware. Whatever the solution looks like in particular, the software layer that lies between the operating system or data repository and the applications on each side of a distributed computing system is the middleware and thus can vary widely in terms of security, concurrency, life-cycle management, transaction, deployment, quality-of-service negotiation, and other services. Interaction of applications with a Web-Services-based middleware layer is usually implemented using RPC (remote procedure call) mechanisms or message-oriented communication where data objects are encapsulated via XML in accordance with the SOAP protocol.

Choices. Among the plethora of middlewares offered—SourceForge[31] alone lists 57 grid-related projects of which 33 range as "middleware"—it is fairly easy to lose ones way. As a rule, one should keep Foster's plea for open standards in mind. In

---

[31] http://sourceforge.net/softwaremap

particular, conformance with the SOA rules should be adhered to. Among some popular Open Source solutions that rank as grid middlewares, UNICORE[32] [41]. from the FZ Jülich, gLite[33] from CERN, GGF's Globus Toolkit (GT)[34] 42, and Gria[35] [43] by Inforsense, currently only the latest version of GT (4.x), offers full WSRF compatibility.

GEMSS. The EU Project GEMSS[36] (Grid-Enabled Medical Simulation Services) [16] has created a grid middleware that can be used to provide medical practitioners and researchers with access to advanced simulation and image processing services for improved preoperative planning and near real-time surgical support. GEMSS builds on top of existing grid and Web service technologies, maintaining compliance with standards, thereby ensuring future extensibility and interoperability. Key aspects of the GEMSS grid middleware include negotiable Quality of Service (QoS) support for time-critical service provision [44], flexible support for business models, authentication, authorization, and security at all levels in order to ensure privacy of patient data as well as compliance to EU law.

The project has created an extensible, interoperable, and collaborative test bed for various medical service applications [45], with varying performance and QoS requirements targeting different medical sectors. The test bed comprises six advanced medical simulation services for maxillofacial surgery simulation, neurosurgery support, radiosurgery planning, inhaled drug-delivery simulation, cardiovascular simulation, and medical image reconstruction. At the core of these simulation services are compute-intensive methods such as finite-element modeling, Monte Carlo simulation, and computational fluid dynamics that are to be executed on remote parallel hardware. These services have been deployed on various high-performance computing platforms in European countries and their integration into the end-users working environments has been evaluated.

The GEMSS infrastructure is based on a service-oriented architecture (SOA) comprising multiple grid clients and grid service providers, one or more service registries, and a certificate authority. Grid service providers utilize the GEMSS service provision framework to expose simulation applications available on clusters or other parallel hardware as services that can be accessed on demand over the Internet. GEMSS services offer a common set of operations for job execution, job monitoring, data staging, error recovery, and application-level QoS support. GEMSS services are exposed via WSDL and securely accessed using SOAP. For large file transfers, SOAP attachments are utilized. The GEMSS Certificate Authority provides the basis for an operational PKI (public key infrastructure) based on X.509 certificates, in order to establish an identity for each client and service provider, as well as to ensure end-to-end security.

---

[32] http://www.unicore.org/
[33] http://glite.web.cern.ch/
[34] http://www.globus.org/
[35] http://www.gria.org
[36] http://www.gemss.de/

The GEMSS design supports a three-step process to job execution. First, there is an initial business step, where accounts are opened and payment details fixed. The pricing model may also be chosen at this stage. Next, there is a quality-of-service negotiation step, where a job's quality of service and price, if not subject to a fixed price model, is negotiated and agreed. Finally, once a contract is in place, the job itself can be submitted and executed.

A key challenge within the GEMSS project was the development of mechanisms for ensuring the timeliness of results for time-critical simulation services used in a clinical environment. To address this issue, GEMSS has developed a flexible QoS infrastructure [44] that supports the dynamic negotiation of Service Level Agreements (SLAs) for ensuring response-time guarantees. GEMSS adopts a reservation-based approach to QoS coupled with application-specific performance models, advance reservation mechanisms [46,47], and client-driven negotiation of service level agreements subject to price constraints. On the basis of these mechanisms, grid clients are able to choose from several service providers before agreeing to book a specific service. Once a client has found a suitable service provider, a corresponding SLA is signed and exchanged to commit both parties before a service is accessed.

The GEMSS middleware has been released as "open source" under the GNU Lesser General Public License (LGPL) Software License Agreement. The GEMSS infrastructure is being utilized and further developed within the EU @neurIST Project [48] (2006–2009), which will create a grid infrastructure for the management of all processes linked to research, diagnosis, and treatment development for cerebral aneurysm and subarachnoid hemorrhage. The @neurIST infrastructure will encompass data repositories, computational analysis services and information systems handling multiscale, multimodal information at distributed sites.

12.2.5.3   Compute Grid

Compute (or "computational") grids can be seen as a subset of parallel, distributed computing solutions. Inspired by experiences from HPC-computing and building on the metaphor of a power grid, the Compute grid is the prototypical grid that has been around longest. Ian Foster and Carl Kesselmann [49] were among the first to attempt a definition (1998) and came up with

A computational grid is a hardware and software infrastructure that provides dependable, consistent, pervasive, and inexpensive access to high-end computational capabilities.

As the world has ever since seen an immense proliferation of grids of all flavors, Foster recently went on to make the following three points:

- Computing resources are not administered centrally.
- Open standards are used.
- Nontrivial quality of service is achieved.

Obviously, this is a "definition" no longer restricted to computational environments.

12.2.5.4   Data Grid

Data grids (DG) [50,51] form the next-generation platform for management of data on the Petabyte scale. Venugopal et al. [52] have identified the following promises for the data grid user:

- The ability to search through numerous available datasets for the required dataset and discover suitable data resources for accessing the data
- To transfer large-sized datasets between resources in as short a time as possible
- To manage multiple copies of their data
- To select suitable computational resources and process data on them
- Ability to manage access permissions for the data

The authors contrast DGs with other distributed data techniques such as content delivery networks, P2P, and Distributed Databases and point to the fact that one of the discerning features of the grid solution on the plus side is the support of VOs. The outstanding demands of a DG, however, is in terms of metadata consistency.

We have seen that data services can be regarded as a kind of specialized compute services whose input is made up of a selection of parts of the underlying data model plus constraints on relations. As most data warehouses nowadays are built on the basis of RDBMSs, the input to a data service will usually be SQL or subsets of it. The second notable part of data sources, XML markup data, is accessible and queryable via XPath and its descendants, but the huge bulk of *a priori* unstructured and thus unindexed data—texts, pictures, binary objects—requires costly full scans and pattern matching. Querying of virtualized data (re)sources cannot get across the data model-dependent limitations and thus has to maintain querying possibilities for all major types of model structure.

OGSA-DAI. OGSA-DAI (Open Grid Services Architecture—Database Access and Integration) [53][37] is a grid middleware component to assist with access and integration of data from separate sources via the grid. It supports the exposure of data resources, such as relational or XML databases, on to grids. Various interfaces are provided and many popular database management systems are supported. The software also includes a collection of components for querying, transforming, and delivering data in different ways, along with a simple toolkit for developing client applications. OGSA-DAI is designed to be extendable, so users can provide their own additional functionality. OGSA-DAI WSRF 2.2 is a Globus Toolkit 4.0.3-based version that, as its name implies, is a WSRF compliant middleware for use as a component of a the GT4 grid environment.

---

[37] http://www.ogsadai.org.uk

12.3   CLINICAL INFORMATION SYSTEMS DATA

Current medical or hospital information systems all require transparent access to and navigation within one or more of the following types of data:

- Clinical histories
- Radiology and pathology reports
- Genomic and image databases
- Technical literature and Web-based resources
- Annotations on any one of the above

With respect to the scales of data origins, one can distinguish between the following 4 levels:

- Population (epidemiology) and
- Patient (case studies) and
- Tissue, organ (anatomy, histology) and
- Molecular biology, genetics

12.3.1   The Electronic Health Record

Electronic health records (EHR) are computer-based patient medical record suggested to facilitate the access of patient data by clinical staff at any given location. They are claimed to be essential for improving health quality and managing health-care delivery, whether in a large health system, hospital, or primary-care clinic. The data itself can be comprised of information from multiple institutions. Among the many promises of electronic records are the accurate and complete claims processing by insurance companies, the feasibility of building automated checks for drug and allergy interactions, and automated scheduling of recurring or single clinical tasks. Data exchange between laboratories is a major issue, as is the patient's data security on its involved path through the institutions. It has been suggested by the Medical Records Institute[38] to subdivide the types of electronic records into the following categories:

The Automated Medical Record, a paper-based record with some computer-generated documents.

The Computerized Medical Record (CMR), which makes the documents of level 1 electronically available.

The Electronic Medical Record (EMR), which restructures and optimizes the documents of the previous levels ensuring interoperability of all documentation systems.

[38]http://www.medrecinst.com/

The Electronic Patient Record (EPR), a patient-centered record with information from multiple institutions

The Electronic Health Record (EHR), which adds general health-related information to the EPR that is not necessarily related to a disease.

Thus, the EHR is the natural primary goal of a data-grid-based CIS that builds upon "conventional" EMRs. Today's solutions have not yet passed the EMR stage. A strategy for joining up the EMR with the remaining parts can go for either a complete fixed and explicit EHR data model or a complete semantical tagging of all relevant data through one global domain ontology, thereby yielding the option of on-demand EHR construction. The latter solution is definitely more costly in terms of retrieval times but allows almost unlimited flexibility, provided that we are dealing with a coherent knowledge schema.

12.4   @neurIST

In this section we bring together the individual technologies introduced above for an architectural sketch of the @neurIST semantic mediation architecture.

12.4.1   Overview

@neurIST is focused on cerebral aneurysms and intends to provide an integrated decision support system to assess the risk of aneurysm rupture in patients and to optimize their treatments. We believe that the current process of cerebral aneurysm diagnosis, treatment planning, and treatment development is highly compromised by the fragmentation of relevant data. Therefore, an IT infrastructure for the management and processing of the vast amount of heterogeneous data acquired during diagnosis is now under development. @neurIST aims at benefiting patients with better diagnostics, prevention, and treatment because it will combine efforts of clinicians and industry. The basis for that aim is seamless access to patient data (see Fig. 12.6), data fusion, and processing of complex information spanning from the molecular to the personal level for finding evidences of links between genomics and cerebral aneurysms and helping clinicians in decision making and selecting more appropriate treatments.

Better insight in aneurysm development and linking modern diagnostic imaging to computational tools will yield a better basis for planning and personalization of minimally invasive interventional procedures for patients. The other main goal is the identification of patients with high risk of rupture by assessing a personal risk factor, thereby reducing the patient's operation risks and anxiety.

The economic and societal impact of vertically and horizontally (semantically) integrated CISs like @neurIST in Europe and beyond is expected to be significant. Personalized risk assessment alone could reduce unnecessary treatment by 50% or more, with concomitant savings estimated in the order of thousand million of Euros per annum. The personal effect of aneurysm rupture is devastating: Morbidity and mortality are high, affecting two-thirds of the afflicted patients.

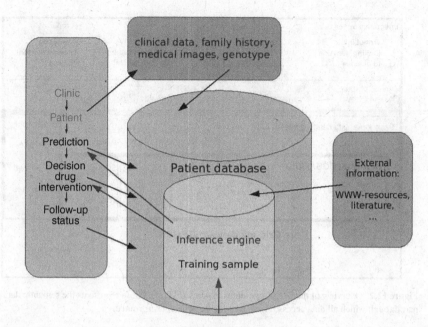

Figure 12.6. Data flow in @neurIST. The CRIM patient database holds the EHR of all patients and is supplemented by external (public and hospital, internally generated) information. The database records are kept updated throughout the therapy process.

A successful particular approach as demonstrated for aneurysms will be extendable to other disease processes and scalable to federate a large number of clinical center and public databases.

12.4.1.1 Application Suites

@neurIST consists of four application suites resting upon two platform suites that make up the compute and the data grid modules of the complete system (see Fig. 12.7).

12.4.2 A Semantically Integrated Data Grid: @neuInfo

@neurIST has three bulk work packages dedicated respectively to the collection, processing, and integration of these data. Data integration relies on an OGSA-DAI-based mediation architecture that draws on a common knowledge model used for mapping and mediation between individual data services. The ontology is comprised of three domains—patient-related, genetics-related, and anatomy-related—that are bound together by relationships for representing risk-inducing influences. Queries concerning individual risk assessment as well as grouped average information are constructed on the basis of this common model and translated to the grid abstraction layer using a MetaQL-to-SQL layer. Queries will be formed using a semantic network browser and constraint entry interface.

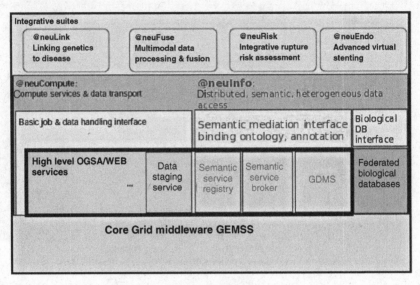

Figure 12.7. Overview of the integrative suites of @neurIST. @neuInfo represents the semantic data grid part through which all data access for the four application suites is routed.

The @neuInfo module was introduced to enable access to clinical and epidemiological data distributed in public and project-specific protected databases. It will provide complex data querying and mediation functionality for the @neurIST grid infrastructure. Different data sources can be searched using a query user interface providing a semantically unified view on an abstract data model that is linked to the actual physical data sources, allowing direct navigation through application-specific knowledge domains like risk assessment, epidemiology, and case history.

12.4.2.1 Medical Information for Aneurysms

The main concern in information integration and information exploitation for a latent condition like aneurysms is necessarily the prediction of risk for acute conditions: aneurysm rupture and stroke. Thus, the different kinds of explicit information available have to obey a unified terminology in order to be put to use. We identified three major different domains of clinically relevant information sources (see Fig. 12.8). Obviously, there is considerable overlap and interdependence between the fields. Building on an existing, standardized vocabulary is therefore essential for interlinking information. The main knowledge domains identified for @neurIST are the following:

1. Clinical medicine (patient-record-centric)
2. Molecular biology (genotypic basis for diseases)
3. Simulation (blood flow in branched vessels, aneurysm formation)

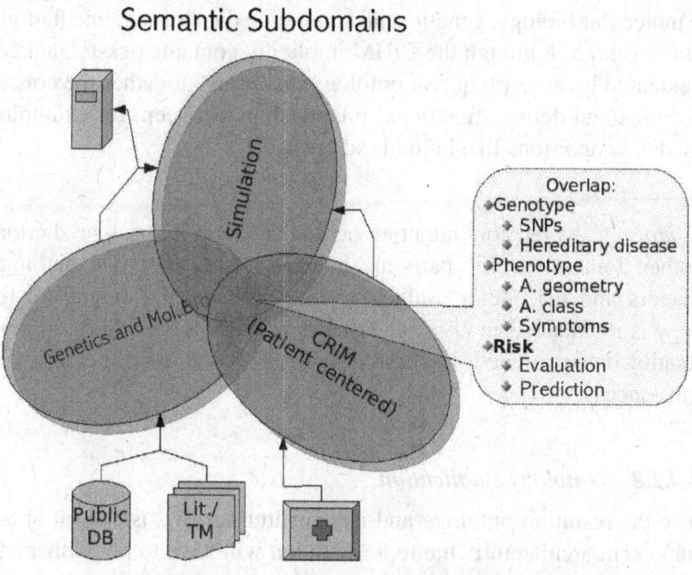

Semantic Subdomains

Figure 12.8. The knowledge domains within @neurIST.

4. Disease and epidemiology
5. Risk factors

where items 4 and 5 have a considerable overlap both with each other and the preceding 3 items. Since risk factor identification is essential for the diagnosis, prognosis, and treatment of aneurysms, it will be at the hub of the final ontology with the other domains yielding auxiliary information. For mediation between the molecular, the simulation, and the clinical domain, ties have to be established that rely on the overlaps depicted in Fig. 12.8. Obviously, the identification and formulation of knowledge domains and their identifying concepts is the *sine qua non* for a semantically enhanced grid infrastructure. Concepts and their relationships should be neither too broad nor too specific and should reflect needs in their respective application field without sacrificing ontological rigor. The common format for all model parts in @neurIST is OWL, because it is a sufficiently matured RDF-based knowledge representation language, for which several extensions related to workflow construction and rule representation (e.g., SWRL) exist.

The knowledge model for @neurIST hinges on the UMLS and two new vocabularies tailored for the purpose.

CRIM. The CRIM (Clinical Reference Information Model) contains all patient-record-centric concepts that are in any way related to risk evaluation branching out from medical history to diagnosis and therapy-related concepts to follow up data terms. The CRIM is meant to serve as the basis for a unified hospital database that dispenses with the need of intrahospital data mediation and offers links for connecting to the molecular biology, genetic, and simulation data through mediation at the inter-hospital level. Even though the CRIM implicitly contains risk-related concepts, it is supplemented by an explicit risk ontology that brings together the concepts from all the domains and defines functional relationships between, for example, anamnesis and medical conditions like high blood pressure.

Risk Ontology. As the core intention behind @neurIST is risk prediction, the CRIM plus other domain-specific parts are bound together in a risk ontology that links risk factors and risk factor evaluation with diseases and diagnostic findings. The ontology is maintained in OWL and makes provisions for adding newly established information onto precoded "textbook knowledge" by allowing new entry of risk factor class instances.

12.4.2.2 Ontology Publication

Because the resulting ontology and its constituting parts is central to all levels of a Semantic grid architecture, the representation will have to be published to a central repository that itself constitutes a data service. The *de facto* standard of RDF/OWL-based ontology representation will be used, which means that a triple store repository is mandatory. Future versions of OGSA-DAI are reported to support a triple store interface of activities, which lends more weight to the approach of a unified access to both relational and RDF data. All references to ontological concepts should be resolved through triple store service access, ideally relying on an appropriate toolkit interface for ontology graph analysis and querying. Such would be the case with the Jena RDF toolkit, for example, that comes with a full triple store persistence layer. A nontrivial requirement for the candidate triple store is the support of ontology versioning. While we do not immediately foresee many significant changes in a release version of the common knowledge model except for additions, the basic fact remains that ontologies are subject to evolution in their life span. The changes can alter their expressive power in many ways. Thus, approaches like the Jena-based SemVersion[39] are among the options to be considered here.

12.4.2.3 Semantic Annotation of Data Services

As discussed in Section 12.2.4.2, data services will implicitly be annotated completely if all data models behind the service are completely annotated. OGSA-DAI supports the retrieval of logical data schemas in XML format that readily lend themselves for annotation. Referencing parts of an XML document can be achieved using a tree index or XPointer,[40] but here we choose a fully qualified name (FQN) of a data schema part

---

[39]http://semversion.ontoware.org/
[40]http://www.w3.org/TR/xptr-framework/

that captures the following parts (optional in brackets):

```
<data service URL>:<database schema>:<schema table>
[:<table column>[:<table row>]]
```

Thus, a data service annotation would be of the form

```
<schema part FQN> instance-of <domain ontology class>
```

12.4.2.4   Data Service Resolution

Putting a global knowledge model to be used on the client side requires the possibility of navigation within the model. User-side navigation of ontologies can be supported by a tree representation of the class hierarchy or a full relational graph. For filtering an ontology graph or equivalently querying an ontology, it is also necessary to set constraints on the ontology class attributes (called properties in RDF/OWL), The navigation process is thus intimately linked with "semantic querying," the search for class instances (individuals in RDF/OWL) that satisfy certain constraints.

Given annotated data services in RDF annotation triples as described above, querying for data services is a matter of finding suitable instances for given combinations of ontology classes and optionally their attributes. Depending on the route taken for annotation publication, there are two methods for querying with different expressive power:

GEMSS registry Unless the user is provided with a semantic navigation interface, it will only be possible to search for regular expression matches for ontology concepts. Given a semantic navigation interface, direct matching can be ensured. Exploitation of the semantic relationships in the knowledge model, however, can only be done through explicit user interaction.

Ontology storage With in-line storage of the data schema FQNs as ontology instances, a host of additional automated search possibilities is opened up, comprising neighbor search, superclass/subclass search, and similarity search.

Irrespective of the way service or data resolution is accomplished, the output will always be a data schema FQN as shown above. In Fig. 12.9, we show an exemplary user front end that would guide a human client through the complete process of ontology navigation, constraint formulation (left panels), and subsequent navigation in the data service instances. This mock-up already exists as a Java implementation with defined API interface and is ready to be used as the basis of future @neurIST developments.

12.4.2.5   Data Querying

If a full semantic annotation of all entity attributes (table columns) from all databases is available, a direct query translation from an RDF query in, for example, SPARQL to SQL can be realized. This is due to the fact that the immediate query results (upper

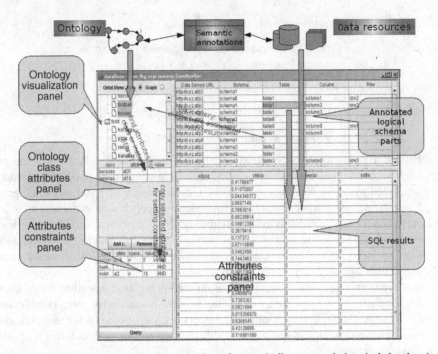

Figure 12.9. The steps in semantic navigation of semantically annotated data include choosing a concept and optionally setting of constraints on the concepts' attributes. The ontology graph query can then be resolved to a data service query and passed on to an SQL query on the data repository.

right panel) are comprised of not only the data service URL (discarding everything behind it in the FQN) but also data schema parts that can be queried immediately (like tables within a schema behind a certain data service). Consequently, a complete annotation of all columns from all constituent data sources, roughly equivalent to an object-relational mapping, would allow direct "semantic" querying of data sources at no additional effort saving the translation from RDF query languages like SPARQL to SQL. Taking into account the extended possibilities of OWL graph-pattern querying, combining queries from different data services should be possible as well.

Given annotated parts of a data service schema (data service URL, database schema, db table, table column, table row), the client is enabled to both retrieve data services and—in a subsequent step—the associated data. The left-hand panels lead the way from ontology concept selection (top), through concept attribute selection (middle), to attribute constraints definition (lower). Given those constraints, an RDF query will retrieve the appropriate data services and logical schema parts that were associated with the concepts during the annotation–publication process. Selection of a data service part can result in direct SQL querying, as shown here, when a table name is selected. Selecting any part of the resulting sets can automatically lead back to the associated parent concepts.

12.4.2.6   Toward Automated Semantic Mediation

MetaQL to SQL. Considering the possibilities offered by a complete "object-relational" mapping outlined in Section 12.4.2.5, a basis for automatic, on-the-fly GDMS mapping construction is created as well. Both goals involve the translation from a metaquery language like SPARQL to a repository-specific query language that without loss of generality can be assumed to be SQL. A provision for mediation rules from semantic annotations would be the representation of transformation rules on the ontology side. Currently, a notable OWL-extension that captures rules for transformations of simple data types (i.e., using arithmetic and string manipulations) is SWRL, the Semantic Web rule language.[41] The transformation facilities are at the heart of the GDMS mapping files and form the basis for set theoretic operations known from SQL like join, union, intersect, and minus of partial result sets. Even without SWRL, all information about the data services and schema parts are already accessible, yielding implicit information about how to map directly matching information from different tables onto each other, making direct SPARQL to SQL translations possible. SWRL, or similar OWL extensions, are the key for yielding the complete GDMS mapping information.

To summarize, given complete semantic annotation and a request for certain concepts with certain restrictions, we can answer the following questions:

1. Which data services are required?
2. Which schemata, tables, and columns from their respective services are required?
3. How do we combine them?
   (a) using transformations where needed,
   (b) using set theoretic operations (join, union, intersect, minus).

Eventually, our goal is to have a knowledge model in SWRL/OWL plus a suitable translation module that completely substitutes hand-written mediations as implemented currently.

12.5   CONCLUSIONS AND OUTLOOK

The emphasis of clinical information systems progresses from the management of billing records and patient tracking toward a more comprehensive view comprising all kinds of patient-related data (images, molecular, epidemiological, etc.) to form the basis for regional and global information networks used for advanced health-care planning and clinical/epidemiological research. In order to allow future meaningful combination of data from various institutions, semantic technologies are key enablers to make hidden knowledge explicit and machine interpretable.

[41]http://www.w3.org/Submission/SWRL/

This chapter introduces the technological basis of the @neurIST semantic data integration approach to provide transparent and intuitive access to distributed, heterogeneous data required by the CIS application suites. Additionally, their interaction and extension to semantic functionality—ranging from service and data annotation—and semantic querying and navigation to service resolution is described. The complete path from semantic annotations to data services based on the logical view of a data sources and a common, centralized, versioned knowledge model represented in OWL, through the publication of annotations and brokering of data (service) requests, to full-fledged data mediation architecture is illustrated.

The service-oriented architecture proposed in this chapter represents an important step toward virtualization of data and compute resources. We use services as wrappers of the various involved resources to provide nonintrusive semantic annotations on different levels. The manner of introducing and exploiting semantic annotations layed out here, while bearing some similarities with existing approaches, is a novelty that offers considerably more freedom in semantic data grid implementation than earlier proposals because the sgSOA is essentially a "pimped-up" SOA that requires minimal changes to a nonsemantic setting.

Automatic on-demand mediation is still very much a research field. With some of the aforementioned modules and tools (GDMS, TUAM, Jena toolkit) already in place, additional efforts will have to be spent on the navigation and querying user interface and the SPARQL-SQL / SPARQL-GDMS mapping translation module. Furthermore, a detailed specification is currently in preparation for all architectural parts beyond the service resolution stage, so we foresee considerable refinement during future research and development steps.

ACKNOWLEDGMENTS

The @neurIST project is supported by the EU as an integrated project IP (project identifier IST-2004-027703).

REFERENCES

1. R.H. Dolin, L. Alschuler, C. Beebe, P.V. Biron, S.L. Boyer, D. Essin, E. Kimber, T. Lincoln, J.E. Mattison, The HL7 clinical document architecture, *Journal of the American Medical Informatics Association* **8**(6), 552–569, 2001.

2. D.A. Lindberg, B.L. Humphreys, A.T. McCray, The unified medical language system, *Methods of Information in Medicine* **32**(4), 281–291, 1993.

3. I. Denley, S.W. Smith, Privacy in clinical information systems in secondary care, *BMJ* **318**(7194), 1328–1331, 1999.

4. E. Torres, C. de Alfonso, I. Blanquer, V. Hernández, Privacy protection in healthgrid: Distributing encryption management over the VO. *Studies in Health and Technology Information* **120**, 131–141, 2006.

5. B. Claerhout, G.J.E. De Moor, Privacy protection for healthgrid applications, *Methods of Information in Medicine* **44**(2), 140–143, 2005.

6. S.E. Middleton, J.A.M. Herveg, F. Crazzolara, D. Marvin, Y. Poullet. GEMSS: privacy and security for a medical grid, *Methods of Information in Medicine* **44**(2),182–185, 2005.

7. R. Haux, Health information systems - past, present, future, *International Journal of Medical Informatics* **75**(3–4),268–281, 2006.

8. V. Breton, K. Dean, T. Solomonides, I. Blanquer, V. Hernandez, E. Medico, N. Maglaveras, S. Benkner, G. Lonsdale, S. Lloyd, K. Hassan, R. McClatchey, S. Miguet, J. Montagnat, X. Pennec, W. De Neve, C. De Wagter, G. Heeren, L. Maigne, K. Nozaki, M. Taillet, H. Bilofsky, R. Ziegler, M. Hoffman, C. Jones, M. Cannataro, P. Veltri, G. Aloisio, S. Fiore, M. Mirto, I. Chouvarda, V. Koutkias, A. Malousi, V. Lopez, I. Oliveira, J.P. Sanchez, F. Martin-Sanchez, G. De Moor, B. Claerhout, J.A.M. Herveg, Healthgrid White Paper collaboration. The healthgrid white paper. *Studies in Health and Technology Informatics* **112**, 249–321, 2005.

9. D. Kalra, P. Singleton, J. Milan, J. Mackay, D. Detmer, A. Rector, D. Ingram, Security and confidentiality approach for the clinical e-science framework (CLEF), *Methods of Information in Medicine* **44**(2),193–197, 2005.

10. J. Choi, S. Yoo, H. Park, J. Chun, Mobilemed: A pda-based mobile clinical information system, *IEEE Transactions on Information Technology in Biomedicine* **10**(3), 627–635, 2006.

11. E.S. Chen, J.J. Cimino, Patterns of usage for a web-based clinical information system, *Medinfo* **11**(1), 18–22, 2004.

12. G. Hripcsak, J.J. Cimino, S. Sengupta, WEBCIS: Large scale deployment of a web-based clinical information system, in: *Proceedings AMIA annual Symposium 1999*, pp. 804–808.

13. H. Matsuda, A grid environment for data integration of scientific databases, in: *Proceedings of the First International Conference on e-Science and Grid Computing, IEEE Computer Society*, Washington, DC, pp. 3–4, 2005. ISBN:0-7695-2448-6 author affiliation: Osaka University.

14. A. Geissbühler, C. Lovis, A. Lamb, S Sphani, Experience with an XML/HTTP-based federative approach to develop a hospital-wide clinical information system, *Medinfo* **10**(121490621), 735–739, 2001.

15. T. Burkle, W. Ruan, A. Michel, J Dudeck, On the way to a Web based hospital information system: Concepts for the use of a medical data dictionary to present context sensitive information in an intranet environment, *Medinfo* **9**(2), 917–921, 1998.

16. S. Benkner, G. Berti, G. Engelbrecht, J. Fingberg, G. Kohring, S.E. Middleton, R. Schmidt, Gemss: Grid-infrastructure for medical service provision, *Methods in Information in Medicine* **44/4**(2), 177–181, 2005.

17. F. Martin-Sanchez, I. Iakovidis, S. Nørager, V. Maojo, P. de Groen, J. Van der Lei, T. Jones, K. Abraham-Fuchs, R. Apweiler, A. Babic, R. Baud, V. Breton, P. Cinquin, P. Doupi, M. Dugas, R. Eils, R. Engelbrecht, P. Ghazal, P. Jehenson, C. Kulikowski, K. Lampe, G. De Moor, S. Orphanoudakis, N. Rossing, B. Sarachan, A. Sousa, G. Spekowius, G. Thireos, G. Zahlmann, J. Zvárová, I. Hermosilla, F.J. Vicente, Synergy between medical informatics and bioinformatics: Facilitating genomic medicine for future health care, *Journal of Biomedical Informatics* **37**(1), 30–42, 2004.

18. L. Sun, E.C. Ifeachor, The impact of grid on healthcare, in: *Proceedings of Second International Conference on Computational Intelligence in Medicine and Healthcare* (CIMED 2005), 29th June–1st July 2005, Costa da Caparica, Lisbon, Portugal, 2005.

19. M. Lenzerini, Data integration: A theoretical perspective, in: *Archive Proceedings of the Twenty-First ACM SIGMOD-SIGACT-SIGART Symposium on Principles of Database Systems*, Madison, Wisconsin, pp. 233–246, 2002, ISBN:1-58113-507-6.

20. A. Wöhrer, P. Brezany, A. Tjoa, Novel mediator architectures for grid information systems, *FGCS* **21**(1), 107–114, 2005.

21. P. Brezany, A. Tjoa, H. Wanek, A. Wöhrer, Mediators in the architecture of grid information systems, in: *Proceedings of the Conference on Parallel Processing and Applied Mathematics*, Czestochowa, September 2003.

22. G. Wiederhold, Mediators in the architecture of future information systems, *Computer* **25**(3), 38–49, 1992.

23. J. Kahan, M. Koivunen, E. Prud'hommeaux, R.R. Swick. Annotea: an open RDF infrastructure for shared web annotations, in: *Proceedings of the WWW10 International Conference, Hong Kong*, May 2001.

24. J. Zvárová, EFMI symposium on "electronic health record, healthcare, registers and telemedicine," *International Journal of Medical Informatics* **75**(3–4), 183–184, 2006.

25. I. Horrocks, DAML+OIL: A description logic for the semantic web, *IEEE Bulletin of the Technical Committee on Data Engineering* **25**(1), 4–9, 2002.

26. A. Gomez-Perez, O. Corcho, Ontology languages for the semantic web, *Intelligent Systems IEEE* **17**(1), 54–60, 2002.

27. P. Haase, J. Broekstra, A. Eberhart, R. Volz, A comparison of RDF query languages, in: *Proceedings of the Third International Semantic Web Conference, Hiroshima, Japan*, November 2004.

28. Oracle, Semantic Technologies Center, WWW, 2006. http://www.oracle.com/technology/tech/ semantic_technologies.

29. B. Popov, A. Kiryakov, D. Ognyanoff, D. Manov, A. Kirilov, KIM—A semantic platform for information extraction and retrieval, *Journal of Natural Language Engineering* **10**(3-4), 375–392, 2004.

30. D. Huynh, S. Mazzocchi, D. Karger, Piggy Bank: Experience the semantic web inside your web browser, in: *International Semantic Web Conference (ISWC)*, 2005.

31. S. Bloehdorn, K. Petridis, C. Saathoff, N. Simou, V. Tzouvaras, Y. Avrithis, S. Handschuh, Y. Kompatsiaris, S. Staab, M.G. Strintzis, Semantic annotation of images and videos for multimedia analysis, in: *Proceedings of the 2nd European Semantic Web Conference*, 2005.

32. S. Handschuh, S. Staab, A Maedche, CREAM Creating relational metadata with a component-based, ontology-driven annotation framework, in: *Proceedings of the 1st International Conference on Knowledge Capture, Victoria, British Columbia, Canada*, pp. 76–83, 2001.

33. E. Bozsak, M. Ehrig, S. Handschuh, A. Hotho, A. Maedche, B. Motik, D. Oberle, C. Schmitz, S. Staab, L. Stojanovic, N. Stojanovic, R. Studer, G. Stumme, Y. Sure, J. Tane, R. Volz, V Zacharias, KAON—Towards a large scale semantic web, in: K. Bauknecht, A. Min Tjoa, and G. Quirchmayr (Eds.), *Proceedings of the 3rd International Conference on E-Commerce and Web Technologies* (EC-Web 2002), Vol. 2455, Springer, Berlin, pp. 304–313, 2002.

34. V. Sinha, D. Quan, D.F. Huynh, D. Karger, Semantic navigation through semi-structured information, Technical report, Student Oxygen Workshop, 2002. Available at http://sow.csail.mit.edu/2002/proceedings/quan-navigation.pdf.

35. A. Chebotko, S. Lu, H.M. Jamil, F. Fotouhi, Semantics preserving SPARQL-to-SQL query translation for optional graph patterns, Technical report TR-DB-052006-CLJF, Wayne State University Department of Computer Science 5143 Cass Avenue, Detroit, Michigan 48202, USA, 2006.

36. M.L. Zloch, Automatic translation of RDQL queries into SQL, Bachelor's thesis, Institut Fiir Informatik, Datenbanken und Informationssysteme, Universitä Düsseldorf, 2005.

37. L.F. Cabrera, C. Kurt, D. Box, An introduction to the web services architecture and its specifications, version 2.0, Technical report, Microsoft Corporation, 2004.

38. K. Kumpf, M Hofmann, Bioinformatics in the semantic grid, *ERCIM News*, **59**, 2004.

39. P. Lord, P. Alper, C. Wroe, C. Goble, Feta: A light-weight architecture for user oriented semantic service discovery, in: *Proceedings of the 2nd European Semantic Web Conference*, ESWC 2005, Crete, Greece, May 2005.

40. M. Wilkinson, H. Schoof, R. Ernst, D. Haase, BioMOBY successfully integrates distributed heterogeneous bioinformatics web services. The PlaNet exemplar case, *Plant Physiology* **138**(1), 5–17, 2005.

41. M. Romberg, The UNICORE grid infrastructure, Special Issue on Grid Computing, *Scientifc Programming Journal* **10**, 149 –157, 2002.

42. I. Foster, Globus toolkit version 4: Software for service-oriented systems, in: *IFIP International Conference on Network and Parallel Computing*, LNCS 3779, Springer-Verlag, New York, pp. 2–13, 2005.

43. M. Surridge, S. Taylor, D. De Roure, E. Zaluska, Experiences with GRIA, in: *Proceedings of the First IEEE International Conference on e-Science and Grid Computing*, 2005.

44. S. Benkner, G. Engelbrecht, I. Brandic, R. Schmidt, and S.E. Middleton, Application-level QoS support for a medical grid infrastructure, in: T.W. Tan, P. Arzberger, and A. Konagaya (Eds.), *Grid Computing in Life Sciences, Proceedings of the 2nd International Workshop on Life Science Grid 2005*, World Scientific Publishing Co., Singapore, 2005. ISBN 981-270-378-0.

45. D.M. Jones, J.W. Fenner, G. Berti, F. Kruggel, R.A. Mehrem, W. Backfrieder, R. Moore, A. Geltmeier, The GEMSS Grid: An evolving HPC environment for medical applications, in: *HealthGrid 2004*, Clermont-Ferrand, France, 2004.

46. J. Cao, F. Zimmermann, Queue scheduling and advance reservations with COSY, in: *18th International Parallel and Distributed Processing Symposium (IPDPS'04), Santa Fe, New Mexico*, 2004.

47. J. MacLaren, Advance reservations: state of the Art, GGF Memo GGF GRAAP-WG June 2003, GGF, 2003.

48. IST-2004-027703, Aneurist, EU IST FP6 Integrated Project, WWW, 2006. Available at http://www.aneurist.org.

49. I. Foster, C. Kesselman, *The Grid: Blueprint for a New Computing Infrastructure*, Morgan Kaufmann Publishers, San Francisco, 2003.

50. A. Chervenak, I. Foster, C. Kesselman, C. Salisbury, S. Tuecke, The data grid: Towards an architecture for the distributed management and analysis of large scientific datasets, *Journal of Network and Computer Applications* **23**(3), 187–200, 1999.

51. W. Hoschek, F. Jaen-Martinez, A. Samar, H. Stockinger, K. Stockinger. Data management in an international data grid project, in: *GRID 2000*, pp. 77–90.

52. S. Venugopal, R. Buyya, K. Ramamohanarao, A taxonomy of data grids for distributed data sharing, management and processing, arXiv preprint GRIDS-TR-2005-3, Grid Computing and Distributed Systems Laboratory, Department of Computer Science and Software Engineering, The University of Melbourne, Australia, June 2005.

53. M. Antonioletti, M.P. Atkinson, R. Baxter, A. Borley, N.P. Chue Hong, B. Collins, N. Hardman, A. Hume, A. Knox, M. Jackson, A. Krause, S. Laws, J. Magowan, N.W. Paton, D. Pearson, T. Sugden, P. Watson, , M. Westhead, The design and implementation of grid database services in OGSA-DAI, *Concurrency and Computation: Practice and Experience* **17**(2–4), 357–376, 2005.

13

BIOINFORMATICS APPLICATIONS IN GRID COMPUTING ENVIRONMENTS

Azzedine Boukerche and Alba Cristina Magalhaes Alves de Melo

13.1 INTRODUCTION

In the last decade, we have observed an unprecedented development in molecular biology. An extremely high number of organisms have been sequenced in genome projects and included in genomic databases, for further analysis. These databases present an exponential growth rate and they are intensively accessed daily, all over the world.

Once a sequence is obtained, its function and/or structure must be determined. Direct experimentation is considered to be the most reliable method to do that. However, the experiments that must take place are very complex and time-consuming. For this reason, it is far more productive to use computational methods to infer biological information from a sequence. This is usually done by comparing the new sequence with sequences that already had their characteristics determined.

Therefore, biologists are now faced with the problem of dealing with very huge databases, in search of meaningful similarities among DNA, RNA, and protein sequences. In order to do that, high computing power and huge storage space are necessary. Moreover, new algorithms must be developed to realistically model the biological relationships between the organisms.

Bioinformatics[1] is a new research area where computational tools and algorithms are developed to help biologists in the task of understanding the organisms, in a functional and evolutionary way.

At the time when the advances were occurring in molecular biology, we observed a fantastic development of the Internet, which made possible the interconnection of millions of powerful machines in a global scale. Several measures were made that stated that, most of the time, the majority of these interconnected machines remain

---

[1] Although most authors consider the terms "bioinformatics" and "computational biology" distinct, they are used interchangeably in this text.

Grid Computing for Bioinformatics and Computational Biology.   Edited by E.-G. Talbi and A.Y. Zomaya.
Copyright © 2008 John Wiley & Sons, Inc.

idle. This led to the idea of metacomputing [1], which proposes the creation of a supercomputer by taking advantage of the idle cycles of the machines connected to the Internet.

Grid computing is considered to be an evolution of metacomputing where not only the computing power of the machines but also several other types of resources such as data, softwares, and specific hardwares [2] are shared. Applications that are developed for grid environments are very complex since they have to deal with a great number of heterogeneous and nondedicated resources placed on multiple administrative domains.

Initially, the efforts in grid computing were concentrated to develop middlewares that were able to offer a wide area infrastructure to support the online processing of distributed applications [3]. The Globus Toolkit [4] is considered to be the *de facto* standard for grid middleware, offering basic solutions for problems such as authentication, resource discovery, access to resources, remote task execution, and data movement, providing the infrastructure where real distributed applications for grid computing can be developed.

Since grid applications are designed to run in a geographically distributed environment, they usually do not have high communication rates and many of them follow the master–slave model [5]. In this case, there is a process (master) that distributes the work among the slaves, which process the work in an independent manner (without communication), sending the results back to the master when the task is finished.

Bioinformatics applications are very good candidates to run in a grid environment since they manipulate an important number of genomic databases that are usually geographically distributed. The most important challenge here is to provide transparent, secure, and scalable bioinformatics grid services. Many efforts to build bioinformatics grids have been made recently. Most of them focus on master–slave bioinformatics applications that, in some cases, can be combined to form workflows.

In this chapter, we present an overview of the state-of-the-art research in grids for bioinformatics. In Section 13.2, we present the biological sequence comparison problem and the most widely used methods to solve it. Section 13.3 presents the main concepts involved in grid computing, with a focus on resource allocation policies. Section 13.4 discusses several grid initiatives for bioinformatics applications and presents a comparative analysis of these approaches. Finally, Section 13.5 presents the conclusions and future research directions.

13.2 BIOLOGICAL SEQUENCE COMPARISON

13.2.1 Basic Concepts

Biological sequence comparison is one of the most basic operations in bioinformatics, given the number and diversity of the sequences and the frequency on which it is needed to be solved daily all over the world [6]. Sequence comparison is very often used as a component to solve more complex problems such as multiple-sequence alignment, protein characterization, and profile alignment [7].

G	A	_	C	G	G	A	T	T	A	G
G	A	T	C	G	G	A	A	T	A	G

+1	+1	− 2	+1	+1	+1	+1	− 1	+1	+1	+1

$$\Sigma = 6$$

Figure 13.1. Global alignment between $s = GACGGATTAG$ and $t = GATCGGAATAG$.

In fact, it is a problem of approximate pattern matching [8] that consists of finding which parts of the sequences are alike. Basically, there are two kinds of comparisons, global and local depending on the interest of the biologist, involving the entire sequences or just parts of them [6].

To compare two sequences, we need to find the best alignment between them, which is to place one sequence above the other making clear the correspondence between similar characters [6]. In an alignment, spaces can be inserted in arbitrary locations along the sequences so that they end up with the same size.

Consider two biological sequences s and t, with sizes n and m, respectively, and an alignment between them. A score can be associated for it as follows. For each column, we associate, for instance, $+1$ if the two characters are identical (match), -1 if the characters are different (mismatch), and -2 if one of them is a space (gap). The score is the sum of the values computed for each column. The maximal score is the similarity between the two sequences. Figure 13.1 shows the alignment of sequences s and t, with the score for each column.

Usually, scoring (or substitution) matrices are used to calculate the mismatch penalty between two different proteins. In Fig. 13.1, we associated a unique value for a mismatch (-1 in the example), regardless of the parts involved. This works well with nucleotides but not for proteins. For instance, some mismatches are more likely to occur than others and can indicate evolutionary aspects [6]. For this reason, the alignment methods for proteins use score matrices that associate distinct values with distinct mismatches and reflect the likelihood of a certain change.

The most widely used scoring matrices are a PAM (Percent Accepted Mutations) [9] and BLOSUM (Blocks Substitution Matrix) [10]. PAM matrices are a result of an extensive work that analyzes the frequencies in which an amino acid a is replaced by an amino acid b during evolution. BLOSUM are scoring matrices generated considering evolutionary rates of a region of a protein (block) rather than the entire protein.

13.2.2 Exact Sequence Comparison

An exact algorithm (NW) based on dynamic programming that obtains the best global alignment between two sequences was proposed by Needleman and Wunsch [11]. In this algorithm, a similarity array of size n x m is built by comparing the prefixes of sequences s and t. This array is filled from top left to bottom right, and the value of each cell $a(i, j)$ depends on three previously calculated values: $a(i − 1, j), a(i, j − 1),$

and $a(i - 1, j - 1)$. At the last row and column of this array, the similarity score can be found. This phase runs on quadratic time and space [11]. In order to retrieve the alignment, a traceback algorithm is executed on the similarity array until position $a(0, 0)$ is reached.

To compute exact local sequence alignments, Smith and Waterman [12] proposed an algorithm (SW), also based on dynamic programming, with quadratic time and space complexity. This algorithm is quite similar to NW but there are three main differences. First, no negative values are allowed at the similarity array. Second, the similarity score is the highest score value that occurs at the array, not necessarily at the last row and column. Third, traceback is done from the similarity score until a zero value is reached.

Hirschberg [13] proposed an exact algorithm that calculates a local alignment between two sequences s and t in quadratic time but in linear space. The approach used splits sequence s in the middle, generating subsequences $s1$ and $s2$, and calculates the corresponding place to cut sequence t, generating subsequences $t1$ and $t2$, in such a way that the alignment problem can be solved in a divide-and-conquer recursive manner. This recursion roughly doubles the execution time, when compared with the original algorithm.

13.2.3 Heuristic Sequence Comparison

Usually, one given biological sequence is compared against thousands or even millions of sequences that compose genetic databases. One of the most important gene repositories is the one that is a part of a collaboration that involves *GenBank* at the National Center for Biotechnology Information (NCBI), the *EMBL* at the European Molecular Biology Laboratory, and *DDBJ* at the DNA Data Bank of Japan. These organizations exchange data daily, and a new release is generated every two months. By now, there are millions of entries composed of billions of nucleotides. Due to the current growth rate, these databases will soon achieve terabytes.

In this scenario, the use of exact methods such as NW and SW is prohibitive. For this reason, faster heuristic methods are proposed that do not guarantee that the best alignment will be produced.

FASTA [14] and BLAST [15] are the most widely used heuristics for sequence comparison, and they use either PAM or BLOSUM matrices (Section 13.2.1) when comparing proteins.

13.2.3.1 FASTA

FASTA (Fast-All) was proposed by Pearson and Lipman [14] in 1988 and its goal is to retrieve good alignments in less time and space than the exact methods. In its first phase, exact pattern matching is done and identical subsequences (*k-tuples*) between s and t are obtained. After that, the *offsets* are calculated that correspond to the diagonals of the similarity array where the *k-tuples* occur.

In the second step, *k-tuples* that occur at the same diagonal and that are close to each other are grouped to form ungapped *regions*. In the step third, these ungapped regions are analyzed and some of them are merged, forming gapped regions. Finally,

Table 13.1   BLAST Family Programs

Program	Database type	Query type	Translation
BLASTN	Nucleotide	Nucleotide	None
BLASTP	Protein	Protein	None
BLASTX	Protein	Nucleotide	Query
TBLASTN	Nucleotide	Protein	Database
TBLASTX	Nucleotide	Nucleotide	Query and database

high scoring regions are realigned using a dynamic programming method (Section 13.2.2) and score matrices (Section 13.2.1).

13.2.3.2   BLAST

BLAST was proposed by Altschul et al. [15] in 1990. Its motivation was to improve the performance of the FASTA algorithm (Section 13.2.3.1). This was mainly achieved by integrating the use of substitution matrices (Section 13.2.1) in the first step of the algorithm. In 1996 and 1997, improved gapped versions of the original BLAST, NCBI-BLAST2 [16] and WU-BLAST2 [17], were proposed.

BLAST provides programs for comparing many combinations of query and database sequence types by translating sequences on the fly. Table 13.1 lists the names of BLAST family programs, the query and database types, and the translations done in a database search.

The BLAST algorithm is divided into three well-defined phases: seeding, extension, and evaluation.

In the first phase, BLAST compares a query sequence s against all sequences in a database, using a scoring matrix (Section 13.2.1). BLAST uses the concept of words, which is defined to be a finite set of letters with length w that appear in a given sequence. For instance, the sequence TCACGA contains four words with length 3: TCA, CAC, ACG, and CGA. The BLAST algorithm assumes that significant alignments have words in common.

The location of all shared w-letter words between the query sequence s and the database sequences is determined by doing exact pattern matching. These locations are known as *identical words*. Only regions with identical words can be used as seeds for the alignment.

For the cases where significant alignments do not contain words in common, the concept of neighborhood is used. The neighbor of a word includes the word itself and every other word whose score is at least equal to the neighbor score threshold (T), when compared through a substitution matrix. For instance, if we consider $T = 11$ and a substitution matrix PAM200, the protein sequences RGD and KGD are neighbors since the score between them is 14 [18].

An appropriate choice of w, T, and the substitution matrix is an effective way to control the performance and the sensibility of BLAST.

The seeds obtained in Phase 1 must be extended in order to generate an alignment. This is done by inspecting the characters near the seed in both directions and concatenating them to the seed until a *drop-off score X* is reached. The *drop-off score* defines how much the score can be reduced, considering the last maximal value. Having the seed *A*, the *X* parameter equal to 4, and a punctuation of +1 for matches and −1 for mismatches, the following result is obtained:

```
ATGC GATA CTA
ATTC GATC GAT
1212 3454 321 <--- score
0010 0001 234 <--- drop off score
```

After that, the algorithm goes back to the best score (in this case, 5) to obtain the alignment. Thus, the extension on the right of the first *A* gives us the alignment:

```
ATGC GAT
ATTC GAT
```

The alignments generated in the extension phase must be evaluated in order to remove the nonsignificative ones. The significant alignments, called high-score segment pairs (HSPs), are the ones whose scores are higher or equal to a threshold *S*. Also, consistent HSP groups are generated that include nonoverlapped HSPs that are near the same diagonal. The consistent HSP groups are compared against a final threshold, known as the *E* parameter [19], and only the alignments that are above this threshold are considered.

Due to the success in obtaining significant alignments fast, many BLAST variations and wrappers were proposed. PSI-BLAST [16], PHI-BLAST [20], Mega-BLAST [21], BLASTZ [22], and MPBLAST [23] are a nonexhaustive list of these variations.

13.3 GRID COMPUTING

The term *grid computing* was conceived in the mid-1990s to denote a new infrastructure of distributed computing for scientists and engineers in a more advanced scope. This name was inspired by the electrical power energy because of its pervasiveness, ease of use, and reliability [4]. More specifically, grid computing can be defined as a type of distributed system the enables the dynamic sharing of autonomous and geographically distributed resources, spread over multiple administrative domains [24].

Grid computing technologies and concepts were initially developed in order to enable resource sharing between scientific institutions with common projects, who needed to share data, software, and computational power.

13.3.1 Grid Middleware Evolution

In developing applications for the grid, it is essential to have an unified middleware to provide a transparent interface to the underlying protocols. The Globus Toolkit [4] emerged in 1998 as an open source project and quickly became a *de facto* standard for grid computing infrastructure. Globus defines and implements a set of protocols,

APIs and services used by hundreds of grid applications all over the world. Moreover, it worked as a pioneer in interoperable grid system development.

In 2002, the Open Grid Services Architecture (OGSA) [3] was introduced by the Global Grid Forum (GGF) to expand standardization. The OGSA provided a new architecture for grid applications based on Web services in order to achieve interoperability using industry standards.

Many OGSA architecture implementations were developed, including one for Globus. Beyond the definition of a set of standardized interfaces, the OGSA architecture provides a framework for portable and interoperable service definition and thus provides a basis for grid development.

In its first specification, OGSA was composed by three modules built upon a Web service layer. The bottom layer of the OGSA architecture was called OGSI (Open Grid Services Infrastructure), which defined mechanisms to manipulate a grid service. Since a grid service is stateful, the traditional concept of Web service was extended to meet this requirement. On top of OGSI, the layers of OGSA services and the OGSA schema were placed. Globus Toolkit 3 was an implementation of the OGSA/OGSI.

OGSI has received many objections from the Web service community, mainly because its specification redefined the concept of Web service, creating a partial incompatibility with the existing tools for manipulating them. Therefore, a great effort was made to obtain a new grid service definition that was adjusted to the existing standards. As a result of this effort, the OGSI layer was totally replaced by a new layer, called WSRF (Web Service Resource Framework). WSRF can be seen as the composition of a Web service and a stateful resource. Globus Toolkit 4 implements the OGSA/WSRF.

13.3.2   Task Execution in the Grid

The process of executing tasks in a grid environment is usually divided in three phases: resource discovery, resource selection, and task execution [3].

The goal of the first phase is to generate a set of resources that potentially can be used to execute a user task. First, an authorization filter is used to determine which resources the user can access. After that, the user specifies a set of characteristics that the resource must exhibit in order to execute the task. For instance, the user can specify the processor architecture, operating system, amount of RAM memory and amount of disk space, among others. These characteristics are then used to find the authorized resources that meet the specified requirements.

The second phase starts by collecting dynamic information such as processor load and amount of free memory. This operation is very complex since the grid is highly dynamic. For this reason, historical information is usually used. Having the dynamic information and the set of resources obtained in Phase 1, a task-scheduling algorithm is executed to assign a set of tasks to a set of resources aiming to maximize the resource utilization and offering high throughput. If the tasks to be scheduled must respect a precedence order, we are dealing with a task-scheduling problem. On the contrary, if there are no precedence relations between the tasks, the problem is called task allocation. Both problems are NP-Complete [25] and, for this reason, heuristics are generally used. This topic will be discussed in detail in Section 13.3.3.

The last phase regards the remote execution of the task. First, the task is sent to the chosen resource (in this case, a machine or a processor). The resource is then configured to correctly execute the task. During the execution, the user usually wants to monitor the task progress and the grid must provide mechanisms that enable him/her to do so. When the task finishes executing, the user is informed and the output of the computation is retrieved. At last, garbage collection is done.

13.3.3 Task Allocation Strategies

A great number of grid applications are modeled as the master–slave model. In the master–slave model, one problem is divided in many independent tasks of smaller size that could be distributed to slave nodes for parallel processing. The slave nodes process the tasks assigned to them in an independent manner and send the result to the master at the end of the computation.

A very important problem to be solved in this context is task allocation. The task allocation problem consists of assigning tasks to processors in order to maximize system performance [26]. In this problem, it is assumed that no precedence relations exist among the tasks. Task allocation is known to be a NP-Complete problem; for this reason, heuristics are used to solve it.

Given a master–slave application composed by a master m and S slaves, the task allocation function allocate(m, s_i, N, S) determines how many tasks out of N must be assigned to a slave s_i. This generic problem is formally described in Equation (13.1) [5]. In this equation, $A(N, S)$ represents a particular allocation policy. The expression WeightFactor(m, s_i, S) was defined by Shao [5] [Equation (13.2)] and provides weights for each slave s_i on the basis its processing rate per task.

$$\text{allocate}(m, s_i, N, S) = A(N, S) * \text{WeightFactor}(m, s_i, S) \qquad (13.1)$$

$$\text{WeightFactor}(m, s_i, S) = \frac{P * \text{WorkerRate}(m, s_i)}{\sum_{i=1}^{P} \text{WorkerRate}(m, s_i)} \qquad (13.2)$$

The function WorkerRate(m, s_i) considers static information previously known from computer nodes and is defined as the task completion rate occurring between master m and worker s_i, in tasks per unit of time.

The following subsections present some task allocation policies. Each strategy is an instance $A(N, S)$ of Equation (13.1).

13.3.3.1 Fixed (Static Scheduling)

The *fixed* [5] strategy distributes all tasks uniformly to slaves nodes. This strategy is appropriate for homogeneous systems whose resources are dedicated and no behavioral variations occur during execution. Also, systems that have high communication latencies benefit from this strategy. Equation (13.3) defines the fixed allocation function.

$$A(N, S) = \frac{N}{S} \tag{13.3}$$

13.3.3.2 Self-Scheduling (SS)

Self-scheduling (SS) [27] distributes single tasks to whatever slave node requests it. The procedure continues until all tasks are allocated. Equation (13.4) presents the SS allocation policy:

$$A(N, S) = 1, \quad \text{while tasks are still left to allocate} \tag{13.4}$$

The self-scheduling principle is to distribute to each node exactly the number of tasks it is able to process. Thus, the maximum idle time a set of nodes could wait for is limited by the processing time of a single task in the slowest node. Nevertheless, self-scheduling points out a potential disadvantage. It demands much communication, since each task retrieved by a slave node requires at least one interaction with the master node.

13.3.3.3 Trapezoidal Self-Scheduling (TSS)

Trapezoidal self-scheduling (TSS) [28] allocates tasks in groups with a linearly decreasing size. This strategy incorporates two variables, steps and δ, that represent the total number of allocation steps and block reduction factor, respectively. Equations (13.5) and (13.6) show how these variables are calculated.

$$\text{steps} = \left\lceil \frac{4NS}{N + 2S} \right\rceil \tag{13.5}$$

$$\delta = \frac{N - 2S}{2S(\text{steps} - 1)} \tag{13.6}$$

The TSS allocation function is presented in Equation (13.7). It calculates the length of the sth block using the difference between the length of the first block and total reduction from the last $s - 1$ blocks.

$$A(s, N, S) = \max \left(\left\lfloor \frac{N}{2S} - [(s - 1) \times \delta] \right\rfloor, 1 \right) \tag{13.7}$$

13.3.3.4 Guided Self-Scheduling (GSS)

Guided self-scheduling (GSS) [29] allocates tasks in groups whose lengths decrease exponentially. The goal is to create a trade-off between the advantages of having few allocation blocks and the advantages of minimizing the discrepancies among the finishing times of slave nodes. The main disadvantage is the potential to allocate large chunks to a slow machine, causing an imbalance in final processing time. Equation (13.8) shows the GSS allocation function.

$$A(s, N, S) = \max \left(\left\lfloor \frac{N \left(1 - \frac{1}{S}\right)^{s-1}}{S} \right\rfloor, 1 \right), \quad s > 0 \qquad (13.8)$$

13.3.3.5   Factoring (FAC2)

Factoring (FAC2) [30] allocates work units in groups organized by cycles. Each cycle consists of S allocation sequences. Equation (13.9) presents the function that determines the cycle number of an iteration s. In FAC2, half of the remaining work units is allocated to active nodes in each allocation round. The FAC2 allocation formula is shown in Equation (13.10). Note that the size of the allocation blocks decrease with an exponential rate of 2. That is why this strategy is called FAC2.

$$\text{round}(s) = \left\lfloor \frac{(s - 1)}{S} \right\rfloor + 1 \qquad (13.9)$$

$$A(s, N, S) = \max \left(\left\lfloor \frac{N}{S \times 2^{\text{round}(s)}} \right\rfloor, 1 \right) \qquad (13.10)$$

FAC2 differs from other allocation strategies mostly by the way it decreases allocation blocks. The length of an allocation block is reduced for all active nodes in a round and not for just an individual node as in other policies.

13.3.3.6   Other Strategies

Weighted Factoring (WF) [31] is in fact an adaptation of FAC2 (Section 13.3.3.5) to heterogeneous environments. Equation (13.10) is modified to include a new variable (W_{pi}) that represents the weight of each processor. This weight depends on the relative power of each processor and thus takes into consideration the heterogeneity of the environment. Also, it must be known previously and does not change in execution time.

Adaptive Weighted Factoring (AWF) [32] proposes a modification on WF that allows the weight of each processor to vary over time. Initially, 1/4 of the total number of tasks are distributed evenly among the processors. The time needed to process this first assignment is reported to the master, which uses this information to estimate the average processing time and standard deviation of each process. A complex probabilistic model is used, then, to calculate how many tasks must be assigned to each processor in the next round. In this case, no history information is discarded, and even very old histories are used to calculate the weight.

The BOLD policy [33] assumes that the average execution time of the tasks and the variancy are known *a priori*. Using statistical formulas, this strategy adaptively reduces the size of the blocks. The overhead introduced to calculate the new sizes is considerable [33].

13.4   INITIATIVES ON BIOINFORMATICS GRIDS

In the past years, many research groups have investigated how to integrate bioinformatics tools into grid environments. Mostly, the biological experiments are expressed as workflows that are potentially composed by many bioinformatics tools. In order to execute them in grid environments, many questions must be answered. First, it must be decided where the biological databases must be placed and whether they must be replicated. Second, a task allocation policy must be used to minimize execution times, considering a heterogeneous and nondedicated environment. Moreover, aspects such as fault tolerance and execution monitoring, among others, must also be addressed.

13.4.1   GADU

GADU (Genome Analysis and Database Update System) [34] is a multi-institutional U.S. project, held mainly at Argonne National Laboratory and University of Chicago. It is proposed as a grid infrastructure to support multiple bioinformatics applications that are modeled and executed as workflows. It is a very complex system that integrates several grid technologies such as Globus 3 (Section 13.3.1), Condor-G [35], and VDL (Virtual Data Language) [36].

GADU has three modules that manipulate genomic data: acquisition, analysis, and storage. The data acquisition module is responsible to periodically search for updates in a set of public genomic databases. These updates are automatically integrated in the GADU system. The data analysis module executes, in a grid environment, workflows that are potentially composed by multiple bioinformatics tools. The results produced by the analysis module are stored in a relational database by the data storage module.

Either predefined or customized bioinformatics workflows are provided that execute well-known tools such as BLAST (Section 13.2.3.2), PFAM [37], BLOCKS [38], and TMHMM [39]. The workflows are translated to a graph of tool invocations. As grid infrastructure, GADU uses Globus 3 and Condor-G. It currently runs on multiple clusters spread over multiple administrative domains.

Figure 13.2 presents a general overview of GADU's architecture. First, automated workflows are created in VDL on the basis of predefined templates. Then, GADU uses Pegasus to generate Condor DAGs from the VDL workflows. These workflows are passed to the DAGMan Condor-G component that submits the workflow to a remote resource through the Globus GRAM (Grid Resource Allocation and Management) component.

The task-scheduling algorithm works as follows [40]. A small test program is periodically submitted to all candidate grid sites to collect their response time. This information is sent to the job-processing server, which labels as *acceptable* all sites that have response times below a given threshold. When a task needs to be scheduled, the job-processing server verifies the size of the Condor ready queue in the acceptable grid nodes. The node selected will be the one with the smaller Condor ready queue.

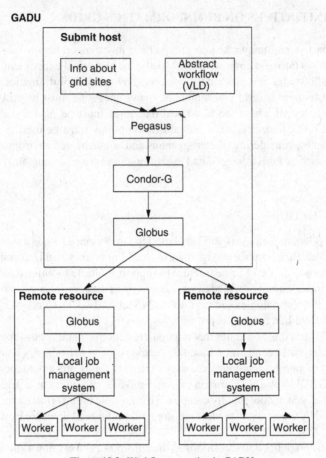

Figure 13.2. Workflow execution in GADU.

GADU was successfully executed in more than 2.3 million BLAST comparison searches on more than 200 nodes, at Teragrid (www.teragrid.org).

13.4.2 GeneGrid

GeneGrid [41] is a collaborative industrial project that is part of the UK e-Science Programme. It is developed mainly at Queen's University of Belfast, and its goal is to provide a *Virtual Bioinformatics Laboratory* where scientists can share resources and experiments in a multi-institutional virtual organization. It is built upon Globus Toolkit 3 and has five main components that are Globus 3 services: workflow management (GWM), resource monitoring and discovery (GARR), data management (GDM), application management (GAM), and portal. Figure 13.3 illustrates the interaction among these components.

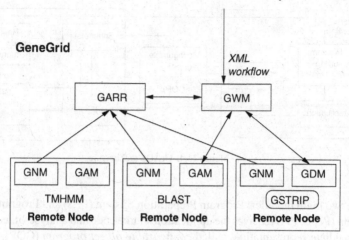

Figure 13.3. Workflow execution in GeneGrid.

When a user wants to execute a bioinformatics application on GeneGrid, he/she must provide an XML workflow description to the GWM component. This component is responsible for identifying the tasks that compose the workflow and assign them to grid nodes. To do so, the GARR service is contacted to retrieve information about the nodes that are able to execute a particular bioinformatics task.

Having decided which node will execute a particular task, the GWM contacts the GAM component in the selected node and the task starts execution. Periodically, a lightweight agent called GNM (GeneGrid Node Monitor) retrieves local information about the grid nodes and sends it to GARR. GARR is a fundamental component of GeneGrid's architecture that keeps information about all grid nodes and services.

The Data Manager Module (GDM) deals with two types of data: biological databases (Swissprot, EMBL, etc.) and GeneGrid information. The latter one is stored in the GeneGrid Status Tracking and Result and Input Parameters (GSTRIP) database. All GeneGrid data are managed by the OGSA-DAI [42] component, which was adapted to GeneGrid.

By now, Genegrid can execute the following applications alone or combined in a workflow: BLAST (Section 13.2), TMHMM [39], ClustalW [43], and HMMER [44].

The task allocation algorithm of GeneGrid assigns the machine with lowest load to a given task. In this decision, only the nodes that are enabled to execute the particular bioinformatics task participate.

GeneGrid successfully used multiple clusters to execute a workflow for detecting antigenic regions.

13.4.3   GrADS for FASTA Applications

GrADS (Grid Application Development Software) [45] is developed at Rice University as a generic framework to execute complex applications on a grid environment.

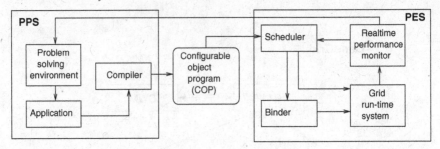

Figure 13.4. GrADS architecture.

It has two main modules: Program Preparation System (PPS) and Program Execution System (PES). PPS receives the application source code and analyses it, generating an intermediate representation, called *configurable object program* (COP), which contains, besides the application code, a performance model and data mappers. The PES is responsible for resource management, including discovery, scheduling, execution, and monitoring. An application-specific performance model is used for task allocation. Having decided the node that will execute a given task, the COP is compiled by the PES to a resource-specific format. The main modules that compose the GrADS architecture are illustrated in Fig. 13.4.

When a user wants to execute a bioinformatics application on GeneGrid, he/she must provide an XML workflow description to the GrADS, which is built upon the Globus Toolkit (Section 13.3) and uses its Monitoring and Discovery System (MDS) as well as the Network Weather Service (NWS) [46] for resource discovery.

Yarkan and Dongarra [47] proposed a master–slave grid-based approach to run FASTA (Section 13.2) on GrADS. The genomic databases are partially replicated in the worker nodes. Task allocation considers some static and dynamic metrics concerning machine and network characteristics, obtained from the resource discovery service. Moreover, some experiments are executed over multiple query sequences and databases, in order to obtain an estimate of the node's execution times. Having these data, the scheduler assigns tasks to nodes using a linear approximation of the performance model and considering data locality. Other task allocation algorithms based on simulated annealing and exhaustive search can also be used.

13.4.4   GridBLAST

GridBLAST [48] is a master–slave grid application based on NCBI-BLAST (Section 13.2.3.2) that uses Globus 2.

It distributes sequences to be compared (queries) among the grid nodes using two task allocation policies: *First Come First Served* and *minmax*. Of those, only the last one takes into consideration the current load and the heterogeneity of the environment. However, to use *minmax*, the total execution time of each BLAST task in each node must be known.

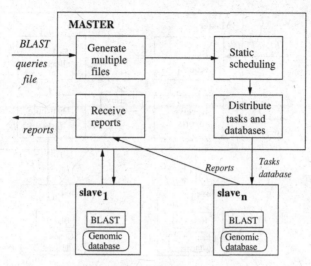

Figure 13.5. GridBLAST architecture.

Having decided which sequences will be compared by each node, GridBLAST sends the sequences, the executable files, and the whole database to be searched to the chosen node, which executes BLAST. If the chosen node is a cluster, the program *Scatter* is used. When the search finishes, the results are compacted and sent to the master node, which gathers all results and places them into a single directory.

Figure 13.5 illustrates the GridBLAST architecture.

The test environment used was a grid composed of three nodes disposed in two different networks and the database searched was *nr*.

13.4.5 GridBLAST Toolkit

GridBLAST Toolkit (GBTK) [49] was developed at the Centre for Development of Advanced Computing, India. It offers a framework and a Web portal to execute BLAST searches in a Web service environment. The authors state that GBTK can be easily extended to run on Globus 3.

All genetic databases that will be used by BLAST are statically placed on the grid nodes (without replication). The BLAST service offered by GBTK is a master–slave application that receives the sequences to be compared and the name of the genetic database to be used (Fig. 13.6). It then verifies if the node that contains the database is available. If so, it is selected to do the search. If the node is not available, the less loaded node is chosen and the database is copied to it.

GBTK also maintains services to obtain CPU load of a given node, detect failures, and transfer and receive files. The CPU load service is responsible to obtain the utilization ration of a given node. Failures are detected by a heartbeat program that is installed in each grid node. The file services are used to copy the genomic databases among nodes.

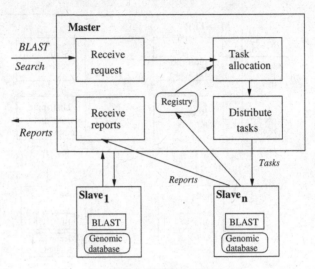

Figure 13.6. GBTK architecture.

The tests were conducted on a set of clusters and desktop machines interconnected by a campus-wide network.

13.4.6   PackageBLAST

PackageBLAST [50] was developed at the University of Ottawa and University of Brasilia. It is a master–slave grid service that executes BLAST searches on segmented biological databases. Segmentation is a well-known technique to reduce input/output (I/O) overhead that splits a database archive in many smaller portions, called segments [51]. In PackageBlast, the genomic database is segmented with an NCBI tool called *formatdb*. The segmented database is fully replicated in all participating nodes.

In order to decide which grid node will process a given database segment, Package-Blast uses an adaptive multipolicy task allocation approach. An allocation framework allows the user to integrate multiple task allocation policies with PackageBLAST. By now, the framework contains five allocation policies: Fixed, SS, GSS, TSS, and FAC2, all described in Section 13.3.

Moreover, a strategy called PSS (Package Weighted Adaptive Self-Scheduling) is used to adapt the chosen allocation policy to a heterogeneous grid environment with local workload. Considering the heterogeneity and dynamic characteristics of the grid, PSS is able to modify the length of the tasks during execution on the basis of the average processing time needed to compare some database segments in each grid node. To distribute database segments to nodes, the master analyzes periodic notifications sent by the slaves, reporting the progress in processing tasks.

PackageBLAST was designed as a grid service over Globus 3 (Section 13.3.1) on the basis of Web Services and Java. Figure 13.7 illustrates the PackageBLAST architecture.

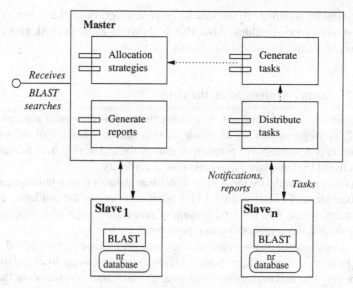

Figure 13.7. PackageBLAST architecture.

The module *Allocation Strategies* contains implementations for the predefined allocation policies—Fixed, SS, GSS, TSS, and FAC2 (Section 13.3.3)—and also makes possible the creation of new allocation strategies through the implementation of the interface *AllocationStrategy* that receives as input parameters the total number of tasks and nodes.

The module *Generate Work Units* is the core of the PSS mechanism. It calculates the weight of each slave node and decides how many work units will be assigned to a particular slave node, according to the current allocation policy.

Distribute Work Units is the module that is responsible for the communication between the master and slaves nodes. It distributes the work units generated by the previous module and collects the notifications.

Finally, the module *Generate Reports* obtains the intermediary outputs sent by the slave nodes through file transfer and merges them into a single BLAST output report.

In general, the following execution flow is executed. The user specifies the sequence to be compared and chooses the allocation strategy through the BLAST submission interface.

The master node starts execution and waits for slave connections. To start processing, a minimum number of slaves must register into the master node, by calling a master grid service. After receiving connections from the slaves, the master uses the Globus 3 notification mechanism to inform them about their initial segments to compare. The slaves process τ database segments and notify the master, which uses this information to compute the next allocation block size on the basis of the selected allocation strategy and the weight provided by PSS. Then, the master sends an XML message to the slave informing its new segments to process. This flow continues until all segments are processed.

The results obtained in a 16-node heterogeneous grid with the *nr* genomic database present very good speedups. Also, PSS is shown to adapt the task allocation policy to short-lived and long-lived local tasks.

13.4.7   Smith—Waterman on the Grid

A master–slave grid approach to execute the Smith–Waterman algorithm (Section 13.2.2) is proposed in [52]. In this algorithm, the computation of the similarity array presents a nonuniform parallelism that evolves as waves over the antidiagonals (wavefront) [51] and has a quadratic time complexity.

In order to parallelize the Smith–Waterman algorithm on a homogeneous cluster, the fixed strategy (Section 13.3.3.1) is often used, where the similarity array is split in P parts, where P is the total amount of processors. Each node calculates a set of columns, and the neighbors communicate with each other.

In a heterogeneous environment such as a grid, this equal workload distribution must be revised. The strategy used in [52] mixes heterogeneous fixed and dynamic load balancing. The heterogeneous fixed strategy takes into consideration the processor speeds and the intercluster network bandwidths to divide the array into sets of adjacent columns equal to the number of clusters. Dynamic load balancing is achieved in the following way. The worker nodes report their progress to the scheduler. Using these notifications, the scheduler produces a new instance of task allocation. A metric called NP (node performance) is used to determine if this new task allocation must be used. If this is the case, the scheduler broadcasts the task allocation instance to the workers, which will adapt their computations by exchanging data between neighbors.

Figure 13.8 illustrates the interaction between the components of this system.

Three 8-node clusters located at two different research centers and interconnected by Myrinet were used to evaluate the approach. A two-layer software architecture is used. The upper layer uses Globus 3 and mpich-G2 to deal with intercluster management and communication. At each cluster (bottom layer), Sun Grid Engine (SGE) is used to allocate tasks within the nodes of a single cluster. Processes on the same cluster communicate through mpich.

13.4.8   Comparative Overview

Table 13.2 presents a comparative view of the systems described in the previous sections. With the exception of GBTK, all analyzed systems use Globus as a grid middleware. This seems to corroborate the idea that Globus is the *de facto* middleware for grid computing.

Moreover, all analyzed systems provide ways to execute sequence comparison bioinformatics applications. Most of them support the execution of BLAST. Smith–Waterman and FASTA are executed by *FASTA on Grid* and *SW on grid*. Besides executing sequence comparison applications, GADU and GeneGrid also execute applications that provide topology prediction of proteins (TMHMM), multiple sequence alignment (ClustalW) and protein profile alignment (HMMER), among

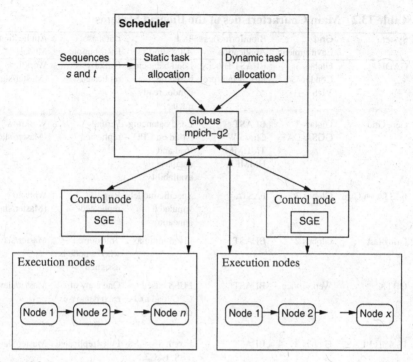

Figure 13.8. Interaction among the components to calculate the similarity matrix in a hierarchical grid.

others. Also, bioinformatics tools that search specific databases (PFAM, Blocks, and Interpro) are provided by GADU.

The task allocation used by a system depends on the class of applications that are addressed. With the exception of SW on grid, all systems focus on master–slave applications. Among those, only GridBlast does not try to achieve load balancing. GADU uses the response time of a test program and the size of the ready queue to choose the less loaded node. GBTK uses a metric to calculate the CPU load combined with the fact that the requested database is local. FASTA on grid uses both CPU and network load metrics. PackageBlast uses the notifications of progress that are periodically sent by the slaves to infer their load. SW on grid uses CPU and network load metrics to decide how to distribute the computation of the columns of the similarity array among the processors. Progress notifications are examined periodically and work redistribution can occur.

Concerning the genomic database placement, three systems (GADU, GeneGrid, and FASTA on grid) use a partial replication strategy. GBTK places only one copy of each database in different nodes, with no replication. PackageBlast uses a full replication strategy, and GridBlast transfers the database to the node, when it is assigned to execute the bioinformatics task. SW on grid does not use genomic databases, since its goal is to compare two biological sequences.

Table 13.2   Main Characteristics of the Biogrid Systems

System	Grid Environment	Bioinformatics Application	Task Allocation	Database Distribution	Application Model
GADU	Globus 3 Condor-G VDS	BLAST Blocks PFAM Interpro	Load balancing based on condor ready queue	Partially replicated	Workflow (Master/slave)
GeneGrid	Globus 3 OGSA-DAI	BLAST ClustalW TMHMM HMMER	Load balancing based on CPU load and database availability	Partially replicated	Workflow (Master/slave)
FASTA on Grid	Globus 3	FASTA	Specific model, simulated annealing	Partially replicated	Workflow (Master/slave)
GridBlast	Globus 2	BLAST	Fixed minmax	Transferred when a node is assigned	Master/slave
GBTK	Web service	BLAST	FCFS based on CPU load and data locality	One copy of each database	Master/slave
PackageBLAST	Globus 3	BLAST	Fixed, SS, GSS TSS, FAC2, others (local load)	Fully replicated	Master/slave
SW on grid	Globus 3	SW	Fixed heterogeneous and dynamic load balancing	NA	Wavefront neighbor communication

As said before, most systems use the master–slave model to execute the applications. Three of them (GADU, GeneGrid, and FASTA on grid) support the execution of workflows, where each component is itself a master–slave application. The most unusual approach is the one adopted by SW on grid, which executes a wavefront parallel application, with communication between the neighbors. In this case, the grid is seen as a set of heterogeneous clusters.

13.5   CONCLUSION

A great number of the advances achieved by molecular biology in the last years were supported by bioinformatics tools and algorithms. However, the huge sizes of the genomic databases and their exponential growth rate indicate that very powerful resources must be aggregated for results to be produced in a reasonable time. Therefore, the execution of bioinformatics tools in distributed platforms such as a grid seems to be a natural evolution.

In this chapter, we discussed in detail the problem of biological sequence comparison, which is a basic problem in bioinformatics, often used as part of the solution for more complex biological applications. We also presented the main concepts involved in grid computing, with emphasis on task allocation. In Section 13.4, seven grid initiatives were discussed and compared.

Grids for bioinformatics is a very recent research area, since most initiatives were proposed after 2003. However, the number of existing projects is growing fast and, in the coming years, we will probably see the bioinformatics grids as a common reality. To achieve that, a lot of work has been done but there is still a lot left to do. One issue that must be addressed is how to provide fault tolerance, since the grid is highly dynamic and composed by autonomous resources. Besides that, scalability issues must be addressed, since next-generation grids will probably be composed of thousands or even millions of resources.

REFERENCES

1. L. Smarr, C.L. Cattlet, Metacomputing, *Communications of the ACM* **35**(6), 44–52, 1992.

2. I. Foster, C. Kesselman, *The Grid: Blueprint of a Future Computing Infrastructure*, Morgan Kauffman, San Francisco, 1999.

3. J. Nabrzyski, J. Schopf, J. Weglarz, *Grid Resource Management: State of the Art and Future Trends*, Kluwer Academic Publishers, Dordrecht, 2003.

4. I. Foster, C. Kesselman, Globus: A metacomputing infrastructure toolkit, *International Journal of Supercomputer Applications* **11**(2), 115–128, 1997.

5. G. Shao, Adaptive scheduling of master/worker applications on distributed computational resources, PhD Thesis, University of California at San Diego, 2001.

6. J.C. Setubal, J. Meidanis, *Introduction to Computational Molecular Biology*, Brooks/Cole Publishing Company, Pacific Grove, CA, 1997.

7. D. Gusfield, *Algorithms on Strings, Trees and Sequences*, Cambridge University Press, New York, 1997.

8. G. Navarro, A guided tour to approximate string matching, *ACM Computing Surveys* **33**(1), 31–88, 2001.

9. M. Dayhoff, R.M. Schwartz, B.C. Ortcutt, A model of evolutionary changes in proteins, *Atlas of Protein Sequence and Structure* **5**, 345–352, 1978.

10. S. Henikoff, J.G. Henikoff, Amino acid substitution matrices from protein blocks, *Proceedings of the National Academy of Sciences of the United States of America* **89**, 10915–10919, 1992.

11. S.B. Needleman, C.D. Wunsch, A general method applicable to the search for similarities in the amino acid sequences of two proteins, *Journal of Molecular Biology* **48**, 443–453, 1970.

12. T.F. Smith, M.S. Waterman, Identification of common molecular subsequences, *Journal of Molecular Biology* **147**, 195–197, 1981.

13. D.S. Hirschberg, A linear space algorithm for computing maximal common subsequences, *Communications of the ACM* **18**(6), 341–343, 1975.

14. W.R. Pearson, D.J. Lipman, Improved tools for biological sequence comparison, *Proceedings of the National Academy of Sciences of the United States of America* **85**, 2444–2448, 1988.

15. S.F. Altschul, W. Gish, W. Miller, E.W. Myers, D.J. Lipman, A basic local alignment search tool, *Journal of Molecular Biology* **215**, 403–410, 1990.

16. S.F. Altschul et al., Gapped blast and psi-blast: A new generation of protein database search programs, *Nucleic Acids Research* **25**(17), 3389–3402, 1997.

17. D.J. States, W. Gish, Combined use of sequence similarity and codon bias for coding region identification, *Journal of Computational Biology* **1**, 39–50, 1994.

18. I. Korf, M. Yandell, J. Bedell, *BLAST—An Essential Guide to the Basic Local Alignment Search Tool*, OReilly Associates, June 2003.

19. S. Karlin, S.F. Altschul, Methods for assessing the statistical significance of molecular sequence features by using general scores, *Proceedings of the National Academy of Sciences of the United States of America* **87**, 2264–2268, 1990.

20. Z. Zhang, A.A. Schaffer, W. Miller, T.L. Madden, D.J. Lipman, Protein sequence similarity searches using patterns as seeds, *Nucleic Acids Research* **26**(17), 3986–3990, 1998.

21. Z. Zhang, S. Schwartz, L. Wagner, W. Miller, A greedy algorithm for aligning DNA sequences, *Journal of Computational Biology* **7**(1–2), 203–214, 2000.

22. S. Schwartz, W.J. Kent, A. Smit, Z. Zhang, R. Baertsch, R.C. Hardison, D. Haussler, W. Miller, Human-mouse alignments using blastz, *Genome Research* **13**, 103–107, 2003.

23. I. Korf, W. Gish, Mpblast: Improved blast performance with multiplexed queries, *Bioinformatics* **16**(11), 1052–1053, 2000.

24. I. Foster, C. Kesselman, Gridbus technologies for service-oriented cluster and grid computing, in: *2nd IEEE International Conference on Peer-to-Peer Computing (P2P 2002)*, September 2002.

25. C. Papadimitriou, *Combinatorial Optimization: Algorithms and Complexity*, Dover Publications, Inc., Mineola, NY, 1998.

26. H.E. Rewini, T.G. Lewis, *Distributed and Parallel Computing*, Manning, Greenwich, CT, 1998.

27. P. Tang, P.C. Yew, Processor self-scheduling for multiple nested parallel loops, *International Conference on Parallel Processing (ICPP)*, pp. 528–535, 1986.

28. T.H. Tzen, L.M. Ni, Trapezoidal self-scheduling: A practical scheme for parallel compilers, *IEEE Transactions on Parallel and Distributed Systems* **4**(1), 87–98, 1993.

29. C.D. Polychronopoulos, D.J. Kuck, Guided self-scheduling: *A Practical scheduling scheme for parallel supercomputers*, IEEE transactions on computers, **36**(12), 1425–1439, December, 1987.

30. S.F. Hummel, E. Schonberg, L.E. Flynn, Factoring: *A method to schedule parallel loops, communications of the ACM* **35**(8), 1001–1016, August, 1992.

31. S.F. Hummel et al., Load sharing in heterogeneous systems via weighted factoring, in: *Proceedings of the 8th Annual ACM Symposium on Parallel Algorithms and Architectures*, pp. 318–328, 1996.

32. I. Banicescu, V. Velusamy, Performance of scheduling scientific applications with adaptive weighted factoring, in: *Proceedings of IEEE Parallel and Distributed Processing Symposium (IPDPS)— Heterogeneous Computing Workshop*, 2001.

33. H. Bast, Provably Optimal Scheduling of Similar Tasks, PhD Thesis, Saarland University, Germany, 2004.

34. D. Sulakhe, A. Rodriguez, M. Wilde, I. Foster, N. Maltsev, Using multiple grid resources for bioinformatics applications in gadu, in: *Proceedings of CCGrid 2006 Workshops (BioGrid)*, 2006.

35. J. Frey, T. Tannenbaum, I. Foster, M. Livny, S. Tuecke, Condor-G: A computation management agent for multi-institutional grids, *Journal of Cluster Computing* **5**, 237–246, 2002.

36. I. Foster, J. Voeckler, M. Wilde, Y. Zhou, Chimera: A virtual data system for representing, querying and automating data derivation, in: *Proceedings of the 14th Conference on Scientific and Statistical Database Management*, 2002.

37. A. Baterman et al., The pfam protein families database, *Nucleic Acids Research* **30**, 276–280, 2002.

38. S. Henikoff, J.G. Henikoff, S. Pietrokovski, Blocks+: a non-redundant database of protein alignment blocks derived from multiple compilations, *Bioinformatics* **15**, 237–246, 1999.

39. E. Sonnhammer, G. von Heijne, A. Krogh, A hidden markov model for predicting transmembrane helices in protein sequences, in: *International Conference on Intelligent Systems for Molecular Biology*, pp. 175–182, 1998.

40. D. Sulakhe et al., Gnare: An environment for grid based high-throughput genome analysis, in: *Proceedings of CCGrid 2005 Workshops (BioGrid)*, 2005.

41. P.V. Jithesh et al., Genegrid: Grid based solution for bioinformatics application integration and experiment execution, in: *18th IEEE Symposium on Computer-Based Medical Systems*, IEEE Computer Society, Los Alamitos, CA, pp. 523–528, June 2005.

42. M. Antonioletti et al., Ogsa-dai status report and future directions, in: *Proceedings of the UK e-Science All Hands Meeting* 2004.

43. J.D. Thompson, D.G. Higgins, T.J. Gibson, Improving the sensitiveness of progressive multiple sequence alignment through sequence weighting, position-specific gap penalties and weight matrix choice, *Nucleic Acids Research* **22**, 4673–4680, 1994.

44. S.R. Eddy, Profile hidden Markov models, *Bioinformatics* **14**, 755–763, 1998.

45. F. Berman et al., The grads project: Software support for high-level grid application development, *Journal of Supercomputing Applications* **15**(4), 327–344, 2001.

46. R. Wolski, N. Spring, J. Hayes, The network weather service: A distributed resource performance forecasting service for metacomputing, *Journal of Future Generation Computing Systems* **15**, 757–768, 1999.

47. A. Yarkhan, J.J. Dongarra, Biological sequence alignment on the computational grid using the grads framework, *Journal of Future Generation Computing Systems* **21**, 980–986, 2005.

48. A. Krishnan, GridBLAST: High throughput blast on the grid, in: *Symposium on Biocomputing*, January 2003.

49. M.K. Satish, R.R. Joshi, GBTK: A toolkit for grid implementation of blast, in: *Proceedings of the High Performance Computing and Grid in Asia Pacific Region, Seventh International Conference on (HPCAsia '04)*, pp. 378–382, January 2004.

50. M.S. Sousa, A.C.M.A. Melo, PackageBLAST: An adaptive multi-policy grid service for biological sequence comparison, in: *2006 ACM Symposium on Applied Computing (SAC)*, ACM, pp. 156–160, April 2006.

51. A. Darling, L. Carey, W. Feng, The design, implementation, and evaluation of mpiblast, ClusterWorld Conference and Expo in conjunction with the *4th International Conference on Linux Clusters: The HPC Revolution 2003*, June 2003.

52. C. Chen, B. Schmidt, An adaptive grid implementation of DNA sequence alignment, *Future Generation Computer Systems* **21**, 988–1003, 2005.

53. G. Pfister, *In Search of Clusters—The Coming Battle for Lowly Parallel Computing*, Prentice-Hall, Engelwood Cliffs, NJ, 1995.

14

RECENT ADVANCES IN SOLVING THE PROTEIN THREADING PROBLEM

Rumen Andonov, Guillaume Collet, J.-F. Gibrat, A. Marin, Vincent Poirriez, and N. Yanev

14.1 INTRODUCTION

Genome sequencing projects generate an exponentially increasing amount of raw genomic data. For a number of organisms whose genomes are sequenced, very little is experimentally known, to the point that for some of them the first experimental evidence gathered is precisely their DNA sequence. In the absence, or an extreme paucity, of experimental evidences, bioinformatic methods play a central role in exploiting the raw data. The bioinformatic process that extracts biological knowledge from raw data is known as annotation.

Annotation is composed of two phases:

1. A static phase whose purpose is to describe the basic "objects" that are found in the genome: the genes and their protein products.

2. A dynamic phase that seeks to describe the processes—that is, the complex ways in which genes and proteins interact to create functional networks that underlie the biological properties of the organism.

The first phase is the cornerstone of the annotation process. The first step consists in finding the precise location of genes on the chromosome. Then, for those genes that encode proteins, the next step is to predict the associated molecular, cellular, and phenotypic functions. This is often referred to as *in silico* functional annotation. Different methods exist for predicting protein functions, and the most important of which are based on the properties of homologous proteins.

Homology is a key concept in biology. It refers to the fact that two proteins are related by descent from a common ancestor. Homologous proteins have the following properties:

Grid Computing for Bioinformatics and Computational Biology. Edited by E.-G. Talbi and A.Y. Zomaya.
Copyright © 2008 John Wiley & Sons, Inc.

- They may have sequences that, despite the accumulated mutations, still resemble the ancestor sequence.
- Their three-dimensional structures are similar to the structure of the ancestor.
- They may have conserved the ancestor function or at least a related function.

Therefore, the principle of *in silico* functional analysis, *in silico* functional analysis based on homology searches, is to infer a homology relationship between a protein whose function is known and the new protein under study, and then to transfer the function of the former to the latter.

The inference of the homology relationship is based on the previously listed properties of homologous proteins. The first developed methods used the first property, and the conservation of the sequences, and were based on sequence comparisons using alignment tools such as PSI-BLAST [1].

These methods are still the workhorses of *in silico* functional annotation: They are fast and endowed with a very good statistical criterion allowing to judge when two proteins are homologous. Unfortunately, they also have a drawback. They are very inefficient when the proteins under study happen to be remote homologs—that is, when their common ancestor is very ancient. In such a case, the sequences may have undergone many mutations and they are no longer sufficiently similar for the proteins to be recognized as homologous.

For instance, when analyzing prokaryotic genomes, these techniques cannot provide any information about the function of a noticeable fraction of the genome proteins (between 25% and 50% according to the organism studied). Such proteins are known as "orphan" proteins. One also speaks of orphan families when several homologous proteins are found in newly sequenced genomes that cannot be linked to any protein with a known function.

To overcome this problem, new methods have been developed that are based on the second property: the good conservation of the 3D structure of homologous proteins. These methods are known as threading methods or, more formally, as fold[1] recognition methods.

The rationale behind these methods is threefold:

1. As mentioned above, 3D structures of homologous proteins are much better conserved than the corresponding amino acid sequences. Numerous cases of proteins with similar folds and the same functions are known, though having less than 20% sequence identity [2].

2. There is a limited, relatively small, number of protein structural families. Exact figures are still a matter of debate and vary from 1000 [3] to, at most, a few thousands [4]. According to the statistics of the Protein Data Bank (PDB),[2] there are about 700 (CATH definition [5]) or 1000 (SCOP definition [6]) different 3D structure families that have been experimentally determined so far.

---

[1] in this context, fold refers to the protein 3D structure.
[2] http://www.rcsb.pdb/

3. Different types of amino acids have different preferences for occupying a particular structural environment (being in an α-helix, being in a β-sheet, and being buried or exposed). These preferences are the basis for the empirically calculated score functions that measure the fitness of a given alignment between a sequence and a 3D structure.

On the basis of these facts, threading methods consist in aligning a query protein sequence with a set of 3D protein structures to check whether the sequence might be compatible with one of the structures. These methods consist of the following components:

- A database of representative 3D structural templates
- An objective function (score function) that measures the fitness of the sequence for the 3D structure
- An algorithm for finding the optimal alignment of a sequence onto a structural template (with respect to the objective function)
- A statistical analysis of the raw scores allowing the detection of significant sequence–structure alignments

To develop an effective threading method, all these components must be properly addressed. A description of the implementation of these different components in the Fold Recognition-Oriented Search Tool (FROST) method [7] is detailed in the next section. Let us note that, from a computer scientist's viewpoint, the third component above is the most challenging part of the treading method development. It has been shown that, in the most general case, when variable length alignment gaps are allowed and pairwise amino acid interactions are considered in the score function, the problem of aligning a sequence onto a 3D structure is NP-hard [8]. Until recently, it was the main obstacle to the development of efficient threading methods. During the last few years, much progress has been accomplished toward a solution of this problem for most real-life instances [9–14].

Despite these improvements, threading methods, like a number of other bioinformatic applications, have high computational requirements. For example, in order to analyze the orphan proteins that are found in prokaryotic genomes, a back-of-the-envelope computation shows that one needs to align $500,000^3$ protein sequences with at least 1000 3D structures. This represents 500 millions alignments. Solving such a quantity of alignments is, of course, not easily tractable on a single computer. Only a cluster of computers, or even a grid, can manage such a amount of computations. Fortunately, as we will show hereafter, it is relatively straightforward to distribute these computations on a cluster of processors or over a grid of computers.

---

[3] This figure corresponds to the number of sequenced genomes (500) times the average number of proteins per genome (3000) times the mean fraction of orphan proteins ($\frac{1}{3}$).

Grids are emerging as a powerful tool to improve effectiveness of bioinformatics applications, particularly for protein threading. For example, the encyclopedia of life project [15] integrates 123D+ threading package in its distributed pipeline. All the pipeline processes, from DNA sequence to protein structure modeling, are parallelized by a grid application execution environment called APST (application-level scheduling parameter sweep template). Another distributed pipeline for protein structure prediction is proposed by Steinke et al. [16]. Their pipeline consists of three steps : a preprocessing phase by sequence alignments, a protein threading phase, and a final 3D refinement. Their threading algorithm solves the alignment problem by a parallel implementation of a branch-and-bound optimizer using the score function of Xu et al. [17]. With a cluster of 16 nodes, they divided by 2 the computation time of aligning 572 sequences with about 37,500 structures from the PDB.

To maintain a structural annotation database up to date (project e-protein[4]), McGuffin and colleagues describe a fold recognition method distributed on a grid with the job yield distribution environment (JYDE) system, which is a meta-scheduler for clusters of computers. To annotate the human genome, they use their mGen THREADER software integrated with JYDE on three different grid systems. On these three independent clusters of 148,243, and 192 CPUs (515 CPUs), the human genome annotations can be updated in about 24 h.

The rest of this chapter is organized as follows. In Section 14.2, we present basic features of the FROST method. Section 14.3 further details the mathematical techniques used to tackle the difficult problem of aligning a sequence onto a 3D structure. Section 14.4 introduces the different operations required in FROST to make the entire procedure modular and describes how the modules can be distributed and executed in parallel on a cluster of computers. Computational benchmarks of the parallelized version of FROST are presented in Section 14.5. In Section 14.6, we discuss future research directions.

14.2 FROST: A FOLD RECOGNITION METHOD

14.2.1 Definition of Protein Cores

Threading methods require a database of representative 3D structures. The PDB that gathers all publicly available 3D structures contains about 40,000 structures. However, this database is extremely redundant. Analyses of the PDB show that it contains at most about 1000 different folds [6]. In theory, only these folds need to be taken into consideration. In practice, to obtain a denser coverage of the 3D structure space, the PDB proteins are clustered into groups having more than 30% sequence identity and the best specimen of each group (in terms of quality of the 3D structure: high resolution, small R factor, no, or few, missing residues) is selected. The final database contains about 4500 3D structures.

[4]http://www.e-protein.org/

For the purpose of fold recognition, the whole 3D structure is not required, but only those parts of the structure that are the characteristic of the structural family need to be considered. This leads to the notion of structural family core. The core is defined as those parts that are conserved in all the 3D structures of the family and are thus distinctive of the corresponding fold.

There are two practical reasons for using cores:

1. Aligning a sequence onto the portions of the 3D structure that are not conserved is likely to introduce a noise that would make the detection process more difficult.

2. By definition, no insertion or deletion is permitted within core elements, since otherwise they would not be the conserved parts of the family structures.

In protein families one often observes that the conserved framework of the 3D structure consists of the periodic secondary structures α helices and β strands, and the loops at the surface of the protein are variable. Acgcordingly, in FROST the core of the protein structures is defined as consisting of the helices and strands.

Hereafter, we will refer to cores instead of 3D structures or folds.

14.2.2 Score Function

To evaluate the fitness of a sequence, for a particular core, we need an objective (or score) function. There are two categories of score functions: "local" and "nonlocal." The former ones are, in essence, similar to the score functions used in sequence alignment methods. The latter ones consider pairs of residues in the core and are specific of threading methods.

In threading methods, a schematic description of the core structure is used instead of a full atomic representation. Each residue in the core is represented by a single *site*. In FROST, it is the Cα of the residue in the structure. Each site is characterized by its *state*, which is a simplified representation of its environment in the core. A state is defined by the type of secondary structure (α helix, β strand, or coil) in which the corresponding residue is found and by its solvent accessibility (buried if less than 25% of the residue surface in the core is accessible to the solvent, exposed if more than 60% is accessible, and intermediate otherwise). This defines nine states, for instance, the site is located in a helix and exposed, or in a strand and buried, and so on.

In FROST we use a canonical expression for the score function. Altschul [18] has shown that the most general form of a score for comparing sequences is a log-likelihood:

$$\text{score}(r_i, r_j) = \log \frac{P(r_i r_j | E)}{P(r_i)P(r_j)}$$

The score of replacing amino acid r_i by amino acid r_j is the log of the ratios of two probabilities:

1. The probability that the two amino acids are related by evolution, that is, they are aligned in the sequence because they evolved from the same ancestral amino acid;

2. The probability that the two amino acids are aligned just by chance.

If the two amino acids, on average, in a number of protein families, are observed to be more often aligned than expected by chance; that is, if the numerator probability is greater than the product of the denominator probabilities, then the ratio is greater than 1 and the score is positive. On the contrary, if the two amino acids are observed to be less often aligned than expected by chance, the score is negative.

These considerations led to the development of empirical substitution matrices (for instance, the PAM [19] or BLOSUM matrices [20]) that gather the scores for replacing a given amino acid by another one during a given period of evolution. Finding the optimal alignment score for two sequences amounts to maximizing the probability that these two sequences have evolved from a common ancestor as opposed to being random sequences (assuming that the alignment positions are independent).

Very similar matrices can be developed for threading methods, except that we now have at our disposal an extra piece of information: the three-dimensional structure of one of the sequences. Therefore, we can define a set of nine state-dependent substitution matrices as

$$\text{score}(R_i, r_j)_{S_k} = \log \frac{P(R_i r_j | E)_{S_k}}{P(R_i)_{S_k} P(r_j)} \tag{14.1}$$

where $P(R_i)_{S_i}$ is the probability of observing amino acid R_i in state S_k, $P(r_j)$ is the background probability of amino acid r_j in the sequence database, and $P(R_i r_j | E)_{S_k}$ is the probability of observing amino acids R_i and r_j aligned in sites with state S_k in protein families. Note that throughout this section uppercases are used for residues that belong to the core and lowercases for residues that belong to the sequence that is aligned onto the core.

This expression represents the score for replacing amino acid R_i by amino acid r_j in a particular state (see Fig. 14.1). In addition, since we know the 3D structure, it is possible to use gap penalties that prevent insertion/deletion in core elements. This provides a score function that is local; that is, a score depends on a single site in a particular sequence. However, with this kind of score, we do not use the real 3D structure but only some of its properties that are embodied in the state (type of secondary structure and solvent accessibility).

In order to explicitly take into account the 3D structure, we must generalize these state-dependent substitution matrices. This is done by considering pairs of residues that are in contact in the core. In FROST, residues are defined to be in contact in a three-dimensional structure if there exists at least one pair of atoms, one atom from each residue side chain, for which the distance is less than a given cutoff value. The

H	H	H	C	C	E	E	E	E	–	–	–	C	C	C
e	e	e	b	b	e	b	b	b	–	–	–	b	e	e
He	He	He	Cb	Cb	Ee	Eb	Eb	Eb	–	–	–	Cb	Ce	Ce
M	F	T	V	N	V	H	I	D	–	–	–	R	L	Y
m	w	t	–	–	v	h	v	e	h	g	v	r	v	y
•							•							

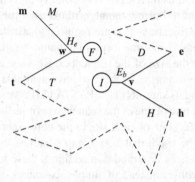

Figure 14.1. Upper part: 1D alignment of two sequences, the query sequence (fifth row) is shown in bold lowercase letters and the core sequence (fourth row) in slanted uppercase letters. The first row is the observed secondary structure: helix (*H*), strand (*E*), or coil (*C*). The second row is the solvent accessibility: exposed (*e*) or buried (*b*). The third row is the corresponding state. Deletion is indicated by dashes. In the core, we focus on the second and eight sites, labeled with black circles. The state of the eight site is *Eb*—that is, an exposed strand. To score this position in the core, we must use score$(I, v)_{E_b}$, the score of replacing an isoleucine by a valine in an exposed-strand environment ($R_i = I$, $r_j = v$, and $S_k = Eb$ in the corresponding equation). Also note that since we are in a strand, a specific gap penalty must be used. Lower part: The 3D alignment of the same two sequences. In the 3D structure, the above two sites are in contact. To score this interaction, we must use score$(FI, wv)_{HeEb}$, the score of replacing the pair *FI* by the pair *wv* in an exposed helical–buried strand environment ($R_i = F$, $R_j = I$, $r_k = w$, $r_l = v$, $S_n = He$, and $S_m = Eb$ in the corresponding equation). Here, since we are in core elements, no insertion/deletion is allowed.

corresponding score function is defined as

$$\text{score}(R_i R_j, r_k r_l)_{S_n S_m} = \log \frac{P(R_i R_j r_k r_l | E)_{S_n S_m}}{P(R_i R_j)_{S_n S_m} P(r_k, r_l)} \qquad (14.2)$$

where $P(R_i R_j)_{S_n S_m}$ is the probability of observing the pair of amino acids R_i and R_j at sites that are in contact in protein 3D structures and are characterized, respectively, by states S_n and S_m. $P(r_k, r_l)$ is the background probability for the amino acid pair $r_k r_l$ in the sequence database. $P(R_i R_j r_k r_l | E)_{S_n S_m}$ is the probability to observe the amino acid pair $R_i R_j$ aligned with the amino acid pair $r_k r_l$ in the structural context described by states S_n and S_m in protein families.

This expression represents the score for replacing the pair of amino acids $R_i R_j$ by the pair $r_k r_l$ in sites that are characterized by states S_n and S_m and are in contact in protein cores (see Fig. 14.1). There are 89 such matrices. This type of score function is nonlocal since it takes into account two sites in the sequence. As we will describe in the next section, the fact that the score function is local or nonlocal has a profound influence on the type of algorithm that needs to be used for aligning the sequence onto the core.

14.2.3   Sequence–Core Alignment Algorithms

For local score functions there exist very efficient algorithms to align sequences with cores. It is sufficient to borrow the algorithms used for sequence alignments and to make the slight modifications that are required to adapt them to our problem. These algorithms are all based on some forms of dynamic programming [21,22] and thus are of $O(N^2)$, N being the size of the sequences. Besides, if the computational requirements are of prime importance, we also have available fast and accurate heuristics (such as BLAST and its variants [1] or FASTA [23]). As shown in Fig. 14.1 the knowledge of the 3D structure of one of the sequence permits the use of substitution matrices that are proper to the state of each site in the core. Secondary structure-specific gap penalties can also be used; that is the, gap penalties that make insertions/deletions more difficult in helices or strands. In addition, these techniques readily enable the use of sequence profiles instead of simple sequences, a procedure that is known to improve the sensitivity of sequence comparison methods [24].

On the contrary, nonlocal score functions do not permit the use of algorithms based on dynamic programming. Indeed, all dynamic programming techniques are based on a recursive procedure whereby an optimal solution for a given problem is built from previously found subproblem optimal solutions. For instance, for sequence alignments, the optimal score for aligning two substrings $s[1 \ldots i]$ and $t[1 \ldots j]$ is obtained from the optimal solutions previously found for aligning substrings $s[1 \ldots i-1]$ with $t[1 \ldots j-1]$, $s[1 \ldots i-1]$ with $t[1 \ldots j]$, and $s[1 \ldots i]$ with $t[1 \ldots j-1]$ by the following recurrence expression:

$$A[i, j] = \max \begin{cases} A[i-1, j] + gp \\ A[i-1, j-1] + c(s[i], t[j]) \\ A[i, j-1] + gp \end{cases}$$

where $A[k, l]$ is the optimal score for aligning substring $s[1 \ldots k]$ with substring $t[1 \ldots l]$, gp is the cost of a gap, and $c(s[i], t[j])$ is the cost for aligning the ith letter of string s with the jth letter of string t.

Nonlocal score functions ruin this recursive procedure since now the score for aligning two sequences not only exclusively depends on the optimal score of previous subsequences but also depends on the interactions with distant residues.

As a consequence, the first threading methods proposed relied on various heuristics to align sequences onto cores, for instance, Madej et al. [25] used a stochastic technique in the form of a Gibbs Monte Carlo.

Lathrop [8] showed that, in the most general case, the problem of aligning a sequence onto a core with a nonlocal score function is NP-hard. A few years later, Akutsu and Miyano [26] showed that it is MAX-SNP-hard, meaning that there is no arbitrary close polynomial approximation algorithm unless P = NP.

Lathrop and Smith [9] were the first to propose an algorithm, based on a branch-and-bound technique that provided, for small instances, an exact solution to the problem. Uberbacher and colleagues [17], a couple of years later, described another algorithm based on a divide-and-conquer approach. These two algorithms were, apparently, rather slow and only able to cope with the easiest problems. They were not implemented in an actual threading method, to the best of our knowledge.

At the turn of the century, new methods based on advanced mathematical programming methods, mixed integer programming (MIP), were developed [10,11,14,27,28] that were able to tackle the most difficult instances of the problem in a reasonable amount of time. Two protein threading packages are currently available that implement exact methods based on the latter approach: RAPTOR[5] [12] and FROST[6] [7]. In Section 14.3, we will describe in more details the FROST implementation of the MIP models. Other interesting integer programming approaches for solving combinatorial optimization problems that originate in molecular biology are discussed in recent surveys [29,30].

14.2.4 Significance of Scores

Equipped with the above techniques, we are able to get an optimal score for aligning any sequence onto a database of cores. We are now faced with the problem of the significance of this score. Let us assume that we have aligned a particular sequence with a core and got a score of 60. What does this score of 60 mean? Is it the representative of a sequence that is compatible with the core? In other words, if we align a number of randomly chosen sequences with this core, what kind of score distribution are we going to obtain? If, for a noticeable fraction of these alignments, one gets scores greater than or equal to 60, it is likely that the initial score is not very significant (unless, of course, all the chosen sequences are related to the core).

Similar questions arise when one compares two sequences. Statistical analyses have been carried out to study this problem, and it has been shown [31] that the distribution of scores for ungapped local alignments of random sequences follows an extreme value distribution. The parameters of this distribution can be analytically calculated from the features of the problem: type of substitution matrix used, size of the aligned sequences, background frequencies of the amino acids, and so on. When gaped alignments are considered, it is no longer possible to perform analytical calculations, but computer experiments have shown that the shape of the empirical distribution is still an extreme value distribution whose parameters can be readily determined from a set of sequence comparison scores.

Such analytical calculation cannot be done for a sequence–core alignment. In fact, we do not even know the shape of the score distribution for aligning randomly chosen sequences onto cores, although some preliminary work seems to indicate that it could also be an extreme value distribution [32].

---

[5]http://www.bioinformaticssolutions.com/
[6]http://genome.jouy.inra.fr/frost/

In FROST, to solve this problem, we adopt a pragmatic but a rather costly approach. For each core, we randomly extract from the database five sets of 200 sequences unrelated to the core. Each set contains sequences whose size corresponds to a percentage of the core size, that is, 30% shorter, 15% shorter, same size as the core, 15% longer, and 30% longer. The assumption behind this procedure is that when a sequence is compatible with a core, its length must be similar to the core length ($\pm 30\%$).[7] We align the sequences of each set with the core. This provides empirical distributions of scores for aligning sequences with different lengths onto the core. For each distribution, we determine the median and the third quartile and we compute a normalized score as

$$S_n = \frac{S - q_2}{q_3 - q_2}$$

where S_n is the normalized score, S is the score of the query sequence, q_2 and q_3 are, respectively, the median and third quartile of the empirical distribution.

This normalized score allows us to compare the alignments of the query sequence onto different cores. The larger the normalized score, the more probable the existence of a relationship between the sequence and the core. Indeed, a large normalized score indicates that the query sequence is not likely to belong to the population of unrelated sequences from which the score distribution was computed. Unfortunately, since we do not know the shape or the parameters of the distributions, we cannot compute a precise probability for the sequence to belong to this population of unrelated sequences. We use empirical results obtained on a test database to estimate when a normalized score is significant at the 99% level of confidence [7,33] (see next section).

When we need to align a new query sequence whose length is not exactly one of the above lengths that were used to precalculate the score distributions, we linearly interpolate the values of the median and the third quartile from those of the two nearest distributions. For instance, if the size of the new query sequence is 20% larger than the size of the core, the corresponding median and third quartile values are given by

$$q_n^{20} = q_n^{15} + \frac{20 - 15}{30 - 15}(q_n^{30} - q_n^{15})$$

where q_n^L represents the median ($n = 2$) or the third quartile ($n = 3$) of the score distribution when sequences of length L are aligned onto the core.

14.2.5   Integrating All the Components: The FROST Method

FROST is intended to assess the reliability of fold assignments to a given protein sequence (hereafter called a query sequence or query for short) [7,33]. To perform this task, FROST uses a series of filters, each one possessing a specific scoring function

---

[7]This is the assumption in case of a global alignment. In Section 14.6 we will consider more general types of alignments, semiglobal and local, for which this assumption does not hold.

that measures the fitness of the query sequence for template cores. The version we describe here possesses two filters.

The first filter is based on a fitness function whose parameters involve only a local description of proteins and corresponds to Equation (14.1). This filter belongs to the category of profile–profile alignment methods and is called a 1D filter. The algorithm used to find the optimal alignment score is based on dynamic programming techniques.

The second filter employs the nonlocal score function (14.2). Because it makes the use of spatial information, it is called a 3D filter in the following. As explained in Section 14.2.3, this type of score function requires dedicated algorithms for aligning the query sequence onto the cores. The algorithm used in FROST, based on a MIP model, is further described in the next section.

FROST functions as a sieve. The 1D filter is fast owing to its dynamic programming algorithm of quadratic complexity. It is used to compare the query sequence with all the database cores and rank them in a list according to the normalized scores. Only the first N cores from this list are then passed to the 3D filter and aligned with the query sequence.

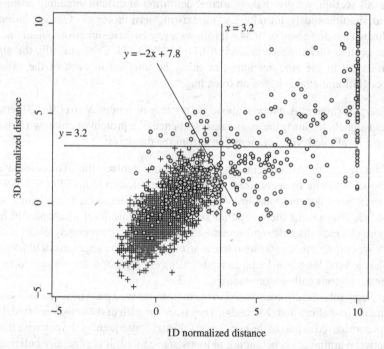

Figure 14.2. Plot of the 1D score (along the x-axis) and the 3D score (along the y-axis) for different (Q,C) pairs (where Q is a query sequence and C is a core). Gray open circles represent (Q,C) pairs that are related, black crosses (Q,C) represent pairs that are not related; that is, respectively, the query sequence is known to have the same 3D structure as the core, and the query sequence is known to have a 3D structure different from the core. The area beyond the lines indicated on the plot contains only 1% black crosses, which are thus false positives. For this example, the recall is 60% [7].

Each of the above N cores is now characterized by two normalized scores, one for the 1D filter and the other for the 3D filter. These scores can be plotted on a two-dimensional diagram. As shown in Fig. 14.2, this allows us to define the area in the diagram, delimited by line equations connecting the scores, that empirically provides a 99% confidence threshold.

Several score functions, other than the ones described in Section 14.2.2, can be developed. The only point that matters is whether these functions are local or nonlocal. The same sieve principle as the one described for the above two score functions is still applicable. The difference is that now the N resulting cores are characterized by a number of scores greater than two. This makes the visual inspection as explained above difficult, and one must rely, for instance, on a support vector machine (SVM) algorithm to find the hyperplanes that separate positive from negative cases.

14.3 FROST: A COMPUTER SCIENCE VISION

14.3.1 Formal Definition

In this section, we give a more formal definition of protein threading problem (PTP) and simultaneously introduce some existing terminologies. Our definition is very close to the one given in [9,34]. It follows a few basic assumptions widely adopted by the protein threading community [9,11,12,17,34,35]. Consequently, the algorithms presented in the next sections can easily be plugged in most of the existing fold recognition methods based on threading.

Query Sequence. A query sequence is a string of length N over the 20-letter amino acid alphabet. This is the amino acid sequence of a protein of unknown structure that must be aligned with core templates from the database.

Core Template. All current threading methods replace the 3D coordinates of the known structure by an abstract template description in terms of core blocks or segments, neighbor relationships, distances, and environments, as explained in Section 14.2.2. This avoids the computational cost of atomic-level mechanics in favor of a more abstract, discrete representation of alignments between sequences and cores.

We consider that a core template is an ordered set of m segments or blocks. Segment i has a fixed length of l_i amino acids. Adjacent segments are connected by variable length regions called loops (see Fig. 14.3a).

Segments usually correspond to the most conserved parts of secondary structure elements (α-helices and β-strands). They trace the path of the conserved fold. Loops are not considered as part of the conserved fold and consequently, the pairwise interactions between amino acids belonging to loops are ignored. It is generally believed that the contribution of such interactions is relatively insignificant. The pairwise interactions between amino acids belonging to segments are represented by the so-called contact map graph (see Fig. 14.3b). Different definitions for residues in contact in the core can be used, for instance, in Reference 12 it is assumed that two amino acids interact if the distance between their C_β atoms is within p Å and they are at least P and q positions

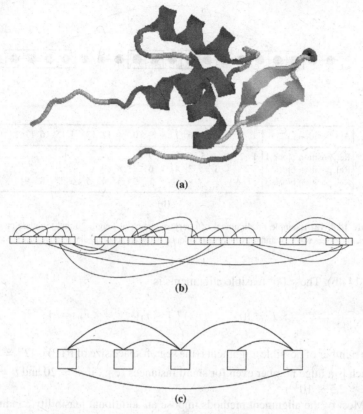

Figure 14.3. (a) 3D structure backbone showing α-helices, β-strands, and loops. (b) The corresponding contact map graph. (c) The corresponding generalized contact map graph.

apart along the template sequence (with $p = 7$ and $q = 4$). There is an interaction between two segments i and j if there is at least one pairwise interaction between amino acids belonging to i and amino acids belonging to j. Let $L \subseteq \{(i, j) \mid 1 \le i < j \le m\}$ be the set of segment interactions. The graph with vertices $\{1, \ldots, m\}$ and edges L is called generalized contact map graph (see Fig. 14.3c).

Alignments. Let us first note that in this section, we adopt an inverse perspective and describe the alignment of a sequence onto a core as positioning the segments along the sequence. The problem remains exactly the same but it is easier to describe this way. Such an alignment is called feasible if the segments preserve their original order and do not overlap (see Fig. 14.4a). an alignment is completely determined by the starting positions of all the segments along the sequence. In fact, rather than absolute positions, it is more convenient to use relative positions. If segment i starts at the kth query sequence character, its relative position is $r_i = k - \sum_{j=1}^{i-1} l_j$. In this way, the possible (relative) positions of each segment vary between 1 and $n = N + 1 - \sum_{i=1}^{m} l_i$ (see

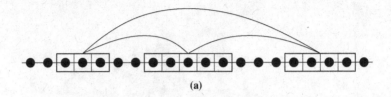

(a)

Abs.position	1	2	3	4	5	6	7	8	9	10	11	12	13	14	15	16	17	18	19	20
Rel. position block 1	1	2	3	4	5	6	7	8	9											
Rel. position block 2				1	2	3	4	5	6	7	8	9								
Rel. position block 3								1	2	3	4	5	6	7	8	9				

(b)

Figure 14.4. (a) Example of alignment of query sequence of length 20 and template containing three segments of lengths 3, 5, and 4. (b) Correspondence between absolute and relative block positions.

Fig.14.4b). The set of feasible alignments is

$$\mathcal{T} = \{(r_1, \ldots, r_m) \mid 1 \le r_1 \le \ldots \le r_m \le n\} \tag{14.3}$$

The number of possible alignments (the search space size of PTP) is $|\mathcal{T}| = \binom{m+n-1}{m}$, which is a huge number even for small instances (e.g., if $m = 20$ and $n = 100$, then $|\mathcal{T}| \approx 2.5 \times 10^{22}$).

Most of the alignment methods impose an additional feasibility condition, upper and lower bounds on the lengths of query zones not covered by segments (loops). This condition can be easily incorporated by a slight modification in the definition of relative segment position.

In the above definition, gaps are not allowed within segments. They are confined to loops. As explained above, the biological justification is that segments are conserved so that the probability of insertion or deletion within them is very small.

14.3.2   Network Flow Formulation

This section follows the formulation proposed in References 10 and 27. In order to develop appropriate mathematical models, PTP is restated as a network optimization problem. Let $G(V, A)$ be a digraph with vertex set V and arc set A. The vertex set V is organized in columns, corresponding to the segments from the aligned core. In each column, each vertex corresponds to a relative position of the corresponding segment along the sequence. Then $V = \{(i, j) \mid i = 1, \ldots, m, \ j = 1, \ldots, n\}$ with m the number of segments and n the number of relative positions (see Fig. 14.4, where $m = 6$ and $n = 3$). A cost C_{ij} is associated to each vertex (i, j) as defined by the scoring function (14.1). The arc set is divided into two subsets : A' is a subset containing arcs between adjacent segments and A'' contains arcs between remote segments. Thus,

$A = A' \cup A''$ with

$$A' = \{((i, j), (i + 1, l)) \mid i = 1, \ldots, m - 1, \; 1 \leq j \leq l \leq n\}$$
$$A'' = \{((i, j), (k, l)) \mid (i, k) \in L, \; 1 \leq j \leq l \leq n\}$$

To each arc $((i, j), (k, l))$ is associated a cost D_{ijkl} as defined by the scoring function (14.2). The arcs from A' will be referred as x arcs and the arcs from A'' as z arcs.

By adding two extra vertices S and T and the corresponding arcs $(S, (1, k))$, $k = 1, \ldots, n$ and $((m, l), T)$, $l = 1, \ldots, n$ (considered as x arcs), one can see the one-to-one correspondence between the set of the feasible threadings and the set of the S-T path on x arcs in G. We say that a S–T path *activates* its vertices and x arcs. A z arc is *activated* by a S–T path if both ends are on the path. We call the subgraph as induced by the x arcs of an S–T path and the activated z arcs *augmented path*. Then PTP is equivalent to finding the shortest augmented path in G. Figure 14.5 illustrates this correspondence.

14.3.3 Integer Programming Formulation

Let y_{ij} be the binary variables associated with vertices in the previous network. Then y_{ij} is one if segment i is at position j and zero otherwise (whether vertex (i, j) is activated or not). Let Y be the polytope defined by the following constraints:

$$\sum_{j=1}^{n} y_{ij} = 1, \qquad i = 1, \ldots, m \tag{14.4}$$

$$\sum_{l=1}^{j} y_{il} - \sum_{l=1}^{j} y_{i+1,l} \geq 0, \qquad i = 1, \ldots, m - 1, \quad j = 1, \ldots, n - 1 \tag{14.5}$$

$$y_{ij} \in \{0, 1\}, \qquad i = 1, \ldots, m, \quad j = 1, \ldots, n \tag{14.6}$$

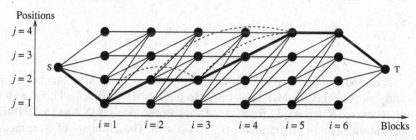

Figure 14.5. Example of alignment graph. The path in thick lines corresponds to the threading in which the positions of the blocks are 1,2,2,3,4,4. Dashed line arcs belong to A'' where the set of segment interactions is $L = \{(1, 3), (2, 5), (3, 5)\}$.

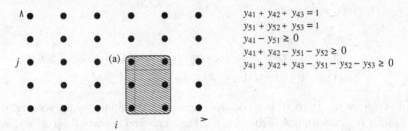

$$y_{41} + y_{42} + y_{43} = 1$$
$$y_{51} + y_{52} + y_{53} = 1$$
$$y_{41} - y_{51} \geq 0$$
$$y_{41} + y_{42} - y_{51} - y_{52} \geq 0$$
$$y_{41} + y_{42} + y_{43} - y_{51} - y_{52} - y_{53} \geq 0$$

Figure 14.6. The effect of constraints (14.4) and (14.5) on zone (a). Exactly one vertex is activated in column four and in column five. Activating a vertex at position $(4, j)$ guarantees that no vertex is activated in column five below j. If a vertex is activated in $(5, j)$, then a vertex must be activated in column four below j.

Constraint (14.4) ensures that each block is assigned to exactly one position. Constraint (14.5) describes a nondecreasing path in the alignment graph. These constraints are illustrated in Fig. 14.6.

In order to take into account the interaction costs, we introduce a second set of variables $z_{ijkl} \geq 0$, with $(i, k) \in L$ and $1 \leq j \leq l \leq n$. These variables correspond to x arcs and z arcs in the network flow formulation. For the sake of readability, we will use the notation z_a for z_{ijkl} with $a \in A$ the arc set. The variable z_{ijkl} is set to one if the corresponding arc is activated. Then, we define the following constraints:

$$y_{ij} = \sum_{l=j}^{n} z_{ijkl}, \qquad (i, k) \in L, \; j = 1, \ldots, n \qquad (14.7)$$

$$y_{kl} = \sum_{j=1}^{l} z_{ijkl}, \qquad (i, k) \in L, \; l = 1, \ldots, n \qquad (14.8)$$

$$z_a \geq 0, \qquad a \in A \qquad (14.9)$$

These constraints ensure that setting variables y_{ij} and y_{kl} to one (the path passes through these two points) activates the arc z_{ijkl}. Finding the shortest augmented path in graph G (i.e., solving PTP) is then equivalent to minimizing the following function subject to the previous constraints:

$$\sum_{i=1}^{m} \sum_{j=1}^{n} C_{ij} y_{ij} + \sum_{a \in A} D_a z_a \qquad (14.10)$$

This model, introduced in Reference 11, is known as the MYZ model. It significantly outperforms the MIP model used in the RAPTOR package [12] for all large instances (see Reference 11 for more details). Both models (MYZ and RAPTOR) are solved using a linear programming (LP) relaxation. The advantage of these models is that their LP relaxations give the optimal solution for most of the real-life instances. They have significantly better performance than the branch-and-bounds approach proposed in Reference 19. Their drawback is their huge size (both the number of variables and the number of constraints), which makes even solving the LP relaxation slow. In the next section, we present more efficient approaches for solving these models. These are based on Lagrangian relaxation (LR).

14.3.4 Lagrangian Approaches

Consider an integer program

$$z_{IP} = \min\{cx : x \in S\}, \quad \text{where } S = \{x \in Z_+^n : Ax \geq b\} \tag{14.11}$$

Relaxation and duality are the two main ways of determining z_{IP} and upper bounds for z_{IP}. The linear programming relaxation is obtained by changing the constraint $x \in Z_+^n$ in the definition of S by $x \geq 0$. The Lagrangian relaxation is very convenient for problems where the constraints can be partitioned into a set of "simple" ones and a set of "complicated" ones. Let us assume, for example, that the complicated constraints are given by $A^1 x \geq b^1$, where A^1 is $m \times n$ matrix, while the simple constraints are given by $A^2 x \geq b^2$. Then for any $\lambda \in R_+^m$ the problem

$$z_{LR}(\lambda) = \min_{x \in Q}\{cx + \lambda(b^1 - A^1 x)\}$$

where $Q = \{x \in Z_+^n : A^2 x \geq b^2\}$ is the Lagrangian relaxation of (14.11), that is, $z_{LR}(\lambda) \leq z_{IP}$ for each $\lambda \geq 0$. The best bound can be obtained by solving the Lagrangian dual $z_{LD} = \max_{\lambda \geq 0} z_{LR}(\lambda)$. It is well known that the relation $z_{IP} \geq z_{LD} \geq z_{LP}$ holds.

14.3.5 Lagrangian Relaxation

We now show how to apply Lagrangian relaxation taking Eq.(14.8) as a complicated constraint. Recall that this constraint insures that the y variables and the z variables select the same position of segment k. By relaxing such a constraint, we relax the right end of a z arcs. This means that an arc can be activated even though its right end is not on the path, as it is illustrated in Fig.14.7a. For a fixed λ, the relaxed augmented path problem obtained in this way can be solved in a polynomial time using a dynamic programming (see Reference 36).

In order to find the Lagrangian dual z_{LD}, one has to look for the maximum of a concave piecewise linear function. This appeals for using the so-called subgradient optimization technique. For the function $z_{LR}(\lambda)$, the vector $s^t = b^1 - A^1 x^t$, where x^t is an optimal solution to $\min_x\{cx + \lambda^t(b^1 - A^1 x)\}$, a subgradient at λ^t. The following subgradient algorithm is an analog of the steepest ascent method for maximizing a function:

- Initialization: Choose a starting point λ^0, Θ_0, and ρ. Set $t = 0$ and find a subgradient s^t.
- While $s^t \neq 0$ and $t < t_{max}$ do $\{\ \lambda^{t+1} = \lambda^t + \Theta_t s^t; \Theta_{t+1} = \rho\,\Theta_t, t \leftarrow t + 1;$ find $s^t\}$

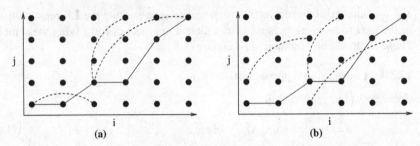

Figure 14.7. Example of a threading instance with $m = 6$ blocks and $n = 5$ free positions. The set of segment interactions is $L = \{(1, 3), (3, 4), (3, 6)\}$. **(a)** The Lagrangian relaxation sets the right end of any arc free. The solution for the relaxed problem could not satisfy the original constraints. **(b)** The Lagrangian relaxation sets both the right and left ends of arcs free.

This algorithm stops either when $s^t = 0$ (in which case λ^t is an optimal solution) or after a fixed number of iterations t_{max}. The parameter $0 < \rho < 1$ determines the decrease of the subgradient step.

Note that for each λ the solution defined by the y variables is feasible for the original problem. In this way at each iteration of the subgradient optimization, we

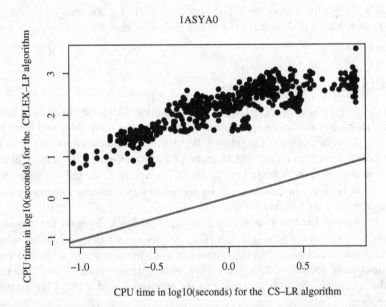

Figure 14.8. Cost-splitting relaxation versus LP relaxation. Plot of times in seconds with the CS algorithm on the x-axis and the LP algorithm from [11] on the y-axis. Both algorithms compute approximate solutions for 962 threading instances associated with the template 1ASYA0 from the FROST core database. The line $y = x$ is shown in the plot. A significant performance gap is observed between the algorithms. For example, point $(x, y) = (0.5, 3)$ corresponds to a case where CS is $10^{2.5}$ times faster than LP relaxation. These results were obtained on an Intel(R) Xeon(TM) CPU 2.4 GHz, 2 GB RAM, RedHat 9 Linux. The MIP models were solved using CPLEX 7.1 solver (see Reference 37 for more details).

have a heuristic solution. At the end of the optimization, we have both lower and upper bounds on the optimal objective value.

Symmetrically, we can relax the left end of each link or even relax the left end of one part of the links and the right end of the rest (see Fig. 14.7b). This approach is used in Reference 14. The same paper describes a branch-and-bound algorithm using this Lagrangian relaxation instead of the LP relaxation. This is the default algorithm in the FROST package.

Another relaxation, called *cost splitting* (CS), is presented in Reference 37. The results presented in this paper clearly show that CS slightly outperforms LR, and both (LR and CS) relaxations are significantly faster than LP (see Fig. 14.8). The interested reader can find further details concerning these approaches in Reference 36.

14.4 DIVIDING FROST INTO MODULES FOR DISTRIBUTION OVER A CLUSTER

The following two sections are based on the results presented in Reference 38.

14.4.1 Amount of Computation to be Done

In Section 14.2.5, we described the FROST functioning. From a computational viewpoint, this procedure can be divided into two phases: The first one is the computation of score distributions (hereafter called phase D) and the second one is the alignment of the sequence of interest with the data set of templates (hereafter called phase E for evaluation) making the use of the previously calculated distributions. These two phases are repeated for each filter (1D and 3D). We denote by Ali1D(Q,C) the process of aligning a query sequence (Q) with a core (C) in the 1D filter and by Ali3D(Q,C) the more computer-intensive alignment process of the 3D filter. Although we have a very efficient implementation of the corresponding algorithm based on a Lagrangian relaxation technique, computing the score distributions for all the templates takes more than a month when performed sequentially.

The whole procedure requires the following computations:

1. Phase D: Align nonhomologous sequences in order to obtain the score distributions for all templates and all filters. Since five distributions are associated to any template and there are about 200 sequences for each distribution, this procedure needs solving about 1,200,000 quadratic problems Ali1D and the same amount of NP-complete problems Ali3D.
2. Phase E: Align the query with the data set of templates that require solving several hundred quadratic problems Ali1D and N NP-complete problems Ali3D (where N is usually 10).

Figure 14.9 shows the distribution of the alignment problems needed to be solved during phase D and gives an idea of the amount of computation required by the 3D filter. The number of the problems is about 1,200,000, while the size of the largest instance is 6.6×10^{77}.

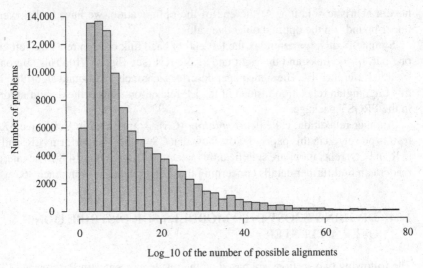

Figure 14.9. Populations of the 3D problems solved during phase D as a $\log_{10}$ function of the size of the search space (number of possible alignments).

Figure 14.10 shows the plot of the mean CPU time required to solve the 3D problems involved in phase D as a function of the number of possible alignments.[8]

The purpose of the procedure proposed in the next section is to distribute all these tasks.

Note that phase D needs to be repeated each time the fitness functions or the library of templates changes, which is a frequent case when the program is used in a development phase.

14.4.2   Distribution of the Computations: Dividing FROST into Modules

The first improvement in the distributed version (DFROST) compared to the original FROST consists in identifying clearly the different stages and operations in order to make the entire procedure modular. The process of computing the score distributions is dissociated from the alignment of the query versus the set of templates. We therefore split the two phases (D and E) that used to be interwoven in the original implementation. Such a decomposition presents several advantages. Some of them are as follows:

- Phase D is completely independent from the query; it can be performed as *a preprocessing stage* when it is convenient for the program designer.
- The utilization of the program is *simplified*. Note that only the program designer is supposed to execute phase D, while phase E is executed by an "ordinary"

---

[8]The mean CPU time here concerns macrotasks, each one containing 10 (gran3D = 10) instances of Ali3D of the same size (see Section 14.4.3).

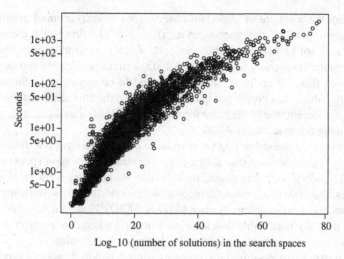

Figure 14.10. Mean CPU time required to solve the 3D problems in phase D as a function of their size.

user. From a user's standpoint, DFROST is *significantly faster* than FROST, since only phase E is executed at his on her request (phase D being performed as a preprocessing step).

- The program designer can *easily carry out different operations* needed for further developments of the algorithm or for database updating such as adding new filters, changing the fitness functions, adding a new template to the library, and so on.
- This organization of DFROST in modules is very *suitable for its decomposition into independent tasks* that can be solved in parallel.

The last point is discussed in detail in the next section.

14.4.3 Parallel Algorithm

We distinguish two kinds of atomic independent tasks in DFROST: The first is related to solving an instance of a problem of type Ali1D, while the second is associated with solving an instance of an Ali3D problem.[9]

Hence phase D consists in solving 1,200,000 independent tasks of types Ali1D and Ali3D, while phase E consists in solving several hundreds of independent tasks Ali1D and 10 independent tasks Ali3D. The final decision requires sorting and analyzing of the N best solutions of type Ali1D and the N best solutions of type Ali3D.

---

[9] In reality, this problem can be further decomposed into subtasks. Although nonindependent, these subtasks can be executed in parallel as shown in References 10 and 11. This parallelization could be easily integrated in DFROST if necessary.

There are a couple of important observations to keep in mind in order to obtain an efficient parallel implementation for DFROST. The first is that the exact number of tasks is not known in advance. Second, which is even more important, the tasks are irregular (especially tasks of type Ali3D) with unpredictable and largely varying execution time. In addition, small tasks need to be aggregated into macrotasks in order to reduce data broadcasting overhead. Since the complexity of the two types of tasks is different, the granularity for macrotasks Ali1D should be different from the granularity for macrotasks Ali3D.

The parallel algorithm that we propose is based on *centralized dynamic load balancing*: Macrotasks are dispatched from a centralized location (pool) in a dynamic way. The work pool is managed by a "master" who gives work *on demand* to idle "slaves." Each slave executes the macrotasks assigned to it by solving sequentially the corresponding subproblems (either Ali1D or Ali3D). Note that dynamic load balancing is the only reasonable task allocation method when dealing with irregular tasks for which the amount of work is not known prior to execution.

In phase E the pool initially contains several hundred tasks of type Ali1D. The master increases the work granularity by grouping gran1D of them into macrotasks. These macrotasks are distributed on demand to the slaves that solve the corresponding problems. The solutions computed in this way are sent back to the master and sorted by it locally. The templates associated with the N best scores yield N problems of type Ali3D. The master groups them into batches of size gran3D and transmits them to the slaves, where the associated problems are solved. The granularity gran1D is bigger than the gran3D granularity. Finally, the slaves send back to the master the computed solutions.

The strategy in phase D is simpler. The master aggregates only tasks in the macrotasks of size either gran1D or gran3D, sends them on demand to idle slaves (where the corresponding problems are sequentially solved), and finally gathers the distributions that have been computed. The master processes the library of templates in a sequential manner. First, it aims at distributing all tasks for a given template to the slaves. However, when the list of tasks for a given template becomes empty but the granularity level is not attained, the master proceeds to distribute tasks from the next template. This strategy allows to reduce globally the idle time of the processors.

14.5 COMPUTATIONAL EXPERIMENTS

14.5.1 Running Times

The numerical results presented in this section (see Table 14.1) were obtained on a cluster of 12 Intel(R) Xeon(TM) CPU 2.4 GHz, 2 Gb Ram, RedHat 9 Linux connected by a 1-GB ethernet network. The behavior of DFROST was tested entirely by computing the phase D of the package—that is, all the distributions for 1125 templates for both filters.

In the case of a 3D filter, solving 1,104,074 alignments in parallel as shown in Table 14.1 is very efficient. The comparison of the total sequential running times with the wall clock time of the master shows that we obtain a speedup of about 12—that is,

Table 14.1   Comparison of the Total Time (in Days, Hours, and Minutes) Taken by a Number of 1D and 3D Tasks with the Corresponding Wall Clock Time After Parallelizing the Program

	Number of Tasks	Wall Clock Time	Total Sequential Time	Speedup
3D filter	1,104,074	3 d 3 h 20 min	37 d 5 h 11 min	11.9
1D filter	1,107,973	31 min	4 h 13 min	8.2
Both filters	2,202,047	3 d 3 h 51 min	37 d 9 h 24 min	11.8

an efficiency close to one. In the case of a 1D filter, for solving 1,107,973 alignments the speedup is lower but then the total sequential time is much shorter than for solving 3D tasks.

These significant results, obtained on such a large data set, justify the work done to distribute FROST and prove the efficiency of the proposed parallel algorithm.

Details from this execution are presented in Table 14.2. The values of the parameters gran1D and gran3D were experimentally fixed to 1000 and 10, respectively.

We can calculate an upper limit for the number of processors beyond which it is not any more possible to benefit from adding more processors. The maximum time for an alignment is 797.4 s, and 14.3 s is the lower limit of the wall clock time for the complete computation of the distributions for Ali3d. The total CPU time necessary to calculate all Ali3D alignments is 3,215,460 s. Thus, adding more than 4032 processors (3215460/797.4) will not further accelerate the global process. This gives a theoretical upper limit. The assumption behind this procedure is that difficult computations are submitted first. This strategy was not implemented in the results presented in Reference 38 since it requires a criterion for a preliminary running time task estimation. Our observation on the code behavior when computing all distributions confirms that a meaningful criterion is the solution in the search space (see Fig. 14.10). Another criterion could be the observance of the past running time for a task.

14.5.2   Statistical Analysis of the Results

Using this parallel algorithm, we were able to compute all distributions for the entire library of FROST templates. This was never done with the sequential code because of large templates such as 1BGLA0 with sequences as long as 528 amino acids, leading to a number of possible alignments as large as 6.647E+77. Statistics concerning the running time distribution are presented in Fig. 14.11.

On average, the running time distribution *of all* Ali1D tasks is characterized by the following data:

Minimum	First quartile	Mean	Third quartile	Maximum
0 s	0.03 s	0.58 s	2.32 s	797.4 s

Note that these times correspond to one alignment.

Table 14.2   An extract from the Execution Times when Computing the 3D Score Distributions

Template	DFROST	CPU tot	Cpu av	NAli
1BGLA0	15455	107569	113	945
1ALO_0	9565	96579	97	995
1CXSA0	5988	55808	58	960
1DIK_0	4506	46855	47	977
1BGW_0	4152	45286	45	1000
1CLC_0	3580	37973	39	969
1AA6_0	3357	35819	38	926
1DJXB0	3025	31276	31	1000
1DAR_0	2705	28671	28	1000
1AOZA0	2477	25156	26	935
1AK5_0	2072	22326	22	979
1AUIA0	2016	22010	22	1000
1AOFB0	2065	21619	21	1000
1BHGA0	1904	20740	21	980
1AORA0	1920	20059	20	995
1AYL_0	1807	18961	19	973
1EUT_0	1753	18883	18	995
1CTN_0	1535	16670	16	1000
1ECL_0	1439	15589	16	953
1ATIA0	1492	15463	15	980
1CIY_0	1441	15044	15	1000
1BYB_0	1307	13892	14	990
1COY_0	1204	13150	13	957
1DLC_0	1104	11825	13	907
1BDP_0	1173	12814	12	995
1AOP_0	1134	12323	12	1000
1AG8A0	1120	12153	12	990
1BMFC0	1094	11338	11	1000
1ECFB0	1052	11254	11	990
1DERA0	1047	11109	11	1000
1ALKA0	1022	10937	11	965
1DPE_0	988	10626	11	957
1DDT_0	973	10349	10	1000
1AC5_0	907	9877	9	1000
1CAE_0	913	9870	9	990
1BMFD0	914	9467	9	998
1DPGA0	875	9092	9	1000
1ASYA0	1102	8634	9	952
1LYLA0	782	8335	8	990

(*Continued*)

Table 14.2 *(Continued)*

Template	DFROST	CPU tot	Cpu av	NAli
1BIF_0	657	7129	7	948
1AD3A0	629	6669	6	1000
1DNPA0	776	6580	6	960

The templates for which the distributions are calculated are listed in the first column. The second column gives the parallel time (the execution time for the master) on a cluster of 12 processors. The third column shows the CPU sequential time (obtained by adding the CPU times from the slaves). The fourth column reports the average CPU time per alignment and the last column shows the actual number of sequences that have been threaded to calculate the distributions. The value of the granularity was fixed to 10.

Table 14.3 Sequential Times in Seconds for Computing the 3D Score Distributions of Four Templates Selected for Their "Difficulty" (Search Space Size)

	Nb Sol	NAli	Min	Q_1	Med	Mean	Q_3	Max
1BGLA0	5.4×10^{27}	55	0.95	0.96	0.98	0.97	0.98	1.02
	1.2×10^{35}	56	0.95	0.96	0.97	0.97	0.98	1.01
	3.5×10^{58}	192	35.6	39.9	42.2	45.2	50.0	73.2
	1.3×10^{70}	199	102.4	116.3	131.0	145.7	164.6	510.0
	6.6×10^{77}	150	203.8	229.7	252.6	291.7	327.5	797.4
1QBA_0	1.6×10^{3}	58	1.82	1.83	1.83	1.84	1.84	1.89
	8.3×10^{37}	57	1.82	1.83	1.83	1.84	1.84	1.89
	5.2×10^{57}	197	27.1	30.2	32.5	36.3	39.8	76.6
	2.8×10^{68}	200	68.4	77.5	86.9	101.4	116.0	354.8
	7.2×10^{75}	200	130.1	154.7	178.3	207.0	239.8	789.8
1ALO_0	3.1×10^{33}	57	0.85	0.87	0.87	0.87	0.88	0.89
	6.0×10^{33}	57	0.85	0.86	0.87	0.87	0.87	0.89
	2.5×10^{57}	190	25.8	29.3	36.1	40.8	46.7	135.2
	1.6×10^{69}	200	67.4	86.3	113.2	123.2	134.8	397.6
	1.3×10^{77}	200	139.9	175.7	231.0	262.2	303.4	735.0
1YGE_0	3.4×10^{23}	61	0.39	0.40	0.41	0.41	0.41	0.43
	2.8×10^{45}	59	0.40	0.41	0.41	0.41	0.42	0.42
	2.1×10^{55}	192	34.8	39.9	43.1	47.5	48.9	139.8
	6.5×10^{61}	173	71.2	80.5	89.5	102.0	115.9	365.1
	4.4×10^{66}	199	120.2	138.5	158.3	178.2	208.9	443.7

For a given template the five rows represent alignment of sets of nonrelated sequences having length, respectively, equal to: -30%, -15%, 0%, $+15\%$, and $+30\%$ of the template length. Nb Sol is the number of possible alignments that can be generated with the sequences and the template. This gives an indication of the difficulty of the problem to solve. NAli is the number of alignments (sequences) in the corresponding set. The last six columns report diverse running time characteristics obtained when aligning the set of sequences with the corresponding 3D structure: Min is the minimum value, Q_1 is the time at the first quartile position, Med is the time at the median position, Mean is the average time, Q_3 is the time at the third quartile position and Max is the maximum value.

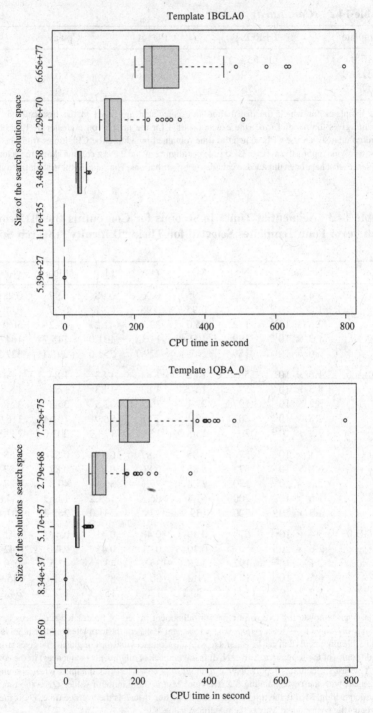

Figure 14.11.

We observed that for 188 templates the computation of the distributions requires more than 1 h CPU time. Statistical details concerning the running time of the four most time-consuming templates are presented in Table 14.3. Remember that a PTP instance (i.e., when the query and the 3D structure are fixed) is considered as an atomic independent task in the current parallel strategy. Yet, as shown in References 10 and 11, such an instance could be further decomposed into subtasks that could be executed in parallel. We studied the need for implementing this parallelization in the package FROST. However, taking in account that (i) the number of independent tasks when computing distributions is very high, (ii) the data from Tables 14.2 and 14.3 as well as their statistical recapitulations in Fig. 14.11 clearly show that really hard-PTP instances are rather rare, and (iii) the speedup reported in Section 14.5 is very satisfactory, we decided, for the time being, to stay with the current parallel strategy.

14.6   FUTURE RESEARCH DIRECTIONS

It is well known that large fractions of the proteins have a modular organization as shown in Fig. 14.12. These proteins are called *multidomain proteins*. These modules can be detected at the level of the amino acid sequence as similar subsequences are found in different protein sequences. In the 3D structure of the whole proteins, these modules correspond usually to one and sometimes to several substructures called structural domains[10] [39] (see the right-hand side of Fig. 14.12).

Several cases can occur when studying such multidomain proteins. Let us illustrate this point with the PEP-utilizers domain presented in Fig. 14.12.

If one wishes to analyze the PEP-utilizers module family, one needs to compare the corresponding sequences over their complete lengths. Using global alignment of the sequences (i.e., gaps before the beginning of a sequence and after its end are penalized) will not give a satisfactory result. If the goal of the study is to search for the PEP-utilizers module in a set of sequences (such as those shown in Fig. 14.12), one must use a semiglobal alignment where the gaps before the beginning and after the end of a sequence are set to zero. This allows the shorter sequence of the PEP-utilizers module to "slide" along the longer sequences until it finds the best match.

---

[10] In the literature, the terms domain and module are often used somewhat interchangeably. In this chapter, we restrict the use of module to subsequences and domain to 3D substructures.

Figure 14.11. Two templates with heavy distribution computations. 1BGLA0 and 1QBA_0 are selected from Table 14.3, and the corresponding box plots of the distribution running time are plotted using the statistical package R [42]. The left and right ends of a box correspond to the lower and upper quartiles, and the middle line corresponds to the median of the distribution. Vertical lines, usually called "whiskers," go left and right from the box to the extreme of the data (here defined as 1.5 times the interquartile range). Outliers are plotted individually. Note that the distribution is not symmetric and exhibits a heavy tail for longer CPU times.

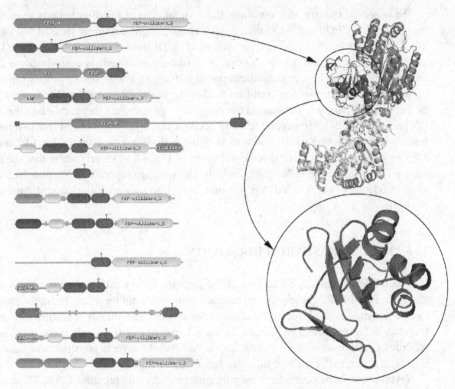

Figure 14.12. Left panel: Schematic representation of protein sequences with different modules (data from the PFAM database [43]). In the figure, we focus on the three modules of the second sequence. These modules are also found in other sequences. Upper right panel: The structure of this sequence (a pyruvate phosphate dikinase) has been solved (PDB code 1dik) and the modules have been drawn in similar shades of gray in the 3D structure. Lower right panel: zoom on the 3D structure of the second module. This module has 102 residues.

The most general case occurs when, comparing two sequences, for instance, the second and the fifth in Fig. 14.12, one is trying to analyze what is common between these sequences. This corresponds to carrying out a local alignment, that is, finding subsequences in both sequences that have the maximum score when aligned (for a given score function).

The local alignment is the most general alignment technique. Accordingly, this is the convenient alignment when comparing an unknown sequence with a database of sequences, since it is unknown beforehand what the similarity is between the query and the database sequences.

Due to the strong analogy that exists between sequence–sequence alignment methods and sequence–structure alignment methods, the above considerations are also valid: *mutatis mutandis* for protein threading methods.

In Section 14.2.4, we mentioned that FROST permits *only* global alignment of a sequence with a core. Even more, to the best of our knowledge, no current protein

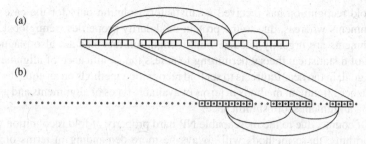

Figure 14.13. Local alignment. (a) A template containing five blocks. (b) A sequence of 58 amino acids. On its right-hand site, this sequence contains a structural domain that exhibits a good similarity to the template when only three blocks are aligned. To obtain this optimal alignment (i.e., giving the best score), two blocks have to be omitted.

threading approach exists that uses nonlocal score functions for providing an exact solution and that is able to carry out semiglobal and local alignments. Some ideas to tackle this problem have been presented by Collet et al. in References 40 and 41 where mathematical formulations based on MIP models for semiglobal and local sequence/structure alignment are discussed. The latest one is also called *flexible alignment* since it allows the omission of blocks during the alignment process (see Fig. 14.13).

Semiglobal and flexible alignments raise a number of new questions. Performing such alignments necessitates the alignment of cores with potentially very long sequences (the largest proteins known are up to 10,000 residues long). The process of computing distributions (see Section 14.2.4) needs to be significantly modified in the context of arbitrarily long sequences. In addition, these types of alignments will drastically increase the solution space and the corresponding running time. In order to manage such an increase of the computational requirements, the future semiglobal and flexible alignment algorithms will need more and more parallel and distributed computing.

14.7   CONCLUSION

Fold recognition (protein threading) is rather typical of problems that occur in bioinformatics. It requires knowledge from different disciplines: biology for the definition of cores, physical chemistry for the development of score functions, computer science for the conception of efficient alignment algorithms, and statistics for the explaination of the significance of the alignment score.

Sequence comparison methods play an outstanding role in exploiting protein sequence data, in particular for *in silico* functional analysis. These methods are versatile and extremely efficient as long as close homologs are considered. Fold recognition techniques are intended to replace them when the much more difficult case of remote homologs needs to be tackled. Unfortunately, fold recognition techniques are computer intensive and, for the moment, are less universal. In particular, the problem of fold recognition has received a satisfactory solution only for the case of global alignments whereas, due to the protein modularity properties, semiglobal and local alignments are urgently needed. Fold recognition methods are also plagued by the lack of a statistical theory permitting to assess the significance of alignment scores. Our goal, in the near future, is to set fold recognition methods on an equal footing with sequence alignment methods in terms of available types of alignments and assessment of the alignment score significance.

Of course, due to the inescapable NP-hard property of fold recognition alignment algorithms, these methods will always be more demanding in terms of computer resources than sequence alignments, although we are able to achieve pruning peak rate as high as 10^{74} per second for global alignments. However, as shown in this paper, it is possible to harness the power of grid computing to perform the heavy calculations that will be needed to analyze the 500 currently sequenced microbial genomes and the further 1000 that are to be released next year.

REFERENCES

1. S.F. Altschul, T.L. Madden, A.A. Schaffer, J. Zhang, Z. Zhang, W. Miller, D.J. Lipman, Gapped blast and psi-blast: A new generation of protein database searchprograms, *Nucleic Acids Research* **25**, 3389–3402, 1997.

2. S.E. Brenner, C. Chothia, T.J. Hubbard, Assessing sequence comparison methods with reliable structurally identified distant evolutionary relationships, *Proceedings of the National Academy of Sciences of the United States America*, **95**, 6073–6078, 1998.

3. C. Chothia, One thousand families for the molecular biologist, *Nature Biotechnology* **22**, 1317–1321, 2004.

4. C.A. Orengo, D.T. Jones, J.M. Thornton, Protein superfamilies and domain superfolds, *Nature* **372**, 631–634, 1994.

5. F.M. Pearl, C.F. Bennett, J.E. Bray, A.P. Harrison, N. Martin, A. Shepherd, I. Sillitoe, J. Thornton, C. A. Orengo, The cath database: An extended protein family resource for structural and functional genomics, *Nucleic Acids Research* **31**(1), 452–455, 2003.

6. A. Andreeva, D. Howorth, S.E. Brenner, T.J.P. Hubbard, C. Chothia, A.G. Murzin, Scop database in 2004: Refinements integrate structure and sequence family data, *Nucleic Acids Research* **32**, 226–229, 2004.

7. A. Marin, J. Pothier, K. Zimmermann, J.-F. Gibrat, Frost: A filter based fold recognition method, *Proteins* **49**(4), 493–509, 2002.

8. R.H. Lathrop, The protein threading problem with sequence amino acid interaction preferences is NP-complete, *Protein Engineering* **255**, 1059–1068, 1994.

9. R.H. Lathrop, T.F. Smith, Global optimum protein threading with gapped alignment and empirical pair potentials, *Journal of Molecular Biology* **255**, 641–665, 1996.

10. N. Yanev, R. Andonov, Parallel divide & conquer approach for the protein threading problem, *Concurrency and Computation: Practice and Experience* **16**, 961–974, 2004.

11. R. Andonov, S. Balev, N. Yanev, Protein threading problem: From mathematical models to parallel implementations, *INFORMS Journal on Computing* **16**(4), 393–405, 2004 (Special Issue on Computational Molecular Biology/Bioinformatics, H. Greenberg, D. Gusfield, Y. Xu, W. Hart, M. Vingro (Eds.)).

12. J. Xu, M. Li, G. Lin, D. Kim, Y. Xu, Raptor: optimal protein threading by linear programming, *Journal of Bioinformatics and Computational Biology* **1**(1), 95–118, 2003.

13. Y. Xu, D. Xu, Protein threading using prospect: design and evaluation, *Proteins* **40**(3), 343–354, 2000.

14. Stefan Balev, Solving the protein threading problem by lagrangian relaxation. in: Jonassen and J. Kim (Eds.), *4th International Workshop on Algorithms in Bioinformatics, Bergen, Norway*, Vol. 3240 of LNCS/LNBI WABI pp. 182–193, 2004.

15. W.W. Li, R.W. Byrnes, J. Hayes, V.M. Reyes, A. Birnbaum, A. Shahab, C. Mosley, D. Pekurovsky, G.B. Quinn, I.N. Shindyalov, H. Casanova, L. Ang, F. Berman, M.A. Miller, P.E. Bourne, in: *The Encyclopedia of Life Project: Grid Software and Deployment*, special issue on Grid Systems for Life Sciences, New Generation Computing, 2003.

16. T. Steinke, Alignment and threading on massively parallel computers, Technical Report, Berlin Center for Genome Based Bioinformatics, 2003.

17. Y. Xu, D. Xu, E.C. Uberbacher, An efficient computational method for globally optimal threading, *Journal of Computational Biology* **5**, 597–614, 1998.

18. S.F. Altschul, Amino acid substitution matrices from an information theoretic perspective, *Journal of Molecular Biology* **219**, 555–565, 1991.

19. M.O. Dayhoff, R.M. Schwartz, B.C. Orcutt, in: *Atlas of Protein Sequence and Structure*, Vol. 5, A model of evolutionary change in proteins, National Biomedical Research Foundation, Washington DC, pages 345–352, 1978.

20. S. Henikoff J.G. Henikoff, Amino acid substitution matrices from protein blocks, *Proceedings of the National Academy of Sciences of the United States of America*, **89**, 10915–10919, 1992.

21. S.B. Needleman C.D. Wunsch, A general method applicable to the search for similarities in the aminoacid sequence of two proteins, *Journal of Molecular Biology* **48**, 1970.

22. T.F. Smith M.S. Waterman, Identification of common molecular subsequences, *Journal of Molecular Biology* **147**, 195–197, 1981.

23. W.R. Pearson, Flexible sequence similarity searching with the fasta3 program package, *Methods in Molecular Biology* **132**, 185–219, 2000.

24. S.E. Brenner, C. Chothia, T.J. Hubbard, Assessing sequence comparison methods with reliable structurallyidentified distant evolutionary relationships, *Proceedings of the National Academy of Sciences of the United States of America*, **95**, 6073–6078, 1998.

25. T. Madej, J.F. Gibrat, S.H. Bryant, Threading a database of protein cores, *Proteins* **23**, 356–369, 1995.

26. T. Akutsu, S. Miyano, On the approximation of protein threading, *Theoretical Computer Science* **210**, 261–275, 1999.

27. N. Yanev, R. Andonov, Solving the protein threading problem in parallel, IPDPS '03, in: *Proceedings of the 17th International Symposium on Parallel and Distributed Processing*, IEEE Computer Society, Washington, DC, page 157.1, 2003.

28. J. Xu, M. Li, G. Lin, D. Kim, Y. Xu, Protein structure prediction by linear programming, in: *Proceedings of the 7th Pacific Symposium on Biocomputing (PSB)*, 2003, pp. 264–275.

29. G. Lancia, Integer programming models for computational biology problems, *Journal of Computer Science and Technology* **19**(1), 60–77, 2004.

30. J. Blazewicz, P. Lukasiak, M. Milostan, Some operations research methods for analyzing protein sequences and structures, *4OR A Quarterly Journal of Operations Research* **4**(2), 91–123, 2006.

31. S. Karlin, S.F. Altschul, Methods for assessing the statistical significance of molecular sequence features by using general scoring schemes, *Proceedings of the National Academy Science of the United States of America* **87**, 2264–2268, 1990.

32. L.A. Mirny, A.V. Finkelstein, E.I. Shakhnovich, Statistical significance of protein structure prediction by threading, *Proceedings of the National Academy of Sciences of the United States of America* **97**, 9978–9983, 2000.

33. K. Zimmermann, A. Marin, J. Pothier, J.-F. Gibrat, Protein threading statistics: An attempt to assess the significance of a fold assignment to a sequence, in: *Protein Structure Prediction: Bioinformatic Approach*, International University line, 2002.

34. J. Setubal, J. Meidanis, *Introduction to Computational Molecular Biology*, PWS Publishing Company, Boston, 1997.

35. R.H. Lathrop, R.G. Rogers Jr., J. Bienkowska, B.K.M. Bryant, L.J. Buturovic, C. Gaitatzes, R. Nambudripad, J.V. White, T.F. Smith, *Computational Methods in Molecular Biology*, Elsevier Science, Amsterdam, pp. 227–283, Chapter 12, 1998.

36. N. Yanev, P. Veber, R. Andonov, S. Balev, Lagrangian approaches for a class of matching problems in computational biology, Rapport de recherche RR-5973, INRIA, August 2006 (to appear in *Computers and Mathematics with Applications*, special issue on Computational Biology, R. Tadei (Ed.)).

37. P. Veber, N. Yanev, R. Andonov, V. Poirriez, Optimal protein threading by cost-splitting WABI'05 (5th Workshop on Algorithms in Bioinformatics), in: *Lecture Notes in Computer Science*, Vol. 3692, Springer, Berlin, pp. 365–375, 2005.

38. V. Poirriez, R. Andonov, A. Marin, J.-F. Gibrat, Frost: Revisited and distributed, IPDPS '05, in: *Proceedings of the 19th IEEE International Parallel and Distributed Processing Symposium (IPDPS'05)—Workshop 7*, IEEE Computer Society, Washington, DC, p. 200.1, 2005.

39. A.M. Lesk, G.D. Rose, Folding units in globular proteins, *PNAS* **78**, 4304–4308, 1981.

40. G. Collet, A. Marin, N. Yanev, R. Andonov, J.-F. Gibrat, Implementing a semi-global alignment algorithm for protein threading methods that use non-local score functions, *Poster of the ROADEF conference*, 2006 (in French).

41. G. Collet, N. Yanev, A. Marin, R. Andonov, J.-F. Gibrat, A flexible model for protein fold recognition, in: A. Denise, P. Durrens, S. Robin, E. Rocha, A. de Daruvar, A. Groppi, (Eds.), *Septièmes Journes Ouvertes de Biologie*, Informatique et Mathématiques (JOBIM), pp. 215–216, 2006.

42. R. Ihaka, R. Gentleman, R, A language for data analysis and graphics, *Journal of Computational and Graphical Statistics* **5**(3), 299–314, 1996.

43. A. Bateman, L. Coin, R. Durbin, R.D. Finn, V. Hollich, Jones Griffiths, A. Khanna, M. Marshall, S. Moxon, E.L. Sonnhammer, D.J. Studholme, C. Yeats, S.R. Eddy, The Pfam protein families database, *Nucleic Acids Research* **32**, D138–D141, 2004.

15

DNA FRAGMENT ASSEMBLY USING GRID SYSTEMS

Antonio J. Nebro, Gabriel Luque, and Enrique Alba

15.1 INTRODUCTION

DNA fragment assembly is a technique that attempts to reconstruct the original DNA sequence from a large number of fragments, each one being several hundred base pairs (bps) long. The DNA fragment assembly is needed because current technology, such as gel electrophoresis, cannot directly and accurately sequence DNA molecules longer than 1000 bases. However, most genomes are much longer. For example, a human DNA is about 3.2 billion bps in length and cannot be read at once.

The following technique was developed to deal with this limitation. First, the DNA molecule is amplified, that is, many copies of the molecule are created. The molecules are then cut at random sites to obtain fragments that are short enough to be sequenced directly. The overlapping fragments are then assembled back into the original DNA molecule. This strategy is called *shotgun sequencing*. Originally, the assembly of short fragments was done manually, which is inefficient and error-prone. Hence, a lot of effort has been put into finding techniques to automate the shotgun sequence assembly. Over the past decade a number of fragment assembly packages [1–3] have been developed and used to sequence different organisms.

The assembly problem is, therefore, a combinatorial optimization problem that, even in the absence of noise, is NP-hard: given k fragments, there are $2^k k!$ possible combinations. Therefore, if we consider large instances of the DNA fragment assembly problem, then the finding of the final sequence is a very time-consuming process, and even the total computing time can be, on the order of hundreds of days. Such high-end computational resources cannot be addressed in normal clusters of machines. In this context, grid computing systems (or grids) [4] appear as a platform that provides the computing power of hundreds and thousands of computers, thus enabling us to execute, in a reasonable amount of time, algorithms that otherwise would be considered unfeasible.

In this chapter, we describe the traditional packages developed to deal with the DNA fragment assembly and the possible extension of these systems to be executed in

---

Grid Computing for Bioinformatics and Computational Biology. Edited by E.-G. Talbi and A.Y. Zomaya.
Copyright © 2008 John Wiley & Sons, Inc.

grid systems. We also present a detailed description of a tool for solving this problem that takes advantage of the features of grid environments.

The rest of the chapter is organized as follows. In Section 15.2, we introduce the DNA fragment assembly problem. In Section 15.3, we analyze related works, and we propose several alternatives to use these tools in grids. A specific package, a grid-based GA for solving the DNA fragment assembly problem, is described in Section 15.4. Finally, some conclusions and open research lines are given in Section 15.5.

15.2   THE DNA FRAGMENT ASSEMBLY PROBLEM

We start this section by giving a vivid analogy to the fragment assembly problem [5]: "Imagine several copies of a book cut by scissors into thousands of pieces, say 10 million. Each copy is cut in an individual way such that a piece from one copy may overlap a piece from another copy. Assume that one million pieces are lost and the remaining nine million are splashed with ink: Try to recover the original text." We can think of the DNA target sequence as being the original text, and the DNA fragments are the pieces cut out from the book. To further understand the problem, we need to know the following basic terminology:

- **Fragment:** A short sequence of DNA with length up to around 1000 bps.
- **Shotgun data:** A set of fragments.
- **Prefix:** A substring comprising the first n characters of fragment f.
- **Suffix:** A substring comprising the last n characters of fragment f.
- **Overlap:** Common sequence between the whole suffix of one fragment and the whole prefix of another fragment.
- **Layout:** An alignment of collection of fragments on the basis of the overlap order.
- **Contig:** A layout consisting of contiguous overlapping fragments. A contig is a sequence in which the overlap between adjacent fragments is greater than a threshold (cutoff parameter).
- **Consensus:** A sequence derived from the layout by taking the majority vote for each column of the layout.

To measure the quality of a consensus, we can look at the distribution of the coverage. Coverage at a base position is defined as the number of fragments at that position. It is a measure of the redundancy of the fragment data. It denotes the number of fragments, on average, in which a given nucleotide in the target DNA is expected to appear. It is computed as the number of bases read from fragments over the length of the target DNA [6].

$$\text{Coverage} = \frac{\sum_{i=1}^{n} \text{length of the fragment } i}{\text{target sequence length}} \tag{15.1}$$

where n is the number of fragments. TIGR [7] uses the coverage metric to ensure the correctness of the assembly result. The coverage usually ranges from 6 to 10 [8]. The higher the coverage, the fewer the gaps are expected, and the better the result.

15.2.1   DNA Sequencing Process

To determine the function of specific genes, scientists have learned to read the sequence of nucleotides comprising a DNA sequence in a process called DNA sequencing. The fragment assembly starts with breaking the given DNA sequence into small fragments. To do that, multiple exact copies of the original DNA sequence are made. Each copy is then cut into short fragments at random positions. These are the first three steps depicted in Fig. 15.1, and they take place in the laboratory. After the fragment set is obtained, traditional assemble approach

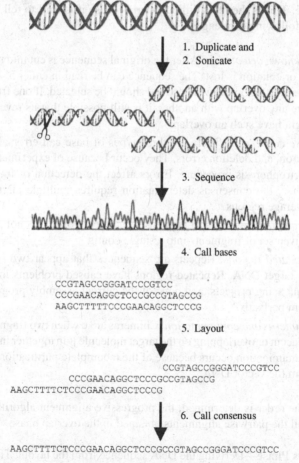

Figure 15.1. Graphical representation of DNA sequencing and assembly [9].

is followed in this order: overlap, layout, and then consensus. To ensure that fragments overlap enough, the reading of fragments continues until the coverage is satisfied. These steps are the last three steps in Fig. 15.1. In what follows, we give a brief description of each of the three phases, namely overlap, layout, and consensus.

Overlap Phase—Finding the overlapping fragments.
This phase consists in finding the best or longest match between the suffix of one sequence and the prefix of another. In this step, we compare all possible pairs of fragments to determine their similarity. Usually, the dynamic programming algorithm applied to semiglobal alignment is used in this step [8]. The intuition behind finding the pairwise overlap is that fragments with a significant overlap score are very likely next to each other in the target sequence.

Layout Phase—Finding the order of fragments on the basis of the computed similarity score. This is the most difficult step because it is hard to tell the true overlap due to the following challenges:

1. *Unknown orientation*: After the original sequence is cut into many fragments, the orientation is lost. The sequence can be read in either 5' to 3' or 3' to 5'. One does not know which strand should be selected. If one fragment does not have any overlap with another, it is still possible that its reverse complement might have such an overlap.

2. *Base call errors*: There are three types of base call errors: substitution, insertion, and deletion errors. They occur because of experimental errors in the electrophoresis procedure. Errors affect the detection of fragment overlaps. Hence, the consensus determination requires multiple alignments in high-coverage regions.

3. *Incomplete coverage*: It happens when the algorithm is not able to assemble a given set of fragments into a single contig.

4. *Repeated regions*: Repeats are sequences that appear two or more times in the target DNA. Repeated regions have caused problems in many genome-sequencing projects, and none of the current assembly programs can handle them perfectly.

5. *Chimeras and contamination*: Chimeras arise when two fragments that are not adjacent or overlapping on the target molecule join together into one fragment. Contamination occurs because of the incomplete purification of the fragment from the vector DNA.

After the order is determined, the progressive alignment algorithm is applied to combine all the pairwise alignments obtained in the overlap phase.

Consensus Phase—Deriving the DNA sequence from the layout. The most common technique used in this phase is to apply the majority rule in building the consensus.

Example: We next give an example of the fragment assembly process.

Given a set of fragments {F1 = GTCAG, F2 = TCGGA, F3 = ATGTC, F4 = CGGATG}, assume the four fragments are read from 5' to 3' direction. First, we need to determine the overlap of each pair of the fragments by the using semiglobal alignment algorithm. Next, we determine the order of the fragments on the basis of the overlap scores, which are calculated in the overlap phase. Suppose we have the following order: F2 F4 F3 F1. Then, the layout and the consensus for this example can be constructed as follows:

```
F2 ->    TCGGA
F4 ->      CGGATG
F3 ->         ATGTC
F1 ->            GTCAG
_____

Consensus -> TCGGATGTCAG
```

In this example, the resulting order allows to build a sequence having just one contig.

15.3 SOFTWARE TOOLS FOR THE DNA FRAGMENT ASSEMBLY PROBLEM

Several software systems have been proposed to solve the DNA fragment assembly problem, but in general they are sequential tools, and they are only able to tackle small to medium instances. A classical package approach is the overlap–layout–consensus one presented in the previous section. Currently, the software is mainly focused on the layout phase, because it is the most complex one. The overlap phase is also very important to obtain accurate results, but from a computer science point of view it is less interesting, since it must mainly be solved by biologists. New approaches different to the overlap–layout–consensus one have also been proposed in the last years. The main tools for all these issues will be presented in following paragraphs. We will also present several approaches to extend current assemblers to grid systems.

Domain-specific tools are mainly focused on the overlap phase. They are based on finding high-quality information about fragments (masking repeat regions and correcting errors) to reduce the complexity of the overlap graph and to alleviate the difficulty of the layout stage, which is generally solved using a greedy method.

PHRAP [2] is the most widely used sequence assembler. Among other features, it allows use of the whole set of fragments and not just the trimmed high-quality part to improve assembly accuracy in the presence of repeats in the overlap phase. A greedy method is used to build the layout order using the calculated overlap information and a ratio score (LLR) on the basis of the probability that the two fragments are from different repeats. A weighted directed graph based on the layout is built to compute the consensus sequence.

The TIGR Assembler [7] has successfully assembled very long sequences. It performs the two first phases of the classical assembly paradigm: overlap and layout (the consensus string is automatically determined by the layout order). The overlap of two fragments is determined by a modified Smith–Waterman algorithm [10]. After computing pairwise overlaps among input fragments, this method uses this information to decide the candidate fragment set that can be merged with the current assembly sequence in each step. The specific fragment that will be included in the assembly is selected according a complex criterion (overlap length, number of local errors, etc.).

STROLL [11] originally provided computational support for the strategy of sequencing by primer walking, but it has evolved into a general-purpose fragment assembler, which supports a wide variety of sequencing technologies. STROLL incorporates base quality information in pairwise comparison to discriminate overlaps, repeats, and chimeras; besides, this method improves sequencing accuracy and solves repeats. STROLL uses incremental multiple alignments to merge one fragment into partial assemblies, a consensus generation phase to determine each base, and gives an associated confidence level.

CAP3 [3] is the third version of the original CAP (Contig Assembly Program). The overlap score among fragments is computed using a variant of the Smith–Waterman algorithm [10]. It also calculates the strength of overlaps and identifies chimeras. In the layout phase, contigs are formed in a greedy fashion by adding the best overlapping fragments one at a time with the help of additional constrains. In the last phase, CAP3 merges groups of fragments to generate consensus sequence.

AMASS [12] is a sequence assembly algorithm that uses exact matches of short patterns randomly selected from fragment data to identify fragment overlaps. It constructs an overlap map and finally delivers a consensus sequence. It starts with sampling patterns of fixed length from shotgun data, and then it finds all occurrences of sampled patterns in shotgun data. The occurrences of patterns are used to detect overlapping fragments and to handle repeats, which is the major hurdle to sequence assembly. Contigs are built in a greedy fashion, adding a fragment with the best score in each step.

The CELERA Whole Genome Assembler (WGA) [13] uses sophisticated string and graph algorithms based on the classical overlap–layout–consensus paradigm. It can handle millions of reads, and it makes extensive use of forward–reverse constraints to address the problem of repeats.

ARACHNE [1] is a system for assembling genome sequences. It employs a traditional overlap–layout–consensus approach, but has a number of well-designed features for large-scale genome projects. It provides an efficient and sensitive procedure for finding real overlaps, a procedure for scoring overlaps that achieves high accuracy by correcting errors before assembly, a reads merger on the basis of forward–reverse links, and a method for detecting repetition of contigs by forward–reverse link consistency.

The previous tools are focused on finding high-quality overlap information that eases the layout phase. To solve the layout itself, they usually apply a greedy method that iteratively adds the best fragment to the current assembly according to the previously calculated overlap information. Currently, new and more intelligent methods have been developed to improve the accuracy of the result of this phase. This problem is closely related to the well-known traveling salesman problem (TSP), although several important differences can be found between the TSP and the layout stage of the DNA fragment assembly. Therefore, generic techniques that have been applied to TSP in the past can also be used to solve this problem. In fact, many evolutionary algorithms [14–16], ant colony systems [17], simulated annealing [18, 19], and artificial neural networks [20] have been successfully applied to solve this problem. Also, several specific methods have been proposed like PALS [21], which uses an estimation of the number of contig to guide the search plus a clustering method [22] that uses clustering concept to order the fragments.

Although the above systems are excellent fragment-assembling tools, a critical analysis of the overlap–layout–consensus paradigm reveals a great difficulty to find efficient solutions of the layout problem. Therefore, new additional approaches have been developed. Pevzner et al. [23] proposed the EULER system that is based on a reformulation of this problem as a Shortest Superstring Problem (NP-hard problem); therefore, they shift from the classical approach to the Eulerian Superpath approach, obtaining promising results in the instances tested.

Also, new sequencing technologies are emerging that produce shorter fragments (80–200 bps) but allow to generate significantly higher coverage (higher than 30) at low cost. Working with small fragments makes the utilization of the previous classical tools difficult, since the shorter the read length, the larger the number of repeats (the main obstacle is to solve fragment assembly problem with classical assemblers). Chaisson et al. [24] presented a modified version of EULER to tackle small fragments.

15.3.1 Grid Approaches

In this section we analyze the requirements that a grid system imposes and how the previous sequential tools can be adapted to profit from the high computational power provided by grid systems.

A grid system can be defined as a large collection of distributed resources connected by a network. In this context, we can distinguish two different software levels. In the top level we find the grid applications, which execute on top of the grid system. In turn, the grid software resides in the bottom level and manages the underlying grid infrastructure, thus enabling the development of grid applications.

The resources in a grid typically share some of the following characteristics [25]:

1. They are numerous.
2. They are owned and managed by different organizations and individuals.
3. They are potentially faulty.
4. They can be added to the grid dynamically.
5. They have different security requirements and policies.
6. They are heterogeneous.
7. They are connected by heterogeneous multilevel networks.
8. They have different resource management policies.
9. They are likely to be geographically separated.

All these issues must be managed to some extent by the grid system software, while only some of them should be taken into account in the level of grid applications. Therefore, they can influence the design of the algorithm.

Analyzing the tools described in the previous section, we can observe that most of them have two common phases: overlap and layout that are prone to be executed in grid systems.

Among the task performed during the overlap stage, the algorithm must perform a pairwise analysis among input fragments. These $(n \cdot n - 1)/2$ calculations are independent, and therefore the can be computed in parallel. Then, a simple strategy to execute them in a grid could be to assign one overlap calculation to each available processor of the grid. The duration of these tasks depends on the fragment length and the particular details of the algorithms. If the execution time of these tasks is too small, it can provoke a high loss of efficiency. To avoid this situation, two or more calculations could be assigned to each processor.

During the overlap phase, the greedy method used by most of the systems compares the current layout with all the remaining fragment. This operation is time-consuming and must be executed n times in each iteration of the greedy algorithm. Here, we can apply the same strategy described above. Another possible approach is to execute a complete greed in each processor, but each one could use a slightly different selection criterion. This simple approach allows to tackle with the characteristics of grid environments. In addition, several metaheuristics have been proposed to solve this stage. Several approaches can be applied: The first one consists in simultaneously launching a metaheuristics start from the same or different solution(s), configured with the same or different parameters in each processor. The algorithms may be independent or cooperative. The independent approach is very suitable to be used in grid systems and allows us to achieve more robust solutions. In its cooperative mode, metaheuristics exchange information during execution and usually allows us to improve the quality of the solutions found. The main issue that should be considered to use this approach in grid systems is that the nodes in the system can vary dynamically. Another approach is the computation of each iteration of the metaheuristics (the transformation/evaluation of the population for population-based metaheuristics or the exploration of the neighborhood for solution-based ones) in parallel. This strategy is similar to the proposed one for greedy method. Finally, both strategies can be combined to generate different approaches. In the next section, we illustrate a possible strategy to use these algorithms on grid systems and also refer the reader to Reference 26 for a complete study of evolutionary algorithms on computational grids.

15.4   AN EXAMPLE: A GRID-BASED EA FOR SOLVING THE DNA FRAGMENT ASSEMBLY PROBLEM

In this section we describe a Grid-based GA for solving the DNA fragment assembly problem [27]. Firstly, we explain the working principles of a sequential GA, and we discuss the details to solve the DNA fragment assembly with a GA; then, we explain our grid approach, and finally, we show experimental results using our GrEA to solve a very complex instance of the DNA fragment assembly problem. The aim of this section is to illustrate how the grid can be actually used in the this problem. Many of the following ideas can be applied to other metahueristics.

15.4.1   Genetic Algorithm Background

A GA is a randomized optimization procedure that uses information about the problem to guide the search (see Fig. 15.2). At each generation (iteration) t, a GA operates on a population of individuals $P(t)$, each one encoding a tentative solution, thus searching in many zones of the problem space at the same time. Each individual is a string of symbols encoding a solution for the problem, and it has an associated fitness value that is computed by the objective function. This fitness function is aimed at ranking the quality of the evaluated individual with respect to the rest of the population. The application of simple stochastic variation operators, such as mixing parts of two strings (*crossover*) or randomly changing their contents (*mutation*), leads this population toward fittest regions in an iterative manner. These operators are used with certain probability p_c and p_m. The algorithm finishes when a stopping condition is fulfilled (e.g., an optimum is found or a number of function evaluations have been carried out).

GAs can work in two basic ways. Firstly, the algorithm produces, from a population $P(t)$, a new population $P(t + 1)$ with the new generated individuals, $P'(t)$, and probably the best individuals of $P(t)$ (*elitism*); it is said then that the GA is *generational*. Secondly, one or two individuals are created at every step and then they are inserted back into the population, consequently coexisting with their parents; this kind of GA is known as *steady state*.

There exist many research lines aimed at improving the efficacy of a GA; one especially successful way to do so is to apply an improvement method to one or more individuals with the aim of accelerating the convergence toward the optimum. The merging of two different techniques in a single new algorithm is named *hybridization* [28].

```
t := 0 ;
initialize & evaluate[P (t)] ;
while not stop_condition do ;
    P '(t) := variation [P (t)] ;
    evaluate [P '(t)] ;
    P (t + 1)  := select [P '(t) ∪ P (t)] ;
    t := t + 1 ;
end while
```

Figure 15.2. Pseudocode describing a sequential genetic algorithm.

The number of iterations required to obtain an acceptable solution (or the optimum) is related to the problem to be solved. In general, it is not unusual that a GA needs to perform tens or hundreds of thousands of function evaluations. In these cases, the computational cost of evaluating each individual has to be taken into account. For example, if we consider the instance of the DNA fragment assembly used here as a working problem (see Section 15.4.4), this cost is around 15 s using a Pentium M 1.6 GHz processor running Suse Linux 10.0. This time does not seem to be very high, but if the algorithm has to carry out 500,000 function evaluations, the total computing time is in the order of 86 days, assuming that all the function evaluations require a constant amount of time. Furthermore, if we want to apply any improvement method that would require, for example, 100 additional function evaluations, the entire task would need around 1700 s. So computing 500,000 of such tasks can be considered as intractable using a single computer. These arguments justify the need of using grid technologies for solving the DNA fragment assembly problem in a reasonable amount of time.

15.4.2   DNA Fragment Assembly Using the GA

To represent an individual in the DNA fragment assembly problem, we have used integer permutations. A permutation encodes a sequence of fragment numbers, where consecutive fragments overlap. This permutation representation requires special operators to make sure that we always get feasible solutions. Two conditions must be satisfied by every individual: All fragments must be presented in the ordering, and no duplicate fragments are allowed.

As to genetic operators, we use binary tournament as the selection scheme. This operator works by randomly choosing two individuals from the population and the one having the best fitness is selected. The crossover operator we have considered is the order-based crossover (OX). This operator was specifically designed for tackling permutation problems. Given two parent individuals, the OX operator firstly copies the fragment IDs between two random positions of the first parent into the offspring's corresponding positions. Then, the rest of the fragments from the second parent is copied into the offspring in the relative order presented in this parent. If a fragment ID is already included in the offspring, it is skipped. Finally, the mutation operator randomly selects two positions from a permutation and then swaps the two resulting fragments. Since no duplicated values are introduced, the mutated individual is always feasible.

In the DNA fragment assembly problem, the fitness function measures the multiple sequences alignment quality and finds the best scoring alignment. Several functions have been used in the literature [17]. For example, one of the most widely used is the following:

$$F1(l) = \sum_{i=0}^{n-2} w(f[i], f[i+1]) \tag{15.2}$$

where w represents the overlap score between two fragments, and $f[i]$ is the ith fragment in the order. This function favors solutions in which strong overlaps occur between adjacent fragments in the layout. But the actual objective is to obtain an order of the fragments that minimizes the number of contigs, being the optimal solution to reach one single contig, that is, a complete DNA sequence composed of all the overlapping fragments. So the number of contigs is used as a high-level criterion to judge the whole quality of the results, since it is difficult to capture the dynamics of the problem into a mathematical function. Contig values are computed by applying a final step of refinement with a greedy heuristic commonly used in this application [22]. We have found that in some (extreme) cases it is possible that a solution with a better fitness (using F1) generates a larger number of contigs (worse solution). Hence, we propose a variation of that equation that also takes into account an upper bound of the final number of contigs ($c(\cdot)$).

$$F(l) = F1(l) \cdot \left(1 + \frac{1}{c(l)}\right) \qquad (15.3)$$

This new equation maximizes the overlap between adjacent fragments and, at the same time, minimizes the upper bound of the number of contigs. Computing the upper bound requires two steps. The first phase divides the solution into contigs. We iteratively check all fragments in the solution, creating a new contig when the overlap score between the current fragment and the next one is less than a threshold. The second phase tries to merge the previous contigs into longer ones by processing all the combinations of the pairs of contigs. Two contigs can be merged if the overlap score between the fragment in the end of the first contig and the fragment in the beginning of the second contig is greater or equal than the cutoff threshold. This phase finishes when all the combinations are processed or only one contig is left.

15.4.3 GrEA: A Grid-Based GA for Solving the DNA Fragment Assembly Problem

In Section 15.3.1, we described the main features of a grid system. In this section, we analyze how they can influence the design of a GA for grids.

The fact that resources are numerous is the leitmotif of grid systems, and it is the main reason why we discard traditional distributed GA (dGA) and cellular GA (cGA) models [29] for our proposal of parallel GA. On the one hand, since the resources are potentially faulty and new resources can be aggregated to the grid system regular topologies such as rings, meshes, and hypercubes are difficult to implement (i.e., the topology should be dynamically reconfigured at runtime). On the other hand, the benefits of individual migration among subpopulations can be difficult to achieve in a system composed of thousands of nodes (e.g., the migration of highly fit individuals using a unidirectional ring topology may not affect long distance subpopulations) in the case of dGA, and the ratio computation/communication can be unfavorable in the case of cGAs. These reasons lead us to consider the panmictic model (one population) with a parallel evaluation of the objective function in our proposal of grid-based GA.

A panmictic GA based on the master–slave model offers several advantages. Firstly, the model is conceptually simple: The master iteratively sends tasks involving the evaluation of individuals to the slaves, which respond with the fitness values; secondly, it requires the use of a star topology, which is simple to implement in a grid; finally, due to the stochastic nature of GAs, the working principles of the algorithm are not highly affected by the potential loss of a slave (just in computing time, which is obvious if one process fails).

Therefore, our GrEA is a steady-state GA following the master–slave parallel model. The basic idea is that a master process executes the main loop of the algorithm and the slaves perform the function evaluations in an asynchronous way. Contrary to a sequential steady-state GA, in GrEA several evaluations are carried out in parallel; ideally, there should be as many parallel evaluations as the available processors in the grid.

The improvement method is based on using a simplified version of the Evolutionary Strategy (ES) method. In concrete, we use a $(\mu + \lambda)$ ES in which the mutation probability does not evolve with the individual; that is, it is fixed. The overall method operates as follows. At each iteration, the ES procedure generates new λ individuals using a mutation operator starting from μ ones. Then, the best μ individuals taken from the μ old ones plus the newly generated λ ones are selected for the next iteration. This process is repeated until a termination condition is met. The mutation operator used for generating the new individuals is the *inversion mutation*. This operator randomly selects two positions from a permutation and then inverts the subsegment between these two fragments.

GrEA has been implemented using MW [30], a software library that enables us to develop master–worker parallel applications on top of the grid system Condor [31] using C++.

15.4.4   Experimental Results

In this section we analyze the behavior of GrEA when it is executed in a grid system. Our condor pool is composed of up to 150 computers belonging to several laboratories at the Computer Science Department of the University of Málaga. The pool includes UltraSPARC 477-MHz processors running Solaris 2.8, and Intel and AMD processors (Pentium III, Pentium IV, Athlon) running at different speeds and executing several flavors of Linux (Suse 8.1, Suse 9.3, RedHat 7.1). We have used Condor 6.7.12 and MW 0.9. All the machines are interconnected through a 100-Mbps Fast Ethernet network.

A target DNA sequence with accession number BX842596 (GI 38524243) was used in this work. It was obtained from the NCBI Web site.[1] It is the sequence of a *Neurospora crassa* (common bread mold) BAC and is 77,292 base pairs long. To test and analyze the performance of our algorithm, we generated a problem instance

[1]http://www.ncbi.nlm.nih.gov/

TABLE 15.1   Parameter Settings of the Experiments

Parameter	Value
Population size	512 individuals
Representation	Permutation (773 integers)
Crossover operator	Order-based ($p_c = 0.8$)
Mutation operator	Swap ($p_m = 0.2$)
Selection method	Binary tournament
Replacement strategy	Worst individual
Improvement operator	$(1 + 10)$ ES
Slave time-out	30 s
Cutoff	30
Stop condition	500,000 task

with GenFrag [32]. The problem instance, 842596_7, contains 773 fragments with average fragment length of 703 bps and coverage 7. This instance is very hard since is generated from a very long sequence using a small/medium value of coverage and a very restrictive cutoff. The combination of these parameters produces a very complex instance. For example, longer target sequences have been solved in the literature [3]; however, they used a larger coverage. The coverage measures the redundancy of the data, and the higher the coverage, the easier the problem. The cutoff value is the minimum overlap score between two adjacent fragments required to join them in a single fragment. The cutoff, which we have set to 30 (a very high value), provides one filter for spurious overlaps introduced by experimental error. Instances with these features have been only solved adequately when target sequences vary from 20k to 50k base pairs [16,22,33].

From previous analyses we observe that the execution time needed by the objective function is variable, especially the time in the last iterations is too small, and it is necessary to increase the computation grain in the slaves when the search progresses. Here, we analyze the use of the $(\mu + \lambda)$ ES described in Section 15.4. As commented in that section, the ES method is engineered by an adaptive behavior to self-adjust its computation during a pre-fixed amount of time. The idea is to establish a time-out so that, when an individual is evaluated, we check if the time-out has elapsed; if not, the ES method is executed with the goal of improving the current individual. The ES main loop is run until the time-out has been consumed. At the end of the computation in the slave, the improved individual obtained by the ES algorithm is returned to the master. Therefore, tasks sent to the slaves may include several individual evaluations.

Once we have established the time-out, we ensure that all the slaves compute during a similar amount of time. As a consequence, the slaves in the fastest processors will make a more intensive search than the ones executing in the slowest processors. Using this strategy, we intend to fix the problem of the unbalanced ratio computation/communication when the quality of the individuals is improved.

The parameter settings of all the experiments are detailed in Table 15.1. The results obtained are included in Table 15.2. Instead of using the speedup to measure the

TABLE 15.2   Results of the Experiments

	Execution 1	Execution 2
Total workers	149	146
Average used workers	138.4	138.2
Wall clock time	40.3 h	41.6 h
Total CPU consumed	187.71 days	191.4 days
Time reduction	111.8	110.5
Parallel efficiency	0.75	0.76
Best fitness found	289,077	287,200
Final number of contigs	2	2

parallel performance (we have not run a sequential version of the algorithm due to obvious reasons of problem complexity), we consider the time reduction, consisting of dividing the total CPU time consumed by the workers by the wall clock time. We will also report on the parallel efficiency, which is computed by dividing the time reduction by the average number of used workers.

In Table 15.2 we can observe that the parallel efficiency in both executions is 0.75. This good result is explained because we have achieved a trade-off between the computation and communication of the worker. The time reduction is important (taking the average of the two experiments, from 380 days to 4 days) and justifies the use of GrEA on a grid system. Anyway, we should expect a better efficiency when solving a larger problem instance.

Considering the found solutions in both executions, they are in the same range of values. It is an expected result, since the algorithm performs the same number of function evaluations in both executions. Also, they obtain the same number of contigs. Although these solutions are not optimal (the optimum value is one contig), they are very accurate, since it is far from trivial to compute solutions with a small number of contigs for real-world instances of this problem.

We have analyzed the behavior of the algorithm observing the trace of the first execution. Concretely, we have measured the following issues at the beginning of each hour of computation time:

- The computing time required by a particular machine in the pool to evaluate the individuals to whom it has been assigned
- The evolution of the best fitness value during the computation
- The number of evaluated individuals per hour

In Fig. 15.3 top left, we show the tracking of the individual evaluation in a particular computer of the grid at the beginning of each computation hour. We observe that in the first 10 h, the times oscillate between 30 and 59 s per execution. This is an expected behavior, because an individual evaluation costs around 30 s at the beginning; thus, if this cost is less than 30 s (the time-out), at least one more evaluation is performed by the ES. Therefore, computing times less than 60 s are foreseeable. The individual

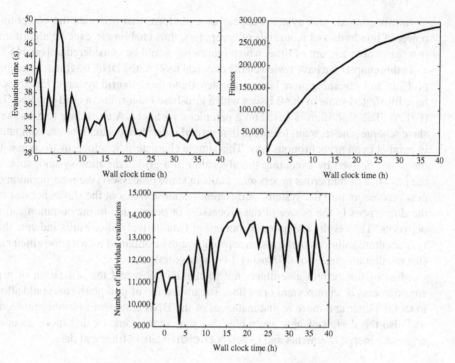

Figure 15.3. Graphical results of analyzing execution 1.

evaluation times after the 10th hour oscillate between 30 and 34 s, which indicates that our approach allows a stable behavior of the slave computations around to a pre-fixed value to be adjusted.

The shape of the curve tracking the fitness value per computation hour (Fig. 15.3, top right) leads us to think that the algorithm is near to converge to an optimum. Given that we do not know the optimal solution to the instance problem being solved, more experiments should be carried out to assess whether we are near the optimal or an suboptimal value.

The number of evaluated individuals per hour (Fig. 15.3, bottom) is kept between 9,000 and 14,000 (Fig. 15.3 bottom), and it indicates that we succeeded to keep the evaluated individuals per hour in a range in which the computation/communication ratio is favorable.

15.5 CONCLUSIONS

The DNA fragment assembly is a very complex problem in computational biology. Since the problem is NP-hard, the optimal solution is impossible to find for real cases, except for very small problem instances. Hence, computational techniques of affordable complexity (like metaheuristics) are needed for it.

In this context, grid systems appear as a platform that provides the computing power of hundreds and thousands of computers, thus enabling to execute algorithms in a reasonable amount of time, which otherwise would be considered unfeasible.

In this chapter we have reviewed the classical tools to the DNA fragment assembly problem and several approaches to execute/extend them to grid systems. Finally, we have illustrated some of these issues with a grid-based algorithm: a Grid-enabled GA (GrEA). The algorithm is based on a panmictic parallel GA according to a master–slave scheme, and its main feature is that several individual evaluations are computed in parallel in an asynchronous way. This simple characteristic allows us to cope with the issues derived by executing the algorithm in a grid computing system, such as the presence of numerous processors, faults in some processors, the incorporation of new processors into the system, or different response times of the slaves because of the differences in the power of the processors or delays due to the communication networks. The results are quite encouraging: Qualitatively, the results indicate that very accurate solutions to the instance problem can be obtained with a good efficiency (the parallel efficiency of 0.75 using 149 processors).

Most of the current assemblers are sequential ones, and the utilization of grid environments is an important open line. The utilization of grid platforms could allow to tackle larger and more realist instances of the DNA fragment assembly problem, and also the design of new assembler that uses more complex and more accurate criteria to merge fragments and to detect errors/repeats in fragment data.

ACKNOWLEDGMENTS

The authors are partially supported by the Spanish Ministry of Education and Science, by European FEDER under contract TIN2005-08818-C04-01 (the OPLINK project, http://oplink.lcc.uma.es) and by the European Union under contract CP3-005 (the CARLINK project).

REFERENCES

1. S. Batzoglou, D. Jaffe, K. Stanley, J. Butler, S. Gnerre, E. Mauceli, B. Berger, J.P. Mesirov, E.S. Lander, ARACHNE: A whole-genome shotgun assembler, *Genome Research* **12**(1), 177–189, 2002.

2. P. Green, Phrap. http://www.phrap.org/.

3. X. Huang, A. Madan, CAP3: A DNA sequence assembly program, *Genome Research* **9**, 868–877, 1999.

4. F. Berman, G.C. Fox, A.J.G. Hey, Grid computing. Making the global infrastructure a reality, in: *Communications Networking and Distributed Systems*, John Wiley & Sons, Hoboken, NJ, 2003.

5. P.A. Pevzner, *Computational Molecular Biology: An Algorithmic Approach*, The MIT Press, London, 2000.

6. J. Setubal, J. Meidanis, Fragment Assembly of DNA, in: *Introduction to Computational Molecular Biology*, University of Campinas, Brazil, pp. 105–139, 1997.

7. G.G. Sutton, O. White, M.D. Adams, A.R. Kerlavage, TIGR Assembler: A new tool for assembling large shotgun sequencing projects, *Genome Science and Technology* **1**(1), 9–19, 1995.

8. S. Kim, A structured pattern matching approach to shotgun sequence assembly, PhD thesis, Computer Science Department, The University of Iowa, 1997.

9. C.F. Allex, Computational Methods for Fast and Accurate DNA Fragment Assembly, UW technical report CS-TR-99-1406, Department of Computer Sciences, University of Wisconsin—Madison, 1999.

10. T.F. Smith, M.S. Waterman, Identification of common molecular sequences. *Journal of Molecular Biology* **147**, 195–197, 1891.

11. T. Chen, S. Skiena, Trie-based data structures for fragment assembly, in: *The Eighth Symposium on Combinatorial Pattern Matching*, Aarhus, Denmark, June 30–July 2 1997, pp. 206–223.

12. S. Kim, A.M. Segre, Amass: A structured pattern matching approach to shotgun sequence assembly, *Journal of Computing Biology* **6**(2), pp. 163–186, 1999.

13. E.W. Myers, G.G. Sutton, A.L. Delcher, I.M Dew, D.P. Fasulo, M.J. Flannigan, S.A. Kravitz, C.M. Mobarry, K.H. Reinert, K.A. Renington, E.L. Arson, R.A. Bolanos, H.H. Chou, C.M. Jordan, A.L. Helpern, S. Lonardi, E.M. Beasley, R.C. Brandon, L. Chen, P.J. Dunn, Z. Lai, Y. Lian, D.R. Nusskern, M. Chen, Q. Zheng, X. Zheng, G.M. Rubin, M.D. Adams, J.C. Venter, A whole-genome assembly of drosophila, *Science* **287**, 2196–2204, 2000.

14. S. Kikuchi, G. Chakraborty, Heuristically tuned ga to solve genome fragment assembly problem, in: *2006 IEEE Congress on Evolutionary Computation*, IEEE Press, pp. 5640–5647, July 2006.

15. G. Luque, E. Alba, Metaheuristics for the DNA fragment assembly problem, *International Journal of Computational Intelligence Research* **1**(1), 98–108, 2006.

16. R. Parsons, S. Forrest, C. Burks, Genetic algorithms, operators, and DNA fragment assembly, *Machine Learning* **21**, 11–33, 1995.

17. P. Mekcangsouy, N. Chakraborty, DNA fragment assembly using an ant colony system algorithm, in: *2003 IEEE Congress on Evolutionary Computation*, IEEE Press, New York, pp. 1756–1763, 2003.

18. C. Burks, M. Engle, S. Forrest, R. Parson, C. Soderlund, P. Stolorz, Stochastic optimization tools for genomic sequence assembly, in: *Automated DNA Sequencing and Analysis*, Academic Press pp. 249–259, 1994.

19. G. Churchill, C. Burks, M. Eggert, M. Engle, M. Waterman, Assembling DNA sequence fragments by shuffling and simulated annealing, Technical Report LA-UR-93-2287, Los Alamos National Laboratory, Los Alamos, 1993.

20. A. Mills, B. Yurke, P. Platzman, Error tolerant massive DNA neural network computation, in: *Fourth International Meeting on DNA-Based Computing*, Baltimore, Pennsylvania, June 1998.

21. E. Alba, G. Luque, A new local search algorithm for the DNA fragment assembly problem, in: *Proceedings of EvoCOP'07*, Valencia, Spain, April, Lecture Notes in Computer Science 4446, 1–12, Springer, 2007.

22. L. Li, S. Khuri, A comparison of DNA fragment assembly algorithms, in: *International Conference on Mathematics and Engineering Techniques in Medicine and Biological Sciences*, pp. 329–335, 2004.

23. P.A. Pevzner, H. Tang, M.S. Waterman, An Eulerian path approach to DNA fragment assembly, *Proceedings of the National Academic of Sciences of United States of America* **98**(17), 9748–9753, 2001.

24. M. Chaisson, P.A. Pevzner, H. Tang, Fragment assembly with short reads, *Bioinformatics* **20**(13), 2067–2074, 2004.

25. A.S. Grimshaw, A. Natrajan, M.A. Humphrey, M.J. Lewis, A. Nguyen-Tuong, J.F. Karpovich, M.M. Morgan, A.J. Ferrari, From legion to avaki: The persistence of vision, in: F. Berman, G. Fox, and T. Hey (Eds.), *Grid Computing: Making the Global Infrastructure a Reality*, John Wiley & Sons., Hoboken, NJ, pp. 265–298, 2003.

26. N. Melab, E.-G. Talbi, S. Cahon, On parallel evolutionary algorithms on the computational grid, in: *Parallel Evolutionary Computations, Studies on Computational Intelligence*, Vol. 22, Springer, Berlin, pp. 117–132, 2006.

27. A.J. Nebro, G. Luque, F. Luna, E. Alba, DNA fragment assembly using a grid-based genetic algorithm, *Computer and Operations Research*, 2007 (to appear).

28. E.-G. Talbi, A taxonomy of hybrid metaheuristics, *Journal of Heuristics* **8**, 807–819, 2002.

29. E. Alba, M. Tomassini, Parallelism and evolutionary algorithms, *IEEE Transactions on Evolutionary Computation* **6**(5), 443–462, 2002.

30. J. Linderoth, S. Kulkarni, J.P. Goux, M. Yoder, An enabling framework for master–worker applications on the computational grid, in: *Proceedings of the Ninth IEEE Symposium on High Performance Distributed Computing (HPDC)*, Pittsburg, Pensylvania, pp. 43–50, 2000.

31. D. Thain, T. Tannenbaum, M. Livny, Condor and the Grid. in: F. Berman, G. Fox, and T. Hey, (Eds.), *Grid Computing: Making the Global Infrastructure a Reality*, John Wiley & Sons, Hoboken, NJ, pp. 299–335, 2003.

32. M.L. Engle, C. Burks, Artificially generated data sets for testing DNA fragment assembly algorithms, *Genomics* **16**, pp. 286–288, 1993.

33. Y. Jing, S. Khuri, Exact and heuristic algorithms for the DNA fragment assembly problem, in: *Proceedings of the IEEE Computer Society Bioinformatics Conference*, Stanford University, IEEE Press, New York, pp. 581–582, August 2003.

16

SEEING IS KNOWING:
Visualization of Parameter–Parameter Dependencies in Biomedical Network Models

Akihiki Konagaya, Ryuzo Azuma, Ryo Umetsu, Shingo Ohki, Fumikazu Konishi, Kazum Matsumura, and Sumi Yoshikawa

> *We should start from the fact that we can know more than we can tell.*
> Michael Polanyi, *The Tacit Dimension*

16.1 INTRODUCTION

One of the great challenges in the postgenomics era is to elucidate dynamic behaviors of biomedical networks that incorporate information on metabolic pathways, signal transduction pathways, gene regulatory networks, and so on [1, 2]. Differential equations and parameter optimization techniques are widely used for representing biomedical networks and for estimating unknown parameter when fitting experimental data [3–5]. However, it is widely recognized that the networks and the parameters obtained do not always reflect biological knowledge in terms of physiological constraints and biochemical data obtained from *in vivo* and *in vitro* experiments, and there is a strong demand for sophisticated methods for validating biomedical network models.

Various sensitivity analysis techniques including flux control coefficient analysis and elasticity analysis, as well as flux variability analysis and robustness analysis, have been used to validate mathematical models and parameter sets for mathematical simulations of biological networks [1, 2]. However, the validation of biomedical network models becomes increasingly difficult as the number of equations increases.

Grid Computing for Bioinformatics and Computational Biology. Edited by E.-G. Talbi and A.Y. Zomaya.
Copyright © 2008 John Wiley & Sons, Inc.

The authors have proposed a new validation technique that visualizes parameter–parameter dependencies (PPD) by means of two-dimensional contour maps (hereafter referred to as PPD contour maps) [6]. PPD contour maps display moment parameters for two control parameters in X and Y axes using a double-logarithmic scale, such as half-life period ($t_{1/2}$), area under curve (AUC), and mean residence time (MRT). In our approach, parameter values obtained from biological experiments are not mandatory for the calculation of PPD contour maps. Rather, it is only necessary to assume the ranges of the parameters used in the mathematical expressions of biomedical networks. The geometrical information from a PPD contour map provides a bird's-eye view in which each point represents a particular biological experiment or an observation with specific values for two control parameters. Interestingly, some PPD contour maps have very similar-looking geometrical patterns over four to six orders of magnitude. Clustering similar PPD contour maps sometimes reveals higher-order control mechanisms such as pseudoequilibrium and feedback control, to name but a few.

In this chapter, the authors focus on the metaphilosophical aspects of biomedical network modeling, simulation, visualization, and interpretation from the viewpoint of the SECI knowledge spiral model proposed by Nonaka. The SECI model consists of a spiral process of explicit and tacit knowledge conversion involving socialization (tacit–tacit), externalization (tacit–explicit), combination (explicit–explicit), and internalization (explicit–tacit) [7]. In this framework the formation of virtual organizations, modeling of bionetworks, simulation and visualization, and interpretation of simulation results can be mapped onto socialization, externalization, combination, and internalization, respectively. Grid plays an important role as "Ba," that is, a place where knowledge is produced in the knowledge spiral. The Grid provides a networked environment where people may form a community and share resources for collaboration, and it also provides a large-scale pool of computational resources for simulation and visualization [8, 9]. Typical PPD contour map analysis requires millions of simulations and produces a huge volume of data when recording time sequences needed for visualization. These data may be on the order of several hundred gigabytes in total [6].

The organization of this chapter is as follows. First, Section 16.2 summarizes Nonaka's knowledge spiral model of tacit–explicit knowledge conversion. Then, Section 16.3 discusses the knowledge creation process for mathematical modeling from the perspective of the knowledge spiral. Section 16.4 introduces the knowledge creation process using PPD contour maps and using the drug metabolic ADME model as an example. Section 16.5 discusses how to use grid computing for PPD contour map creation, and Section 16.6 will conclude with a summary of parameter–parameter dependency analysis.

16.2   TACIT KNOWLEDGE, EXPLICIT KNOWLEDGE, AND KNOWLEDGE SPIRAL

Michael Polanyi, a twentieth-century philosopher, commented in his book, *The Tacit Dimension*, that "we should start from the fact that we can know more than we can tell." This implies that we should consider tacit knowledge in human beings as well as explicit knowledge represented by language, symbols, and programs when dealing with "knowledge" using computers.

Nonaka proposed the SECI model of the knowledge spiral theory [7] in which knowledge is created in a cyclic process of conversion between tacit knowledge and explicit knowledge involving the following stages: (1) socialization (tacit-to-tacit knowledge), (2) externalization (tacit-to-explicit knowledge), (3) combination (explicit-to-explicit knowledge), and (4) internalization (explicit-to-tacit knowledge). The SECI model provides a general framework for the creation of new knowledge through the mutual conversion of tacit knowledge and explicit knowledge.

The knowledge spiral begins with socialization, that is, the formation of a community such as a virtual organization in grid computing. In general, we can assume that experts in some community have already shared both tacit and explicit knowledge to some extent through face-to-face meetings, conferences, journals, and so on.

Externalization is a knowledge creation process performed by human experts who transform tacit knowledge into explicit knowledge. The process corresponds to the intellectual activity of creating new ideas and new concepts. Modeling mathematical biomedical networks is a typical example of elaborate knowledge-intensive work categorized as externalization.

Combination is a knowledge creation process producing new explicit knowledge by modifying existing explicit knowledge. Typical examples of collections of explicit knowledge include knowledge bases, databases, text bases, and program libraries. Logical inference, data mining, and mathematical simulation are typical techniques for producing new explicit knowledge from knowledge bases, databases, and simulation models with computer systems, respectively.

Internalization is a knowledge creation process producing new tacit knowledge from explicit knowledge through experience. Generally speaking, explicit knowledge is easy to access and share but learning from experience sometimes plays an essential role in understanding the true meaning of explicit knowledge, that is, proverbs. The processes described above can be repeated in a spiral fashion and can help human experts and communities to produce and share both tacit and explicit knowledge.

16.3 SECI VIEW OF BIOMEDICAL NETWORK MODELING AND SIMULATION

16.3.1 Grid as an Infrastructure for Socialization

Grid is one of the most attractive cyber infrastructures for sharing resources over a network in a secure fashion [10]. Resources include computers, databases, applications, services, and knowledge. Grid is also helpful for the formation of a community or virtual organization [8]. In this sense, grid may be considered as an important infrastructure for socialization. However, it should also be noted that a key to socialization is the establishing of relationships with mutual trust among communities rather than the building of network infrastructures [11].

16.3.2   Mathematical Modeling as Externalization

The mathematical modeling of biomedical networks involves knowledge-intensive work to extract key control mechanisms of bimolecular interactions orchestrated by hundreds and thousands of molecules. The main objective of biomedical network modeling is to highlight key molecules and interactions that characterize biological phenomena of interest. A deep understanding of target phenomena is necessary in order to determine the network topology and parameters involved in simulating the phenomena. In other words, biomedical networks reflect the modeler's knowledge including his or her understanding and curiosity regarding the target phenomena. The selection of key molecules and network topology are highly knowledge-intensive tasks involving the conversion of experts' biomedical knowledge into explicit knowledge in mathematical form on computers.

Figure 16.1 shows three examples of drug metabolism schemes and corresponding PPD contour maps when hepatocytes are dosed with irinotecan (CPT-11, a prodrug for the treatment of colon cancer, malignant lymphoma, and lung cancer [12]). A PPD contour map represents a double-logarithmic plot of the half-time period of SN-38 concentration with respect to irinotecan dosage and CYP3A4 enzyme concentration. Figure 16.1a represents the minimal model of CPT11 metabolism occurring in hepatocytes [13]. In addition to this, the effect of the reabsorption of intestinal SN-38 produced by the deconjugation of glucuronate in SN-38G through intestinal bacteria with beta-glucuronidase is taken into account in the second model (Fig. 16.1b) [14]. In the third model, it was necessary to take into account urinary and fecal excretions of APC and NPC (Fig. 16.1c) [15].

It is apparent that the three models have different PPD contour maps for the same irinotecan dosage and CYP3A4 concentration. This means that each model reveals a different half-time period for the same drug dosage and enzyme concentration. In other words, each model reveals different parameter values when fitting unknown parameters to biological experimental data. It is not fruitful to discuss which model is correct, since the differences result from the varied focal points of each model. Each model is correct in the sense that it reflects the irinotecan metabolic process to some extent, and each model is incorrect in the sense that it does not reflect all molecular interactions occurring during the irinotecan drug metabolic process. The lesson observed here is that simulation results are strongly dependent on the selection of network topology and parameters, and artifacts may be observed when parameter values exceed the ranges which are meaningful in a physiological sense.

16.3.3   Visualization as Combination

It is often observed that a set of data provides new information that is difficult to detect with individual data. PPD contour maps are one such example, producing higher-order information from a set of simulation results. PPD contour maps represent higher-order

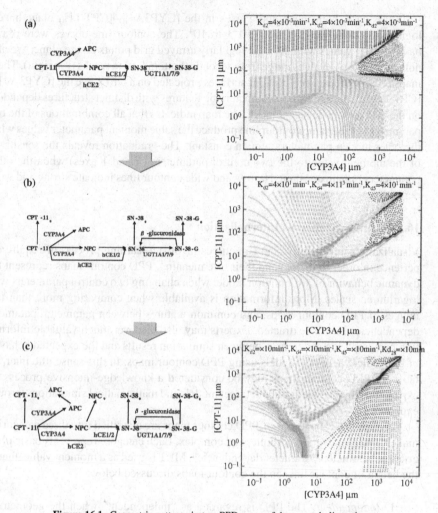

Figure 16.1. Geometric patterns in $t_{1/2}$ PPD maps of drug metabolic pathways.

information as the geometrical patterns of moment values. In this sense, visualization may be considered as part of a process for creating new explicit knowledge from a combination of existing explicit knowledge. The plotting process for a contour map such as that in Figure 16.1 is as follows:

1. Define a pathway scheme.
2. Define reaction equations, parameters, and initial concentrations.
3. Define ($[[CYP3A4]_0$, $[[CPT-11]_0$) values.
4. Simulation: solve differential equations.
5. Calculate half-life period ($t_{1/2}$), AUC, and MRT values.
6. Plot contour line curves.

In this case, both the X and Y axes in the $[CYP3A4]_0$–$[CPT-11]_0$ plane have a logarithmic scale ranging from 10^{-1} to 10^4. The contour line curves were drawn based on $t_{1/2}$ values with 20×20 regularly arrayed grid points on the plane. We also note that these $t_{1/2}$ values range from seconds (bottom left) to weeks (top right). These maps provide view of $t_{1/2}$ contour surfaces projected on a bird's-eye the $[CYP3A4]_0$–$[CPT-11]_0$ plane, and exhibit characteristic features with distinct structures depending on the pathway models generated. The map indicates that all combinations of the two parameters on the same contour line produce the same moment parameter values when the other hidden parameters remain constant. The graduation reveals the sensitivity of the moment value to the two control parameters (X and Y axes) when the other parameters remain constant. Narrow and wide contour lines indicate strong and weak dependencies, respectively.

16.3.4   Interpretation as Internalization

Visualizations are intuitive but sometimes involve a learning process or require experience in order to understand their true meaning. PPD contour maps represent the dynamic behavior of a simulation model when changing two control parameters with logarithmic scales. More information is available when comparing more than two images of PPD contour maps, and common features between parameter–parameter dependencies may be extracted. Experts may also discover much valuable information by comparing differences between simulation results and the expected behavior of biomedical network models using PPD contour maps. In this sense, the interpretation of PPD contour maps may be considered a knowledge-intensive process for expanding tacit knowledge about target models and mathematical simulations through experience.

The geometrical patterns of PPD contour maps are classified into three categories, namely, independent, hyperbolic, and complex. Each category represents basic properties of parameter–parameter dependencies. MRT is used as a moment value, that is, the height of contour lines in the contour maps discussed below.

1. *Independent*: The PPD is regarded as "independent" when the geometrical pattern of contour lines is determined by only one of the two parameters, as shown in Fig. 16.2a. Each of these 2D images exhibits juxtaposed lines with a vertical or horizontal orientation.

2. *Hyperbolic*: The PPD is regarded as "hyperbolic" when the values of moment parameters in some area adjacent to the periphery of the window linearly depend on one of the two parameters and become saturated at the other side of the window, as seen in Fig. 16.2b. In hyperbolic patterns, the two parameters are in a trade-off relationship in terms of the moment parameter. In a typical case as in Fig. 16.2c, moment values depend on the product of two parameters. These dependencies become more complex when hyperbolic and stepwise behaviors are mixed.

3. *Complex*: The PPD is regarded as "complex" when the moment values depend nonlinearly on the parameters, as seen in Fig. 16.2c. The geometrical patterns

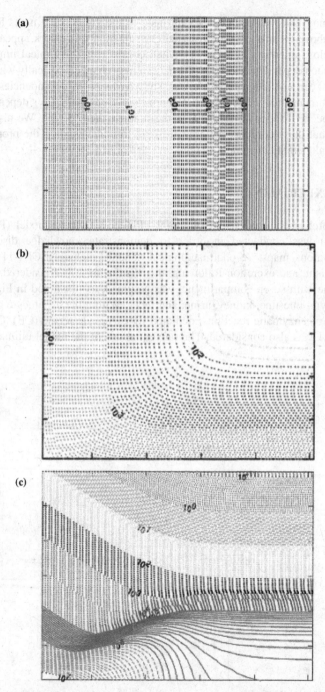

Figure 16.2. Categories of geometrical patterns in PPD contour maps: **(a)** independence, **(b)** hyperbolic, and **(c)** complex patterns.

may involve dependencies intrinsic to individual PPD maps for which the above-mentioned pattern-based classification framework appears useless. A close attention is necessary when considering the clinical implications for such dependencies. The PPD pattern may change drastically when the values of certain hidden parameters are shifted (due to the dependencies in the higher dimensional space). We note here that strong parameter dependencies may be involved with artifacts in the mathematical model. We also emphasize that these complex patterns are keys to understanding the properties of the mathematical model.

16.4 EXPERIMENTS

A comprehensive analysis of binomial PPD in a CPT-11 model (PPD-binomial analysis) was conducted in order to demonstrate knowledge discovery using PPD contour maps. A pharmacological scheme including CPT-11 distribution, metabolism, and excretion following an i.v. infusion was considered. Specifically, a scheme with seven compartments was assumed, as illustrated in Fig. 16.3: vein, hepatocyte, intestine, kidney, urine, and feces. Within the hepatocyte compartment, a series of enzymatic reactions mediated by carboxylesterase (CE), CYP3A4, and UGT1A1 was also considered. The rate equations of the model ultimately involved

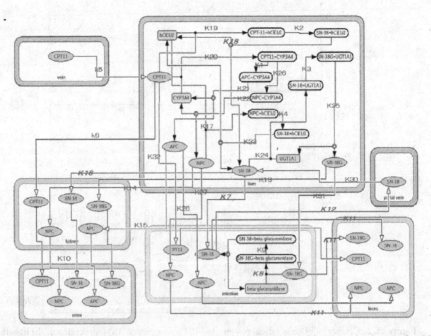

Figure 16.3. CPT-11 pharmacology scheme with physiological considerations implemented with CellDesigner^{TM}.

Table 16.1   List of Parameters and Their Ranges Used in the PPD-Binomial Analysis

Type	Parameter	Range
Catalytic reaction rate coefficient	K1, K2, K3, K4, K9, K26	2×10^{-5}–2×10^{0} min
Transportation rate coefficient	K5, K6, K7, K10, K11, K12, K13, K14, K15, K16, K27, K28, K30, K31, K32	2×10^{-5}–2×10^{0} min
Initial concentrations	$[CYP3A4(liver)]_0$, $[hCE1/2(liver)]_0$, $[CPT11(vein)]_0$, $[UGT1A1(liver)]_0$, $[\beta\text{-glucuronidase(intestine)}]_0$	2×10^{-2}–$2 \times 10^{4} \mu M$ 2×10^{-2}–$2 \times 10^{4} \mu M$

32 and 41 parameters for kinetic coefficients and initial concentrations, respectively. Twenty-six parameters of interest were selected from among them (see Table 16.1). MRT contour maps were obtained for all of the binomial combinations among them, that is, $_{26}C_2 = 325$. Hence, each of these maps provided a two-dimensional PPD in a rectangular area determined by the ranges shown in Table 16.1, while other parameters were fixed at intermediate values satisfying physiological conditions. The PPD-binomial analysis was found to provide useful information for understanding the properties of a mathematical model because it revealed that some dependencies in the maps appeared to be linked to a particular substructure of the network scheme.

Some features of interest exist in the dynamic properties that reflect network structures. One is the plateau associated with a region of constant moment parameter values, governed over several decades of the parameter range. Such a plateau often corresponds to the saturation of MRT at maximum or minimum values. Another feature of interest is the linear dependency of the rate constants (or the kinetic and transportation coefficients) in the mathematical model. We hypothesize that this linear dependency arises from pseudoequilibrium between input and output streams for a given molecular concentration.

Some of the maps reveal very similar geometric patterns as shown in Fig. 16.4. Groups of triadic kinetic parameters were obtained based on these patterns as shown in Fig. 16.5. The triadic relations can be classified into three groups: (K11, K12, (K2, K4, K5)), (K13, K31, (K2, K4, K5)), and (K1, K26, (K2, K3, K5, K9, K30)), This diagram aids in the determination of how the MRT of SN-38 is controlled by parameter–parameter dependencies such as K11 versus K12, K13 versus K31, and K1 versus K26 Fig. 16.6. One interesting observation that is common to all the groups is that these three pairs occur at branching pathway substructures as shown in Fig. 16.3. The curled structure occurring in the corner characterizes the appearance of the map. This feature was found to be associated with a very simple and common substructure in the pathway scheme: a molecule/complex with a single influx and a pair of competitive effluxes (consisting of routes for excretion and downstream feedback), as listed in Table 16.2.

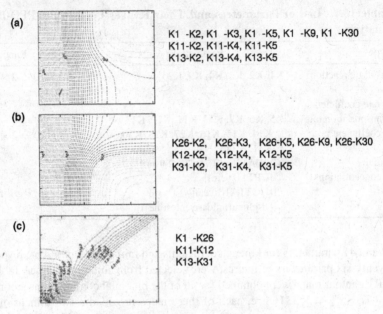

(a)

K1 -K2, K1 -K3, K1 -K5, K1 -K9, K1 -K30
K11-K2, K11-K4, K11-K5
K13-K2, K13-K4, K13-K5

(b)

K26-K2, K26-K3, K26-K5, K26-K9, K26-K30
K12-K2, K12-K4, K12-K5
K31-K2, K31-K4, K31-K5

(c)

K1 -K26
K11-K12
K13-K31

Figure 16.4. Common hyperbolic patterns.

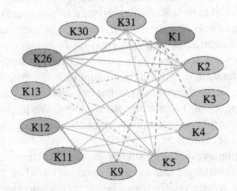

Figure 16.5. Triadic relations in hyperbolic patterns.

Table 16.2   List of Reactions with the Branching Parameter Group

Molecule/Complex	Influx	Efflux
SN-38 in intestine	K7	K11 and K12
SN-38G in hepatocyte	K25	K13 and K31
CPT11–CYP3A4 complex in hepatocyte	K20	K1 and K26

Table 16.3   Total Loop Length, Data Size, and Cumulative CPU Time Used for a PPD-Batch Calculation for a Simple Enzyme Reaction Model

Loop Length	Data Size	CPU Time
$25 \times 21 \times 16^3 = 2,150,400^a$	334 GB[b]	$25\ min^c \times 16^3 = 71$ days

[a]25×21 stands for parameter points required for a single 2D PPD map on $[S]_0$ versus $[E]_0$. 16^3 is the data space for the slider scrolls with K1, K2, and K3.

[b]The data size of a single PPD map that corresponds to around 90 MB.

[c]The cumulative CPU time for a single PPD map.

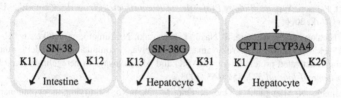

Figure 16.6. Branching patterns and their associated pathway substructures.

16.5   GRIDIFICATION OF BIOMEDICAL NETWORK SIMULATION

The PPD contour map visualization system is available on both PC clusters and grids. The grid version incorporates a global scheduler (CONDOR) in order to make multiple PC clusters available as a simulation engine. The overhead time required by this global scheduler is measured to account for nearly 10% of the total processing time. In the interactive mode, the real time required for the back-end process has been measured to be 25 min or 256 s with the use of a single CPU or a PC cluster with 16 CPUs, respectively. In addition, the PPD batch calculation was applied to a simple enzyme reaction model in order to reveal the scale of the calculation involved. The total loop length, data size, and cumulative CPU time are shown in Table 16.3.

16.6   CONCLUSION

Visualization plays an essential role in understanding the dynamic behavior of mathematical models. Parameter–parameter dependency contour maps facilitate a comparison of the effectiveness of control parameters and network topologies according to a bird'-eye view. The significance of PPD contour maps can be recognized in terms of two roles from the perspective of Nonaka's knowledge spiral theory. One is the creation of new explicit knowledge by combining hundreds of simulation results in geometrical patterns. The other is the creation of new tacit knowledge regarding the understanding of PPD maps through experience. The distinction between these two roles sheds light on the fundamental properties of visualization, that is, how to bridge human knowledge and computer simulation. The Grid plays an important role in sharing not only computational resources but also knowledge among virtual organizations. We strongly believe that a combination of social communication systems and grid computing is the key to promoting the knowledge spiral in a cyber infrastructure.

REFERENCES

1. D. Fell, *Understanding the Control of Metabolism*, Portland Press, Seattle, WA, 1997.

2. B.O. Palsson, *Systems Biology Properties of Reconstructed Networks*, Cambridge University Press, New York, 2006.

3. M. Hatakeyama, S. Kimura, T. Naka, T. Kawasaki, N. Yumoto, M. Ichikawa, J.H. Kim, K. Saito, M. Saeki, M. Shirouzu, S. Yokoyama, A. Konagaya, A computational model on the modulation of mitogen-activated protein kinase (MAPK) and Akt pathways in heregulin-induced ErbB signaling, *Biochemical Journal* **373**, 451–463, 2003.

4. H. Imade, N. Mizuguchi, I. Ono, N. Ono, M. Okamoto, Gridifying, an evolutionary algorithm for inference of genetic networks using the improved GOGA framework and its performance evaluation on OBI Grid, *Grid Computing in Life Science (Lecture Notes in Bioinformatics)* **3370**, 171–186, 2005.

5. S. Kimura, K. Ide, A. Kashihara, M. Kano, M. Hatakeyama, R. Masui, N. Nakagawa, S. Yokoyama, S. Kuramitsu, A. Konagaya, Inference of S-system models of genetic networks using a cooperative coevolutionary algorithm, *Bioinformatics*, **21**, 1154–1163, 2005.

6. A. Konagaya, R. Azuma, R. Umetsu, S. Ohki, F. Konishi, K. Matsumura, S. Yoshikawa, Parameter mining: Discovery of dynamical characteristics using geometrical patterns of parameter–parameter dependencies on differential equations, LSGRID2006, pp. 137–149, 2006.

7. I. Nonaka, R. Toyama, N. Konno, SECI, Ba and leadership: A unified model of dynamic knowledge creation, *Long Range Planning*, **33**, 5–34, 2000.

8. A. Konagaya A, Trends in life science grid: From computing grid to knowledge grid, *BMC Bioinformatics* **7** (Suppl. 5), S10, 2006.

9. A. Konagaya, OBIGrid: Towards the 'Ba' for sharing resources, services and knowledge for bioinformatics, CCGRID2006, BioGrid Workshop, 2006.

10. P.W. Arzberger, A. Farazdel, A. Konagaya, L. Ang, S. Shimojo, R.L. Stevens, Life sciences and cyberinfrastructure: dual and interacting revolutions that will drive future science, *New Generation Computing* **22**, 97–110, 2004.

11. A. Konagaya, F. Konishi, M. Hatakeyama, K. Satou, The Superstructure toward Open Bioinformatics Grid, *New Generation Computing* **22**, 167–176, 2004.

12. N. Hariparsad, S.C. Nallani, R.S. Sane, D.J. Buckley, A.R. Buckley, P.S. Desai, Induction of CYP3A4 by Efavirenz in primary human hepatocytes: Comparison with Rifampin and Phenobarbital, *Clinical Pharmacology* **44**, 1273–1281, 2004.

13. E. Raymond, M. Fabbro, V. Boige, O. Rixe, M. Frenay, G. Vassal, S. Faivre, E. Sicard, C. Germa, M. Rodier, L. Vernillet, J.P. Armand, Multicentre phase II study and pharmacokinetic analysis of irinotecan in chemotherapy-naive patients with glioblastoma, *Annals of Oncology* **14**, 603–614, 2003.

14. R. Garcia-Carbonero, J.G. Supko, Current perspectives on the clinical experience, pharmacology, and continued development of the camptotecines, *Clinical Cancer Research* **8**, 641–661, 2002.

15. V. Charasson, M.C. Haaz, J. Robert, Determination of drug interactions occurring with the metabolic pathways of irinotecan, *Drug Metabolism and Disposition* **30**, 731–733, 2002.

16. M. Kageyama, H. Namiki, H. Fukushima, Y. Ito, N. Shibata, K. Takada, *In vivo* effects of cyclopor in A and Ketoconazole on the pharmacokinetics of representative substrates for *p*-glycoprotein and cytochrome P450 (CYP) 3A in rats, *Biological and Pharmaceutical Bulletin* **28**, 316–322, 2005.

17. R. Mathijssen, R.J. van Alphen, J. Verweij, W.J. Loos, K. Nooter, G. Stoter, A. Sparreboom, Clinical pharmacokinetics and metabolism of irinotecan, *Clinical Cancer Research* **7**, 2182–2194, 2001.

18. T. Ishikawa, A. Tamura, H. Saito, K. Wakabayashi, H. Nakagawa, Pharmacogenomics of the human ABC transporter ABCG2: From functional evaluation to drug molecular design, *Naturwissenschaften* **92**, 451–463, 2005.

INDEX

Ab initio calculations, 188
Actual load distribution process, 30
Adaptive weighted factoring (AWF), 310
Alignment cache, 138
Allocation strategy, 317
Annotation systems, 274
Application-level scheduling parameter
    sweep template (APST), 328
Area under curve (AUC), 376
Artificial neural networks
    (ANNs), 2
Automated semantic mediation, 295

Basic local alignment search tool
    (BLAST), 168
Berger–Munson algorithm, 28
Berkeley open infrastructure for network
    computing (BOINC), 4, 72, 251
Best multilinear regression (BMLR), 7
BIOINFOMED project, 269
Bioinformatics, 47, 48, 199, 301, 302
Bioinformatics Research Center
    (BIRC), 89
Biomedical network simulation, 377
    gridification of, 385
    SECI view, 377
Blocks substitution matrix (BLOSUM), 303
BOLD policy, 310
Brookhaven Protein Data Bank, 110
Bus networks
    heuristic strategies for, 33
    idle-time insertion strategy, 34
    performance evaluation of, 35
    reduced set-processing
        strategy, 34
    sequence matching on, 28

Cellular GA (cGA) models, 367
Chemical data bank (CDB), 4
Clinical information systems (CISs), 267
Clinical reference information model
    (CRIM), 291
Comma-separated value (CSV), 271
Common object resource broker architecture
    (CORBA), 226
Common prefix–suffix tree (CPST), 101
Community authorization service (CAS), 72
Computerized medical record (CMR), 287
Configurable object program (COP), 314

Database access tool, 8
Database-driven grid computing, 247
Database of interacting proteins (DIP), 5
Data indexing, 164, 171
    mechanisms, 170, 171
    structures, 166
Data-intensive resources, 257
Data syndication techniques, 157
Data warehouse, 8
Decision support system (DSS), 236
Directed acyclic graph (DAG), 276
Distance-based methods, 127
Distributed hash table (DHT), 164
Distributed resource management
    (DRM), 89
DNA sequencing process, 359
Domain-specific tools, 361
Drosophila melanogaster, 98, 100
Drug discovery
    grids for, 3

Electronic health record (EHR), 267, 287,
    288

Grid Computing for Bioinformatics and Computational Biology. Edited by E.-G. Talbi and A.Y. Zomaya.
Copyright © 2008 John Wiley & Sons, Inc.

y Series on

aformatics: Computational Techniques and Engineering

ormatics and computational biology involve the comprehensive application of
natics, statistics, science, and computer science to the understanding of living
s. Research and development in these areas require cooperation among specialists
e fields of biology, computer science, mathematics, statistics, physics, and related
s. The objective of this book series is to provide timely treatments of the different
of bioinformatics spanning theory, new and established techniques, technologies
ls, and application domains. This series emphasizes algorithmic, mathematical,
al, and computational methods that are central in bioinformatics and computational

Editors: **Professor Yi Pan** and **Professor Albert Y. Zomaya**
pan@cs.gsu.edu   zomaya@it.usyd.edu.au

---

dge Discovery in Bioinformatics: Techniques, Methods, and Applications
a Hu and Yi Pan

omputing for Bioinformatics and Computational Biology
by El-Ghazali Talbi and Albert Y. Zomaya

rmatics Algorithms: Techniques and Applications
ndiou and Alexander Zelikovsky

s of Biological Networks
by Björn H. Junker and Falk Schreiber

Printed in the United States
By Bookmasters